Unraveling Vietnam

Unraveling Vietnam

*How American Arms and Diplomacy
Failed in Southeast Asia*

William R. Haycraft

McFarland & Company, Inc., Publishers
Jefferson, North Carolina, and London

LIBRARY OF CONGRESS CATALOGUING-IN-PUBLICATION DATA

Haycraft, William R. (William Russell), 1929–
   Unraveling Vietnam : how American arms and diplomacy failed in Southeast Asia / William R. Haycraft.
      p.   cm.
   Includes bibliographical references and index.

   ISBN 0-7864-2354-4 (softcover : 50# alkaline paper)

   1. Vietnamese Conflict, 1961–1975 — United States.
2. Vietnam — History — 20th century.   3. United States — History —1945– . I. Title.
DS558.H39   2005
959.704'3373 — dc22   2005026339

British Library cataloguing data are available

©2005 William R. Haycraft. All rights reserved

No part of this book may be reproduced or transmitted in any form or by any means, electronic or mechanical, including photocopying or recording, or by any information storage and retrieval system, without permission in writing from the publisher.

Cover photograph ©2005 Brand X Pictures

Manufactured in the United States of America

McFarland & Company, Inc., Publishers
  Box 611, Jefferson, North Carolina 28640
    www.mcfarlandpub.com

To Carol

Contents

Preface	1
Introduction	5
1. Ho Chi Minh's Vietnam	9
2. The Origins of U.S. Involvement: 1945-1960	34
3. The Kennedy Years	60
4. Johnson Takes Charge	105
5. Lyndon Johnson's War	129
6. Richard Nixon's Peace	177
7. The Aftermath	210
8. Conclusion	220
Notes	227
Bibliography	249
Index	253

Preface

With the passage of time, writing about the Vietnam War will, if it has not already done so, soon pass *entirely* into the hands of persons who were not there and had no part in the events. This is, of course, inevitable with every historical event — for example, the American Civil War — but that does not seem to diminish interest in nor the steady outpouring of books on that subject. While I would not dare to predict that 100 years hence, the Vietnam War will sustain the level of interest of the Civil War, there is little doubt, as evidenced in the 2004 presidential election, that the Vietnam War continues to excite powerful emotions in this country, emotions that also pique the interest of young people to know more about that intensely controversial event in American history.

I am one of those who was not there and had no role in the Vietnam War. I join the already substantial number of authors who fit this category, and there will undoubtedly be a much greater number who will join in the future. So the question arises, why did I write this book?

The race goes to the swift, so writers who were fastest off the blocks with well-written, persuasive books on the Vietnam War were able to preempt the field in molding American opinion about that unhappy national experience. In those days of the late 1960s and through the 1970s, when the war was going badly and the U.S. was withdrawing or had finally lost the war, most Americans, reeling from the tragedy, were in no mood to read books that upheld the country's costly and unsuccessful efforts to preserve South Vietnam, Laos, and Cambodia from a Communist takeover. So it was not surprising that the books that did appear at that time were almost universally critical of America's role in Southeast Asia while almost nothing was published that took the countervailing view. These books were highly acclaimed by the predominantly liberal critics, won coveted literary prizes, and were and still are widely read. They were strongly influential in gaining ascendancy for the orthodox view of Vietnam, that is, inter alia, that America pursued a fundamentally flawed policy in Southeast Asia for 25 years, that Southeast Asia was not an area of strategic importance; that it was misguided to attempt to contain Communism in Southeast Asia; that U.S. intervention was immoral and anyway, the war was unwinnable; that North Vietnam was the innocent, aggrieved party; that the integrity of the U.S. guarantee was not at stake in Vietnam; and variations on these themes. In the aftermath of the U.S.'s defeat, these arguments were almost universally accepted in academia and gained credence with the general public. Gradually, however, a few books began to appear that challenged the received wisdom, but having established the earlier, orthodox view, academia labeled these as revisionist.

One of the best recent books on the subject is Michael Lind's *Vietnam: The Necessary War*, published in 1999. Lind's principal theme is that the Vietnam War, as a proxy in the Cold War, was one the U.S. had no choice but to fight, but that in allowing the war to become drawn out, the U.S. was doomed to fail. He focuses on the geopolitical factors that drove the decision to intervene and the geopolitical fallout from America's defeat. He also does a superb job of thoroughly skewering the myths about Vietnam nurtured by the liberal left. Although I do not agree with all his assertions, overall, I believe his perceptions are highly accurate.

For my part, I read those early critical works at the time of publication and continued to read prominent books on the subject as they came out over the years, but I was never fully persuaded to the orthodox view. At a point in the late 1990s, I began a more concerted study of the Vietnam bibliography, including works that had received less critical notice. From my reading I reached conclusions that differed in almost every respect with the orthodox version. Certainly I am not the first to arrive at this point; however I was not able to find any one account that I felt adequately explored the reasons behind the U.S.'s failure in Vietnam. Thus, my two goals in writing this book: first, that it be comprehensive, encompassing not only the two Indochina Wars but also the years leading to the 1946 start of the first war and those that followed the 1975 collapse of South Vietnam and the end of the second war, to provide perspectives on the origins of the wars and America involvement and the repercussions in Vietnam and worldwide of the ultimate Communist victory in this dangerous episode of the Cold War; and second, that it challenge the orthodox version with reasoned arguments that support my contrary views.

Those who write history have an important advantage — they usually have more information than those who wrote before, and thus I had the benefit of a great deal of primary material much of it published in the past decade, not available to earlier writers. The memoirs of the protagonists have now been written, and it is unlikely that many more first-hand accounts will be forthcoming due to the passage of time. I was able to write this book by sifting through the memoirs and biographies, the documentary material and what has been written by others to evaluate the arguments surrounding this very controversial event and to arrive independently at my own conclusions.

A primary source was the United States Government Printing Office-published series *Foreign Relations of the U.S.* (*FRUS*) relating to Vietnam, covering in 10 volumes the period 1955 through 1966, seven of which were published since 1990 with the volume on 1966 having been published as late as 1998. Later material from this source is not yet available.

Another very important source was *U.S. Government and the Vietnam War: Executive and Legislative Roles and Relationships*, parts I through IV, covering the period 1945 through 1967. Commissioned by the Committee on Foreign Relations of the U.S. Senate and compiled by William Conrad Gibbons of the Congressional Research Service of the Library of Congress, it takes on a quasiofficial nature. Originally published by the USGPO and reprinted by Princeton University Press, this massive work has appeared at intervals beginning with Part I in 1984 and continuing through Part IV in 1994. Part V covering the period January 1968 to May 1975 has yet to appear.

From the foregoing, one can see that two extremely valuable sources, *FRUS* and Gibbons' work, did not go beyond 1966 and 1967 respectively and so do not cover the Nixon administration nor the postwar period, but I was able to draw on memoirs and biographies, accounts of officials, and the works of historians to bring my story through to its conclusion in the 1990s. Kissinger's *The White House Years* provides a unique window into the protracted secret negotiations between himself and Le Duc Tho that led to America's disengagement but did not end the war. Nixon's memoirs are invaluable in corroborating and sometimes diverging from Kissinger's version, and later, Alexander Haig's 1992 memoirs add another valuable source on the Nixon years. Duiker's *Vietnam Since the Fall of Saigon* and Lamb's *Vietnam Now: A Reporter Returns* provided valuable material on postwar conditions in South Vietnam under Communist rule as did, to a lesser extent, Sheehan's *After the War Was Over: Hanoi and Saigon*.

Not surprisingly, most books on the Vietnam War by American authors focus on events in Washington and South Vietnam and have very little to say about conditions in North Vietnam and the actions of its leaders. To a degree this is understandable due to the closed nature of that society; but this lack of balance, whether by default or design, has resulted, more often than not, in the reader's receiving one-sided and usually negative views of the government of South Vietnam and the U.S.'s purposes and actions in Indochina while the grim totalitarian Hanoi regime and its relentless war on South Vietnam go unremarked. This made Duiker's works particularly valuable in providing insights into the inner workings of the Democratic Republic of Vietnam from its inception in 1945 into the postwar years of the early 1980s. Less objective but still useful are Jean LaCouture's 1966 work *Vietnam: Between Two Truces* and his 1968 hagiography of Ho Chi Minh. LaCouture was regarded as friendly by Hanoi and thus had access to North Vietnam during the period. (He later repudiated the Hanoi regime.) A little known biography of Ho Chi Minh is David Halberstam's *Ho*, published in 1971. This fawning paean is wholly derivative, devoid of documentation and not useful as a source. Halberstam would probably prefer that this book remain obscure. John F. Cady's 1974 work *His-*

tory of Post-War Southeast Asia is useful up to 1963 after which he focuses on South Vietnam to the almost complete absence of material on North Vietnam while drawing heavily on the *New York Times* and its version of *The Pentagon Papers* for documentation. We also have the noted Vietnam scholar Joseph Buttinger's 1973 work, *A Dragon Defiant*, although his interpretation of the Second Indochina War faithfully adheres to the Hanoi version. Bernard Fall has provided valuable material on North Vietnam in *The Two Vietnams*, of 1963, and *Viet-Nam Witness: 1953–66*, of 1966, and finally we have American scholar Gareth Porter's 1975 work, *A Peace Denied*, which traces the peace negotiations and final events of the war from Hanoi's perspective. With the exception of Halberstam's book, all of these were used for background on North Vietnam.

Though *FRUS* was my preferred source for documents, *The Pentagon Papers* as published by the *New York Times* (1971) had a few documents not in *FRUS*, but I avoided drawing on the narrative portions of that book because by then the *Times* had abandoned all pretense of objectivity on the Vietnam War.

No discussion of sources on the Vietnam War would be complete without commenting on four works that are standards on the subject. These are historian George C. Herring's *America's Longest War: The United States and Vietnam, 1950–1975* (first edition 1979, second edition 1986) and three works by journalists: Stanley Karnow's *Vietnam: A History* (1983); Frances fitzgerald's Pulitzer Prize-winning *Fire in the Lake* (1972); and Halberstam's widely read *The Best and the Brightest* 1972. While these books were useful as general background, I rarely cited them because, writing at a later time, I had sources not available to them which I believed were more authoritative or objective. However, for background on the members of Kennedy's New Frontier, Halberstam is excellent.

And so, in the sincere hope that readers will find its arguments well founded, useful and informative, I submit this book as my contribution to the ongoing Vietnam War debate.

William R. Haycraft
Fall 2005

Introduction

With the signing of the Paris agreement in January 1973, Americans were told the nation had achieved a "peace with honor" and could withdraw from Vietnam with heads high, leaving a strong, independent South Vietnam capable of defending itself against the Communists. But the realists in Washington and Saigon knew that South Vietnam probably would not survive the inevitable trial of arms with the North without renewed intervention by American air power, and within six months of the conclusion of the agreement, that possibility was effectively obviated by an intractable Congress. And when the expected attack quickly brought the collapse of the Republic of Vietnam, what had been a peace with honor was derisively labeled "a decent interval."

There was no disguising the collapse of South Vietnam as anything but a humiliating defeat for American arms and diplomacy. Some in the radical antiwar movement took a perverse pleasure in the outcome, but the mass of everyday Americans reacted with a mixture of shock, sadness, and bitter anger to the fact that the United States had lost the war and the Communists had won. What had gone wrong? How could a small Southeast Asian country of 20 million people with a primitive economy defeat the world's most powerful nation? Were the tragic sacrifices of some 58,000 American dead, not to speak of the untold billions of dollars in costs, all for nothing? Why, in the first place, did America fight a war to prevent the Communist takeover of a small country in Southeast Asia? What would an undisguised defeat in Vietnam mean for American prestige with uncommitted nations in the global Cold War? Did America's loss of political will mean its guarantee was no longer credible? Thus began the tendentious debate that is still ongoing in America over the Vietnam War and its consequences.

Was it worth it? Even in 1973, few Americans would argue that the Paris agreement had redeemed so massive a sacrifice, and two years later, after the collapse of South Vietnam, almost no one argued that the war had been worth it. America will always mourn the loss of so many, but with the passage of nearly 30 years, emotions have cooled, and it is possible to examine from a longer perspective the imperatives driving U.S. foreign policy in the 1950s and 1960s which led to the costly and ultimately tragic U.S. intervention.

Over a half century ago President Truman made the decision to support France in the First Indochina War, putting the U.S. on a path that led, 25 years later, to the indisputable defeat of America in the Second Indochina War. Between those two points in time, a great many other decisions relating to Southeast Asia were made by presidents Eisenhower, Kennedy, Johnson and Nixon, each contributing incrementally and cumulatively to the final outcome. While as chief executives they had the ultimate responsibility, others with prominent roles in formulating and executing American policy in Vietnam included Dean Acheson, John Foster Dulles, Dean Rusk, Henry Kissinger, McGeorge and Bill Bundy, Robert McNamara, Clark Clifford, Melvin Laird, Averell Harriman, Henry Cabot Lodge, Maxwell Taylor, William Westmoreland, and Creighton Abrams. With a few exceptions we now have their memoirs or biographies, and since the war's end we have a wealth of other sources such as *The Pentagon Papers, Foreign Relations of the U.S.*, and the various presidential libraries as well as the works of others who, from the perspective of important secondary level positions, have made valuable contributions. Finally, historians and journalists have mined the archives and the presidential libraries to produce numerous books in which they give us their exegeses of events, so there is no shortage of material that purports to explain, to justify, to rationalize or to condemn American policy and strategies in Vietnam. The record is now probably almost complete, but the interpretation of that record continues.

This book is a yet another interpretation of the record, of why the U.S. was there, why the U.S. stayed for nearly 25 years and why the U.S. was defeated. It argues that American aims in Southeast Asia were honorable; that the American presence there *was* in the national interest; and that American objectives in Southeast Asia could have been achieved and at a far lower cost, both human and material, had different strategies been pursued. These arguments run directly counter to the standard or "orthodox" version of America's role in Vietnam that takes as settled facts that the Communists, not the United States, held the moral high ground in the war, that the vital interests of the United States were not at stake in Southeast Asia and that the war was "unwinnable" for a variety of reasons.

How was the term "vital national interest" to be defined? There were those on the liberal left who argued that Southeast Asia was peripheral to national interests, but did this mean that all such areas of the world were to be passively conceded to the international Communist bloc? Indeed, those same elements later argued that America should not contest Communist encroachment even within our own hemisphere, in Chile, Nicaragua and El Salvador. If the U.S. had pursued this policy, just where on the periphery *would* it fight? And having engaged a guarantee to support South Vietnam in its struggle to resist absorption by the Communist North, how could the U.S. withdraw when the stakes were raised in the mid–1960s as the contest became clearly a proxy in the Cold War?

The orthodox view is that the Viet Cong or National Liberation Front were nationalist patriots who were fighting to reunify Vietnam, a goal desired by all Vietnamese people, and that therefore, there was something inherently immoral in America's support of a separatist South Vietnam. Few would deny that a unified Vietnam would be a natural and desirable state of affairs, but it is entirely debatable that all Vietnamese people wished to be unified under Hanoi-style totalitarian Communism, and there was certainly nothing immoral in aiding those who wished to avoid that outcome. In any case, after 1968 those "heroic" Viet Cong patriots so admired by writers like Frances Fitzgerald had become almost irrelevant in the conventional war being conducted by the invading North Vietnam regular forces that eventually overwhelmed the South. Considering that almost 30 years after the war an unelected Communist hierarchy still rules in Vietnam as it does in North Korea and Cuba, are there still critics who argue that America's efforts on behalf of an independent non–Communist South Vietnam were immoral?

That the war was unwinnable was the line propagated by antiwar groups and elements of the media and Congress during the war, and this is now deeply embedded in orthodox histories to the extent that to argue otherwise is to be labeled revisionist. But considering the gross disparities in the military power of the adversaries, to assert that the war was inherently unwinnable by the U.S. is absurd on its face. Still, if the predominant military power dissipates nearly four years in pursuit of wrongheaded, costly and futile strategies then, indeed, the war can become unwinnable, not in the sense that the U.S. no longer had the means to force North Vietnam to desist, but that President Johnson had so badly divided the nation and forfeited its confidence that disengagement had become the only feasible alternative.

It was never the aim of the U.S. to force a World War II–style unconditional surrender on the Democratic Republic of Vietnam or to unify Vietnam under a regime friendly to the West. On the contrary, the U.S. objective in Vietnam was straightforward and nonthreatening to China: to sustain an independent non–Communist South Vietnam, and this was never qualified throughout the period of U.S. involvement. A win for the U.S. would occur when the DRV withdrew its forces and ceased its support of the insurgency in the South either through a tacit stand-down in the fighting or a negotiated cease-fire. The disjunction between what were and were not U.S. objectives brought confusion to the selection of American strategy and gave rise to the concept of limited war. Johnson and his advisors committed the fatal error of conflating limited war with limited means, adopting the flawed strategy of graduated response and applying a variety of crippling political restraints to the conduct of the war. Perhaps Johnson's most egregious error was his refusal to mobilize the nation, a deliberate decision motivated by domestic political considerations to avoid arousing the people while he led them toward his Great Society. His guns-and-butter policy not only undermined the nation's resolve but brought pernicious economic consequences.

The book deals in some depth with events in Southeast Asia between the end of World War II and the beginning of the Kennedy administration because a knowledge of this period is basic to understanding how the U.S. came to be so deeply involved in Vietnam. The critical significance of the failure of Kennedy's diplomacy in Laos and of his backing of the overthrow of Diem, matters that receive rather cursory treatment in standard works on the war, are thoroughly explored. The book documents the deepening and ultimately tragic involvement of the U.S. in Vietnam during the Kennedy and Johnson administrations, focusing on the principal protagonists in Washington and Vietnam and their roles in the decision-making processes as the policies and strategies were developed that governed the U.S.'s relationship with Vietnam and its conduct of the war. It examines the consistent disconnect between policy and the supporting strategies that were a hallmark of Vietnam involvement and provides an exegesis of why those strategies failed.

Richard Nixon, anathema to the liberal media and academia even before Watergate, has always been more heavily criticized by them for his conduct of the negotiations and disengagement than are his predecessors for creating the conditions that forced the U.S. to disengage. Could he have ended American involvement sooner? No doubt, but only by conceding the independence of South Vietnam to an implacable Communist North while sacrificing the integrity of the U.S. guarantee. Equally, Hanoi could have opted to end the war at any time, a point rarely acknowledged by Nixon's critics who place the onus for the drawn-out negotiations entirely on him. This book holds that Nixon was correct in holding out in the face of Communist obduracy and that the Paris cease-fire agreement was the best outcome realistically obtainable, given the intense domestic pressure to end American involvement. Did Nixon really intend to enforce the agreement? That we will never know because Watergate stripped him of moral authority while Congress stripped him of the power to act.

In the years following the 1964 Tonkin Gulf Resolution, the executive branch dominated the Vietnam debate, but with the disgrace and resignation of Richard Nixon and America's defeat in Southeast Asia, power shifted to Congress and to those in that branch who had most strongly opposed our Vietnam policy. This was seen by the Communist bloc, our allies, and the uncommitted nations of the Third World as a loss of will, a retreat from America's forward position since World War II in the Cold War struggle to contain Communism, and the Soviet Union and its allies did not hesitate to exploit this palpable weakness in a new and more dangerous Cold War.

Ronald Reagan pulled the nation out of the slough induced by the bitter Vietnam experience, infused a renewed national will, and wresting control from an isolationist Senate, launched a revanchist foreign policy that posed new challenges to a Soviet Union riven with deep-seated internal weaknesses. The 45-year Cold War, in which the proxy war in Vietnam was a pivotal event, ended with the collapse of the Soviet Union in 1991.

1

Ho Chi Minh's Vietnam

The southeast corner of Asia is capped by Vietnam, an elongated and sinuous country that forms a narrow veneer on the land mass behind it. It could be called the balcony of Southeast Asia from its strategic position overlooking the Gulf of Tonkin, the South China Sea and the Gulf of Siam and the shipping lanes to and from China and Japan. The shape of the country has been likened to a flattened S with over 2,100 miles of coastline in contrast to a length as the crow flies of some 1,000 miles from its southern tip in roughly 8 degrees 30 minutes north latitude to its northernmost point on the border with China. Lying entirely between the equator and the Tropic of Cancer, Vietnam is tropical in climate.

Some have also seen in the shape of Vietnam a likeness to a dragon rampant, its head formed by the northern hinterland with the tip of its tail at Camau Point, the dividing point between the South China Sea and the Gulf of Siam. The head of the dragon forms the widest part of the country, extending northwest from the coast some 300 miles inland to a range of mountains while at its narrowest point in the dragon's midsection, the country is only some 30 miles wide. Aside from its unusual shape, the country is unique in that two of Asia's major rivers, the Red and the Mekong, pass through it and form fertile deltas where they join the sea. The appropriately named Red River, the smaller of the two at about 800 miles long, rises in the mountains of China's Yunnan Province and flows through northern Vietnam. The Mekong, one of the world's longest (2,800 miles) and largest rivers, rises in the mountains of Tibet, touches Burma and Thailand and passes through Laos and Cambodia before reaching southern Vietnam. The Mekong is navigable by oceangoing vessels well into Cambodia.

The deltas of these rivers are of particular significance in the history of the country in that their fertility naturally attracted ancient agricultural civilizations. It appears that what became the Vietnamese people originated in prehistoric times in the area of the Red River delta, but apparently very little is known of their origins. In any case, the first record of these people is found in Chinese history when in 208 BC a Chinese general conquered the area that became northern Vietnam, beginning more than 1,000 years of Chinese dominion. It is truly remarkable that despite strenuous efforts over a millennium, China was not able to eradicate the Vietnamese through assimilation so that in 939 when an uprising drove China out, the Vietnamese had survived as a distinct people. Thus began the second millennium of Vietnam's recorded history in which as a feudal society it was ruled by a succession of Vietnamese dynasties. Though they had expelled the hated Chinese, Vietnamese culture, art, literature, religious teachings (Buddhism), and system of government were heavily influenced by the Chinese experience.

Chinese control had extended only as far south as the present-day location of Danang. Southern Vietnam was populated by peoples ethnically distinct from the Vietnamese with cultures that owed their origin to Indian influences. Of these, the Chams who formed the powerful and advanced Champa nation had, with the support of Cambodia, repeatedly but unsuccessfully attacked the Vietnamese until the Vietnamese finally destroyed them in 1471. This opened the way for gradual southward migration of the Vietnamese which took place over a period of some 300 years, culminating in 1757 with the annexation of the Mekong Delta from a Cambodia in decline

The Coming of the French

The great Portuguese seafarers who led the way into the Pacific during Portugal's dynamic period of exploration in the 16th century were the first Europeans to arrive in Vietnam. They were followed by the Dutch, the English and the French, all hoping to establish trading operations. It was the practice of the Catholic nations of Europe to send out their explorers with a dual mission, to establish trade and to save souls, and thus the vanguard of these expeditions always included missionaries. This was the pattern during the early European penetrations of Vietnam in the 16th and 17th centuries. During this period the saving of souls met with moderate success, but little progress was made in establishing trade, causing all the colonial powers but France to gradually to lose interest in Vietnam. Never hospitable to Western influences, in the 18th century the rulers of Vietnam began to persecute the missionaries and native converts, leading some in France to begin contemplating military conquest. Increased persecution of missionaries during the reign of Emperor Minh Mang (1820–1841) caused growing agitation among French Catholics for action in Vietnam, and the strongly imperialistic Emperor Napoleon III acted in 1857 to acquire Vietnam by conquest, perhaps motivated less by a desire to protect missionaries than by a need to avoid being left out in the scramble for colonial possessions then underway among the major European powers.

After a four-year campaign, in 1862 the French were able to force the Vietnamese emperor to cede Saigon, and in 1867 France annexed all of Cochin China, the name it applied to southern Vietnam. With Cochin China as a base, it was able to mount a successful attack against Hanoi, forcing the Vietnamese to submit to a French protectorate over Annam and Tonkin, signed August 25, 1883. Having already established a protectorate over Cambodia in 1863, France did the same over Laos in 1893, forming what was known, for the next 60 years, as French Indochina.

Cambodians and Laotians were rather tranquil and submissive peoples who were not difficult to rule, but such was not the case with the Vietnamese, a proud and martial race that never ceased to resist French control. And soon after the French had completed their conquest of Vietnam, an individual was born in an Annamese village who was destined to lead the nation out of its subjugation by France.

That individual was Ho Chi Minh. No understanding of the events that are the subject of this book would be possible without a knowledge of this man whose iron will and charismatic leadership over several decades led a small, backward Asian nation to defeat two major Western powers and unify Vietnam under Communism.

Ho Chi Minh — His Early Life

Until he emerged as president of the Democratic Republic of Vietnam (DRV) in 1945, Ho Chi Minh's life had been lived in the shadows. Thus, much of his early life is a blank page to biographers, but there is much on which there is apparent agreement although documentation is decidedly meager.

His life was closely bound up in the history of French involvement in Indochina. The official date of his birth as observed in Hanoi today is May 19, 1890, only seven years after the French had forced the Vietnamese emperor to accept a protectorate over Annam and Tonkin.

Over the course of his life he used many aliases, not adopting Ho Chi Minh (He Who Enlightens) until about 1942, but for simplicity, the name Ho will be used throughout. He was born Nguyen Tat Thanh in a northern Annam village near the city of Vinh. His father was a Confucian scholar and minor mandarin official in the imperial government who either resigned his position or was dismissed by the French, in either case because of his opposition to French rule. Tutored by his father, Ho also attended a lycée but never a university. In 1908, as a student, Ho became involved in an anti–French political demonstration that resulted in his being dismissed from the lycée, ending his formal education. He then became a language teacher in the small town of Phan Thiet in southern Annam.[1] At this point, he was probably fluent in Mandarin and French as well as his native tongue, skills that would fit him well for his future employment in the Communist International (Comintern).

London and Paris

Ho left Saigon at the end of 1911 aboard a merchant ship, spending most of the next two years as a seaman.[2] He gave up the seafaring life in late 1913 and ended up in London where he remained for most if not the duration of World War I, moving to Paris at some point between late 1917 and late 1918. In Paris he quickly became involved in leftist activities and joined the Socialist Party. He with other Vietnamese émigrés prepared a program for Vietnamese independence for presentation to the Versailles Conference, but it failed to receive consideration. He participated in the Socialist Congress at Tours in December 1920, joining a radical breakaway group which formed the French Communist Party (FCP), affiliated with the Communist Third International (Comintern). During his over five years in Paris, he appears to have been engaged almost full time in political activities.[3]

To Moscow

Such a man could not escape the notice of the Comintern which was seeking promising recruits among expatriate Asian radicals for agitation and propaganda work in the Far East, and so Ho was called to Moscow in 1923 to work in the Comintern and receive training at the Stalin School for the Toilers of the East.[4] During his time in Moscow he consistently stressed the importance of the role of the peasantry in revolution in economically backward countries, a view that would prove more prescient of the realities in the Far East than Marxist-Leninist orthodoxy which placed the proletariat in the vanguard.[5]

China

In late 1924 or early 1925, he was sent by the Comintern to Canton, China, to work under Michael Borodin, the Comintern's chief political emissary to the Kuomintang. At that point, the Chinese Communist Party, in line with Comintern instructions, was cooperating with the Nationalist Kuomintang so that Ho was able to discreetly carry out his true purpose in Canton, which was to begin organizing for a Communist revolution in Vietnam. As a first step, in June 1925, he set up the Vietnamese Revolutionary Youth League (in Vietnamese, shortened to Thanh Nien[6]), a semiopen organization (but required to operate underground in Vietnam) aimed at bringing together progressive Vietnamese nationalists of all classes and political stripes. The stated goal of Thanh Nien was an anti–French nationalist revolution in Vietnam, but with Ho as leader and an inner core of Communists, Thanh Nien was intended by Ho to form the nucleus of a future Vietnamese Communist Party.[7] Under Ho's leadership, Thanh Nien grew rapidly and by the late 1920s rivaled in influence the largest of the many other nationalist organizations which operated clandestinely in Vietnam.[8]

Vietnamese Nationalist Groups

In describing the numerous non–Communist nationalist groups that existed at this time, it is important to recognize that they included many individuals whose credentials as legitimate nationalists and patriots equaled or exceeded those of Ho Chi Minh, but once the Democratic Republic of Vietnam was established, the Communists, through assassinations and forced exiles, were able to eliminate individual nationalists they believed were potential rallying points for opposition to the regime. Of course, as the ultimate victors, the Communists wrote the history in which only Ho and his associates emerged as patriotic nationalists, and the others have passed into obscurity.

Probably the strongest of the non–Communist groups was the Nationalist Party (VNQDD), a revolutionary organization of Tonkinese origin with close ties to the Kuomintang in South China. Organized at about the same time as Thanh Nien, VNQDD was quick to recognize the underlying Communist orientation of Thanh Nien behind its nationalist façade. Another group, the Viet Nam Restoration League (Phuc Quoc) had been organized in 1911 by Vietnamese political refugees who had fled to Japan. With strong ties to Japan, it had monarchist and racial "Asia for the Asians" tendencies.[9] The New Revolutionary Party (Tan Viet), an Annamite group, was leftist but with no connection to the Comintern. These radical nationalist groups were intent on expelling the French by means of armed revolution. Finally, there were the Trotskyites, centered in Saigon, with whom the Communists cooperated until the late 1930s when Moscow ordered an end to the relationship. They were exterminated by the Vietminh in 1946.

Two other groups, formed later, also had important roles in the turbulent Vietnamese revolution and subsequent wars. In 1939, a pro–Japanese faction broke away from VNQDD to form the Great Viet Nam Nationalist Party (Dai Viet Quoc Dan Dang, or Dai Viet) which was able to survive in the South until the end of the republic. The role of Ho in Dong Minh Hoi, a coalition of Vietnamese nationalist groups formed in South China in 1944 under the aegis of the Kuomintang, will be discussed later.

These were but a sampling of the numerous factions across the spectrum of Vietnamese opposition to French rule.[10] Factionalism was the bane of Vietnamese non–Communist nationalism, opening the way for the unified and disciplined Communist Party.

Return to Moscow

Although he had successfully launched Thanh Nien, Ho's time in China was foreshortened when in 1927 Chiang Kai-shek turned on the Communists in a bloody purge that almost destroyed the Chinese Communist Party. Ho and other members of the Comintern delegation in Canton had to flee for their lives to Russia, and the Communist nucleus of Thanh Nien was scattered, some able to reach the safety of Hong Kong where, though weakened, the organization continued to function.[11] By then, Thanh Nien was, for all practical purposes, a proto–Communist party.

Ho was back in Moscow for the Sixth Comintern Congress in 1928 at which a new line was laid down by Stalin — Communist parties were no longer to cooperate with nationalist and non-Communist parties of the left. Socialist and Social-Democratic parties were now labeled social-Fascists, and Communist organizations worldwide were instructed to increase their organizing and agitprop activity among workers and peasants in preparation for the revolutionary wave that Stalin believed was imminent.[12] While the new line was aimed principally at Europe where organized Communist parties existed in every country, as will be seen it also affected the situation in Vietnam where no Communist Party yet existed.

Formation of the Indochinese Communist Party

In late 1928 Ho was again sent to the Far East, this time to Siam (now Thailand) which was then a far safer place for Comintern agents than China. Ho spent at least part of his time in Siam disguised as a bonze, a Buddhist monk as a cover for his work as a Comintern agent.[13]

Meanwhile, in Vietnam the more radical elements of Thanh Nien began agitating for the formation of a Communist Party, and lacking Ho's steadying hand, the league, in typical Vietnamese fashion, broke into squabbling factions. Alarmed at these developments, in 1930 the Comintern ordered Ho to Hong Kong to bring order to this chaos. Calling a conference between representatives of the factions, Ho quickly succeeded in bringing unity to the situation, resulting in the formation of the first official Indochinese Communist Party and the dissolution of Thanh Nien. For the first time, a Communist Party was operating in Vietnam, but under deeply clandestine conditions. Ho remained undercover in Hong Kong where he acted as the Comintern's representative for Southeast Asia.[14]

Yen Bay and the Nghe An Uprisings

The formation of the Communist Party seemed timely — the country was seething with discontent over French rule. In February 1930, an uprising organized by the VNQDD was attempted by Vietnamese garrison troops at the town of Yen Bay in Tonkin but was quickly and bloodily suppressed by the French. This episode demonstrated to the revolutionaries that it would require much more than isolated military putsches to succeed in dislodging the French.[15]

A second event of 1930 of much deeper significance to the Communists was a peasant insurrection in Ho's native Nghe An Province in northern Annam. At the outset, it may have been spontaneous, but it is hardly credible that the subsequent actions of simple, untutored peasants in organizing soviets would have occurred without Communist direction. The uprising failed to spread, remaining localized in northern Annam, and was soon suppressed. Those not killed by the French were rounded up, leading to the arrest of many of the future leaders of the DRV, including Pham Van Dong, Vo Nguyen Giap and Truong Chinh, who were tried and imprisoned.[16] The nascent Indochinese Communist Party was nearly destroyed, putting it in a decline from which it did not recover until the early 1940s.[17]

Out of it all, Ho's location and identity as a Comintern agent and the party's gray eminence were disclosed. He was arrested by British authorities in Hong Kong, and the Sûreté requested his extradition. Had the British complied, Ho would probably have gone to the guillotine in Hanoi, but though he was jailed, he was granted the right of political asylum and never extradited. He was held for a time by the British in Hong Kong, and although the final disposition of his case is not clear, it appears he was either released or escaped in 1932 and was spirited out of Hong Kong by supporters, eventually regaining contact with the Comintern which was able to bring him back safely to the Soviet Union in early 1934.[18]

Return to Moscow — The Great Terror

Nineteen thirty-four marked the beginning of The Great Terror, Stalin's murderous purges of the party, the Communist International and the Red Army that continued in waves into 1939. If Moscow in the mid-thirties was not a safe place even for Old Bolsheviks, it was still more insecure for failed Comintern agents like Ho Chi Minh.

Ho was criticized in Moscow for failing to follow the 1928 shift in the party line away from cooperation with non–Communist parties. His Thanh Nien was condemned for opportunism in its willingness to collaborate with right-wing nationalist and bourgeois elements, and he was blamed for the erroneous policy followed by the Nghe An soviets as inconsistent with the party line.[19] That Stalin did not begin his wholesale purge of the Comintern until 1937 may have given Ho time to rehabilitate himself, but nonetheless, his escape from being purged was nothing short of miraculous. Of those in the International who, like Ho, had ever been denounced for errors and deviations, few survived.

One did not survive this harrowing experience without being hardened by the ruthless methods employed in eliminating real (and imagined) opposition nor perceiving the need for slavish obedience to the twists and turns of the party line and to the person of the leader himself. Such lessons could not have been lost on Ho. Later, in the early days of the Vietminh struggle for power, similar tactics were employed in Ho's name to eliminate his non–Communist Vietnamese nationalist rivals who were perceived as obstacles to the cause.

Ho attended the Seventh (and last) Congress of the Third International in Moscow in 1935 where the Indochinese Communist Party received formal recognition, but, significantly, Ho was not even a member of the Vietnamese delegation, and at that point Le Hong Phong, not Ho, was regarded by the Comintern as the leader of the ICP.[20] Ho's subsequent rise to leadership occurred at least partially by default through the elimination in Vietnam of Phong and other potential rivals by the French Sûreté.[21]

Hitler's rise to power in 1933 foreshadowed a new party line announced at the Congress: Communist parties worldwide were now to join with bourgeois parties and the non–Communist left to form anti–Fascist popular fronts. The following year, the Popular Front government of Socialist Leon Blum was formed in France, supported by the French Communist Party. The practical effect of this in Vietnam was that the colonial authorities were ordered by Paris to permit the ICP to operate openly, and party leaders imprisoned after the Nghe An uprising were released.[22]

World War II Begins — Defeat of France

But the honeymoon ended abruptly in August 1939 with the signing of the Soviet-German Non-Aggression Pact followed by their joint attack on Poland and the start of World War II. The governments of France and England, lulled by several years of Soviet propaganda on the need for a common front against Fascism, turned on the Communists, now regarded as Hitler's allies. In Indochina the ICP was declared illegal, and the Sûreté, which had never really relaxed its vigilance, went back to its old habits of hunting down Communists.

The defeat of France in June 1940 and the establishment of the Petain-led Vichy government had a decisive influence in Indochina. Indochina remained under the control of Vichy, but the Petain government was powerless to augment its forces in the Far East to defend French possessions there. Quick to take advantage of this weakness, Japan opened what were very one-sided negotiations with Vichy that resulted, in July 1941, in the peaceful occupation of Indochina by Japanese forces. Thus, until March 1945, the existing colonial administration ran Indochinese civil affairs while French colonial armed forces coexisted peacefully with the Japanese army. This démarche by Japan not only outflanked China on the south but provided a base from which Japanese forces later attacked the Dutch East Indies, Malaya and Burma. During their occupation, the Japanese remained largely aloof from involvement in Indochinese political affairs, leaving the colonial forces free to continue their extirpation of nationalist and Communist revolutionary groups.[23]

Formation of the Vietminh

Meanwhile, beginning with his arrest in Hong Kong in 1931, Ho Chi Minh had been remote from direct involvement in the Far East[24] although he undoubtedly remained well informed of events through the Comintern's Moscow bureaucracy. In 1938, the Comintern sent him back to China, and after spending over a year with Mao's Chinese Communists in Yenan, he was able to make his way to south China in the spring of 1940.[25] There he met Pham Van Dong and Vo Nguyen Giap along with other ICP members who had fled French repression.[26] Elements of various Vietnamese non–Communist nationalist émigré groups were also present in the area.

The sudden shift in status from legal to illegal following the Soviet-German Non-Aggression Pact had put heavy pressure on the ICP from French colonial authorities so that Ho found a much-weakened party on his arrival in south China. Under these conditions, Ho used a standard Comintern tactic when the party was weak or vulnerable — organize a front to attempt to draw other Vietnamese nationalist organizations into support of what appeared to be a common cause. Although a Kuomintang-sponsored front of Vietnamese nationalist organizations was set up with Ho's involvement in late 1940,[27] Ho and the ICP Central Committee, meeting secretly at Pac Bo just inside North Vietnam in May 1941, set up a new, rival front called the League for the Independence of Vietnam, the true and enduring Vietminh Front.[28]

The Vietminh Front welcomed the participation of all revolutionary patriotic elements in achieving the goal of independence for Vietnam while temporarily subordinating the class struggle aspects of the Communist program as a tactic to avoid alienating moderate groups. Although the ICP continued to exist separately,[29] the Communist-led Vietminh Front became the core organization responsible for the forwarding of the revolution and later the war against France.

On a trip into China in August 1942, Ho was arrested near the border by Chinese authorities who found his papers suspicious. As a result, he spent over a year in Nationalist jails where eventually his identity as an Indochinese Communist and possibly as an agent of the Comintern became known,[30] putting Ho in a very delicate position, but his luck held. In September 1943 he was released from jail by warlord Gen. Zhang Fakui (Chang Fa-kwei) commanding Nationalist forces in Kwangsi province who believed that Ho could be useful to him.[31]

The Dong Minh Hoi

General Zhang had been the power behind the original Kuomintang-sponsored front organization set up in late 1940, but the covert involvement of the Communists could not be long disguised. When it was revealed, the front disintegrated. But Zhang was still determined to form a Chinese-controlled front of anti–French, anti–Japanese Vietnamese revolutionaries, so after another abortive attempt, he succeeded in March 1944 in establishing the VNQDD-dominated Dong Minh Hoi. This time Zhang permitted Communist participation, and Ho became a member of the executive committee, but actual Vietminh involvement was nominal and entirely self-serving.[32] It used its ostensible alliance with other nationalist groups in Dong Minh Hoi to establish credibility in the hope of receiving material support from the Chinese and American military and OSS groups, but the Ho-led Vietminh had no intention of participating in any revolution it could not eventually control.

In August 1944 Zhang allowed him to return to Vietnam, perhaps in the naive belief that Ho could more effectively advance the interests of the Zhang-backed Dong Minh Hoi there than in China.[33] Whatever Zhang's motive, the Chinese hope to control the Vietnamese revolution disappeared with this act.

During Ho's two-year absence from Vietnam, Giap worked to consolidate small, poorly armed guerrilla groups which were forming in remote areas of Vietnam near the Chinese border and to bring them under Vietminh control. This activity was intensified after Ho's return, but though it was still far from anything that could be called large-scale guerrilla warfare, the French colonial forces had begun to notice. They made plans in the spring of 1945 to attack into the areas of guerrilla infestation, and with the balance of forces then so heavily favorable to them, they would almost surely have been successful in breaking up the Vietminh had not a totally unforeseen event intervened.[34]

The Japanese Coup d'Etat

On March 9 the Japanese occupation forces effected a coup d'état throughout Indochina in which French military units were disarmed and interned along with French colonial authorities and influential French civilians. The Japanese action was intended to forestall an anticipated Indochinese uprising by Gaullist sympathizers after the Allies' liberation of France and the demise of the Vichy government in 1944. It was probably one of the greatest strokes of luck ever to befall a group of revolutionaries.[35] Vietnam, with the exception of Cochin China, was declared independent as were Laos and Cambodia, all under Japanese tutelage. The Vietnamese emperor Bao Dai, a puppet under the French administration, formed another puppet government under the Japanese to administer Annam and Tonkin from the imperial capital of Hue while the Japanese retained full control in Cochin China.[36]

The Democratic Republic of Vietnam

With these developments, the Vietminh's growth and influence progressed rapidly, unhindered by French opposition. The enemy was now declared to be the Japanese, but this was largely empty rhetoric because in the interim between the coup d'état in March and Japan's surrender in August, no serious operations were undertaken by the Vietminh against the Japanese.[37] Instead, the Vietminh, not wishing to arouse the sleeping tiger, concentrated on enlarging the area under its influence through the activities of its propaganda brigades.[38] As the Pacific War entered its final days, the Japanese forces isolated in Indochina became increasingly demoralized and uncertain, creating a growing power vacuum. The capitulation of Japan on August 15 removed any legitimacy from the Japanese occupation, and with the weak Bao Dai puppet government unable to exercise control, the power vacuum was complete. The watchful Ho had anticipated these events, and the Vietminh, well prepared to flow into the vacuum that existed in Hanoi, seized power there on August 19, 1945. Japanese forces could easily have batted down the relatively weak Vietminh, but not only did the Japanese choose to stand aside, they continued to hold the interned French, clearing the way for an almost uncontested Vietminh takeover in Tonkin. On September 2, President Ho Chi Minh proclaimed the formation of the Democratic Republic of Vietnam to a large crowd in Hanoi. Ho, then 55 years of age, had reached the first plateau in his lifelong struggle to unify and impose Communism on Vietnam.[39]

In the brief interregnum between the Vietminh's seizure of power in Hanoi in late August and the arrival of British and Chinese occupying forces in Vietnam beginning the second week of September, the Vietminh constituted the only significant armed group in Vietnam aside from the Japanese, who were passive. The Vietminh used this opportunity to round up and eliminate as many opponents as possible among prominent Vietnamese. It was during this period that Ngo Dinh Khoi, an anti–Communist former government official and brother of Ngo Dinh Diem, the future president of South Vietnam, was assassinated by the Communists.[40]

Postwar Occupation

At the July 1945 Potsdam conference the U.S., Britain and the USSR agreed that responsibility for postwar occupation of Indochina and the disarming and repatriation of the Japanese forces there would be assigned to Britain south of the 16th parallel (Cochin China and southern Annam) while the Chinese Nationalists would take everything north of that line. Thus, in mid–September, a small British-Indian Army contingent arrived in Saigon while no less than 152,000 Nationalist Chinese troops moved into their zone of occupation,[41] creating an entirely new situation for the Vietminh.

Although at this point the Cold War still lay in the future, Ho knew it was absolutely vital that the Vietminh present itself as a nationalist front and disguise as best it could the Marxist orientation of its leadership. To gull his nationalist opponents as well as the Nationalist Chinese into believing he had no hidden agenda, in mid–November Ho dissolved the ICP replacing it with Marxist study groups.[42] Those who were meant to be deceived would have to have been incredibly naive and devoid of any knowledge of Communist practices to be taken in by this purely tactical move.

The Chinese would have been content to see France permanently expelled from Indochina and a weak indigenous government installed and thus were tolerant of the aspirations of the DRV as long as its government included members of Chinese-backed organizations like the VNQDD and Dong Minh Hoi. Although anti–Communist, the Nationalist Chinese were prepared to tolerate a few Vietnamese Communists whom they believed they could control in preference to the French whom they could not.[43]

On the other hand, Britain, itself a major colonial power, was only too aware of the implications to its own colonies if a revolutionary nationalist group were to succeed in expelling the French by force from Indochina. Thus, in its area of responsibility the British took strong measures to suppress the very radical Vietminh organization in Saigon while at the same time releasing and arming the interned French. The Vietminh were forced out of Saigon into the countryside where they began to conduct the guerrilla warfare that lasted nearly 30 years.[44]

Expeditionary forces from France began arriving in Saigon in early October where they were welcomed by the British, but no French forces could be introduced into Tonkin until France negotiated the withdrawal of the Chinese and the future status of the DRV. Step one was to get the Chinese out which was accomplished by a Sino-French agreement signed February 28, 1946, in which France ceded all extraterritorial concessions it had held in China going back to the 19th century in return for Chinese evacuation of northern Vietnam by March 31, 1946.[45]

Negotiations with France

The future status of the DRV was the subject of negotiations in Hanoi beginning in October 1945 between Jean Sainteny acting for France and Ho Chi Minh. Of course, Ho's initial negotiating position was complete independence for a unified Vietnam. France, recognizing the realities, was prepared to recognize the Democratic Republic of Vietnam as a "free state" with a degree of autonomy within an Indochinese federation as part of the French Union but only for the protectorates of Tonkin and Annam. The status of the colony of Cochin China that it considered a part of France was to be determined by a future referendum of the people there. After drawn-out negotiations and pressured by the imminent arrival of French troops in Haiphong, Ho signed the Provisional Ho-Sainteny Agreement on March 6, 1946, the same day French troops began arriving in Tonkin. Ho, believing the DRV was unprepared for a military trial of strength with France and unable to extract major concessions, had signed an agreement that was closer to the French than to the Vietminh position, and Ho and his Vietminh associates were hard pressed to justify the unpopular agreement to the nationalists and the populace at large.[46]

As a follow-up to the Ho-Sainteny Agreement, talks between the DRV and France were held at Fontainebleau in the summer of 1946 to flesh out and formalize a final understanding, but the conference broke up in failure due to inflexibility on both sides, and Ho returned to Hanoi empty handed.[47] After Fontainebleau, negotiations between a succession of French governments and Ho's regime continued sporadically into late 1947. Once fighting began, France insisted, as a prerequisite to concessions, that order be restored which the Vietminh interpreted as requiring its surrender, and differences persisted on the issue of the free state within the French Union versus full independence.

The Lien Viet Front

The unpopular Ho-Sainteny agreement had weakened the Vietminh, so in an attempt to recoup the position, Ho resorted to the standard Communist tactic in these situations—a new front. In May 1946 he formed the National

United Front of Vietnam (Lien Viet), aimed at attracting the support of moderate nationalist elements (Catholics, Buddhists and splinter parties) which had declined to join the Communist-dominated Vietminh Front.[48] The formation of the Lien Viet failed to lull the VNQDD and other nationalist groups that were working to inform the public in Hanoi through newspapers and broadcasts as to the true nature of the Vietminh. Its more subtle measures having failed, the Vietminh resorted to open repression in the summer of 1946. Prominent opponents who were not assassinated fled to China, and opposition print and broadcast organs were closed.[49] From this point forward, the DRV was effectively a one-party state although the Vietminh, led by dedicated and well-armed Communists, always took pains to make it appear otherwise by permitting complaisant progressive parties and individuals to hold cabinet positions and a few seats in the nonfunctional National Assembly.[50] And while differences existed from time to time within the DRV leadership, genuine opposition to the Communist regime was no longer feasible.

The First Indochina War Begins

Meanwhile, the Vietminh's armed forces in Tonkin had been steadily building strength so that as the year wore on, the more militant elements believed they were now ready and should attack before the French became too strong. Whether Ho Chi Minh endorsed this position or wished to continue negotiating is not clear, but in any case, by late fall 1946, negotiations were at an impasse. The French military leadership was taking an equally hard line. After a number of incidents and growing tension during the fall, on December 19, 1946, the Vietminh launched a coordinated attack on French forces in Hanoi and Haiphong, and the First Indochina War was underway.

Under the determined attacks of the French, the Vietminh were unable to hold their positions in Haiphong and Hanoi and retired to the hinterlands of Tonkin. The DRV became a rump government exercising administrative control only in the limited areas it actually held. Ho's stature as president and focus of the revolutionary forces was undiminished, but Giap, as the Vietminh's military commander, assumed the critical role of directing the war. Initially, the French held the military initiative while the Vietminh conducted low-level guerrilla activities and built its strength.[51]

At the beginning of the war, Vietminh strength was 50,000 men throughout Vietnam, including regional guerrillas, and two years later this figure was alleged to be 250,000 although not all of this number were armed.[52] This raises the question of how a government isolated in the mountains of northern Vietnam with few resources was able so quickly to obtain large quantities of arms since, at this point, the Soviet Union had not recognized the DRV and was providing no overt support of any kind, and the Chinese Communists in far-off north China were in no position to offer aid. While one can only speculate, it seems almost certain that initially the chief source of arms was Nationalist China whose shortsighted and corrupt generals were always ready to take bribes in return for rifles. Also, although the U.S. was officially neutral on political developments in Vietnam in 1945–46, some OSS agents on the scene in 1945 were openly sympathetic to the Vietminh, and an undetermined quantity of arms came from that source.[53] But from 1945 until 1949, the DRV's sources of foreign exchange to import the large quantities of arms, ammunition and medical supplies required to carry on its war against the French remain a mystery.

After 1947, the war entered a period in which neither side was able to gain a decisive advantage. The French held the cities and major provincial towns, but their forces were never large enough to clear and hold large areas of the interior while the Vietminh continued to build its strength and enlarge the rural areas under its control. But in the fall of 1949, an event occurred which ultimately doomed the French effort to regain Indochina — the victorious Chinese Communists had defeated Chiang Kai-shek's Nationalists. The DRV was no longer alone. It now had a major ally on its northern border who could supply all the military and economic aid it would need to carry on the war indefinitely.[54]

Formation of the Dang Lao Dong — Vietnamese Workers' Party

In January 1950, the newly proclaimed People's Republic of China became the first world power to recognize the DRV, and not to be outdone, the Soviet Union followed two weeks later. These developments coupled with an adverse trend in U.S. policy led the DRV to conclude it was pointless to maintain the now transparent tactical fiction that it was a coalition front of patriotic nationalist groups, and accordingly, Ho's DRV openly allied itself with the international Communist bloc.[55] The Indochinese Communist Party, allegedly dissolved in 1945, of course had never ceased to function behind the thinly disguised screen of Marxist study groups, and in 1951 it was reconstituted as the Dang Lao Dong Viet Nam or Lao Dong, the Vietnam Workers' Party (VWP).[56] At the same time, because "Vietminh" had become almost synonymous with "Communist," another attempt was made to submerge it in the Lien Viet Front,[57] but until the end of the First Indochina War, the DRV leaders never succeeded in eliminating the close association, especially outside Vietnam, of Vietminh with Communism. These moves in Hanoi marked a sharp shift away from Ho's softer, more inclusive approach to a much harder leftist line, mirroring that of the Chinese Communists. Ho was elected chairman of the VWP but party power was shared with the pro–Chinese general secretary, Truong Chinh, a veteran Communist who was the party's chief theoretician. He and Ho had had prior differences of doctrine and strategy, but the more charismatic and pragmatic Ho had always maintained ascendancy over the doctrinaire Chinh. Other top members of the leadership at this time were the always militant and aggressive Giap and Pham Van Dong, who ran day-to-day government affairs. These four shared in the decision-making process with Ho as primus inter pares.[58]

At the same time the VWP was created, separate Communist parties were formed for Laos and Cambodia which, under the guidance of the VWP, would lead the revolutions in those countries.[59]

The War Wears On

Ho and the leadership in Tonkin had little influence on the fighting in the South where the Vietminh conducted guerrilla warfare in what became a sideshow to the fighting in the North. The assassinations and terror tactics employed by the Vietminh in the South had exceeded anything done in the North, alienating the moderate elements, so in 1951 direction of the war in the South was turned over to a new Central Office for South Vietnam (COSVN) under Le Duan reporting directly to the Central Committee of the VWP. Over the course of the two Indochina Wars, Le Duan's star was to rise steadily in the party hierarchy.[60]

In Tonkin, the main arena of the war, the area under French control steadily contracted. With the influx of arms, training and advice from the PRC, in the fall of 1950 the Vietminh armed forces, now called the Peoples' Army of Vietnam or PAVN, launched attacks against the isolated French strong points along the northern border, forcing the French to pull back into the Red River Delta. With these successes, Giap convinced his compatriots that the time was ripe for a shift to direct frontal attacks by his main force units to defeat the enemy in 1951, but this strategy proved premature when the PAVN was thrown back by a strong French defense. With the failure of the offensive, over the next two years the DRV pursued a strategy of gradually wearing down the French forces.[61]

Although the financial costs of the war were increasingly being borne by the U.S., French casualties continued to mount, and French public opinion on the war had shifted from support to apathy to opposition. By 1953, after seven years of war under a succession of governments, Paris was beginning to accept that a military victory was no longer possible and that negotiations were inevitable to end the fighting. But with U.S. encouragement it was decided to make one last maximum effort to gain military victory or force the Vietminh to negotiate under unfavorable conditions—thus, the origin of the Navarre Plan, a new strategy to defeat the Vietminh and bring the war to an end.[62]

Dien Bien Phu

Although at the end of 1953 newly appointed Gen. Henri Navarre had about 500,000 men under arms in his French Indochina Command, only about

150,000 were well-equipped, high-quality troops capable of mobile offensive operations with the balance lightly armed French Union and indigenous military and paramilitary units, suitable mainly for static defensive purposes.[63] Against these forces, Giap had 300,000 fighters of which about 150,000 were organized into regular Vietminh units.[64] Still, Navarre planned to wrest the military initiative from the Vietminh, and central to this was a strategy to draw main force PAVN units into set-piece battles where superior French firepower could be brought to bear. In retrospect, it appears Navarre's strategy was unsound in almost every respect. A decisive aspect of the plan was the establishment in late 1953 of the redoubt at Dien Bien Phu in northwest Tonkin astride the Vietminh's line of communication into Laos. In the ensuing siege, Giap used 50,000 regular troops backed by over 55,000 support troops and 100,000 transport workers to overwhelm the isolated 16,000-man garrison and inflict a major defeat on the French. To do it, he took 23,900 casualties including nearly 8,000 dead, but effectively, the battle ended the First Indochina War.[65]

The Geneva Conference

The surrender of Dien Bien Phu on May 7, 1954, was well timed for the DRV, occurring the day before the convening of the Geneva conference called by the Soviet Union, France, Britain and the U.S. to take up the issue of Indochina. In addition to the four major powers, the People's Republic of China was also represented, as were Laos, Cambodia, the Bao Dai-headed Associated State of Vietnam and the DRV with Pham Van Dong leading its delegation. In the chapter "Origins of U.S. Involvement," the positions of the participants with respect to the Geneva negotiations and the consequences of the Accords on U.S. policy in Southeast Asia will be fully discussed.

However, with respect to the DRV, it is sufficient here to say that its hopes that the conference would result in the unification and independence of Vietnam under DRV control were not fulfilled. While the Accords did end the war and established the DRV unequivocally as a fully independent state free of French political and military influence, the agreement granted the DRV control of only the northern portion of Vietnam. The Accords created a temporary partition of Vietnam at the 17th parallel, a provision which Ho was persuaded by PRC foreign minister Zhou Enlai to accept with the understanding that a plebiscite would be held in July 1956 on the question of unification.[66] This outcome of the conference was received with great bitterness by the Vietminh militants who believed that their patrons, the USSR and the PRC, had negotiated away their hard-won victory.[67]

The Agreement on Cessation of Hostilities in Vietnam was signed in Geneva on July 20, 1954, by representatives of the French Union Forces and the People's Army of Vietnam. The conferees, with the U.S. and the Bao Dai government abstaining, endorsed the Final Declaration of the Geneva Conference by voice vote on July 21.[68] Separate agreements were also concluded for Laos and Cambodia.

It is important to note that while the unspoken but anticipated outcome of the Geneva Accords was that the projected 1956 plebiscite would create a unified Vietnam under DRV control, the Accords nevertheless left Bao Dai's Associated State of Vietnam as an *independent nation*, recognized as such by the major Western powers just as the DRV was recognized by the Communist bloc. Thus, the Geneva Accords produced an anomaly in which there were, effectively, two independent states each claiming sovereignty over the same territory, so contrary to some interpretations of the Final Declaration of the Geneva Conference, there was nothing provisional or interim in the status of the Bao Dai and later the Diem regime.

With the Geneva Accords, Ho Chi Minh had reached another plateau in his struggle. Although forced by their allies to accept less than they believed they had won on the battlefield, Ho and his compatriots saw their goal as tantalizingly near. They were confident the plebiscite, if held, would result in unification under the DRV, but were alarmed at the growing U.S. support for the Diem government.

DRV Decision to Build Socialism

With the war's end, the leadership in Hanoi quickly established a "people's democratic dictatorship" instead of the usual Communist "dictatorship of the proletariat" and began a program to build socialism in the DRV.[69] Under pressure from the doctrinaire general secretary of the VWP, Truong Chinh, and with Ho's agreement, it was decided to give top priority to land reform which had as an underlying purpose the purging of any remaining elements of opposition to the regime.[70] Using methods modeled on the Stalinist and Maoist experiences of class warfare, the program created chaos in the villages where alleged rich peasants, landlords and counterrevolutionary elements were denounced, tried, imprisoned and often executed by kangaroo courts usually made up of poor, often landless peasants encouraged by doctrinaire cadres.[71] After reaching a peak of excesses in 1955, the program was labeled a blunder by Ho, who tried to stop it, but it had achieved a momentum of its own. In late 1956, a peasant protest near Ho's birthplace in Nghe An Province grew into an uprising that had to be put down brutally by a regular division of the PAVN in tactics reminiscent of French colonialism. Estimates of the number of victims of the program and subsequent uprising range from 50,000 to 100,000 killed or imprisoned.[72] In the aftermath, scapegoats for the land reform debacle had to be found, but President Ho would not be one of them. As the "soul of the revolution" he was untouchable, but Truong Chinh was vulnerable, and he was sacrificed, losing his position as general secretary of the party. Ho agreed to serve temporarily as his replacement.[73] It is interesting to note that the intensive coverage by the Western news media of the Soviet Union's bloody suppression of the Hungarian Revolution crowded out the concurrent Nghe An uprising, giving the DRV a gratuitous pass from the extremely negative publicity suffered by the Kremlin.

Unification Plebiscite Is Denied

To add to the problems brought about by the brutal land reform program, the regime was forced to accept that the plebiscite on unification would not occur. Ngo Dinh Diem, who was now firmly in power as president of the Republic of Vietnam, had no intention of permitting it, at least not under the terms of the Geneva Accords. Recognizing that peaceable reunification would not occur, Hanoi debated whether to continue focusing resources on building socialism in the DRV or shift to a policy aimed at bringing about reunification by force. Ho counseled patience, and for the moment this policy was adopted although the "stay behind" cadres and supporters in the South under the leadership of Le Duan were reactivated and instructed to step up recruiting and renew the terror tactics that had been discontinued while there was still a hope for a plebiscite on unification. At the Eleventh Plenum of the VWP Central Committee, held in December 1956, a secret policy was approved calling for a buildup of the revolutionary organization and the selective punishment of "reactionary" elements in South Vietnam. Within months this was reflected in a rise in terrorist activities that took the form of the murder and kidnapping of South Vietnamese government officials, village leaders, medical personnel and teachers.[74] Ignoring these facts, the version presented by writers sympathetic to the DRV is that the DRV did nothing to encourage the insurrection until 1959 and then only in response to appeals from their persecuted compatriots in the South.[75]

A Declaration of War — Resolution 15

For many years, Ho had been both president and prime minister (chief of state and head of government) of the DRV, but in 1955 he devolved the prime ministership on Pham Van Dong. As related earlier, as a measure to restore party unity after the land reform crisis and the dismissal of Truong Chinh, President Ho had also become party general secretary, but this was more a matter of form than substance. Someone was needed who could conduct party affairs on a full-time basis, and the Central Committee chose Le Duan to become acting general secretary while Ho remained chairman.[76] With the selection of Le Duan in early 1957, the balance of power in the Central Committee began to shift in favor of reunification by force as Duan gradually replaced supporters of Ho and Truong Chinh with his own men.[77] An Annamese by birth (Quang Tri province), Duan had fought in the South throughout the war against the French.[78] He was single-minded in his devotion to the cause of reunification so that in early 1959 at the Fifteenth Plenum of the Central Committee the militants were able, through Resolution 15, to effect a tentative change to a more interventionist policy in the South.[79] Tentative because the regime had first to consult its patrons, the Soviet Union and the PRC, both of which had been counseling caution lest the U.S. be drawn into open intervention. The attitude of the Soviet Union was especially doubtful since Khrushchev at this point was pursuing a line of peaceful coexistence with the West. Ho Chi Minh traveled to Beijing and Moscow to seek approval for the shift in policy without which it is unlikely that vital military supplies would have been forthcoming. Apparently he was successful because in May 1959 the Central Committee formalized the crucial decision to place the highest priority on achieving reunification through revolutionary war in the South.[80] This was, effectively, an unannounced declaration of war by the DRV on the Republic of Vietnam and marked the true beginning of the Second Indochina War.

Following the 1954 Geneva Accords, Ho's influence in Hanoi's decision-making councils began to diminish. During the war against France, important decisions, though made collectively, almost always had reflected his opinions, but after Geneva his pragmatism and willingness to compromise began to erode his influence with the hard liners. In the high councils of the late 1950s, his voice was still being heard respectfully, but after 1957, Le Duan's influence as party general secretary began to predominate in Hanoi. The regime continued to draw on Ho's valuable personal relationships with other leaders in the socialist camp, and it was in the national interest that Ho continue to appear to be the central figure of the regime, so if anything, Hanoi's propaganda mills intensified production of adulatory material on the kindly, simple "Uncle Ho," the soul of the revolution, the founder of the party, the father of the nation, lover of children, etc., making him into a national icon like Stalin, Mao, Castro, Kim Il Sung, et al.[81]

The National Liberation Front

As guerrilla warfare intensified in the South, the Hanoi Politburo recognized the need for a new organization there to provide reliable, correct political guidance and coherence in the revolutionary war that was formally launched by Resolution 15 against the Diem regime. In the time-honored Communist method, the solution was to create a front organization in the South, and thus, in December 1960, the National Liberation Front was willed into being. Like the Vietminh Front when it was formed, the NLF was intended to bring together "progressive" nationalist patriots, regardless of class, in a unified front with the objective of achieving reunification by displacing the incumbent regime using whatever means were necessary. Of the delegates who met at a location somewhere in the South to set up the front, none could claim to represent any large constituency in South Vietnam. Their principal common characteristic was opposition to the Diem regime, and although mostly leftist in orientation, few were *openly* Communist. Throughout its existence, the NLF always had prominent non–Communist figures in its leadership, standard procedure in the common-front strategy which the Communists used so masterfully on so many occasions, but the Communists were always able ultimately to dominate and exercise control. From its inception, the NLF was a creature of the Lao Dong (VWP) Central Committee, but the Hanoi regime always maintained the transparent fiction that such was not the case.[82] For its part, the NLF leadership may have nursed an illusion of independence, but as later events would demonstrate, it was just that, an illusion.

The usual Communist tactic when forming a front was to attempt to pull together non–Communist political organizations in support of what was represented as a common cause, and then through subversion, co-optation and other methods, to absorb, smother and otherwise render harmless or destroy its partners in the front. This is precisely what occurred with the Vietminh and later, the Lien Viet. The unique aspect of the NLF was that no non–Communist organization of any significance in the South formally joined the Front, only individuals from a variety of backgrounds (Buddhists, Catholics, Socialists, Cao Dais, Hoa Haos, intellectuals, students, Montagnards, military deserters, etc.) whose common attribute was opposition to Diem but who did not, in any formal sense, represent an organization or constituency.[83] Therefore, the Communist Lao Dong nucleus found it necessary *to create, after the fact,* the organizations which, along with itself, would make up the front.[84] The result was a number of functional liberation associations created at the village level including the Farmers' Liberation Association, Women's Liberation Association, Workers' Liberation Association, Youth Liberation Association, Student Liberation Association, and Cultural Liberation Association (for the intellectuals).[85]

The fundamental objective of these sociopolitical organizations was to gain control of the people at the village level. In this the associations functioned as communication channels for peasant indoctrination as a means of mobilizing support for the People's Liberation Armed Forces (Viet Cong), and as devices for exercising discipline in the villages. They were intended to be revolutionary mass organizations with the peasant farmer as the base of this organizational effort. Thus, the NLF regarded the Farmers' Liberation Association as the most important and put its initial emphasis there, claiming a membership of 1.8 million in 1963. To build associations of this scale and effectiveness in a scant two to three years was truly a tour de force on the part of the NLF, and there is no question they played a major role in its success in areas under NLF control and in contested areas, but later, as the GVN was able to expand the areas under its control, the farmer as an intensely self-interested individual was quite prepared to transfer his allegiance if he believed it was to his advantage. In the early 1960s, it was NLF doctrine that these well-organized village-level associations would soon form the vanguard in a General Uprising that would overthrow "the Diem clique and the U.S. imperialists,"[86] and as will be seen, this was an unfulfilled expectation of the 1968 Tet offensive.

In the West, those who may have been predisposed to sympathize with the goals of the DRV were only too ready to believe that the NLF *was* truly an autonomous organization. This was most emphatically the case with the young American antiwar marchers who bleated, "Ho, Ho, Ho Chi Minh, the NLF is going to win," and even many of their more mature leaders may have believed in the autonomy of the NLF. Left-wing journalists helped to propagate the line. Thus, for example, Lacouture asserted, "the Lao Dong was to *authorize the creation* in the southern Zone of a genuine revolutionary organization: the National Liberation Front. This organization was to be *autonomous*... ." Then he undermines his argument by adding, "but was evidently going to be *tied rather closely* to the Lao Dong in order to be able *to demand from it* aid against the Saigon regime."[87] Further, "And at that time the situation developed ... into a regular war between a *popular organization* (the NLF) with a rather vague ideology *controlled by communists*... ."[88] These references make it clear Lacouture knew the NLF was set up at the instance of the Lao Dong and was dominated by it, but later he repeatedly advances the hardly credible thesis that the NLF could claim to represent some legitimate southern constituency in which the Communists were only one factor and that it acted independently of the Lao Dong. Without belaboring the point, one has only to consider that after its victory in 1975 Hanoi exercised complete control in governing South Vietnam to the almost total exclusion of any meaningful role for the Provisional Revolutionary Government, the successor to the NLF.

On the day it was formed, the NLF, as if it were an independent voice, issued a 10-point program outlining its goals. There was assuredly nothing in them that deviated from anything the DRV could not wholeheartedly endorse, but Point One was the only one that mattered: *Overthrow the camouflaged colonial regime of the American imperialists and the dictatorial power of Ngo Dinh Diem, servant of the Americans, and institute a government of national democratic union.*[89] This phrase set the stage for another 15 years of war for when the DRV issued its Four Point "peace program" in 1965 as a basis for negotiations, Point Three called for the resolution of the internal affairs of the South *in accordance with the program of the NLF.*

The People's Revolutionary Party (PRP)

In a follow-on to the formation of the NLF, in January 1962 Hanoi transformed the covert southern branch of the Lao Dong into the People's Revolutionary Party in the South and joined it to the NLF. The PRP, as an openly Communist party and a clear adjunct of the Lao Dong,[90] would provide the Marxist-Leninist internal framework of the NLF.[91] Had the government of South Vietnam agreed in the early 1960s to negotiate an end to the war, the PRP, as the mirror image of the Lao Dong, would have had underlying control of NLF participation in any resulting coalition government in Saigon.

Hanoi's Four Points

Throughout the Second Indochina War, the DRV was always ready to negotiate a takeover of South Vietnam but until 1972 was never prepared to yield meaningful political concessions. So despite claims to the contrary by

Western partisans of the DRV or NLF, in the early 1960s there was no real basis for a peaceful settlement in Vietnam other than as a disguised surrender of South Vietnam in the form of its acquiescence to a coalition government dominated by the Hanoi-controlled NLF-PRP that, based on experiences in Eastern Europe, would lead, in short order, to a complete Communist takeover of the South.

In April 1965 the DRV launched a peace campaign when Pham Van Dong announced its Four Points[92] which with slight modifications were to stand as its basis of negotiations for the next seven years. In abbreviated form these were:

(1) The U.S. to withdraw all troops, cancel its military alliance with South Vietnam and stop all acts of war against the DRV;

(2) While Vietnam was divided, strict adherence to the 1954 Geneva Accords; no foreign military bases in either territory;

(3) Internal affairs in South Vietnam to be settled in accordance with the program of the NLF; and

(4) Reunification of Vietnam to be settled by the Vietnamese people without foreign interference.

All but Point Three were regarded by the U.S. and South Vietnam as negotiable and probably could have been successfully negotiated in the mid-sixties, but Point Three, the issue of who would have political control of the South, required another 10 years of war to resolve.

The overthrow and assassination of Ngo Dinh Diem and his brother Nhu on November 1, 1963, created a degree of uncertainty among the leaders in Hanoi. On the one hand, the event rid them of an implacable enemy who, more than any other individual, had so far frustrated their plans for a takeover of South Vietnam, but at the same time, the replacement of Diem by a potentially more popular regime could be a cause for concern. Informants in Saigon had undoubtedly kept Hanoi fully informed of the rather poorly concealed role of Washington and Ambassador Lodge in the plot to overthrow Diem, and the more perceptive observers in the DRV may have realized that this portended a dangerous increase in U.S. involvement in the affairs of South Vietnam.[93]

Rapprochement with Moscow

In the schism between Moscow and Beijing, the DRV had tilted to Beijing because the doctrinaire leaders in Hanoi believed China's position followed the more orthodox Marxist line. In late 1964, Nikita Khrushchev was overthrown in a Kremlin coup led by Leonid Brezhnev, and soon after, a DRV diplomatic mission to Moscow was pleased to find a reorientation of Soviet policy vis-a-vis the U.S. from peaceful coexistence to one of a more confrontational nature.[94] The new leaders in the Kremlin had decided they had nothing to lose by transforming the war in Vietnam into a proxy war in which their client state would do the fighting with the Americans while the Soviets supplied the weapons.

Moscow's intentions became evident when the following February a high-level military and economic mission headed by Soviet premier Alexei Kosygin visited Hanoi. This visit proved to be a watershed for Hanoi because from this point forward, the DRV was the recipient of a continuous flow of Soviet high-tech weaponry, including the radar-controlled antiaircraft artillery and surface-to-air missiles which made later air attacks very costly to the U.S.[95] In addition, for the remainder of the war, the Soviets supplied trucks, tanks and the petroleum products to support them, artillery, rockets, munitions and other military equipment to the extent that by the end of the war the PAVN had become truly a world-class fighting force. Despite persistent diplomatic efforts, the U.S. was never able to induce the Soviets to discontinue military aid to the DRV.

U.S. Escalation Begins

As it happened, the Kosygin mission overlapped one to South Vietnam by McGeorge Bundy, the president's national security advisor, presenting the Viet Cong with a very exploitable situation. On February 7, they carried out a major attack on the U.S.–ARVN base at Pleiku, an act interpreted by the U.S. as a deliberate provocation given Kosygin's presence in Hanoi at the time. American analysts believed the attack was ordered by Hanoi to invite U.S. reprisal raids while Kosygin was present, thus humiliating Kosygin with the objective of binding the Soviets more closely to the DRV, or alternatively, if the U.S. did not react, to demonstrate that the U.S. was a paper tiger. In any case, Bundy, getting his first taste of the war, and Ambassador Taylor strongly recommended reprisal air strikes which were approved by Johnson and conducted the next day on targets near the DMZ.[96] As will be seen, Johnson's approval of these reprisal attacks seemed to break down whatever remained of his restraint and marked the beginning of direct U.S. intervention in the Second Indochina War.

Ho — His Death and Legacy

In 1967, Ho Chi Minh's health began to fail, and he began making protracted visits to Beijing and Moscow for medical treatment.[97] He had ceased being the indispensable man in Hanoi although he continued as the much-revered chief of state, but Le Duan had clearly supplanted Ho as de facto leader of the DRV. Duan and his Politburo associates made the decision to launch the January 1968 Tet offensive in Ho's absence although he was consulted after the fact for pro forma approval, but the decision to open the Paris peace talks the following May was made without consulting him.[98] Peace talks were ongoing at the time of Ho's death on September 2, 1969, but he had no direct role in them and little apparent influence on decisions in Hanoi during this period.

When he died at 79 on the 24th anniversary of the proclamation of the Democratic Republic of Vietnam, his goal of unification of Vietnam was, after his 45-year struggle,[99] just six years away. Ho had one thing in common with Lenin and Mao—the underlying backbone of their movements was a disciplined Communist Party based on doctrinaire Marxism, but Ho was also able to incite and harness a strong nationalism among his followers, first to expel the hated French and, after Vietnam was divided in 1954, to unify the country under the control of the Hanoi regime.

The characterization of Ho painted by Hanoi's propaganda mills as the gentle "Uncle," kindly lover of children, was accepted not only by the unquestioning North Vietnamese people but also has been endorsed widely in the Western media. Ho's admirers in the West invariably emphasize his nationalism while minimizing his deep-dyed Communism, but his nationalism and his Communism were not separable, and thus the fight for independence and the imposition of Communism on Vietnam would go hand in hand under him. That he was a nationalist is indisputable, but he was by no means *the* sole legitimate nationalist. And while Ho could never be ranked with Stalin when it came to murder, there is certainly no doubt that in the process of consolidating power, the Ho-led Vietminh, using the methods of Stalin's NKVD, liquidated a great many non–Communist rivals who had equally valid nationalist credentials.

And so we probe the question of who and what was Ho Chi Minh? In examining the evidence, it is clear that Ho's career paralleled that of his compatriots in the pantheon of Communist leaders: early adoption of Marxism as a personal creed; many years of clandestine revolutionary work in agitation, propaganda and subversion; slavish obedience to the twists and turns of the Comintern line; clever use of fronts to manipulate and dupe non–Communist groups; seizure of power by force of arms; ruthless elimination of political opponents by violence; establishment of a one-party "people's democratic dictatorship," suppression of freedom of speech, association, and the press; imposition of a collectivized economy; and support of subversion of neighboring states.

While history credits Ho Chi Minh as being the father of modern Vietnam, was he in fact uniquely indispensable to the creation of the Democratic Republic of Vietnam and the ultimate reunification of the country? Ho founded the Vietnamese Communist Party in 1930, but he himself did not personally lead it during the 1930s. From his departure in 1911 until his return to form the Vietminh Front in 1941 he was never physically present in Vietnam, and it was only in 1941 that he began his actual hands-on leadership of the movement from within Vietnam.[100] From that point through the creation of the Democratic Republic of Vietnam in 1945, the defeat of the French, and the 1954 Geneva Accords, the Vietnamese Communists operated through collective leadership, but there was no doubt Ho was *the* paramount first among equals, and it was in this formative period that Ho's charismatic leadership had a decisive impact on the fortunes of the DRV.

So, was Ho indeed the indispensable man? The answer would be a qualified yes in that he laid the groundwork and led his movement through its formative years and the First Indochina War, but it was left to others, building on his foundation, to conduct the war with the Americans and South Vietnamese leading to the ultimate victory But in a symbolic sense, Ho *was* unquestionably the indispensable man since every revolution needs a heroic central figure, and Ho filled this need

In a final irony, on Ho's death the hierarchy in Hanoi chose to disregard his wishes to be cremated and have his ashes scattered. He was too valuable a commodity, even in death, for the regime literally to cast away. Technicians were sent to Moscow to consult with those responsible for the preservation of Lenin's remains, and thus, in emulation of Lenin's tomb in Red Square, Ho is now on view in a specially constructed mausoleum in Hanoi.[101]

2

The Origins of U.S. Involvement: 1945–1960

Perhaps because America itself was once colonies, Americans have always disapproved of the practice of colonialism that was so avidly pursued by the Western European powers. Although the annexation of the Philippine Islands in 1898 was a source of discomfort to some Americans, it was generally rationalized as benefiting the natives by exchanging an allegedly backward and corrupt Spanish rule for a progressive and benevolent American one. In any case, the American experience with the Philippine colony (or commonwealth) was short lived, ending in 1946 with the creation of the Philippine Republic. At the Versailles Conference Wilson's Principles gave promise of independence for colonized peoples, but the outcome was merely a shift in ownership of certain colonies and the establishment of a new form of colonialism called the mandate.

Roosevelt and Indochina

Franklin D. Roosevelt shared the bias of most Americans toward colonialism and during World War II, as eventual Allied victory became certain, he foresaw the opportunity, even the requirement, to bring independence to many of the colonized peoples around the world. Perhaps because of the wartime behavior of the Vichy government or his dislike of de Gaulle, when he reverted to the issue at Cairo, Tehran and Yalta, Roosevelt focused on the French colonies and most specifically on Indochina, but his close associate, ally and friend, Winston Churchill, who was probably the world's leading imperialist, was having none of it and effectively squelched discussion of the matter at the Great Powers conferences.

Why Indochina when there were a variety of misgoverned colonies around the world to choose from? Roosevelt's knowledge of Indochina was superficial, but his attention had been drawn to that remote and obscure place by events there in 1940 and 1941 that were a proximate cause of the war in the Pacific. As already related, in 1940 the Vichy government of France, bowing to Japanese pressure, granted Japan the right to station troops in Vietnam. This move southward toward the oil-rich Dutch East Indies set off alarm bells in Washington, London and The Hague and caused the U.S. to embargo the shipment of aviation gasoline, aircraft engines and parts and steel scrap to Japan. When in July 1941 Japan occupied all of Indochina and established a protectorate, Roosevelt froze Japanese assets. This halted shipments of U.S. petroleum products that were vital to the maturing war plans of Japan, and it made inevitable a Japanese grab for control of the Dutch East Indies that would entail, as a corollary, control of the Philippines, moves which were certain to bring war in the Pacific.[1]

As the Japanese-American relationship rapidly deteriorated in the fall of 1941, Indochina was a major source of friction between the two countries, culminating on December 6, the day before Pearl Harbor, with Roosevelt's direct appeal to Emperor Hirohito to use his influence to preserve peace and to withdraw troops from Indochina.[2]

Although FDR cloaked his animus toward the French in Indochina in terms of sympathy for the aspirations of the Indochinese people, at bottom it was probably the behavior of the Vichy government and the wartime collaboration of the French Indochinese colonial administration with the Japanese that was at the root of Roosevelt's opposition to the reestablishment by the French of their prewar position in Indochina. Toward the end of the war, Roosevelt was thinking in terms of some form of trusteeship for Indochina for 25 years or so, "until we get them on their feet. Just like the Philippines,"[3] but Churchill, ever sensitive to Britain's own colonial empire, was not receptive to Roosevelt's half-formed ideas for the postwar treatment of Indochina. In March 1945, it was reported that the Allies were to discuss the trusteeship with France,[4] but with Roosevelt's death on April 12, the idea died with him. The State Department was never enthusiastic, and Truman had a great many more weighty and immediate matters bearing in on him than the pursuit of secondary issues like the future of Indochina.

U.S. Air Attacks

During the war, Indochina remained out of the mainstream of hostilities. Although landings there were briefly considered by the U.S., the idea of an invasion of the Asian littoral was discarded in favor of the naval island-hopping campaign and the reconquest of the Philippines. Indochina was bypassed, but it did not escape air attacks beginning in 1943 conducted from China by the U.S. Army Air Force and later by carrier-based aircraft. These attacks, gradually increasing in frequency and intensity, were targeted against Japanese bases in the Hanoi, Haiphong and Saigon areas, railroads and bridges, merchant shipping and naval units, and coupled with submarine warfare, by 1945 had largely isolated the Japanese forces in Indochina without hope of reinforcement or evacuation.

Enter Ho Chi Minh

An outgrowth of the air campaign was the need to rescue fliers downed in Indochina, and this resulted in contacts between the Vietminh and U.S. personnel in South China. In November 1944, Army Lt. Rudolph Shaw was forced to parachute from his reconnaissance plane over Tonkin and was picked up by Vietminh guerrillas and brought to Ho Chi Minh at his headquarters near the Sino-Vietnamese border. Ho realized the rescue of this downed pilot was a heaven-sent opportunity to be of service to the U.S. and thus to establish contact, ingratiate himself and his movement and, hopefully, to gain U.S. political and material support. Accordingly, Ho personally escorted Shaw to safety across the border and into the hands of the Kunming-based U.S. Air Ground Aid Services (AGAS) which had been set up to recover downed fliers. Ho was able to parlay this incident into a subsequent interview with none other than Lt. Gen. Claire Chennault, commanding officer of the U.S. Fourteenth Army Air Force in Kunming. At this meeting, which was essentially social in nature, Ho requested a signed photograph of Chennault that the latter was only too flattered to provide. In the coming months, Ho would cleverly put this photo to good use to impress leaders of other Vietnamese nationalist factions that the Vietminh had the backing of the U.S.[5]

OSS Role in Indochina

Not only was the downing of Lieutenant Shaw a tremendous stroke of luck for Ho, but the timing was also fortuitous since it brought him to Kunming at precisely the right moment. The March 9, 1945, Japanese coup d'état had closed off the meager flow of information from clandestine sources in Indochina to the Office of Strategic Services and other U.S. intelligence groups in China. The U.S. desperately needed to establish new intelligence sources in Vietnam to provide target information, bomb damage assessments, and Japanese army order of battle information. At the time of Ho's visit to Kunming, AGAS had just been authorized to expand its mission to include intelligence gathering, and here was a man right in Kunming who said he had an organization in Vietnam that was capable and eager to fulfill this role for the Americans. At this point AGAS should have been able to learn from the OSS that Ho was a Communist, but that may not have been considered relevant. The need for a network in Indochina trumped ideology. Thus, in April, a radio with an OSS-trained Vietnamese radio operator was sent back to Vietnam with Ho, but AGAS was under strict instructions to avoid involvement in Vietnamese-French politics. Although Ho had failed to gain U.S. political and military backing for his movement, he had made contact with key American

2. The Origins of U.S. Involvement: 1945–1960

officials in China and laid the groundwork for what would develop into a productive relationship for the Vietminh.[6]

The role of the OSS with respect to Ho and the Vietminh was highly ambiguous. It acted as the channel for what was probably the first direct approach by the Vietminh to the U.S. when in August 1944 the OSS delivered a letter from the Vietminh organization in south China to U.S. consul general William Langdon in Kunming appealing for aid and offering to fight alongside the Allies against the Japanese in Indochina. This letter was actually the product of a collaboration between OSS and Office of War Information personnel on the one side and representatives of the Vietminh on the other with a view to obtaining the services of Ho and the Vietminh in projected OSS activities in Vietnam.[7] At this point, the OSS, which had been shut out by the Chinese and Free French intelligence organizations from participation in their operations in Vietnam, was clutching at straws in a desperate effort to start its own independent network in Vietnam. Langdon subsequently had a friendly meeting with Vietminh representatives in which he diplomatically avoided any expressions of support but promised to pass on their letter to the ambassador.[8] Nothing came of this episode.

On April 13, 1945, Capt. (later Maj.) Archimedes L. A. Patti arrived in Kunming from Washington to join the OSS team. Assigned responsibility for OSS activities in Vietnam, Patti came with a strong bias against French colonial policies in Indochina.[9] Learning of the AGAS arrangement, Patti met with Ho near the Chinese border and became convinced the Vietminh could meet American short-term goals of providing intelligence and fighting the Japanese in Vietnam even though Ho and the Vietminh had by then been clearly identified as Communist, and Ho made no secret of his intention to fight any postwar French effort to reestablish control of Indochina.[10] Thus, the OSS became involved in supporting the Vietminh by expanding the AGAS plan to include a group of OSS officers and enlisted men called the Deer Team, the first contingent of which was parachuted in to Ho and the Vietminh on July 16, a month before the war ended. In addition to intelligence gathering, the team was to arm and train about 200 handpicked Vietminh in guerrilla tactics.[11] Again, the Americans were instructed to avoid involvement in Vietnamese-French political matters. The military impact of the OSS team on Japanese forces was negligible, but the political fallout of the American presence was to increase the prestige of the Vietminh in the eyes of other Vietnamese at a time when Ho's name was not well known in Vietnam, and he and the Vietminh were struggling to establish ascendancy over other nationalist organizations. Also, the actual amount of arms provided to the Vietminh by the OSS remains shrouded in mystery, raising the likelihood that it was far more than has ever been admitted.[12]

The sudden end of the war in mid-August ended the need for this relationship, but this neither deterred the OSS mission from involving itself politically with Ho nor from allowing itself to be used as a conduit for communications from Ho directed to higher U.S. officials asking for American support for his government.[13] On August 22, three days after the Vietminh had taken over Hanoi, Patti, leading a small team of agents, was flown in with the mission of seeing to the welfare and repatriation of Allied prisoners of war in the area and making preliminary arrangements for the surrender of Japanese forces in northern Vietnam, but he was instructed to remain aloof from political matters. However, beginning August 26, the day after Ho's arrival in Hanoi, Patti and Ho had frequent meetings that were intrinsically political in nature over the course of which they developed a close rapport.[14] Ho was intent on persuading Patti that he was not a real Communist but a nationalist leading the Vietminh, "a coalition endorsed by a majority of non–Communist groups" which clearly was not true. The VNQDD, Dai Viet and Dong Minh Hoi, the largest non–Communist nationalist groups, were rivals of the Vietminh at that time.[15] When Ho proclaimed the Democratic Republic of Vietnam on September 2, Patti and others of his uniformed OSS team were conspicuously present at the public ceremony which risked being interpreted by observers as U.S. support of Ho or even as implicit recognition of the DRV.[16] Ho never ceased attempting to use Patti, with some success, as a conduit in seeking the recognition and support of higher American officials in China and Washington, but by this time the U.S. had adopted a firm hands-off policy in Indochina and moreover no longer had any illusions as to Ho's political orientation. When Patti's persistent involvement in Vietnamese political matters, contrary to instructions, became known to Gen. Patrick Hurley, the U.S. ambassador in Chungking, Hurley was infuriated, and Patti's mission to Hanoi very nearly came to an abrupt conclusion.[17] In any case, President Truman, who regarded the freewheeling OSS as a loose cannon, brought an end to its activities by terminating the agency by executive order effective October 1, 1945, and Patti departed Hanoi for Kunming on October 1, followed soon after by the remaining OSS personnel.[18]

U.S. Postwar Role, 1945–1950

Chinese occupation troops began arriving in Hanoi in early September followed by Brig. Gen. Philip E. Gallagher, U.S. advisor to Gen. Lu Han, the commander of Chinese Occupation Forces for Indochina.[19] The formal Japanese surrender was accepted by Gen. Lu Han on September 28 at a brief ceremony at which neither the French nor the Vietminh were officially represented.[20] U.S. Army advisors to the Chinese departed with the withdrawal of Chinese forces in mid–1946, turning U.S. representation over to the State Department which established a consulate in Hanoi accredited to France, not the DRV. The consulate remained the sole outpost of the American flag in northern Vietnam even after the French withdrew in mid–1955 following the Geneva Accords, but subsequently, American unwillingness to extend diplomatic recognition to the DRV made the existence of the consulate increasingly tenuous. It was closed at the end of 1955.[21]

In September 1945 the U.S. had no official role in southern Vietnam

2. The Origins of U.S. Involvement: 1945–1960   39

because it came under the administrative control of British admiral Louis Mountbatten, South East Asian Theater commander, in New Delhi. Nevertheless, American authorities in New Delhi saw fit to insert a small OSS team under Lt. Col. A. Peter Dewey whose assignment was to see to the well-being and repatriation of Allied POWs and civilian internees, determine the status of U.S. property (which was nil), investigate war crimes and carry out other OSS instructions.[22] Since this assignment largely duplicated that of the British, who felt fully capable of carrying out their responsibilities, they naturally regarded the Dewey mission as unwarranted interference and withheld their support. Acting on his own, Dewey quickly inserted himself into the very complex and volatile Saigon political situation even though his grasp of the Vietnamese personalities and their aims and the interplay among the factions vying for power could not have been profound, given his brief experience on the scene. His mixing in Saigon politics resulted in his being declared persona non grata and ordered out by General Gracey commanding British forces in southern Vietnam. Just before his departure, on September 26, Dewey was assassinated,[23] becoming the first of some 58,000 Americans to die in Vietnam. His death is usually attributed to the Vietminh, but whether it was a calculated or random act has never been clear.

With the winding down of the OSS, the remaining members of the Dewey team were withdrawn from Saigon, leaving the U.S. with no official or unofficial military representation there. As in Hanoi, the State Department assumed responsibility for representing American interests by establishing a legation. There the situation remained until 1952 when, after the U.S. had extended recognition to Bao Dai's Associated State of Vietnam, the Saigon legation became an embassy with Donald R. Heath as ambassador.[24] The embassy provided a base of operations for the growing number of Americans that began arriving to administer the economic aid programs the U.S. was extending to the Bao Dai regime. In the fall of 1950, the U.S. military reappeared in Saigon when a 65-man Military Assistance and Advisory Group (MAAG) began coordinating the flow of American war materiel with the French command in Vietnam.[25] The MAAG role in Vietnam grew steadily in importance with Lt. Gen. John M. O'Daniel's assignment in March 1954 as chief, and in size, reaching 342 by July 1954 when the Geneva Accords were signed.[26]

Although the official U.S. presence in Vietnam between 1946 and 1952 was minimal, Washington was watching events there closely. In the postwar 1940s, there continued to be strong anticolonialist sentiment in Washington in support of the principle of self-determination for Indochina, but this had to be balanced against the delicate political situation in France and the extreme sensitivity of the French government to American "meddling" in what the French regarded as purely an internal matter.

It is this juncture (1945–1947) in the formulation of American policy toward Vietnam that many historians identify as the fateful turning point that led, step by step, to our eventual involvement. Their arguments proceed along the following lines:

- The U.S. followed a misguided policy in allowing the dominant Europeanist faction of the State Department to override the (wiser, more farseeing?) Asian specialists who correctly foresaw the coming cataclysm in Asia, and in so doing, the U.S. hypocritically sacrificed America's cherished principles as well as those in the Atlantic Charter and the San Francisco Declaration by failing to support Vietnamese aspirations.[27]

In late 1945 and 1946, a controversy did indeed exist within the State Department between the Europeanists and the Asian specialists over the correct U.S. position vis-a-vis Indochina, with the Europeanists, who had traditionally dominated the State Department, easily prevailing.[28] Thus, in May 1945 at the San Francisco Conference the U.S. privately assured France that the U.S. did not envision a postwar trusteeship status for Indochina without French agreement, something that was highly unlikely, and that, therefore, French sovereignty over Indochina was not in question. In August, Acting Secretary of State Dean Acheson affirmed internally that the U.S. would not oppose reestablishment of French control of Indochina,[29] and from the end of World War II until early 1950 the U.S., in fact, pursued this policy but always with the caveat that in reestablishing control, France would work toward granting increased autonomy to the Vietnamese leading to eventual independence, and in friendly and delicately phrased diplomatic terms the U.S. persistently encouraged France to this end.[30]

Those who question the correctness of U.S. policy in giving primacy to our interests in Western Europe do so only with the benefit of several decades of hindsight. At the time, all of Eastern Europe including Poland, the Baltic states, Hungary, Rumania, Bulgaria, Yugoslavia, Albania and East Germany had already fallen under Communist control. The status of Austria, Czechoslovakia and Finland was in the balance. West Germany, under Allied occupation, was still a political cipher. The Communists under Togliatti were rampant in Italy. France, our traditional ally, seemed our best and perhaps our only hope to retain a bridgehead of Western democracy in a major country on the Continent. But France, too, was under threat that the French Communist Party, at the head of a coalition, could form a government.

Among the proudest of nations, France had been deeply humiliated by her defeat by Germany, her ancient enemy, and the nation was seeking scapegoats for the debacle. The issue of "who lost the war" was lacerating the French polity in the immediate postwar years, and it was in the midst of this bubbling cauldron that the question of Indochina arose. To the French nation, regaining control of its prewar possessions was a key element in the restoration of France to its former grandeur as one of the world's great powers. Thus one can appreciate that at this point, among French political parties, it was absolutely imperative to avoid being "the party that lost Indochina," the jewel of the French colonial empire.[31] Even the French Communist Party, following Moscow's lead,[32] believed it expedient to support the French government's Indochina policy into 1948 when the party went into opposition on an unrelated domestic issue.

2. The Origins of U.S. Involvement: 1945–1960

Under these conditions, for the U.S. to refuse to recognize French sovereignty in Indochina or to recognize Ho Chi Minh's government and to provide it with material support would have been regarded in Paris as an utter betrayal and repudiation of an ally and faithful friend. Franco-American relations would have been so severely damaged that the balance of French public opinion could indeed have tipped in favor of the Soviet Union, which was then supporting the French government's position on Indochina. Thus, in Washington's foreign policy councils, pragmatism trumped altruism. Clearly, U.S. interests were best served by recognizing French sovereignty while encouraging negotiations between the French and the Vietnamese for the establishment of real democratic institutions and the granting of increased autonomy to the Vietnamese people.

- We ignored or pigeonholed numerous communications from Ho Chi Minh appealing for U.S. support because State Department policy makers wrongly labeled him a Moscow-controlled Communist, thus driving him to seek Communist bloc support.[33]

This is the theory that the U.S. missed an opportunity in 1945–47 to "Titoize" Ho when he was seeking support wherever he could find it.[34] Of course, in those years the Tito model of deviationism did not exist since his open break with Moscow did not occur until June 1948 when Yugoslavia was expelled from the Cominform (successor to the Comintern). Putting this aside, while Ho and Tito were indeed strong nationalists, both were also dedicated Communists, and after the schism with Moscow, the Tito regime remained fully collectivist, and the opening with the West took several years to mature.

As to Ho, by mid-1945 if not earlier, top officials in the State Department knew of his record as an agent of the Comintern, yet in all his contacts with Americans Ho always stressed that his main objective was independence, not Communism,[35] something that was truthful in a narrow sense. But few if any Americans were familiar with Ho's writings, going back to 1926 with his book, *The Revolutionary Path*, which had described the revolution as a two-stage process, the first stage leading to national independence and the second to the class struggle resulting in the final destruction of capitalism.[36].

If Washington had been willing to disregard the disastrous effect on U.S.-French relations of extending recognition and aid to Ho, in return the DRV would doubtless have been prepared to make a temporary accommodation with the U.S., that bastion of capitalism, but Ho could not have sustained this façade for long and retained the loyalty of the more radical and doctrinaire Marxist elements of the Vietminh leadership where decisions were made collectively.[37] And certainly any Tito-like stance would have collapsed when the victorious Chinese Communists arrived on the northern border, and a break with the U.S. would have been inevitable. No, the Hanoi politburo's plans for the DRV and eventually for all of Vietnam were for a fully collectivized economy in a one-party state aligned with the international

Communist bloc, plans that were hardly compatible with U.S. support in the Cold War period.

Thus, while it is seductive for historians retrospectively to criticize U.S. policy in Southeast Asia in the postwar 1940s, when alternatives facing policy makers *at the time* are considered, America's larger interests were best served by sustaining an ally in Paris and nonintervention in Indochina while encouraging negotiations toward eventual independence for Vietnam.

* * *

The Shift in U.S. Policy

Triggered by the imminent collapse of Greece and Turkey, the announcement of the Truman Doctrine in March 1947 signaled formal adoption by the U.S. of a policy of containment of Communism followed three months later by the launch of the Marshall Plan (European Recovery Program). These two initiatives, along with the establishment of NATO in 1949, effectively blunted Communist penetration in Western Europe and the Eastern Mediterranean and deflected the Kremlin's focus to what appeared to be more fertile fields in the Far East. In 1945 the Soviets, in an opportunistic last-minute entry into the Pacific War, occupied Manchuria and North Korea. The last Soviet occupation troops left North Korea in late 1948, leaving behind the radical and bellicose Kim Il Sung Communist regime. In Manchuria, the Soviet presence made difficulties for Chiang's overextended Nationalist forces and facilitated the infiltration of the Chinese Communists whom they supplied with captured Japanese arms. By the end of 1948, Mao's forces controlled Manchuria and most of China north of the Yangtze,[38] and by mid–1949, the collapse of the Nationalists was complete. On October 1, 1949, the People's Republic of China was proclaimed, and Chiang Kai-shek fled to Taiwan. The Communist victory in China shook America to the core, creating an uproar in Washington with long-lasting partisan repercussions that would have a direct bearing on our policies in Indochina.

As these adverse developments unfolded in China and Korea, the U.S. gradually came to a resolution regarding our ambiguous policy toward Indochina. While Washington was under no illusions that the 1949 Elysée agreements that established the Associated States of Indochina within the French Union meant genuine independence for Vietnam, still they represented movement in the direction we had been encouraging since the war, and the U.S. gave diplomatic recognition to Laos, Cambodia and the Bao Dai Vietnam regime in February 1950.[39] At the same time, it had come to be accepted in Washington that the Ho Chi Minh regime was thoroughly Communist but not necessarily a Kremlin-directed brand of Communism, and some even argued it was a benign, nationalist form of Communism. (The nationalist character of the regime was never in question, and events were to show that it was definitely not Kremlin-directed, but it was anything but benign.) But whether nationalist or Kremlin-directed, it nevertheless was viewed as representing the threat of Communist penetration into an unstable Southeast Asia already in turmoil.

Paralleling the French in Indochina, the Dutch had battled since 1945 to reestablish themselves in Indonesia (formerly the Dutch East Indies), but unlike the French, in December 1949 the Dutch gave up the fight and granted full independence to Indonesia under Sukarno, a nationalist whose political leanings were not yet clear.[40] In Malaya, beginning soon after the war, the British struggled for a decade and ultimately succeeded in defeating a Communist insurrection by ethnic Chinese, and in the newly independent Philippines, the Communist-led Hukbalahap insurrection was in full swing. These adverse developments all came piling in on a very alarmed Washington in the 1948–1950 period.

By early 1950, it was clear that France was not going to succeed in reestablishing its authority in Indochina without a far greater commitment of its armed forces, entailing a significantly reduced contribution to NATO while at the same time further crippling its already overburdened finances. Further, Washington policy makers believed that Chinese support of the Vietminh was now a certainty and that China might even intervene openly in Indochina. So, the French appeal for help in the struggle with the Communist Vietminh got a sympathetic reception in Washington, even though there was no avoiding the fact that France's principal objective was to regain control of its prewar colonies, not to contain Communism. So shortly after recognizing the Associated State of Vietnam in early 1950, the U.S. announced a small program of military aid to the French forces there, but the start of the Korean War in June and Chinese intervention in the fall brought large increases in aid to the French in Indochina[41] as the Truman administration, Congress and the American public quite naturally made a connection between these events. There is no need here to detail the amounts and forms of aid provided by the U.S. between 1950 and the cease-fire in 1954. Suffice it to say the total monetary contribution to France over the period came to over $2.7 billion, divided almost evenly between between war materiel for Indochina and financial support of the French national budget. In fiscal year 1954, the last year of the First Indochina War, the U.S. was covering 78 percent of the monetary cost.[42] Thus, from a small commitment to help the French in the spring of 1950, the U.S. was steadily drawn into the struggle, and Vietnam became the place where the U.S. would commit its prestige against the further advance of Communism in Asia.

The Decision to Support France

After faulting the policy of giving primacy to Western Europe and citing the "missed opportunity" with Ho Chi Minh in 1945–47, next, historians of the orthodox school have criticized the decision to provide military support to the French in Indochina.[43] For a fair reading, this decision must be viewed in the context of 1949–50, a period that saw an almost unbroken stream of adverse developments for the U.S. in Europe and Asia[44] that gave Washington every reason to believe the West was losing the battle against Communism. Some have charged that the French cleverly manipulated Washington's fear of Communism to gain American support in Indochina,[45] but Washington was not so obtuse that it did not recognize that France's first interest in Indochina was to restore its authority there. Thus, Washington's wish to forestall Communist encroachment in Southeast Asia had to be set against its need to avoid being seen as supporting a colonial war. In the end, the Truman administration swallowed its misgivings and decided to support the French.[46] Aside from resisting the spread of Communism, Washington reasoned that aid would entitle it to a voice on French policy in Indochina, i.e., that Paris could be persuaded to recognize the futility of its policy and grant true independence to the Indochinese states, thus erasing the colonialist stigma and undermining the Vietminh, which claimed sole legitimacy as fighters for independence. But despite the fact it was only American aid that enabled France to continue fighting in Indochina for another four years, French pride would never concede the U.S. a voice in policy or military strategy there,[47] and the Associated States negotiated full independence only after France had determined to end the war.

What if Truman had chosen to stand aside, to do nothing in 1950? One could speculate endlessly on the probable outcomes, but with the benefit of hindsight, it seems highly likely that all of Indochina would have been under Communist control over 20 years sooner than the actual event.

One could rightly argue, with perfect hindsight, that this outcome at no cost in American lives would have been immensely superior to the same outcome 25 years later at the cost of 58,000 Americans and perhaps 2 million Vietnamese. But we are dealing in the context of 1950 when NSC-68 [48] and the Domino Theory began driving American thinking about Southeast Asia. NSC-68, a joint State-Defense paper, was the postwar turning point in American policy toward the aggressive expansion of Soviet Communism. It analyzed the threat and capabilities of our adversary and recommended actions to stem what had been, since the war, its steady advance. This included large increases in spending on defense and greater preparedness to support other free societies and emphasized the need to unify the American public behind this new course. NSC-68 was adopted as national policy on April 25, 1950. What had been piecemeal and ad hoc responses to Communist thrusts would become, after NSC-68, a concerted global effort, and the decision to aid France in Indochina was consistent with this policy.[49]

The Domino Theory, this well-known and much-maligned principle, held that the loss of Vietnam would trigger in quick succession the fall to Communism of the other nations of Southeast Asia.[50] It is the current fashion to ridicule this theory because events have proven it wrong, but perhaps the very reason it has been proved wrong had everything to do with American intervention in Southeast Asia. As discussed earlier, in 1950 an unstable Southeast Asia lay wide open to Communist penetration. The Vietminh were winning the war in Vietnam, Vietminh-sponsored guerrilla groups were forming in Laos and Cambodia and strong Communist movements existed in Malaya, the Philippines, Burma and Indonesia. A weak Thailand watched developments apprehensively. With historical interests in the Philippines, the U.S. was helping to defeat the Communist-led uprising there, but elsewhere in Southeast Asia the U.S. had never had close commercial or cultural ties with any of the nations. Thus, a passive attitude by the U.S. to events in the area would naturally have been interpreted by the Soviets and Chinese as giving them a free hand there, and one can easily visualize the successive collapse of these weak countries to Communism. But the U.S. decision to support the French, and later the Republic of Vietnam, had two results:

- It put the Soviet-Chinese bloc on notice that the U.S. intended to contest Communist encroachment in Southeast Asia, making the area an arena of potential conflict. After the Korean War, China sought to avoid another armed confrontation with the U.S. and thus followed a policy of restraint to avoid U.S. military intervention.
- It bought time. By the mid–1950s, the Communist insurgencies in Malaya and the Philippines had been defeated, and a stronger Thailand was firmly aligned with the West. South Vietnam had been stabilized and appeared to be on its way to becoming an independent, democratic state capable of resisting Communist penetration. The strong U.S. presence in Southeast Asia unquestionably stiffened the Indonesians later in their successful struggle to defeat a Communist coup d'état.

Influence of the European Defense Community

Criticism of the decision to support France in Indochina also gives little weight to or disregards altogether the containment strategy the U.S. was pursuing in Western Europe in which France played a key role. The principal element of this strategy was the U.S.-supported European Defense Community (EDC), a pooling of the armed forces of the Western European nations that would entail rearming West Germany. This was *the* primary American foreign policy initiative in Western Europe in the early 1950s, but given French fear of a rearmed Germany, persuading France to agree to the EDC would require delicate diplomacy. Thus, a sympathetic U.S. response to French pleas for support in Indochina could be called a quid pro quo, but it was also *realpolitik*.[51] In the event, France stalled final ratification of the EDC for over three years while the war in Indochina continued. The center-right Gaullist Rally of the French People (RPF Party) was torn between strong support for the Indochina war and violent opposition to the rearming of Germany, but when the Geneva Accords ended the war in July 1954, the RPF quickly joined with the French Communist Party in rejecting the EDC in the Chamber of Deputies.[52]

Effect of the Korean War

As related above, the decision to aid France in Indochina was driven initially by European policy considerations, but the onset of the Korean War gave

Indochina new significance on its own merits. The keystone of American postwar policy in Asia was Japan where, by encouraging an early economic recovery, the U.S. hoped to bring stability to the region. South Korea and Taiwan, as traditional sources of rice for Japan, had an important role in this plan, but the flight of large numbers of Nationalists from the mainland to Taiwan had drastically reduced the rice surplus there, and the Korean War effectively eliminated Korea as a source. Thus Indochina, as a rice surplus area, took on new importance in U.S. plans for Japan and added to the urgency that control of Vietnam remain in friendly hands. In addition, with the loss of China as a market, Japan badly needed a friendly Southeast Asia as an outlet for its manufactured goods.[53]

The U.S. at Geneva

Although the U.S. had briefly considered the idea of unilateral intervention during Dien Bien Phu, the Eisenhower administration concluded the U.S. would go in only as a part of a unified action with Britain, but Britain demurred, placing its hopes for a settlement on the upcoming Geneva talks. Washington did not welcome these talks, knowing even before the Dien Bien Phu debacle that France was desperate to end the war and was prepared to make major concessions in the hope of salvaging something of its economic and cultural position in Vietnam.

Secretary of State Dulles knew that with the bitter Korean War having ended only a year earlier in an inconclusive stalemate, the American people would be strongly opposed to any agreement that would sanction the establishment of yet another Communist regime in Asia, and that therefore the U.S. could not be a signatory or guarantor of any such agreement.[54] He instructed Walter Bedell Smith, the head of the American delegation, to disengage from the negotiations and assume the stance of an observer. The U.S. continued to exercise its influence through private talks with Britain and France but took a passive role in the general negotiations.[55]

Facing the reality that the war was going to end, Vietnam was going to be partitioned, and at a minimum, the Communists were going to gain control of northern Vietnam, Dulles sought to obtain an outcome from the Geneva talks that would minimize Communist gains and create a postwar situation in Indochina in which stable non–Communist regimes could be established and sustained in Laos, Cambodia and the lower half of Vietnam. In private talks, Dulles and Anthony Eden, the British foreign secretary, developed a seven-point list of principles which if adhered to in the negotiations would produce an agreement the U.S. and the Great Britain would be willing to respect. France was able to negotiate these principles into a final cease-fire agreement which the U.S. believed was as good as could be expected, considering the weak negotiating position of the Western powers.[56]

Dulles foresaw that the outcome was going to leave three very weak nations—Laos, Cambodia, and what remained after the partition of Vietnam — all highly vulnerable to a Communist takeover, and he knew that to forestall this the U.S. would have to fill the void created by the withdrawal of the French. So the State Department began planning for U.S.-backed nation-building programs in all three countries and some form of multilateral regional security organization in the area — the genesis of the Southeast Asia Treaty Organization.

Southeast Asia Treaty Organization

Regarding the 1954 Geneva Accords as a diplomatic defeat for the West that could lead to further Communist encroachment in Southeast Asia, Dulles did not delay in forming a collective defense treaty à la NATO (but without the teeth of NATO). Thus, SEATO was signed in Manila in September 1954, a bare 60 days after the conclusion of the Geneva Accords, and ratified by the U.S. Senate in February 1955. Signatories were the U.S., Britain, France, Australia, New Zealand, Thailand, Pakistan and the Philippines. Of the other Southeast and South Asian states, the so-called Colombo Pact nations of India, Ceylon, Burma and Indonesia maintained a nonaligned stance, declining to join, and Malaya was still a British colony. A provision of the 1954 Geneva Accords prohibiting military alliances prevented South Vietnam, Laos and Cambodia from joining, but the treaty unilaterally placed them under the umbrella of its protection as protocol states.[57] Neutralist Cambodia soon renounced protection under the pact, and as will be seen when the Laotian neutralist coalition government was formed in 1962 one of its first acts was to repudiate its status as a protocol state, leaving Vietnam as the only protocol state of SEATO. In Vietnam, U.S. involvement initially was justified under SEATO, but after the passage of the Tonkin Gulf Resolution in August 1964, President Johnson no longer needed the fig leaf of SEATO as a legal basis for American intervention.

Enter Ngo Dinh Diem

At this point we will digress to introduce a figure who had a central role in the story of America's involvement in Vietnam — Ngo Dinh Diem, the father of the Republic of Vietnam, a dedicated Vietnamese nationalist and patriot whose credentials in that respect were fully as valid as those of Ho Chi Minh. That Diem created the nation is indisputable, though this is regarded as a perverse accomplishment by some, but in retrospect his critics have not been able to suggest a credible alternative who could have succeeded, as he did, in consolidating an anti–Communist government in Saigon.

When the 1949 Elyseé Agreements established the Associated State of Vietnam within the French Union, Paris induced Bao Dai, who had resigned as the puppet emperor of the protectorate in 1945, to return as head of state under French tutelage. With the conclusion of the Geneva Accords, Bao Dai sought a prime minister to form a new government to administer his domain, i.e., that portion of Vietnam below the 17th parallel which would constitute the de facto Associated State of Vietnam. The 53-year-old Diem, with a reputation as a lifelong anti-communist and untainted by collaboration with the French, got the job, and on July 7, 1954, took power in Saigon.

Few new national leaders in history have faced the problems confronting Diem as he took office. Since its formation in 1949, the Associated State of Vietnam had been kept afloat by French subventions and U.S. economic aid, but Diem knew that after Geneva he could not count on continued financial support from France. The Eisenhower administration quickly realized that South Vietnam would not survive without financial support, and in August Diem received Eisenhower's qualified pledge of support followed in October by firm assurances of aid.[58]

In undertaking to support the Bao Dai-Ngo Dinh Diem regime in 1954, the principal U.S. objective was to block the anticipated Communist expansion into Southeast Asia. It hoped to do this by providing economic and military backing to the Associated State of Vietnam and in the process to create an economically strong, independent and democratic state capable of resisting Communist encroachment and subversion.[59] During the first year, the chances of success seemed slim indeed as chaos reigned in South Vietnam, and Washington's support of Diem began to waver badly.

Lansdale and Diem

On June 1, 1954, Col. Edward G. Lansdale, USAF,[60] arrived in Saigon at the head of the Saigon Military Mission (SMM), a 10-man CIA team assigned to undertake paramilitary operations and to wage political-psychological warfare against the Vietminh, working with the Vietnamese while keeping the French as friendly allies, "as far as possible."[61] The U.S. Military Advisory and Assistance Group (MAAG) was used as the cover for the SMM, but Lansdale reported nominally to the U.S. ambassador, Donald Heath. The exploits of the team are related in its report,[62] so will not be recounted here other than to say that in terms of actual damage to the Vietminh, little of real significance was accomplished despite the exaggerated claims of the report, but what was of major importance in the history of South Vietnam and its relationships with the U.S. was Lansdale's crucial role in the survival of Diem as the leader of South Vietnam. Lansdale was to gain a position of trust with Diem that was never equaled by any other American official.

In 1954 Lansdale was fresh from his experiences in the Philippines where he had worked with Ramon Magsaysay in defeating the Communist-led Hukbalahap insurrection. In Saigon, he quickly solidified his position when he helped Diem defeat an incipient coup by the Vietnamese army chief of staff.[63]

In November 1954, when Gen. J. Lawton Collins, President Eisenhower's special representative with the rank of ambassador, arrived in Saigon, Diem's grip seemed tenuous indeed, and influenced by the anti–Diem bias of General Ely, the French high commissioner, Collins soon began lobbying in Washington for Diem's removal. Thus, the U.S. was in the anomalous position of having, on the one hand, a CIA man helping Diem to retain power and, on the other, the president's special representative recommending that Diem be replaced. In the event, Lansdale's advice to Diem proved more effective than Collins' advice to Eisenhower because, with the defeat of the sects, Washington decided definitively to throw its support behind Diem. In the face of French opposition to Diem, this decision was the final breaking point with France over Vietnam policy.[64] Collins' usefulness in Saigon was at an end, and he returned to the U.S., to be replaced by Ambassador G. Frederick Reinhardt in May 1955.[65]

The Refugee Problem

Diem's first challenge was the influx of 860,000 refugees from the North who, under the terms of the Geneva Accords, had chosen to regroup to the South. Under the agreement, only 300 days were permitted for the regroupment, creating a massive flow of homeless people that had to be fed, housed and resettled. Some find it difficult to accept that so many would voluntarily opt out of the socialist DRV and so attribute the massive emigration of Catholics to anti–Vietminh fear propaganda generated by shadowy American agents.[66] In fact, the Catholics, encouraged by their priests, chose to leave for the South because their treatment under the Communist DRV was highly uncertain.[67] In the South, about 100,000 Vietminh and sympathizers regrouped to the North, but the Vietminh was careful to leave in place a nucleus of hard-core cadres estimated at from 5,000 to 15,000 people.[68] The successful absorption and resettlement of nearly 1 million refugees, carried out by a new government in a highly unstable period, was probably Diem's outstanding accomplishment.

The Sects

In his first six months as premier, Diem laid the groundwork for resettling the hordes of refugees from the North and gained control of the Vietnamese National Army when the French high commissioner relinquished command to Diem's government, but his struggle to consolidate his regime was not over. He still had to deal with that unique phenomenon of South Vietnam, the sects, which were, for all practical purposes, operating as autonomous states within a state.

Of these, the two major religious sects, Cao Dai and Hoa Hao, numbered between them 3 million to 4 million adherents and controlled significant areas of South Vietnam with private armies of some 30,000 irregulars. The much smaller Binh Xuyen, on the other hand, was devoid of pretensions to any religious creed or political program. Rather, it was a criminal organization engaged in various illegal activities, but incredibly it controlled the Saigon police, something that could have occurred only through a profoundly corrupt arrangement with Bao Dai and the French. The Binh Xuyen army of about 2,500 well-armed men was concentrated in the Saigon-Cholon urban area.

Such was the challenge facing Diem in early 1955 — to break the power of these disparate and unruly states within a state, to gain their allegiance or, failing that, to destroy them. Knowing that the sects would never stay unified, his tactic was divide and rule. When Diem brought the religious sects under control in the spring of 1955, Lansdale was alleged to have been the bagman for the CIA funds that were used to bribe certain sect leaders,[69] and after several weeks of fighting, the national army destroyed the Binh Xuyen. Diem had won.[70]

Formation of the Republic

There still remained one more step in Diem's consolidation of his government — ridding itself of the baggage of Bao Dai, the absentee monarch and chief of state. He laid the groundwork for this on July 7, 1955, the first anniversary of his rise to power, when he announced a referendum for October 23 on the issue of monarchy versus republic. From his perch in Cannes, Bao Dai, knowing his monarchy was doomed, attempted to forestall the vote by dismissing Diem, but Diem ignored him. In a foregone conclusion, Bao Dai was repudiated by the people of South Vietnam by 98.2 percent of the vote. On October 27, 1955, Diem proclaimed the Republic of Vietnam with himself as president.[71] Lansdale drew on his civilian experience in advertising to advise Diem in preparing for the referendum, but it is doubtful Lansdale's advice was entirely responsible for the lopsided vote.

It was now left to Diem only the task of providing the trappings of democracy to his nascent republic. A 123-member Constituent Assembly was elected March 6, 1956, which, not surprisingly, was almost entirely free of opposition to Diem, and in July the assembly approved a Diem-drafted constitution providing for a strong executive form of government with Diem as president for a six-year term. On October 27, the first anniversary of the republic, the constitution was officially promulgated, Diem inaugurated, and the Constituent Assembly transformed into the first National Assembly. Thus South Vietnam, which had been regarded by the Communist bloc (and some in the West) as purely a weak, temporary entity pending takeover by the DRV, had confounded everyone by becoming an independent republic recognized by all the major Western powers. That the U.S. backing was crucial to this unlikely outcome is indisputable, but in the end it was the courage and tenacity of Diem that shaped the result.[72]

While these internal developments were underway, in February 1956 Diem moved to end the last major French presence in Vietnam when he requested the withdrawal of French troops. The French High Command in Saigon was dissolved on April 26, 1956, and thus, the only Western signer and a putative guarantor of the Geneva Cease-Fire Agreement departed Vietnam, abandoning the field to the U.S. as the protecting power of non–Communist Indochina.[73]

In another crucial step, he formally repudiated that part of the Geneva Accords calling for a plebiscite on unification no later than July 1956. Diem's position was that South Vietnam was not bound by the accords because, first, the truce agreement had been between *France* and the DRV, and second, the Final Declaration was unsigned, and in any case, had not been adhered to by the Associated State of Vietnam (of which he was then premier). Hanoi strongly protested Diem's démarche, but it was met with only mild diplomatic remonstrations by the USSR and the PRC. The U.S. and Britain supported Diem.[74] Thus, the line of the 17th parallel delineating the two regroupment zones which the Geneva Accords stated was "provisional and should not in any way be interpreted as constituting a political or territorial boundary,"[75] became the de facto border between the DRV and the Republic of Vietnam.

Diem now had all the levers of power firmly in his hands. It was a golden time for him, but from late 1956 when his popularity was at the flood, it began to recede like an ebbing tide. Although the republic had all the trappings of democracy — a constitution, a legislature, and a judicial system — Diem, trained in the mandarin tradition, did not believe a representative government on the model of America and Western Europe was appropriate for his young country, especially at a time when his nation was under threat of armed Communist insurgency.

Rather, he believed the politically unsophisticated people of his underdeveloped nation needed a highly centralized, authoritarian government and in this he was not greatly different from the leaders of other Southeast Asian nations nor those in other less-developed areas of Africa and South America. In his government all power was centralized in the presidential palace in the persons of Diem and Nhu, his brother and chief advisor. The National Assembly never sought to oppose him, the judiciary became his willing tool while the cabinet was largely comprised of technicians. The concept of loyal opposition was foreign to him — one could not oppose him without being considered disloyal.[76]

Diem the Liberator

Compared to the turbulent two years leading to the proclamation of the republic in October 1956, the years 1957 and 1958 were for Diem probably the most tranquil of his nine years in power. He was now secure in his role as the unquestioned leader of the republic. While not all elements of South Vietnam were wholeheartedly supportive, he had the backing of the U.S., and more importantly the loyalty of the army. During the dark times of 1954 and 1955 when his regime was tottering, his support in Washington had wavered badly, but in the end, U.S. support held fast, largely by default, because no one could identify an acceptable alternative.[77] Now he was being lauded in the American media as a hero, a genius, and Southeast Asia's bulwark against Communism. In May 1957 he made a triumphal 13-day visit to the U.S. during which he addressed a joint session of Congress and the National Press Club and was awarded honors and feted at every turn. The *New York Times* hailed him as the liberator of South Vietnam.[78] In 1959, he received the U.S. Freedom Foundation award for resistance to Communism, and a *New York Times* editorial hailed the award.[79] Later that year, a *Times* editorial cited his fifth anniversary as president and the gains under his administration.[80] Still, there were disquieting signs, beginning in 1957, that guerrilla activity was again on the increase, manifested by the growing number of assassinations of minor government officials and village leaders.[81]

Civilian Advisory Teams

With Diem now in less need of his advice, in 1956 Lansdale was reassigned to the Pentagon,[82] but as will be seen, his influence on affairs in Vietnam was not at an end. With the consolidation of the Diem regime in 1955, numerous American civilian technical advisors contracted by the U.S. government began arriving in Saigon. The new advisors included some 50 scholars and public administration experts from Michigan State University who were to advise on reorganizing the South Vietnamese government, the police and the Civil Guard. Their leader was Dr. Wesley Fishel, a very early supporter of Diem and probably his closest American friend. Some of their recommendations did not sit well with Diem. For example, their concept of a Civil Guard was modeled on the Michigan State Police under central government control while he preferred a paramilitary organization and more fragmented control by the province chiefs. Although the Civil Guard was centralized under the Ministry of Interior, later, at Diem's behest, it was moved to the Ministry of Defense, becoming a well-armed paramilitary organization contrary to the recommendations of MSU. Diem also had difficulty with MSU concepts of academic and press freedom. Ultimately, some MSU faculty members, on their return from Vietnam, wrote articles for academic journals critical of the regime. Cumulatively, these problems led to nonrenewal of MSU's contract when it expired in June 1962.[83] Several years later it was revealed, much to the embarrassment of MSU, that its work in Vietnam had been partially funded by the CIA.

Land Reform

With the encouragement of his French and American advisors, in 1955 Diem embarked on a land reform program.[84] The French motivation stemmed from the recognition that the days of absentee French ownership of agricultural lands in Vietnam were over and that French landowners were unlikely to receive any compensation whatever from the Vietnamese government. Accordingly, France purchased rice land from its nationals in francs at nominal rates and turned it over to the Diem government; however, non-rice land was exempt from the program. Thus, the largely French-owned rubber plantations, a primary source of foreign exchange, continued to operate under French control. The American motivation was driven by the conviction that the family farm was the "bulwark of democracy" and further, that it was imperative to counter Viet Cong land reform propaganda initiatives.

It is intended here to provide only a brief overview of Diem's program and its effectiveness. The program had three parts: 1) to resettle peasants on abandoned agricultural land and on undeveloped land in the public domain; 2) to safeguard tenants' rights by means of land tenure contracts; and 3) to redistribute land from large holders to landless persons. The first part of the program was pressed upon Diem by the influx of refugees from the North and was carried out quickly and fairly successfully. The second part involved the development of a model lease for use between landowner and tenant, to run for three to five years, the principal provision of which stipulated that annual rent could not exceed 25 percent of the yield. The contract, being compulsory, produced an immediate benefit for the tenants, and by mid–1959, 800,000 contracts had been registered.

The first two parts of Diem's plan were relatively noncontroversial, but the third part, redistribution, the heart of any land reform scheme, was less successful. The principal problem was the numerous exemptions. Under certain conditions, the owner of rice land could keep 284 acres (116 hectares), an excessively generous amount considering the very large number of landless farmers in the country. This plus the total exemption of foreign exchange-producing rubber, tea, and coffee plantations acted to severely reduce the amount of land available for redistribution. U.S. advisors recommended a lower exemption, and perhaps the Diem government would have agreed if the U.S. had been willing to provide the $30 million needed to pay off the landowners.[85] Any meaningful land redistribution program requires the taking of land, but the American advisors who had guided the program knew that expropriation was a supersensitive issue in the U.S. Congress where private property was sacrosanct. Congress was not asked nor did it volunteer to appropriate funds to pay landowners.

Overall, the resettlement and land tenure aspects of the program were reasonably successful, but redistribution failed. It was reckoned in late 1962 that only about 10 percent of an estimated 1 million to 1.2 million tenant households had obtained land under the program. Part of the reason for failure, as cited above, was the inherent flaws in the program, but beginning in the early 1960s the growing insurgency and accompanying disorders in the countryside and the shift of focus first to agrovilles and then to strategic hamlets simply overwhelmed the government's tenuous ability to administer the land reform program. The failure of most peasants to obtain land under Diem's program was a rich source of propaganda for the NLF.[86]

The Military Assistance and Advisory Group (MAAG)

Initially established in 1950 with a small staff to coordinate U.S. military aid to the French, the MAAG had grown slowly but steadily. Although the U.S. did not adhere to the Final Declaration of the 1954 Geneva Accords, it took note of the agreement and adopted a policy of respecting its provisions which, in practice, froze the MAAG at the August 11, 1954, staff level of 342 advisors.[87] At that point, responsibility for the training of South Vietnamese armed forces rested with the French. Negotiations had begun earlier between Generals Collins and Ely for the U.S. to assume the training responsibility which in April 1955 resulted in an informal agreement to establish a joint training organization commanded by MAAG chief General O'Daniel but under the overall command of Ely, an awkward arrangement but one that permitted the French to begin gracefully to disengage from a burdensome and unwanted task.[88]

Prior to this, MAAG officials had already recognized the size of their staff was inadequate to train the Army of the Republic of Vietnam (ARVN) which by then had an authorized strength of 150,000, and MAAG chief Lt. Gen. Samuel T. Williams, who had replaced General O'Daniel in October 1955, was casting about for a means to increase staff without violating the Geneva Accords, which at that time the U.S. was still respecting. Eventually, by arguing that it should be entitled to compensate for the loss of French training personnel, in early 1958 the U.S. gained ICC agreement to increase the MAAG by 343, and thus, it reached 685 where it remained through the end of the Eisenhower administration.[89]

Reorganization of the ARVN

With the impending withdrawal of the French army, in 1955 General O'Daniel recognized that the ARVN, while continuing its original mission of internal security, now had to become capable of resisting external attack. O'Daniel had a daunting task because of the dire shortage of Vietnamese officers with experience commanding even battalion-size units.[90] To fulfill the dual mission, O'Daniel set about organizing the ARVN into four field divisions, six light divisions and 13 territorial regiments for regional security but capable of consolidation into three or more light divisions if necessary. The field divisions, organized like American infantry divisions but about half the size, were intended to resist invasion while the smaller light divisions, with minimal transport and no artillery, were set up to fight the guerrillas.[91]

Whatever the merits of the light divisions and territorial regiments in combating the guerrillas, they were never given a chance to prove themselves for when O'Daniel was succeeded by. General Williams, the latter chose a different approach. Williams, who was convinced a North Vietnamese invasion constituted the principal threat, had by 1960 reformed the ARVN into seven standard infantry divisions of 10,450 men each and three corps headquarters. Suppression of guerrilla activity was to be the responsibility of the Civil Guard, which at that point was a disorganized and poorly armed branch of the Ministry of Interior.[92]

In a February 12, 1960, meeting with Ambassador Durbrow, Diem expressed concern that not enough attention was being given by the MAAG to training the ARVN for antiguerrilla warfare.[93] In fact, since 1955 when the MAAG had taken over the responsibility for ARVN training from the French, very little specific antiguerrilla training of any kind had been conducted. The MAAG staff was oriented to training for conventional warfare and had few officers qualified to conduct any other form of training. Prior to his discussion with Durbrow, Diem had already taken matters into his own hands when, without consulting the Americans, he ordered the ARVN to form ranger companies trained in antiguerrilla warfare. When MAAG chief General Williams heard of the plan, he tried to dissuade Diem, arguing that a well-trained and equipped conventional army supplemented by an effective Civil Guard were all that were needed to defeat the guerrillas, but he succeeded only in persuading Diem to reduce the planned number of rangers from 10,000 to 5,000, on a trial basis. While the idea of forming ranger units was by no means a panacea for defeating the Viet Cong, it did show that perhaps Diem understood better than the MAAG what it would take to defeat unconventional warfare.[94]

Arriving in 1960 as Williams' replacement, Lt. Gen. Lionel C. McGarr brought fresh thinking on what was now being called counterinsurgency. He recognized this as a different kind of warfare that called for unconventional measures, as reflected in his support of Diem's ranger concept.[95] But by mid-1961, there were still only 9,096 ARVN Rangers and a few hundred CIA-trained personnel in special units[96] which could be considered as more or less prepared to cope with guerrilla tactics while the remainder of the ARVN was still conventionally organized, equipped, and trained to meet a main force invasion by the DRV which, after the Geneva Accords, had immediately begun to enlarge and reequip the People's Army of Vietnam (PAVN).[97]

Although the inability of the ARVN to suppress the guerrillas in the 1959–65 period has been at least partially attributed to wrongheaded training, in fairness to the American military advisers and trainers, they could not completely disregard the possibility that an attack from the North could occur.[98] Also, critics conveniently ignore the fact that after the 1968 Tet Offensive, the war transitioned into one between conventionally organized PAVN and ARVN forces including two undisguised invasions of South Vietnam by the regular forces of the DRV.

Diem's Preoccupation with Security

Despite Diem's efforts to extirpate them, the remaining Communists in the South were tenacious and, reinforced by infiltrated regroupees from the North, during 1957 they began to recover their strength as measured by the increased number of incidents, i.e., assassinations, kidnappings, sabotage and attacks on police posts. While never complacent about internal security, Diem became steadily more preoccupied with it, and this led eventually to a basic difference between Diem and the U.S. Embassy. U.S. intelligence sources were leading the American staff to believe, into late 1959, that security was well in hand when actually it was deteriorating rapidly. The depth of American misperception of the security situation is shown in a long despatch of December 7, 1959, from Ambassador Durbrow to the Department of State assessing the overall progress of Diem's regime but commenting only briefly on the security situation, stating, "One of the major advances made by the government has been in the field of public order and security. Communist and bandit armed gangs or assassination teams still exist and strike, but their threat to public order is certainly not what it was five years ago. The armed gangs are generally restricted to jungle hideouts or safe havens over the Cambodian border, and communism is now more a clandestine and underground problem *rather than a danger to the security of the state*"[99] (*emphasis added*).

The Americans were blissfully unaware that seven months prior to this reassuring message, Hanoi had covertly declared war on the South through ratification of Resolution 15 which placed the highest priority on achieving unification through revolutionary war in the South.

But only three months later, another long Durbrow dispatch to State on March 3, 1960 described the serious state of internal security and said, "Developments during the last month or so have, however, awakened Diem and other officials to the gravity of the present internal security and political situation." [100] Obviously, it was not Diem but the U.S. Mission that had awakened since Diem's perception of the actual security situation all along was more realistic than that of the Americans. Durbrow spent most of 1960 haggling with Diem over budgetary details while the security situation deteriorated. In *Foreign Relations of the U.S., 1958–1960, Vol. 1, Vietnam*, a majority of the 1960 documents relate to internal security. Diem wanted an increase in the national army of 20,000 to 170,000, increased antiguerrilla training for the army, and better arms for an augmented Civil Guard (national police) and the Self Defense Corps, essentially all of which would have to be paid for by increases in U.S. aid. Durbrow believed Diem consistently overemphasized security while neglecting development while Diem was convinced that security had to *precede* development. The U.S. was later to learn from experience that development projects designed to "win the hearts and minds of the people" could not be conducted successfully in areas that were not secure.

Using his powers to rule by decree, Diem issued draconian ordinances and laws giving government authorities wide arbitrary powers of arrest and detention of those considered "a danger to the state." An example was Law 10 of 1959 which provided for military courts to judge offenses under the general heading of security. Those suspected of guerrilla activity could be tried in these courts and summarily convicted and sentenced with no right of appeal.[101] These measures were thought necessary to combat the growing emergency of Communist insurgency in the country but gave the government all the trappings of a police state. And yet there was no unanimity among observers on how all-encompassing the police-state system of South Vietnam really was, and voices of opposition could still be heard.[102]

The Counterinsurgency Plan

McGarr's arrival was timely for in late 1960, Washington, alarmed at the deterioration in security situation in Vietnam, directed the embassy and MAAG to collaborate in developing a counterinsurgency plan to defeat the Viet Cong and restore stability to the country.[103] Thus, for the first time, an effort was made to develop a comprehensive and coordinated plan among the various American civil and military groups working to aid the government of Vietnam, but the plan failed to resolve the fragmentation of the American effort.

MAAG's principal recommendations supported Diem's wishes to increase the size of the army by 20,000 and transfer the Civil Guard from the Interior to the Defense Ministry while changing its nature from a police to a paramilitary organization. Ambassador Durbrow opposed both these actions, believing they reflected Diem's preoccupation with military at the expense of political responses to the Viet Cong.[104] He believed the size of the army was already adequate, and while conceding the Civil Guard needed upgraded training and equipment, he viewed the move to Defense as a backdoor means of increasing the size of the ARVN. Durbrow's recommendations focused on getting actions from Diem — broadening the base of his government by including opposition elements, relaxing press censorship, allowing real political parties to function, increasing the powers of the National Assembly, and others — which Durbrow believed were the recipe for improving popular support for the regime. While Durbrow deemed these actions political, their principal effect would be to placate the intellectual and political classes of Saigon, but they would do little to counter the inroads of the Viet Cong in the villages where the peasants lacked appreciation for such nuances.[105]

At this point, in 1960, neither the ambassador, who was focused on Diem; the U.S. Operations Mission, which was oriented to development projects; nor the MAAG, which thought only in military terms, had yet grasped the need for a political strategy by the government of Vietnam aimed at countering the Viet Cong in the villages. Thus the Counterinsurgency Plan became a laundry list of pet programs and desiderata of the various American agencies, many of which were doubtless beneficial, but it failed to offer solutions to the most critical problem. There were some Americans who did understand the need — CIA Saigon station chief William Colby, and Edward Lansdale back in Washington — but their voices were lost in the cacophony. It would be over five years before the U.S. fully grasped the necessity of fighting the political war in the villages, under the labels of pacification, Revolutionary Development, and Civil Operations and Revolutionary Development Support (CORDS).

Elections

On the political front, Diem's government conducted elections August 30, 1959, for a new National Assembly to replace the one elected in 1956 as a Constituent Assembly and then converted to a National Assembly after the proclamation of the republic. Of the 123 seats, 78 were taken by Diem's National Revolutionary Movement and 36 by independents with the remainder taken by splinter parties, but an analysis of the results by the embassy showed that overall, 114 were supporters of the government. Observers believed the actual voting to be relatively free of manipulation or intimidation, with a voter participation of about 85 percent nationally. While the vote counting was not administered as it was in the 1956 referendum, in fact, through charges of election law violations the regime did keep certain opposition candidates off the ballot or refuse to seat them after they won. In the provinces where Diem's National Revolutionary Movement won heavily, the election was more a process of education of an electorate with little or no experience in casting a ballot. By Western standards, the elections were not democratic, and the embassy concluded that the conduct of the campaign showed no progress toward liberalization of the regime. While the Americans, who were pushing to make South Vietnam into a liberal, Western-style democracy, were not satisfied, the elections were nevertheless a move in that direction, something that was far from happening in the North where no elections had been held for a national assembly since the first one was formed in 1946. Undoubtedly sensing its vulnerability on the issue, the DRV launched a fierce propaganda campaign against the "Diem machinations for illegal parliamentary elections ... under conditions of terror and fraudulent methods...."[106]

Diplomatic Relationships, 1954–1960

As related earlier, President Eisenhower's October 1954 letter to Diem pledged American support conditioned on the regime's performance in establishing democratic institutions and resisting Communism, and with the Communist insurgency not assuming serious proportions until 1959, the emphasis of the Eisenhower administration was on advising Diem on governmental organization and on provision of economic and military aid. During the period 1954–60, the State Department, under Dulles and, on his death, Christian Herter, was in control of relationships with Vietnam with the Defense Department taking its lead, sometimes reluctantly, from State.

During the tenure of Ambassador Reinhardt (1955–57), the State Department watched with growing dissatisfaction the lack of progress in Vietnam toward Western liberal democracy, but during these years Diem, America's ally and the "bulwark of Southeast Asia," was receiving very favorable treatment in the American media, and thus, it was thought unwise to risk antagonizing him through the application of excessive pressure to accept American recommendations. Still, Diem listened politely to the ambassador's suggestions, accepting those he liked while rejecting the rest.

Believing that a fresh messenger was needed, in March 1957 Washington replaced Reinhardt with Eldridge Durbrow, like Reinhardt a career foreign service officer but one considered a more forceful personality.[107] As will be seen, Durbrow did, indeed, increase the pressure on Diem by vigorously recommending sweeping changes in his regime. Needless to say, these recommendations put Durbrow and Diem at loggerheads aggravated by Diem's wish to increase the size of the armed forces, a move Durbrow opposed as unnecessary.

During the development of the Counterinsurgency Plan of 1960, Durbrow believed increasing the size of the army, though he opposed it, should be used as a bargaining chip with Diem in exchange for obtaining the political changes Durbrow was pressing for. McGarr disagreed, believing the security situation in the country had become so serious that the 20,000-man increase in the ARVN should be agreed to unconditionally. In this he was backed up by Edward Lansdale from his position in the Pentagon as a counterinsurgency specialist. Lansdale wrote that to treat Diem " ... as an opponent to be beaten to his knees" would be fruitless and counterproductive.[108] In the end, Diem won the argument but not until after the Kennedy administration took office.[109]

The End of the "Quiet" Period

From the Geneva Accords into 1957, Communist guerrilla activity in South Vietnam had remained at a relatively low level, but when it became clear that the 1956 plebiscite would not be held, guerrilla activity began to intensify, and beginning in mid–1959 rapidly increased. Still, the relatively quiet early years of the republic had given Diem breathing space for consolidation and the U.S. time to organize and train the ARVN, strengthen the country economically and encourage Diem to create liberal political institutions on the model of Western democracies. How had South Vietnam progressed since 1954? Diem had certainly succeeded in consolidating his regime, so much so that effective political opposition had been largely suppressed. Thus, little progress had been made toward American liberal political goals for South Vietnam. Compared to 1954, the economy had been strengthened, but the government was hardly closer to being able to survive without U.S. subsidies. The U.S. MAAG had created an army out of the disorganized fragments left by the French, but the ARVN had not yet shown it was capable of coping with the Viet Cong.

Overall, the relationship between the U.S. as patron and Diem as client had not followed accepted patterns. The intractable Diem had rejected a great deal of American advice, and when an issue had come to the test almost invariably he won. Although the U.S. was by no means satisfied with the regime, Communist expansion in Southeast Asia had indeed been blocked by the American-sponsored Republic of Vietnam.[110]

3

The Kennedy Years

When Kennedy loyalists refer to John F. Kennedy's inaugural address, the passage usually cited is the famous line, "ask not what your country can do for you — ask what you can do for your country."[1] Eloquent and moving words indeed ... words that evoke the spirit of Patrick Henry and Nathan Hale, but there is another passage in that address with a similar heroic ring that is less often cited but which had a much more profound effect on the nation:

> Let every nation know, whether it wishes us well or ill that we shall pay any price, bear any burden, meet any hardship, support any friend, oppose any foe to assure the survival and success of liberty.[2]

Thus the foreign policy of the incoming Kennedy administration was announced to the world. It was a ringing declaration that the torch had been passed to a dynamic new administration that would be courageous, selfless, determined and yes, tough, in defending freedom against that implacable enemy, international Communism, wherever it might be found. Stirring words, delivered in the bravura Kennedy style, and well received by the American people and the media. But words have consequences, and those consequences began to flow with terrible swiftness in the first months of the Kennedy administration with the crisis in Laos, the Bay of Pigs and Vietnam where those brave sentiments were quickly put to the test.

* * *

The Foreign Policy Team

It was the New Deal of 1933 all over again. The New Frontiersmen who swept into Washington in January 1961 were mostly young (early 40s), with little or no experience in high government councils, but, in a word used frequently by David Halberstam in *The Best and the Brightest*, they were "brilliant," they knew they were brilliant, and they were cocksure there was no problem that would not succumb to sheer intellect. Most had degrees from Harvard, Yale or MIT in their backgrounds, and Ph.D.s and Rhodes Scholars abounded. Those selected to work in the foreign policy area were deeply committed to the vision enunciated in Kennedy's inaugural address, but of course none of them had any inkling of the tragedy their hubris would lead the nation into.

Perhaps the biggest prize that Kennedy was able to lure to his foreign policy team was McGeorge Bundy, dean of Harvard College, who came in as the president's special assistant for national security affairs. Bundy, from an aristocratic Boston family, had a record of academic brilliance, first at Groton, then Yale, followed by a Junior Fellowship at Harvard. When the war came, family connections got him a spot as an army second lieutenant aide to Vice Adm. Alan Kirk, who commanded the Western Task Force at D-Day.[3]

After the war, he worked briefly with the Council on Foreign Relations, the conservative establishment bastion which had influenced American foreign policy for years and where Bundy, by birth already a member of the Establishment, undoubtedly made some valuable connections. In 1949 it was back to Harvard as a lecturer in foreign policy, and in 1954, at the age of 34, he was appointed dean of the College of Arts and Sciences. making him the youngest dean in the history of Harvard.[4]

Kennedy had to be impressed by this intellectually gifted man who, it was said, actually ran Harvard University even though he was only dean of the college. Bundy was an elitist Establishment figure with a sharp analytical mind but whose foreign policy credentials were, at best, slender. Although he had taught the subject for several years, he had done no serious scholarly work in the field,[5] or for that matter in any field. (He was not Dr. Bundy, never having earned a Ph.D.) Unlike Henry Kissinger, a later national security advisor, Bundy kept a low public profile and never saw the need to compete with others for power. He was much more the behind-the-scenes manipulator using his superior access to the president and control of the national security papers that Kennedy saw to influence decisions. Still, the influential media ranked him as the brightest star in the firmament of Kennedy advisors, but the same media would later turn on him, and now, most Vietnam War scholars agree he was one of the principal authors of the escalation of U.S. involvement.

Of the top three cabinet posts of State, Defense and Treasury, Kennedy had the most difficulty making his decision on State. Initially, Robert Lovett, a well-known Eastern Establishment figure who as a Republican had served with distinction in previous Democratic administrations, was offered his choice of the three jobs, but Lovett demurred for health reasons. It would not have been a popular appointment among loyal Democrats. Adlai Stevenson seemed a logical candidate to many Democrats but was thought too controversial on Capitol Hill, so he became ambassador to the UN. Averell Harriman, a longtime liberal and loyalist Democrat, lobbied hard for the job, but because of his age (he was 69) and for other reasons he was ruled out. He was made a roving ambassador. Other candidates were discarded for one reason or another or given another job. Finally, Lovett suggested Dean Rusk, whose name seemed to be second on everybody's list.[6] Almost by default, he got the job.

Rusk was then president of the Rockefeller Foundation, a prestigious job that brought him into contact with the cream of the Establishment, but he himself was not of the Establishment. Born in 1909 on a hard-scrabble farm in north Georgia and educated in public schools, with work and a scholarship he was able to attend Davidson College, a small Presbyterian liberal arts school in North Carolina where he was Phi Beta Kappa. He became a Rhodes Scholar, the one distinction he shared with many of his future colleagues in the Kennedy administration, and in 1934 he joined the faculty of Mills College in Oakland, California, as an instructor in international relations. Like Bundy, he too became a young dean of the college, but Mills was a long way, both in miles and prestige from Cambridge, Massachusetts. A reserve officer from college ROTC, he was called to active duty in 1940 as an infantry captain, but his educational background quickly led to staff work, and he became a highly regarded deputy chief of staff for Gen. Joseph Stillwell in the China-Burma-India Theater headquarters in New Delhi, ending the war as a colonel. Postwar, as a War Department staff officer, he was spotted by Secretary of State General George Marshall, who brought him in to head the United Nations desk in 1947.

Rusk was comfortable in the structured bureaucracy of State, moving up steadily, and by 1950, he was assistant secretary for Far Eastern affairs (FE) in the Acheson regime. That year he joined the board of trustees of the Rockefeller Foundation, and two years later John Foster Dulles, his predecessor at the Rockefeller Foundation and a close friend, got him the presidency in the dying days of the Truman administration. As a diplomat and administrator, Rusk was probably all that Kennedy hoped for at State but as a foreign policy fresh thinker and presidential advisor, he fell well below Kennedy's expectations. In every crisis, in the large, unstructured meetings typical of the Kennedy White House, on Laos, the Bay of Pigs, the Cuban Missile Crisis, Berlin, Diem and escalation in Vietnam, the inscrutable Rusk would sit Buddhalike, listening to the back and forth, staying low in the boat and sensing the wind, and then sometimes staying after the meeting and giving his advice privately to the president. Later, this fitted well with Johnson, who liked secrecy and kept his circle of advisors very small, but according to Arthur Schlesinger, Kennedy was dissatisfied with Rusk and planned to dump him after he was reelected in 1964.[7] In eight years as secretary of state, he left few footprints, but of the key foreign policy players brought in during 1961, he was, incredibly, the last man standing at the end of 1968. He was a part of the New Frontier but never of the Camelot inner circle, nor did he wish to be. He was far more comfortable later with his fellow southerner, Lyndon Johnson.

With Bundy and Rusk, the third member of Kennedy's foreign policy team was Robert Strange McNamara, who was tapped as secretary of defense. Again, Lovett played a role, suggesting McNamara, who had just become president of Ford Motor Company. McNamara had impressed Lovett during the war when, as assistant secretary of war for air, Lovett had brought him in from Harvard as a systems analyst.[8] Kennedy liked McNamara's qualifications for the Defense job and settled on him very quickly.

Born in 1916, a year before Kennedy, he grew up in a middle-class setting around Oakland, California. He was a product of the public schools, including the University of California at Berkeley where he majored in economics with minors in philosophy and mathematics, but from his subsequent career, mathematics; seems to have been his natural field. He was Phi Beta Kappa. From Berkeley, he went on to Harvard Business School where his talents in the field of management accounting were so outstanding that, after graduating in 1939, he was invited back as an instructor. Soon after the U.S. entered the war, Harvard Business School was asked by the Army Air Corps to train officers in statistical control, a new management technique being applied with excellent results to aircraft procurement, deployment and reliability issues. Col. Charles B. "Tex" Thornton, the program manager under Lovett, quickly spotted McNamara as especially talented, and in early 1943, he was persuaded to join the Thornton group as a civilian consultant, later obtaining a direct commission as an Army Air Force captain. During the war the group honed its analytical techniques, developed a new discipline called systems analysis, and with McNamara in the forefront made a valuable contribution to the war effort. With the war winding down, Thornton conceived the idea offering the talented group as a package to private industry. Henry Ford II, now running Ford Motor Company after years of mismanagement by Henry Sr. and his cronies, desperately needed management talent and jumped at the idea, and nine of the group, including McNamara, joined Ford in early 1946.[9]

Thornton soon left, but McNamara stayed. He installed a management control system at Ford that may very well have saved the faltering company, and young Henry Ford recognized his genius and rewarded him with broader responsibilities. But overall, the evidence from his years at Ford shows McNamara as less well equipped to deal with intangibles that could not be reduced to numbers. Coping with ambiguity was not his forte.[10]

Kennedy believed that McNamara, the management genius, could work the same miracles at the Department of Defense that he had worked at Ford, and McNamara did introduce sweeping changes in the way that amorphous agency was run. And when Kennedy, in November 1961, sought someone to be the administration's point man in Vietnam, McNamara volunteered even though at that point the issues were more political than military.[11] Southeast Asia was clearly going to be where the action was, and McNamara grabbed for it. Six years later a bitterly disillusioned McNamara had learned that wars are not won by concepts like cost effectiveness and marginal utility, and in the end, he was humbled by the ambiguities of the Vietnam War.

These then were Kennedy's and for a time Johnson's principal foreign policy advisors, Bundy, Rusk and McNamara. Of the three, only McNamara fell under the Kennedy spell and became a member of Camelot. Bundy, the cool, distant Cambridge patrician, qualified but remained aloof, and Rusk was never invited.

No discussion of the Kennedy team would be complete without reference to Vice President Lyndon Johnson whose presence, in contrast to the other principals who were chosen after the election, was the result of a political compromise before the election. Aside from balancing the ticket, both men believed Johnson's experience and influence in the Senate would be invaluable in moving Kennedy's legislative program, but neither reckoned on how jealously Johnson's old Senate colleagues would defend the separation between the legislative and the executive branches and how quickly Johnson's influence evaporated.[12] Far from being one of the most powerful men in Washington, a disillusioned Johnson had to accept that as vice president he would be one of the least powerful figures in the administration and as such was not really a member of the team.

Below the principals was a second tier of advisors whose influence on policy was pervasive and whose names would later appear frequently on documents in the Pentagon Papers. Prominent among this group was George W. Ball, who was appointed undersecretary for economic affairs, the number three job at State, and later moved up to undersecretary when Kennedy reshuffled State in November 1961. Ball had an impeccable liberal pedigree going back to 1933 when he came to Washington from Chicago to become a New Deal lawyer. Later in the '30s he was associated with Adlai Stevenson in a Chicago law firm, and after the war he practiced international law in Washington. He became closely identified with the liberal wing of the Democratic Party and was a leading backer of Stevenson in 1952 and 1956. While most of the second tier of advisors initially were hawks on Vietnam, Ball was unique in consistently advising Kennedy and later Johnson against becoming more deeply involved in Vietnam. His advice disregarded, in September 1966 he resigned to return to his law practice.[13]

There was William P. Bundy, assistant secretary of defense for international security affairs and key aide to McNamara in the area where Defense interfaced with State. The older brother of McGeorge, Bill Bundy had Groton, Yale and Harvard Law in his background, and had chosen a career in public service, coming to Defense from the CIA He was the son-in-law of Dean Acheson.[14]

Later, in early 1964 when Bundy moved to State to replace Roger Hilsman as assistant secretary for Far Eastern affairs, his successor was John McNaughton, another Harvard man who was teaching law there when invited to join the administration. McNaughton, a midwesterner, was ambitious to gain acceptance as an important player in the Washington bureaucracy and was McNamara's alter ego and chief aide on Vietnam during the 1965–66 escalation years. Halberstam deals with McNaughton sympathetically, depicting him as a closet dove, apparently on the testimony of Michael Forrestal, but with his name on many hawkish Vietnam papers, McNaughton remains an equivocal figure. He and his family died tragically in a plane crash in mid–1967.[15]

Michael Forrestal, the son of the illustrious James V. Forrestal, the first secretary of defense, was one of a triumvirate that played the central role in triggering the end of the Diem regime in 1963. He was a product of Phillips Exeter Academy, Princeton and Harvard Law. A Wall Street lawyer and at 34 young even by New Frontier standards, he got his White House job through the influence of Averell Harriman, whose protégé he was. Coming in 1962, he joined McGeorge Bundy's national security staff as a Southeast Asia specialist although he had no experience in the area. Young, single, and good looking, Forrestal was quickly enfolded into Camelot.[16]

The second member of the triumvirate was Roger Hilsman, Jr., who came in from the faculty of Johns Hopkins as director of State's Bureau of Intelligence and Research (INR). A 1943 West Point graduate, he had been one of Merrill's Marauders, a commando-type unit that fought behind Japanese lines in Burma in World War II. Postwar he had CIA experience, then took a Ph.D. at Yale in 1951 followed by 10 years of academic and think-tank work relating to international affairs. His war experience fitted well with Kennedy's fascination for counterinsurgency as a means of meeting the Communist guerrilla threats that were popping up in underdeveloped areas around the world, so when Kennedy set up the Counterinsurgency Committee (Special Group [CI]) in late 1961, chaired by Gen. Maxwell Taylor, Hilsman was a member. His position at INR gave him an ideal forum from which to propagate not only his ideas on counterinsurgency but his strongly held views on Vietnam as well. In April 1963 his promotion to assistant secretary of state for Far Eastern affairs placed him in an even better position to influence administration policy on Vietnam.[17]

The leader of the triumvirate, W. Averell Harriman, was one figure in the Kennedy administration who could never be accused of dilettantism in foreign affairs. The son of E. H. Harriman, the railroad baron, Averell Harriman was involved in the international shipping business while still in his 20s. In 1926, before U.S. diplomatic recognition of the U.S.S.R., he was negotiating mining concessions with Leon Trotsky in the Kremlin.[18] With the coming of the New Deal, the liberal Harriman made a commitment to public service and began what would be a long series of appointments under Roosevelt and Truman, including manager of Lend-Lease in London, wartime ambassador to the Soviet Union, secretary of commerce and Marshall Plan administrator in Paris. He nurtured unrealistic ambitions to the presidency, making weak bids for the Democratic nomination in 1952 and 1956. To bolster his standing as a serious candidate for the nomination, he ran for governor of New York in 1954 and won but lost his bid for reelection to Nelson Rockefeller in 1958, thus ending his hopes for high elective office.

So, when the New Frontier swept in, Harriman, who had been on the sidelines for eight years, desperately wanted back in, but never very politically astute, he had failed to support Kennedy early enough in the presidential race. When he realized his error and jumped on the bandwagon, it was too late to gain a favored position. The job he wanted was secretary of state, only to lose out to Rusk, someone Harriman regarded as little more than a clerk. Harriman swallowed his pride and took what was offered, ambassador-at-large, far below his hopes, but at least he was in. He quickly set about ingratiating himself with Kennedy, and someone later observed that Harriman was the only ambitious 70-year old in Washington. Kennedy was not slow in recognizing how useful this experienced diplomat could be.[19]

Another key player in the unfolding Vietnam drama was Walt Whitman Rostow, 45, Yale Ph.D., Rhodes Scholar and MIT faculty member since 1950. He was on the staff of the prestigious MIT Center for International Studies and had written prolifically on the subject. Rostow had been in Kennedy's pre-election cabinet of intellectuals and so was assured of a policy job in the administration. His scholarly credentials exceeded those of McGeorge Bundy except that Rostow lacked that special Harvard cachet, so he was named Bundy's deputy for Southeast Asia. From the start, Rostow would be an unwavering hawk on Vietnam, perhaps a bit too hawkish even for Bundy. In less than a year, he was moved over to State as counselor and chairman of the policy planning council, State's think tank. When Bundy left government in early 1966, Rostow replaced him as Johnson's national security advisor, and like Rusk, when the Johnson administration ended in 1968, he too was still standing.[20]

These then were the key players, appointed by Kennedy and retained by Johnson, in what was to become the tragedy of Vietnam, a group whose advice and decisions would, step by step, lead the nation into the longest war in its history and would irrevocably change American society. They saw themselves as realists, activists, hawkish, tough, in the Kennedy mold, believers that we should "pay any price meet any hardship, support any friend, oppose any foe to assure the survival and success of liberty." Most of the civilians had never had power before, certainly not this kind of power, and it was thrilling. And even after Kennedy's death, they hung on because they liked the power although it was not quite the same under Johnson because the New Frontier was over. But by the end of 1966, when they were better able to see the cumulative results of their advice in innumerable draft memos and meetings and the decisions that were taken based on that advice, the realities of power began to come home, and it was no longer so thrilling, and the exodus from government began.

* * *

The Crisis in Laos

The first grave international crisis of the Kennedy administration occurred in a small, remote country landlocked in the midst of Southeast Asia. In the late 19th century, as France extended its reach in Indochina, Laos was the last to come under its control when a protectorate was established in 1893. Because of its inaccessible location and mountainous terrain, its natural resources remained largely unexploited, and thus, French commercial activities were minimal, and the French presence and influence on the culture were less than in Vietnam. By nature, the Laotians were a passive people, deeply committed to Buddhism and content to live quietly in rural hamlets where they engaged in subsistence farming.[21] Opposition to French rule existed in the small educated class, some of which became émigrés, but there was never the underlying ferment nor occasional outbreaks of violence that characterized Vietnam. The Indochinese Communist Party had little support in Laos except among Vietnamese nationals.[22]

In the final days of World War II when the Japanese forces occupying Indochina declared Laos to be independent under Japanese tutelage, many of the émigré opponents of the French returned, but the French quickly reestablished control everywhere in Indochina except Tonkin, where they were disputed by the Vietminh. In 1949, Laos was granted independence within the French Union, which in practice was a façade for continued French control.[23] Closely watching the progress of the revolutionary war against the French in Tonkin, many of the disillusioned leftist Laotian nationalists, including Prince Souvannaphong of the Laotian royal family, decided to seek the support of the Vietminh and joined it in the mountains of northwest Vietnam.[24] As related earlier, with the formation of the Vietnam Worker's Party in 1951, a separate Laotian Communist Party was formed which became the Pathet Lao (Land of Lao) led by Prince Souphanouvong. As the Laotians were not a warlike people, the Pathet Lao was slow in developing into an effective guerrilla force and so did not contribute materially to the war against the French. When the Vietminh attacked French-held Laos in 1953, the Pathet Lao was a part of the invading force, but the fighting was done by the Vietminh. To cut the invasion route and to bring Vietminh main force units to battle, the French established the fortified redoubt at Dien Bien Phu in northwest Vietnam, a few miles from the Laotian border, and as related earlier, this proved to be the decisive miscalculation of the First Indochina War.

Just prior to the July 1954 Geneva Accords, the French granted Laos unconditional independence under the king.[25] The provisions of the accords affecting Laos were: 1) a cease-fire throughout Indochina; 2) the withdrawal of all Vietminh and all French combat forces (a small French military contingent was permitted for training the Laotian national army); 3) the establishment of a regroupment zone in the two northern Laotian provinces to which the Pathet Lao forces were to withdraw; and 4) the establishment of an International Control Commission (ICC) to monitor the agreement. A political settlement to determine the make-up of the Laotian government was to be the subject of negotiations among the contending Laotian parties.[26]

In the event, the 1954 Geneva Accords affecting Laos failed in almost every respect. A fragile cease-fire did come into effect but only temporarily. The French did withdraw their combat troops, but the Vietminh never fully withdrew their forces from eastern Laos nor did the Pathet Lao fully regroup in the designated areas. The ICC (India-Canada-Poland) could never achieve the unanimity required for action on violations of the accords so it proved totally ineffectual in its monitoring role. The protracted political discussions between neutralist Prince Souvanna Phouma and his half brother, Pathet Lao leader Prince Souphanouvong, ended in November 1957 with the formation of a neutralist–Pathet Lao coalition government with Souvanna as premier.

Of the states of Southeast Asia, only Laos borders on China, North Vietnam, South Vietnam, Cambodia, Thailand and Burma. Because of the critical strategic location of the country, the U.S. was alarmed by the provisions of the Geneva Accords which it regarded as a sellout to the Vietminh–Pathet Lao, and the Eisenhower administration believed unless it took steps to establish a pro–Western, anti–Communist government in power there, Laos would be a conduit for Communist infiltration and subversion of Thailand, Cambodia and South Vietnam. So as the French troops departed, the U.S. moved in with a nation-building program involving large amounts of economic aid and a buildup of the Laotian national army. Although Premier Souvanna Phouma claimed to be neutralist, the Eisenhower administration distrusted him, believing he was under the influence of the Pathet Lao, and through the machinations of the CIA he was ousted in 1958 in favor of a rightist government. Reinstalled in a neutralist coup in 1960, he was again ousted in late 1960 by another U.S.-supported rightist coup. Prince Boun Oum, premier of the new government, was a figurehead for the real power, Defense Minister Phoumi Nosavan, who was the U.S. candidate to lead the country to the desired position. Souvanna Phouma fled to Cambodia and his neutralist forces decamped from Vientiane to set up headquarters in an area of Laos controlled by the Pathet Lao.[27]

In the period following the 1954 Geneva Accords the Pathet Lao, with the support of the Democratic Republic of Vietnam, had been quietly building its strength, and in 1959 it resumed the fighting.[28] By 1960, tensions between the Soviet Union and the People's Republic of China had broken into the open, setting off a bitter rivalry for the role of leader of the international socialist bloc. To forestall the spread of Chinese influence in Southeast Asia, in December 1960 the Soviets stepped in to support the Pathet Lao by airlifting arms from Hanoi, creating the potential for a dangerous confrontation between the U.S. and the Soviet Union. And with the U.S.-backed Phoumi forces showing a marked distaste for battle, the Pathet Lao–DRV forces gradually gained the upper hand so that by early 1961 they controlled the entire northern and eastern parts of the country and appeared poised to take the two government centers—Vientiane, the political capital, and Luang Prabang, the imperial capital.

Kennedy's First Test

On Eisenhower's last day in office, he briefed Kennedy on Laos, calling the situation there the most serious international crisis then facing the U.S. and suggesting that unilateral military intervention might be necessary.[29] Thus the Laos crisis was thrust upon Kennedy, becoming the first issue to test his foreign policy team.

Kennedy recoiled at the suggestion of U.S. military intervention in Laos, and at his first presidential press conference on January 25 he addressed the issue, stating that Laos should be neutral and independent,[30] an ideal solution but one that did not take into account North Vietnam's vital interests in that country. In February, he established a Laotian Task Force to study the issue and make recommendations as to how this neutrality was to be brought about, the objective being a neutralist government which did not include the Pathet Lao. The task force concluded that the Communists would first have to be rolled back by force to strengthen the position of the Laotian government in establishing itself as a truly neutral nation, but the issue became moot when Phoumi's forces were attacked and defeated by DRV-led Pathet Lao forces in March, creating an even more adverse military situation for the Boun Oum-Phoumi government. These events forced the issue of SEATO intervention onto the table, and it seemed there was no other solution if Laos were to be saved.[31]

But SEATO was rapidly proving to be a paper tiger. The Washington planners believed the involvement of North Vietnam in support of the Pathet Lao constituted foreign aggression, and thus, under the treaty, members of SEATO were obligated collectively to consult on action in defense of Laos. But these consultations soon proved fruitless. France, having recently extracted itself from an eight-year war in Indochina, declared unequivocally that it would not participate in military intervention in Laos. Britain, too, was decidedly unenthusiastic, and Australia and New Zealand were lukewarm That left the U.S. with the support of the slim reeds of SEATO members Thailand, the Philippines and Pakistan plus the Diem government of South Vietnam. At a series of National Security Council meetings in March and April, Kennedy's civilian and military advisors were nearly unanimous in recommending intervention, advancing various proposals for deployment of U.S. troops in Laos, but with Kennedy's continued reluctance to agree, the planners were reduced to concocting schemes involving joint action by the Royal Laotian Army (Phoumi's forces), Thailand and South Vietnam at minimum cost to the U.S. These came to nothing since Thailand would move only in concert with U.S. forces, Vietnam had no troops available for adventures in Laos, and Phoumi's army was then incapable of offensive action.[32]

The Geneva Conference on Laos

Kennedy had not given up on the idea of a negotiated political solution although he realized now that a coalition government would have to include the Pathet Lao. While deliberations on intervention were underway, the U. S. was supporting a British initiative to obtain a cease-fire followed by the convening of a conference in Geneva to take up the question of Laos. To convince the Soviets of U.S. determination to intervene if necessary, the Seventh Fleet was moved into the South China Sea and a token force of 500 marines was flown into Thailand. On April 20, 1961, the American military effort in Laos was upgraded to a Military Assistance and Advisory Group (MAAG), and the U.S. military advisors already there in civilian clothes were ordered to don their uniforms.[33]

Even though their Pathet Lao clients held a clear military advantage on the ground, in April the Soviets agreed to the British proposal for a cease-fire preceding a new conference, and the opposing parties in Laos negotiated a tenuous cease-fire on May 1.[34] What motivated Khrushchev to agree? Arthur Schlesinger saw it as a retreat or knuckling under by Khrushchev to Kennedy's threats of intervention.[35] The reality was otherwise. With the Soviets then confronting the U.S. over the status of Berlin, Khrushchev actually might have welcomed American intervention in this remote backwater since it would entail a further drain on U.S. military resources, which were already stretched. On the other hand, he had to weigh the possibility that U.S. intervention might draw the Chinese into an active military and political role in Indochina, something the Russians wished to avoid. It is highly unlikely the Soviets ever remotely contemplated confronting the Americans militarily in Laos simply because they believed their objective of a Communist Laos would be achieved without it. In the end, from the Soviet perspective, there was little downside to agreeing to a cease-fire and negotiations. A settlement could solidify the Pathet Lao's favorable position on the ground and get the Americans out of Laos while locking them into a diplomatic agreement that would, in practice, restrict their room for maneuvering both diplomatically and militarily, and indeed, this was the outcome.

With military victory within their grasp, the Pathet Lao and DRV were forced by the Soviets to acquiesce to a conference of the major powers reminiscent of Geneva in 1954, but as later events would show, in Laos the Soviets had adroitly averted U.S. intervention while preserving the advantages the Pathet Lao and North Vietnamese had won on the ground and setting the stage for a future Communist takeover.

Since taking office, Kennedy had been seeking to avoid intervention in Laos, so the prospect of a cease-fire and negotiations were welcomed by the administration with great relief. After three months of indecision, on May 2 Kennedy, still reeling from the Bay of Pigs fiasco, put in abeyance the question of intervention, although contingency planning for it could continue.[36] Khrushchev's agreement to negotiate had relieved Kennedy of the need for a decision he wished to avoid.

On May 11 the conference convened in Geneva, and after the opening round Rusk turned the negotiations over to Averell Harriman, then an underemployed ambassador-at-large. Harriman, unhappy with his marginal position in the hierarchy, seized on this assignment as an opportunity to enhance his role and ingratiate himself with Kennedy. Harriman's orders were to achieve a neutralist Laos, and this he set out to do with single-minded determination.[37]

But the U.S. had few bargaining chips other than on the one hand to withdraw the small contingent of military and CIA advisors and on the other to intervene militarily, a sham alternative since Kennedy was determined to avoid it. Thus Harriman was forced to play a hand without trumps. The Geneva negotiations devolved into sometimes tendentious bilateral discussions between Harriman and G. M. Pushkin, the Soviet representative, while parallel negotiations among the Laotians dragged on as the rightist, neutralist and Pathet Lao factions jockeyed for power in a future government.[38] The U. S. ultimately found itself in the equivocal position of backing neutralist Souvanna Phouma as premier of the future government while at the same time providing support for rightist General Phoumi Nosavan's army. Harriman was frustrated by his inability to control the recalcitrant Phoumi who, with CIA support, opposed Souvanna Phouma and neutralization of Laos.[39] In the meantime, the cease-fire broke down, so that fighting and talking were occurring simultaneously.

In late 1961 a major breakthrough (or at least what Harriman and Kennedy chose to regard as one) occurred on the political side of negotiations when the Soviets agreed to guarantee the observance of the agreement by the Communist signatories, i.e., the DRV, the PRC and the Pathet Lao.[40] At this point, the U. S. should have asked itself: a) how would the Soviets exercise this responsibility should their fellow Communists choose to violate the agreement? And b) what recourse would the U. S. have if the Soviets failed to hold to their promise? Even if the Soviets were sincere, they had no realistic means of enforcing this agreement short of putting in troops, which they certainly would not do, or cutting off military aid to the DRV and Pathet Lao, which would only invite in the Chinese. And the U. S. would have no recourse other than hollow diplomatic remonstrations with the Russians[41] or intervening with troops, the latter being in contradiction of the whole object of the exercise on the part of the U.S. Harriman and Kennedy chose to accept the Russian promise at face value, knowingly choosing to ignore these awkward questions.[42]

The Russians and Chinese also agreed to a provision prohibiting the presence of foreign (Vietminh) troops in Laos and the use of Laos as a corridor to South Vietnam and Cambodia (the Ho Chi Minh Trail),[43] again raising the question of enforcement. The Communists felt themselves quite safe on these points, knowing from experience with the 1954 Geneva Accords how ineffectual the ICC would be in policing them.

In fact, the real sticking point in the negotiations was policing the accords, that is, the issue of the ICC's authority to travel freely throughout Laos to verify compliance. The Communist side insisted on unanimity among the three Laotian government factions to authorize ICC inspections which, in practice, would mean no ICC travel to sensitive areas in eastern Laos under Communist control. In his zeal to get an agreement and over the vehement objections of State, Harriman persuaded Kennedy to compromise and give way on this point.[44] The U.S. got nothing in return, but the DRV got precisely the key concession it wanted from the entire negotiation: a sacrosanct eastern Laos with unrestricted access to the Ho Chi Minh Trail, free from embarrassing inspections. This proved to be the underlying crux of the entire negotiations, and one as astute as Harriman must have understood this. With this concession,

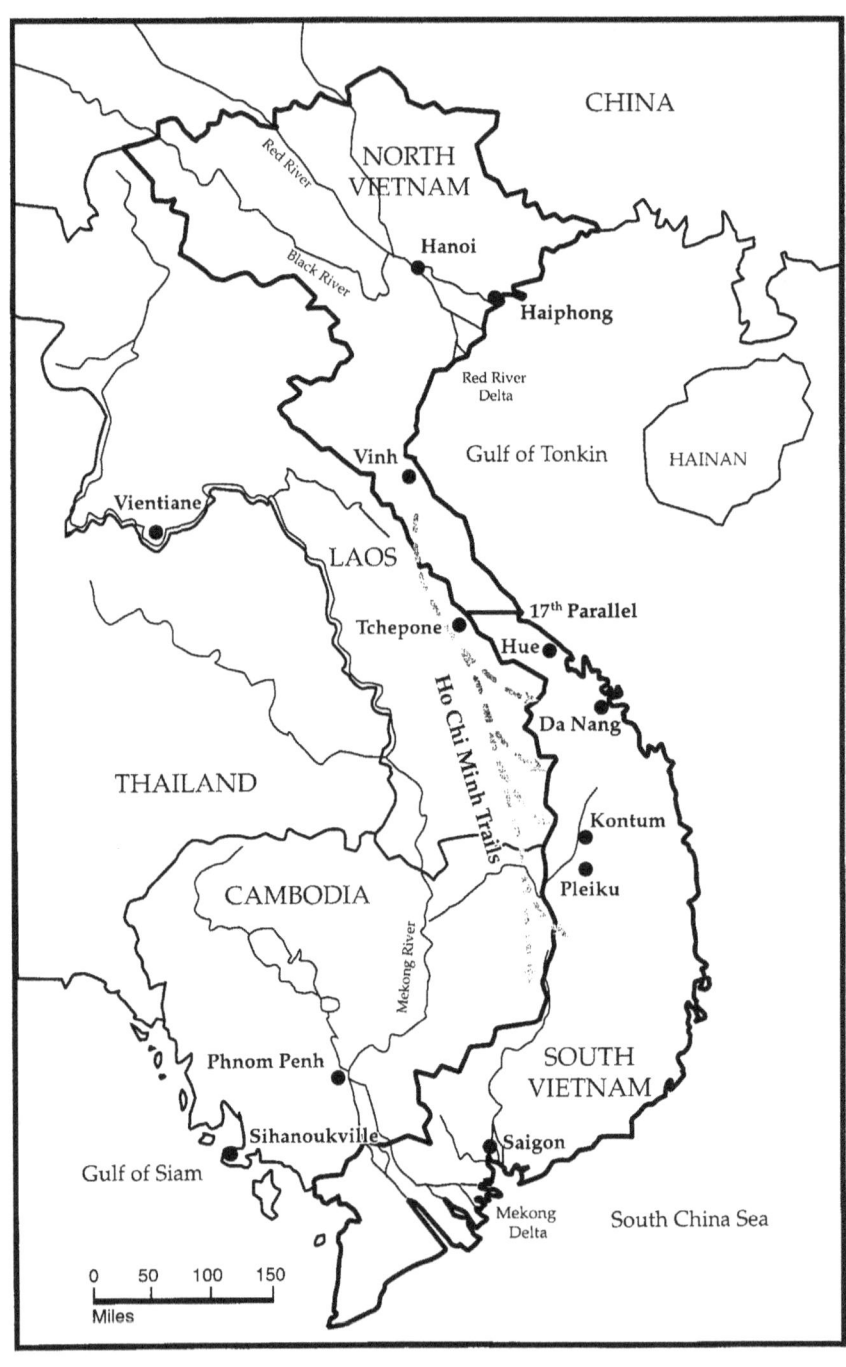

the whole game was given away.[45] While Communist control of the thinly populated, mountainous eastern Laotian panhandle would have little strategic value within Laos itself, as a corridor to South Vietnam[46] and Cambodia, it proved to be a decisive factor in the war in South Vietnam. That Kennedy could have been unaware in 1961 of the vital significance of this corridor is not credible since the (Joint Chiefs of Staff), State Department officials and members of the White House National Security staff had recognized it and warned that Communist control of it would make the defense of South Vietnam virtually impossible.[47]

The implications of this concession and other trends in the negotiations were not lost on the South Vietnamese, who expressed serious concern about the lack of guarantees for North Vietnamese withdrawal from eastern Laos. Accordingly, Kennedy wrote Diem a stiff letter telling him Laotian neutrality was the best possible solution and *in the best interests of South Vietnam*.[48]

When Kennedy reorganized his State Department at the end of November 1961, he asked Harriman to become assistant secretary for Far Eastern affairs, technically a demotion from ambassador-at-large, and Harriman, anxious to please, accepted while continuing as chief negotiator in Geneva.[49] He had been ordered to get a neutral settlement, and he was determined to brush aside anything standing in the way, thus becoming captive to his own negotiations. When Communist obduracy led to impasses in the negotiations, these were met by more unreciprocated concessions by Harriman.[50] In the face of Phoumi's recalcitrance, Harriman maneuvered in Washington to undercut him. As a means of whipping Phoumi into line, in January he succeeded in getting a cutoff of economic aid, thus putting the U.S. in the anomalous position of withholding economic aid to the Laotian government while simultaneously supplying arms and equipment to the Laotian army.[51] In early May, after Phoumi's army suffered a serious reverse in northern Laos, Phoumi finally caved in to the pressure and agreed to join a neutralist coalition headed by Souvanna and including the Pathet Lao leader, Souphanouvong, and Phoumi as vice premiers. Officially formed on June 23, the government's first acts were to proclaim a cease-fire, renounce SEATO protection[52] and declare Laos neutral. The Geneva conferees signed the Declaration on the Neutrality of Laos and the military protocols on July 23, 1962.[53]

The Aftermath

The small U. S. and allied military contingents began withdrawing immediately and were completely out of the country by early October, but only 40 of an estimated 10,000 North Vietnamese troops ever passed through the ICC checkpoints.[54] Unlike the 1954 accords, there was nothing in the 1962 agreement requiring the Pathet Lao to withdraw to regroupment areas.

Harriman had loyally carried out Kennedy's orders and brought in an agreement establishing a putative *neutral government* in Laos, but the real objective, a *neutralized* Laos, was not achieved. The agreement was a sophistry which had two main outcomes: a de facto partition of Laos and the provision of a fig leaf behind which Kennedy was able to save face and avoid intervention. Harriman, Rusk and Kennedy all knew the agreement was a sham, but that did not deter them from heralding it as a great step in pacifying Southeast Asia. Schlesinger had to admit, ruefully, that the agreement did not work, but he was still able to find a silver lining in that "the new policy brought clear gains.... The result was to localize the crisis, stop an imminent Communist takeover, place the Pathet Lao in the role of breakers of the peace, block the southward expansion of China and win the American position international support."[55] These "gains" were ephemeral when compared with the real advantages on the ground that were pocketed by the Communists. The reality was that when it became clear that the 1956 plebiscite on unification of the two Vietnams would not take place, North Vietnam determined to take control of eastern Laos which was strategically vital to Hanoi's plans to unite Vietnam by other means, and it would be truly ingenuous to believe that the existence of a neutralist coalition would have deterred North Vietnam from doing so.

The coalition held up for two years, collapsing in 1963 with the withdrawal of the Pathet Lao.[56] The neutralist forces largely remained loyal to the Souvanna government so that world opinion now cast the Pathet Lao as the clear aggressor for whatever that was worth. U.S. military and economic aid to Laos continued but without military advisors, however the CIA did remain active in support of government forces by various means. In December 1964 the U.S. began bombing the infiltration trails in eastern Laos and the panhandle in Operation Barrel Roll, sustaining these attacks until the final U.S. withdrawal from Vietnam, but though they may have slowed the flow somewhat, they never succeeded in stopping it.[57]

Thus, the war in Laos continued for 11 more years with the DRV-supported Pathet Lao gradually gaining the upper hand. Parallel with the January 1973 Paris agreement on Vietnam, a cease-fire was negotiated February 21 between the Laotian government and the Pathet Lao, and like the Paris agreement, the cease-fire did not hold. In 1975 the Pathet Lao achieved complete victory.[58]

So, in hindsight, the Kennedy decision in 1961–62 not to intervene in Laos contrary to the advice of his chief advisors may well have been the pivotal decision of the Second Indochina War. Although his advisors could not foresee how deeply the U.S. would become involved in the Second Indochina War, they did grasp the strategic importance of eastern Laos to the futures of South Vietnam and Cambodia, and they repeatedly advised Kennedy of this.[59] But Kennedy had by then decided to concede Laos and to make a stand against the Communists in Vietnam, believing that Vietnam was a better place than Laos to do this because the Vietnamese were better fighters and the logistics would be more favorable.[60] While these were indeed valid considerations, the decision ignored the crucial fact that North Vietnam's control of eastern Laos with the supply routes and sanctuaries it provided would make it nearly impossible to defeat the Communist insurgency in South Vietnam. It was a matter of pay now or pay later, and Kennedy's decision caused the U. S. to pay a very high price later.

Intervention in Laos

The final question is: would U.S. military intervention in Laos in 1961–62 have caused the People's Republic of China to enter the fighting as it did in Korea? With the costly Korean War still fresh in its memory, China was anxious to avoid provoking another armed clash with America, especially at a time when Chinese relations with the Soviet Union were steadily deteriorating. So despite its bellicose rhetoric, it did not want the Laos crisis to escalate into a major international confrontation. Chinese behavior after the U.S. intervened in Vietnam indicates that in the Laos case, China would have provided the DRV–Pathet Lao with all-out material support but would have stopped short of direct involvement as long as U.S. forces did not threaten its borders.

Kennedy's decision not to intervene in 1961–62, based on his very laudable but unrealistic wish for a neutral Laos, was the first in a sequence of major mistakes during the next decade of American involvement in Southeast Asia. It grew out of a failure to grasp the vital importance of Laos to North Vietnam in its plan to gain control of South Vietnam by subversion and force of arms, and, influenced by Harriman, Kennedy's subsequent actions over the course of the Geneva negotiations displayed a dangerous insouciance with regard to Communist aims and negotiating techniques. He was bested in the Laos negotiations but would not live to see the result.[61]

Attention Turns to Vietnam

During 1960, Edward Lansdale, now a brigadier general in the Pentagon, had been lobbying for authority to visit Vietnam in his capacity as a counterinsurgency specialist but was meeting resistance from the State Department which regarded him as a loose cannon with an anti–State attitude.[62] He had few friends at Defense either, where he was labeled "too political." In November, Ambassador Durbrow reluctantly authorized a visit which took place in the last month of the Eisenhower administration. In Vietnam he met with his old friend Diem, MAAG officials, Durbrow and mission staff, and CIA station personnel, and traveled to threatened areas of the country. His report stressed the seriousness of the trend in the security situation and called for fundamental changes in the way both Diem and the U.S. were approaching the situation. His recommendations were primarily political in nature, urging the appointment of a new American team in Vietnam whose members would be qualified by background and experience to deal with the insurgency and with Diem and his regime. It was, in effect, an implicit nomination of himself to the job of ambassador.[63]

The report worked its way through the bureaucracy until in late January it reached Deputy National Security Adviser Rostow on the White House staff who showed it to President Kennedy. In his preinaugural briefings, Kennedy had been led to believe that Laos was the main trouble spot in Southeast Asia, but Lansdale's report opened his eyes to the rapidly deteriorating situation in Vietnam which the incoming administration had thought was fairly secure.[64] Lansdale's report also succeeded in cutting the ground from under Durbrow, and it almost succeeded in getting Lansdale the ambassador's job when Kennedy let it be known that he was his choice to succeed Durbrow. But Kennedy was quickly dissuaded by Rusk and his State Department colleagues. Lansdale had to be satisfied with an appointment to Kennedy's Vietnam Task Force while Frederick E. Nolting, Jr., a career foreign service officer, was named to replace Durbrow who, by his persistence in pressing for improvements, had overdrawn on his credit with Diem.[65] Nolting planned to take a softer, less demanding line, building goodwill with Diem in the belief that he could later draw on that goodwill to gain the desired improvements.[66]

One can only speculate on what course events might have taken if Lansdale, with counterinsurgency experience and Diem's confidence, had been appointed, but there is no doubt his report had a pervasive influence on Kennedy and U.S. policy in Vietnam. The confrontational approach of Durbrow was replaced by clear assurances of continuing U.S. support from the softspoken new ambassador and reinforced by the visit in May by Vice President Lyndon Johnson.

As authorized by Kennedy, Johnson proposed to Diem that there be a U.S.-Vietnam mutual defense pact and that U.S. combat troops be sent to Vietnam. Diem declined both proposals, but notwithstanding, Johnson praised him extravagantly in a statement to the press, calling him "the Winston Churchill of southeast Asia."[67]

The Counterinsurgency Plan

In early January 1961 the counterinsurgency plan developed by Ambassador Durbrow and General McGarr arrived in Washington.[68] It included the ARVN and Civil Guard increases wanted by the MAAG and Diem, but in return for this increased assistance, the Diem government was expected to take the political and economic measures called for by Durbrow. At the end of January, the overall plan was approved by Kennedy, but since the military, political and economic parts of the plan had involved tradeoffs *among the Americans* with no commitment from Diem, implementation was another matter. In the meantime, the administration's attentions were diverted to Laos and then to the Bay of Pigs, and in the interim no action was taken on the counterinsurgency plan. The idea of an Vietnam Task Force, dormant since Kennedy had seen Lansdale's report in early February, was activated April 20, led by Deputy Secretary of Defense Roswell Gilpatrick and including Lansdale and Rostow.[69] However, before they had compiled their recommendations, Defense, at an April 29 National Security Council meeting, preempted the task force

3. The Kennedy Years

by gaining Kennedy's approval to several key military recommendations of the counterinsurgency plan—chiefly the increase of twenty thousand soldiers in the ARVN, an increase in MAAG staff of 100, and transfer of Civil Guard support and training from the civilian U.S. Operations Mission to the Military Assistance Program, i.e., the MAAG.[70] The recommendations of the task force, presented to Kennedy on May 10, reaffirmed the need for the actions already approved and added a long list of other actions in the military, economic, psychological and covert areas. Prominent among these were the deployment of 400 Special Forces to Vietnam for training of ARVN personnel in counterguerrilla tactics. Covert actions under the heading of "Unconventional Warfare" included, " In North Vietnam, using the foundations established by intelligence operations, form networks of resistance, covert bases and teams for sabotage and light harassment," a grossly unrealistic plan that achieved almost nothing and resulted in the deaths of many brave South Vietnamese volunteers. Completely absent from the task force recommendations was any recognition of the need for comprehensive political programs at the village level to counteract Viet Cong influence.

The following day National Security Action Memorandum (NSAM) 52 was issued, signed by McGeorge Bundy, approving essentially all the task force's recommendations.[71] This NSAM may well have been the most critical document of the entire U.S. experience in Vietnam in that it made a commitment and authorized actions that went well beyond anything done by the previous administrations of Truman and Eisenhower and thus should be considered the first step in the long series of escalations that followed. Referring to the task force report, the opening statement said: "The U.S. objectives and concept of operations ... are approved: to prevent Communist domination of South Vietnam; to create in that country a viable and increasingly democratic society, and to initiate, on an accelerated basis, a series of mutually supporting actions of a military, political, economic, psychological and covert character designed to achieve this objective." While some have argued that Kennedy always held back from making an unequivocal commitment to Vietnam, the words of NSAM 52 speak otherwise. Having waffled on Laos, he had chosen Vietnam as the ground on which he would show his mettle in resisting the encroachment of international Communism.

The deployments of 400 Special Forces and the 100-man increase in the MAAG were done covertly since they put the U.S. over the 685-man ceiling of the Geneva Accords. Thus, Kennedy established the precedent for what became a long sequence of U.S. government actions in Vietnam that were kept from the American people. The May 11 actions also marked the point at which Washington policy makers dropped the pretense of strict adherence to the Geneva Accords.

In addition to the increase in the ARVN to 170,000, NSAM 52 also authorized an assessment by U.S. military planners of the utility of a further increase to 200,000, but this study had hardly begun when in early June Kennedy received the letter from Diem urging that the ARVN be increased to 270,000 and that this be accompanied by a buildup of "selected elements" of U.S. armed forces.[72] A compromise was reached in August when the 200,000 level was authorized but with no increase in the MAAG. This only postponed the decision to increase the number of U.S. advisers.

Significantly, the actions required of Diem in the original Counterinsurgency Plan in return for the increased military and economic support had been completely dropped from NSAM 52, but the memo authorized Ambassador Nolting "...to begin negotiations looking toward a new bilateral arrangement with Vietnam, but no firm commitment will be made to such an arrangement without further review by the President."[73] Nothing had yet been done by Nolting on this point when on September 30 Diem surprised the administration when he suddenly reversed the position he had taken during Vice President Johnson's May visit and requested a bilateral security treaty with the U.S.[74] In response, Kennedy resorted to a device that would become standard practice on Vietnam in his and his successor's presidencies— send a fact-finding mission.

The Taylor-Rostow Mission

Gen. Maxwell D. Taylor, the president's personal military adviser, was designated to head a team including Rostow and Lansdale. Kennedy instructed Taylor to take into account not just military but also political, social, and economic elements in formulating his recommendations on the courses of action by the U.S. to assist South Vietnam in overcoming the current threat and assuring the country's continued independence.[75]

Taylor was the one military figure present throughout the Kennedy and Johnson administrations and is deeply woven into the Vietnam story. After distinguished service in World War II and Korea, he had become army chief of staff in 1956 during a period when the Dulles massive retaliation doctrine effectively was reducing the army's role in national security. Although Taylor disagreed with the policy, he supported it loyally, but after retiring in 1959 he wrote *The Uncertain Trumpet*[76] in which he advanced his doctrine of flexible response. This meshed perfectly with Kennedy's thoughts for restructuring the armed forces and also fitted well with his counterinsurgency ideas, so Taylor was a prophet who would have to be brought onto the Kennedy team. This was done when Taylor, as a civilian, was asked by Kennedy to head a group to do a post mortem on the Bay of Pigs. The relationship was formalized in mid-1961 when he became Kennedy's personal advisor on military affairs, an appointment that was not well received by the Joint Chiefs of Staff who believed they were the legally constituted military advisors to the president. When the Special Group (CI) was established in late 1961 to advise on counterinsurgency matters, Taylor chaired it.[77] Actually, Kennedy was only holding his favorite general in readiness, awaiting the opportunity to make him chairman of the JCS, which came October 1, 1962.[78]

After a whirlwind two-week visit to Vietnam, Taylor's team repaired to

Baguio in the Philippines to formulate its report. Although Taylor, in two meetings with Diem, had given the latter ample opportunity to request American combat troops (indeed, almost invited him to do so), again Diem demurred. Undeterred by Diem's reserve on this point, Taylor nevertheless recommended the introduction of an 8,000-man U.S. combat engineer unit, ostensibly to assist in recovering from floods that recently had ravaged the Mekong Delta but whose real purposes were to provide a U.S. military presence capable of raising morale, conducting such combat operations necessary for self defense, and providing an emergency reserve for the ARVN.[79] It was particularly ironic that this recommendation came not from the Pentagon but from Kennedy's favorite general. Kennedy did his best to prevent Taylor's troop recommendation from becoming public knowledge.[80]

Taylor's recommendations also included the deployment of military support units and personnel — helicopter and light reconnaissance aircraft, naval patrols, communications and intelligence — and a substantial increase in the size of the MAAG while shifting its charter from "an advisory group to something nearer — but not quite — an operational headquarters in a theater of war.... The U.S. should become a limited partner in the war...."[81] The report focused on military aspects, but did recommend "a high-level government advisor or advisors" in key ministries and in this connection mentioned that Diem had specifically requested Lansdale. Since State considered its ambassador as Diem's principal American civilian advisor and regarded Lansdale with deep suspicion, there was no chance it would agree to this. Taylor also included a statement which must go down as one of the classic misjudgments in American military history: "The risks of backing into a major Asian war by way of SVN are present but are not impressive."[82]

On November 8, Defense Secretary McNamara provided Kennedy with his and the Joint Chiefs' conclusions on the Taylor report. His memo was carefully hedged and full of ambiguities. It framed the basic issue as whether the U.S. should:

a. Commit itself to the clear objective of preventing the fall of South Vietnam to Communism, and

b. Support this commitment by necessary military actions.

The memo foresaw accurately that preventing the fall of South Vietnam would require the introduction of substantial forces and went on to estimate the likely maximum U.S. forces required. (In the event, his estimate of 205,000 troops was wildly optimistic. Peak deployment reached about 545,000 in early 1969.) It concluded that unless the U.S. committed firmly to the objective, major forces should not be sent and "we [McNamara and the JCS] are *inclined* to recommend that we do commit the U.S. to the ... objective ... and that we support this commitment by the necessary military actions." And finally, "*If such a commitment is agreed upon*, we support the recommendations of General Taylor as the first steps" (emphasis added). After sending the memo,

McNamara worried that it would appear too bellicose for Kennedy. He would soon learn that such memos should initially be put only in draft form so they would not be considered firm recommendations and could be modified when he had learned which way the wind blew in the White House.[83]

Another more pleasing memo had to be produced, this time jointly by McNamara and Rusk.[84] Though they persisted in recommending a commitment to the objective of preventing the fall of South Vietnam to Communism, they backed off from outright combat troop commitments. Instead, they divided the troops issue into two categories: (A) support units of modest size, and (B) larger units with an actual or potential military mission. They recommended adoption of the items in Taylor's report that fitted under Category A but that Defense only *plan* for the possibilities of Category B.

In the end, the McNamara-Rusk Category A–type recommendations were approved, but even though he had approved NSAM 52, Kennedy continued to equivocate on the basic commitment to prevent the fall of Vietnam to Communism which was the underlying premise for the actions proposed.[85] Thus, the buildup in Vietnam was authorized by a president who may have harbored private reservations about the objective being served. The first two helicopter companies arrived in December and by year's end, the U.S. had over 2,000 uniformed personnel in Vietnam.

The entire package of actions was wrapped up in NSAM 111 of November 22 entitled "First Phase of Vietnam Program." Included was an upgrading of the MAAG from an advisory and assistance group to a Military Assistance Command-Vietnam or MACV under a four-star general. Nolting was told to inform Diem that in return for increased military support, Washington expected Diem to change his autocratic ways and to broaden the base of his regime and that the U.S. expected "... to share in the decision-making process in the political, economic and military fields as they affect the security situation." Nolting reported back that Diem reacted very adversely to this, saying, "Viet Nam did not want to be a protectorate." In the face of this resistance, the U.S. softened its stand to accepting a close partnership and frequent consultation rather than insisting on participating in decision-making.[86] Diem had won again.

While no decision had been made to commit combat troops, the decisions flowing from the Taylor-Rostow mission marked the point at which Rusk and State lost primacy over Vietnam policy to McNamara and Defense. The White House and Defense believed Vietnam was essentially a military, not a political problem, and Rusk acquiesced in this view over the opposition of lower levels at State. The aggressive McNamara flowed quickly into the opening created by Rusk's passivity and thus became Kennedy's and later Johnson's point man on Vietnam.[87] For the next six years, those few isolated voices (Colby and Lansdale were the most prominent) who stressed the need for actions on the political side were ignored while the military buildup continued.[88]

The MACV was established to have an *operational* role as contrasted to the MAAG's purely advisory role, and its chief would enjoy equal status with the ambassador. Clearly, McNamara and the Joint Chiefs were laying the groundwork for a much larger future role for the U.S. military in Vietnam.

When the formation of the MACV and appointment of Lt. Gen. Paul Harkins to head it were announced on February 8, 1962, the administration's increased commitments to the war in South Vietnam could no longer be hidden, and the resulting clamor in the House and Senate and in the press forced Kennedy to divulge at least a part of his new policy.[89] In a *New York Times* column, James Reston wrote that "everyone but the American public knows the U.S. is involved in an undeclared war."[90]

A Wave of Optimism

U.S. military personnel edged closer to combat when U.S. advisors were authorized to accompany their ARVN units into combat, and U.S. Air Force pilots began flying close support missions in propeller-driven South Vietnamese aircraft while ostensibly training Vietnamese pilots in the back seat (Operation Farmgate).[91] These changes plus the mobility provided by the American-flown helicopters produced a diminution of guerrilla activity in the first half of 1962. This combination of events produced what proved to be an unwarranted optimism among the Americans advisors in Saigon and officials in Washington.

Accordingly, in July 1962, at one of his periodic Honolulu conferences, McNamara ordered Harkins to prepare a plan for phasing out the MACV over the next three years.[92] McNamara credits himself as the originator of this initiative, based on the military situation,[93] but Schlesinger states that in July 1962, "Kennedy instructed McNamara to start planning for the phased withdrawal...."[94] For Kennedy loyalists this is a pivotal issue in their effort to support their assertion that Kennedy planned to withdraw from Vietnam. In any case, there almost certainly were domestic political considerations underlying McNamara's order to Harkins. He knew that Kennedy, looking ahead to the 1964 elections, was anxious that the U.S. appear to be reducing, not increasing, its commitments in Vietnam, so the ground was being prepared in mid–1962.[95] Meanwhile, the buildup of American military advisors and support personnel continued apace. By the end of 1962 the number was over 11,000.[96]

The Mansfield Report

In early December 1962, Senator Mike Mansfield led a Senate Foreign Relations Committee fact-finding mission to Vietnam. Mansfield had been one of Diem's earliest and most ardent supporters in the early 1950s when Diem was an émigré in the U.S., and thus, it came as a rude shock to Diem when the very critical nature of Mansfield's report became public. The report questioned if the American commitment to Vietnam could be justified by U.S. security interests in Southeast Asia, criticized Diem's lack of progress in establishing a stable government despite massive American aid and implied that if greater efforts were not forthcoming from the Saigon government, the U.S. should reduce or abandon its support. But in the end, the report urged continuation of the U.S. effort at the present level. (It was in discussing the report with Mansfield that Kennedy allegedly told the latter of his, Kennedy's, intention to withdraw from Vietnam after he was reelected in 1964, but that to do so prior to the election would create a political firestorm that might endanger his reelection.[97]) Knowing Mansfield's influential position in Washington, Diem interpreted the report as presaging a change in U.S. policy, and it took all the persuasive powers of Nolting and Rusk to reassure him such was not the case.[98]

The Strategic Hamlet Program

Diem understood clearly that the issue in South Vietnam ultimately would be resolved by the side that controlled the peasantry, the 85 percent of the population residing in the villages, and that it was vital for the government to take measures in the villages to counter the inroads of the NLF.[99] In the spring of 1962, the Diem government launched its most important nonmilitary initiative, the strategic hamlet program. Directed by Nhu, the objectives of the program were similar to the earlier failed agroville program[100]— to provide the people with improved security and social and health services while denying the NLF access to the peasantry. It was a political, not a police or military, program, and thus, in concept, was precisely the right program for the time, but, like the agroville program, it was flawed in execution. The huge scope of the undertaking is indicated by the fact there were about 16,000 hamlets in South Vietnam of which about 14,000 (later revised to 11,000) were to be included, all to be completed in 14 months. U.S. aid consisted of funding, barbed wire and building materials, but the program was a South Vietnamese initiative. The concept involved the stockading of the hamlets through the use of fences of mud, wood or barbed wire, sharpened stakes and ditches, but unlike the agrovilles, the inhabitants remained in or near their homes. Also, each hamlet was to organize its own militia as defense against outside attack. By the spring of 1963 over 8,000 hamlets had been stockaded. The capacity of the hamlets for self-defense varied, but it quickly became clear that isolated hamlets outside areas of government control usually could not successfully resist Viet Cong attacks. Also, the scope of the program and the haste with which the hamlets were built were such that it was beyond the government's ability to provide everywhere the promised improvements in social and health services.

Almost every critic states, inaccurately, that the genesis of the program was a system used by the British to defeat the insurgency in Malaya, a system which the critics believed was totally inappropriate for the situation in Vietnam.[101] In fact, the program was not based on the Malayan system, as related in the authoritative account of the origins of the program by William Colby who was then

CIA station chief (later director of the CIA) and a confidant of Nhu.[102] Duncanson's account of the origins of the program,[103] although somewhat different from Colby's, also contradicts the Malaysian theory. In any case, the origins of the program were completely irrelevant. The only issue was its effectiveness.

As to its effectiveness, Pike, an acknowledged expert on the NLF, writes: "The period also witnessed, in late 1962 and early 1963, a major crisis for the NLF, the growth of the GVN's strategic-hamlet program. This program not only forced NLF village leaders to flee but it offered alternative social and political organizations to the villagers. Moreover, since the program relocated villagers and thus mixed people from different villages, efforts by NLF agents to rebuild the network inside the strategic hamlet became increasingly complicated and less successful...."[104] And again, "This attitude [of the NLF] of the late 1961 and early 1962 period gave way to grim pessimism a year later as a result of two developments: the advent of massive American aid, and the GVN's strategic-hamlet program."[105] Further, in commenting on Hanoi's reasons for founding the People's Revolutionary Party: "Countering the GVN's strategic-hamlet program especially required stronger organizational methods than previously had been necessary...."[106]

Also, one could always detect when a program or activity was especially damaging to the Communists by the frequency and stridency with which it was denounced in their pronouncements and propaganda. Thus, the strategic hamlet program was always high on the NLF's list of nefarious schemes of the Diem regime which had to be attacked or which would be abolished after the NLF took power.[107]

Critics of Diem and Nhu were totally fixated on reporting weaknesses and failures while ignoring the larger issue of the rightness of the objectives of the program in countering the NLF. As Colby said, "The strategic hamlets program seized the initiative in the contest with the Communists for the first time" but "The urban elite focused on the failures in the program and transmitted their complaints to the foreign civilians and media communities...."[108] With no knowledge of its impact on the NLF, the journalists took their cue from the chattering classes in Saigon and it was quickly written off as a failure.

After the overthrow of the Diem regime and the wholesale dismissal of Diemist officials in the provinces and districts by the short-lived Minh military regime, the program was allowed to disintegrate, although some strategic hamlets continued in existence. When in turn the Minh junta was overturned by Gen. Nguyen Khanh, the program was reestablished under a new name, New Life Hamlets, which deemphasized stockades and self-defense while serving principally as a channel for distributing aid to the villages.[109]

Press Relations

As the focus of the Kennedy administration shifted from Laos to Vietnam in late 1961, the attention of the American news media likewise was drawn to this deepening confrontation between the U.S. and its Communist bloc adversaries. As it became clear that America was drawing a line in the sand there, Vietnam began to deserve closer coverage, and soon most major American television and print media had a full- or part-time representative in Saigon. Many of these correspondents were young, impressionable and hungry for recognition, but lacked experience in the Far East and knew little about Vietnam. In the hothouse atmosphere of fractious Saigon, it was not difficult to establish contacts with critics of the Diem regime, including young staffers in the U.S. Embassy, a few outspoken U.S. military advisors and disgruntled Vietnamese intellectuals, not to mention other Western news correspondents. Gradually, beginning about 1960, the American media shifted from what had been since 1954 a pro–Diem stance to a more guarded, neutral one, and by 1962, this attitude had become critical if not openly hostile to his regime.

Three correspondents who probably had the greatest influence on the spin being received by the American public at this point were David Halberstam of the *New York Times*, Malcom Browne of the Associated Press and Neil Sheehan of United Press International. The three, all in their 20s, became friends, sharing rumors, experiences and convictions and fast coming to the shared conclusion that "*we* could not win the war" with Diem heading the government of South Vietnam. Effectively, they became advocates of this point of view, and their reporting reflected it. What made their reporting so influential in Washington was the extremely low tolerance of the Kennedy administration and John Kennedy personally to media criticism, especially in the *New York Times*, of administration policy in any area. Nothing stirred the thin-skinned Kennedy to anger quicker than a negative story in the *New York Times*.[110]

New grounds for criticism of the regime were not long in coming when on January 2, 1963, in a battle in the Mekong Delta near the hamlet of Ap Bac, a VC battalion, although heavily outnumbered and surrounded by ARVN forces, was able to inflict casualties of 51 dead (including three Americans) and over 100 wounded while downing five U.S. helicopters and then slip out of the trap.[111] The battle seemed to bear out earlier press criticism of Diem's conduct of the war and accordingly the Ap Bac engagement was reported as if it had been the turning point, the Gettysburg or Stalingrad of the Vietnam War. The *New York Times* gave it extensive play on page one on January 3 with continued commentary and editorials for six days, and while Ap Bac was certainly not the turning point of the Vietnam War, it may well have been the turning point in the *Times*' editorial position on the war.

American officials in Saigon and Washington became increasingly concerned over what they viewed as a tendency among American correspondents to emphasize reputed failures of the Diem regime and ARVN defeats while ignoring positive developments. Washington believed this was having an adverse effect on the American public's attitude toward the war and was undercutting efforts of the U.S. Embassy to work with Diem and Nhu and to establish harmonious relationships with Vietnamese counterparts. The problem fed on itself as negative material in the U.S. media caused increased hostility to the correspondents among Vietnamese officials which led to further deterioration in press relations and even more adverse reporting.[112]

By early 1963, the Viet Cong had adjusted their tactics to meet the new ARVN tactics made possible by the American helicopters. Heavy machine guns had been infiltrated from the North for use against the helicopters leading U.S. advisors to call for faster, more heavily armed aircraft. The U.S. was beginning to lose helicopters with their air crews from VC ground fire, and the number of advisors killed in action with their ARVN units was also increasing, but U.S. casualties were still at a level at which the press was reporting as an individual news item the death in action of a single American serviceman or the loss of a helicopter. The number of killed in Vietnam had gone from 16 in 1961 to 53 in 1962 and reached 118 in 1963. (In the first major engagement after the deployment of combat troops, the Ia Drang Valley battle in November 1965, the U.S. lost 240 killed in action in two weeks.[113])

The Buddhist Crisis

While the negative media treatment of Diem brought discomfiture in the Kennedy administration, it was not yet of the gravity to bring down the Diem regime. Rather, it was an incident in Hue in early May 1963 which actually lit the fuse to a train of events that ultimately brought an end to the Diem government and to the lives of Diem and Nhu. It started innocently enough with the Buddhist celebration of Wesak, the birthday of Buddha, an annual public holiday in Vietnam. A dispute arose over the flying of the Buddhist flag without an accompanying national flag as required by a government regulation. Even though the minister of interior agreed to make an exception for the occasion, a leading local bonze, Thich Tri Quang, who appeared to be seeking a pretext for a confrontation, was not mollified, and charging government discrimination against Buddhism, organized protest processions with banners demanding religious equality with Catholics. What began as a peaceful protest ended in disorders, and the Civil Guard was called in to disperse an unruly crowd. Exactly what happened next is in dispute, but the outcome was nine Buddhists dead. Quang now had his martyrs.[114]

Compared to Ceylon, Burma and Tibet where Buddhism was firmly implanted as the state religion, in South Vietnam, Buddhism coexisted with Catholicism and the Cao Dai and Hoa Hao religious sects. (Though they incorporated some aspects of Buddhism, the sects were not recognized by the Buddhist hierarchy.) In recent years, Vietnamese Buddhists had become more militant, perhaps in response to Catholicism which was gaining strength throughout Vietnam. This rivalry was probably intensified by the accession of the Catholic Ngo family (one of whom was a bishop) to power in South Vietnam in 1954, the influx of over 600,000 Catholics refugees who regrouped from the North, and Diem's selection of a disproportionate number of Catholics for important positions in his government. Some take the latter as evidence on its face of malign discrimination against Buddhism by the Diem government when in filling top positions, like all politicians, Diem had a natural and legitimate inclination to choose from loyal supporters, people he knew, trusted and believed were qualified. (American presidents follow the same practice.) This is not to say that his cabinets were exclusively Catholic as all included some Buddhists, and a majority of the top army officers were non–Catholic although not necessarily practicing Buddhists.[115]

Although the image of the Buddhist held by most Westerners was one of the passive ascetic devoted to quiet meditation in his pagoda, free of all worldly concerns, such was far from describing the leaders of the Vietnamese Buddhist uprising beginning in 1963. Thich Tri Quang and his fellow bonzes were thoroughly politicized individuals with a flair for manipulating their following and the media using techniques not acquired through the practice of yoga. Thus, the Hue incident was followed by the establishment of press relations offices, the issuance of communiqués to the media and the marshalling of the Buddhist faithful for demonstrations in Central Vietnam and Saigon, demanding that the government admit responsibility for the Hue incident, that the flag regulation be rescinded and that technical differences be eliminated in laws having to do with incorporation of church bodies which the Buddhists believed favored Christian religions. These issues were characterized in communiqués as official and systematic persecution of Buddhism by the Diem regime,[116] and an appeal was even dispatched to the secretary-general of the United Nations who sent a fact-finding mission to Vietnam.[117] It appeared the Buddhists' true objective was to bring down the Diem regime, but it was never clear what the Buddhists, from their obscurantist rhetoric, wanted to put in its place.

As the disturbances continued and media criticism of the Diem regime intensified in the U.S., the State Department began to panic. In a June 11 message to the U.S. embassy, Rusk described Buddhist demands as "reasonable and/or insubstantial," recommended that Diem accede to them and closed by saying, "If Diem does not take prompt and effective steps to reestablish Buddhist confidence in him we will have to reexamine our entire relationship with his regime."[118] Before any of this could be conveyed to Diem, this position was leaked to the *New York Times* for on June 14 a front-page article stated inaccurately that the U.S. had warned Diem it would publicly condemn his treatment of the Buddhists unless he took prompt action to meet their grievances. Halberstam was contributing to U.S.-Diem tension through provocative articles in the *Times* such as one stating that American officials in Saigon had reversed their opinion on Diem and wanted a new government and that ARVN officers were ready to overthrow him.[119]

By midsummer other disaffected elements, including the Cao Dai, Hoa Hao, students and intellectuals, had taken advantage of the turmoil and jumped on the bandwagon. Diem was astute enough to recognize at the outset that the disturbances had little or nothing to do with religion and everything to do with politics but not astute enough to recognize that he could not handle this in the usual high-handed manner that he had applied successfully to other political situations. The crux of the problem was Diem's unwillingness to fully conciliate the demands of the Buddhists for fear this would serve as a precedent for other dissatisfied interest groups which would then begin lodging their own demands. His initial attempts at stonewalling only exacerbated the clamor, allowing it to build for over one month until finally, on June 11, an event occurred which took any possibility of controlling the unrest entirely out of Diem's hands. An elderly bonze, Thich Quang Duc, immolated himself by fire publicly on a street corner in Saigon, and alerted by the Buddhist press relations staff, the Western press was able to witness and photograph the happening. If any single event could be identified as bringing the dénouement of the Diem regime, it would be this one.[120]

The reaction in the West was one of deep shock and horror. Up to this point, Americans typically had not shown intense interest in events in far-off Vietnam. They knew the U.S. was helping South Vietnam fight the Communists and may have been vaguely aware of the current unrest in the country, but this event riveted their attention as never before. The coterie of anti–Diem correspondents in Saigon had been handed an unparalleled news coup with which to smite the regime, and they took full advantage of it. The general line played by the American media was that the immolation was the supreme protest against the oppressive Diem government which had been persecuting the peaceable Buddhists even though they comprised the majority of the people.[121] Every right-thinking American knew that religious persecution was wrong and, ergo, the regime must be evil, and from this point, American public opinion turned on the Diem regime. Thus, the Kennedy administration found it necessary to distance itself from the Diem government and, eventually, to sacrifice him.

The immolation of Thich Quang Duc was followed by five or six others before Diem was finally toppled, but after the first two or three, it was no longer news. Immolations continued after the fall of Diem, but these received little notice in the Western media. These events never took place without prior notification of the foreign press corps by representatives of the Buddhist press relations office. The profound cynicism of the Buddhist leaders in using the immolations of bonzes, monks and nuns to further the underlying political aims of the dissidents was ignored in American press and television reports. Concessions by the successor Minh and Khanh governments to the Buddhist activists were only met with new demands. The Buddhists were unappeasable.

Stunned by the overwhelmingly adverse publicity in the West and the growing anarchy in Vietnam, as the summer wore on Diem alternated between concessions and repression, but neither was effective in resolving the crisis. U.S. officials, whose grasp of the true nature of the controversy was superficial at best, were advising him to make concessions to the Buddhists[122] while his brother Nhu was counseling him to take a hard line. In the end, it was Nhu who carried the day.

Lodge Appointed Ambassador

In late June, Kennedy changed ambassadors. This decision was influenced by a backstage campaign to oust Nolting orchestrated by Undersecretary of State Harriman who believed Nolting too pro–Diem, and abetted by Hilsman, assistant secretary for the Far East, and Forrestal of the White House National Security staff. Perhaps the most overtly active member of this triumvirate was Forrestal, Harriman's protégé and willing tool whose position in the White House was used by Harriman to get his views before Kennedy. Following a brief trip to Vietnam by Hilsman and Forrestal, their lengthy report of January 25 to Kennedy included a section on their evaluation of the performance of the U.S. Mission. Without actually naming Nolting, they cited various alleged shortcomings which could only be attributed to him and recommended replacing him.[123] In a February 4 memo to Kennedy, Forrestal said, "If you approve, Governor Harriman and I will start a quiet campaign in the appropriate departments for the following objectives" one of which was to replace Nolting when his two-year term was up in April.[124] Thus did Harriman work his will within the Kennedy administration, and as will be seen, the intrigue of this triumvirate ultimately would have a decisive influence on U.S. policy in Vietnam.

On June 28, Kennedy announced the appointment of Henry Cabot Lodge, Jr., as ambassador to Vietnam. After years of foreign service professionals in Saigon, the appointment of a Republican politician to this high-profile post was a surprise. While the Kennedy administration was filled with establishment figures, Lodge's background transcended the mere establishment — he was from a patrician Boston Brahmin family with connections to people like Theodore Roosevelt, Edith Wharton and Henry Adams. Grandson of the Republican senate leader and adversary of Woodrow Wilson, he was raised in a political milieu leading inevitably to a career of public service. In 1936, at the age of 34, he was elected to the U. S. Senate, defeating James Curley, no small feat in a landslide Democratic year. After 16 years in the Senate (with two years out for World War II service), when running for reelection in 1952 he had the misfortune to have as his opponent John F. Kennedy, bringing an end to his years of elective office but not his career as an influential Republican politician. He served the Eisenhower administration as ambassador to the UN and was Nixon's running mate in 1960, again being defeated by Kennedy.[125]

Arthur Schlesinger would have it that the idea of Lodge's appointment was advanced originally by Rusk, and that Kennedy was motivated, at least partially, by magnanimity toward the man he had twice defeated.[126] In fact, it seems rather doubtful that there was the slightest shred of magnanimity in the appointment. Given that Kennedy could have chosen from a number of capable Democrats, the selection of Lodge, a Republican, was coolly calculated for no other reason than to give Kennedy political cover in case things went badly in Vietnam. But Kennedy failed to calculate that Lodge, the imperious mandarin, would be his own man in Saigon, and thus beyond Kennedy's power to control. In any case, the appointment was to prove the most fateful of any made over the entire course of U.S. involvement in Vietnam.

The Crisis Deepens

In a July 8 appraisal of the situation, the CIA indicated an awareness of coup plotting among at least three different groups in Saigon and observed that the militant Buddhists now appeared to be transferring their struggle to the political realm in an effort to overthrow Diem.[127] Meanwhile, as the crisis deepened, the regime seemed to be drifting between honoring and repudiating a June 16 agreement with the Buddhists. As the drift continued and coup rumors grew stronger, the anti–Diem clique in the State Department began to envision Diem's removal,[128] but at this point, in late July and early August, involvement of U.S. personnel in Vietnamese coup planning had gone no further than a contact by one group of coup plotters with CIA agent Lucien Conein.[129]

On August 20, Diem acted to quell the chaos. According to Duncanson, at a conference with the top generals, he obtained their signatures to "a remonstrance calling on the Government to seize and silence the ringleaders."[130] Diem then declared a state of siege in Saigon, and the next day placed the country under martial law. On the night of August 21-22, units of Nhu's Special Forces and the police conducted a raid on the Xa Loi pagoda, the principal Buddhist center in Saigon, arresting some 400 monks and nuns[131] while other units raided pagodas in Hue, Da Nang and other cities and town. The detention of large numbers of Buddhist dissidents along with martial law temporarily quieted the disturbances in Vietnam, but the manic press coverage by American correspondents only exacerbated the distress in official circles in Washington.

The American correspondents in Saigon had a field day with the raids on the pagodas, identifying Nhu as the force behind them and ignoring the complicity of the army generals.[132] In the raids on pagodas outside Saigon, the army clearly furnished troops, but that did not fit the anti–Nhu spin which charged he had falsely implicated the army. The generals were quite happy to go along with the reporters' version of events. But in the days after the raids, the truth began to trickle out when the *New York Times* reported that U.S. officials believed some ARVN generals persuaded Diem to proclaim martial law and crack down on the Buddhists.[133]

The declaration of martial law on August 20 followed by the raids on the pagodas were pivotal points in the 25-year history of U.S. involvement in Vietnam. Although the embassy had clear indications that martial law had been recommended by the top ARVN generals and that the role of the generals in the pagoda raids was at least ambiguous if not actually complicit,[134] Washington, undoubtedly influenced by press reports from Saigon, placed responsibility for the situation entirely on Nhu.[135] Long considered by embassy officials and American press corps in Saigon as the evil *eminence grise* of the regime and the nexus of U.S. problems in Vietnam, Nhu now became the object of frenzied resentment in Washington.

In the meantime, Lodge arrived in Saigon on the evening of August 22. Based on his actions throughout the ensuing crisis that culminated with the death of Diem on November 2, there is little doubt Lodge came on the scene predisposed to the overthrow of the Diem regime. Even before he knew he would have any role in Vietnam, Lodge expressed serious reservations about the Diem government to Harriman,[136] and this attitude was probably reinforced by briefings from Harriman and Hilsman in preparation for his assignment.

Deptel 243

The Harriman-Hilsman-Forrestal triumvirate saw this situation as ideal for a move against the Diem regime, which it had opposed with growing stridency.[137] Accordingly, they decided to take matters into their own hands. Harriman, a veteran of Washington intrigue, cleverly chose to act on a Saturday, August 24, when all of the principals — Kennedy, Rusk, McNamara, Taylor of the JCS and McCone of the CIA — were away or not readily available, to draft a cable to Lodge which became the fateful Deptel 243.[138] The principal draftsman of the cable was Hilsman with Harriman's approval, but Forrestal played his part by preparing the ground with Kennedy. First was a memo for Kennedy's weekend reading in which Forrestal stated, "Agreement is also developing that the US cannot tolerate a result to the present difficulties in Saigon which leaves Brother Nhu in a dominating position ... *Averell, Roger and I* now agree that we must move before the situation in Saigon freezes"[139] (emphasis added). And a telegram on August 24: "Harriman, Hilsman and Forrestal have drafted following telegram to Saigon.... Since situation in Saigon may not remain fluid for long, *Department* believes desirable transmit this message tonight"[140] (emphasis added). A first draft of what became Deptel 243 was attached.

The three, along with Undersecretary of State George Ball, then proceeded to obtain clearances of the message by a process which has been the subject of widely varying accounts by the participants, Vietnam scholars and journalists alike but which, on consensus, would be described as dubious, deceptive, or dishonest.[141] It was a kind of whipsaw game in which the clearer's approval was obtained conditioned on the approval of the others, but no clearer actually discussed the cable with another in the circle. No principal actually saw the draft, but it was read to Rusk over an open phone line. Rusk later claimed he was told at the time that Kennedy had already approved it.[142] Roswell Gilpatrick, deputy secretary of defense acting for McNamara, also was told by Forrestal it had already been approved by Kennedy and that he was being advised for information only.[143] Taylor was not contacted prior to transmittal of the message.[144] Kennedy, at Hyannisport, did not see the final draft, the relevant passages being read to him over a secure phone. In any case, having been assured by the triumvirate that it had been cleared by the appropriate officials, Kennedy approved its transmittal which occurred at 9:36 P.M., August 24. Karnow's account of this event concludes with the insouciant observation: "Most probably, Kennedy was not paying close attention to the details."[145]

Though Deptel 243 is lengthy, its impact on subsequent events in Washington and Saigon was too critical to permit paraphrasing here. The text follows:

"243. Eyes only Ambassador Lodge. For CINCPAC/POLAD exclusive for Admiral Felt. No further distribution. [Here follow references to previous communications.] It is now clear that whether military proposed martial law or whether Nhu tricked them into it, Nhu took advantage of its imposition to smash pagodas with police and Tung's Special Forces loyal to him, thus placing onus on military in eyes of world and Vietnamese people. Also clear that Nhu has maneuvered himself into commanding position.

US Government cannot tolerate situation in which power lies in Nhu's hands. Diem must be given chance to rid himself of Nhu and his coterie and replace them with best military and political personalities available.

If, in spite of all your efforts, Diem remains obdurate and refuses, then we must face the possibility that Diem himself cannot be preserved.

We now believe immediate action must be taken to prevent Nhu from consolidating his position further. Therefore, unless you in consultation with Harkins perceive overriding objections you are authorized to proceed along following lines:

(1) First, we must press on appropriate levels of GVN following line:
(a) USG cannot accept actions against Buddhists taken by Nhu and his collaborators under cover martial law. (b) Prompt dramatic actions redress situation must be taken, including repeal of decree 10, release of arrested monks, nuns, etc.

(2) We must at same time also tell key military leaders that US would find it impossible to continue support GVN militarily and economically unless above steps are taken immediately which we recognize requires removal of Nhu from the scene. We wish give Diem reasonable opportunity to remove Nhus, but if he remains obdurate, then we are prepared to accept obvious implications that we can no longer support Diem. You may also tell appropriate military commanders we will give them direct support in any interim period of breakdown central government mechanism.

(3) We recognize the necessity of removing taint on military for pagoda raids and placing blame squarely on Nhu. You are authorized to have such statements made in Saigon as you consider desirable to achieve this objective. We are prepared to take same line here and to have Voice of America make statement along lines contained in next numbered telegram whenever you give the word, preferably as soon as possible.

Concurrently with above, Ambassador and country team should urgently examine all possible alternative leadership and make detailed plans as to how we might bring about Diem's replacement if this should become necessary.

Assume you will consult with General Harkins re any precautions necessary protect American personnel during crisis period.

You will understand that we cannot from Washington give you detailed instructions as to how this operation should proceed, but you will also know we will back you to the hilt on actions you take to achieve our objectives.

Needless to say we have held knowledge of this telegram to minimum essential people and assume you will take similar precautions to prevent premature leaks. End text.[146]

Deptel 243 was a major shift in U.S. policy, but it is almost certain that Kennedy did not grasp the full import of what he had approved. In the Kennedy administration, policies were established or changed only after long and tortuous discussion and debate among the principals and their assistants in numerous White House meetings, usually with Kennedy presiding. But back in Washington on Monday morning, the full significance of Deptel 243 came home to him when he was confronted with a raging controversy over the way the telegram had been slipped through the system without adequate deliberation of the principals. McNamara, Taylor and McCone were particularly incensed over the last paragraph that said, "we have held knowledge of this telegram to the minimum essential people." which had not included them.[147]

Kennedy's response was to call a White House meeting of the Executive Committee (EXCOMM) for noon that day, August 26. He was faced with a dilemma: if he pulled back from this ill-considered message, it would be a tacit admission that he really had not paid attention to what he was approving. Embarrassing leaks would be inevitable, and he would lose face all around, in the media, with his cabinet and with Lodge. No, he had to brazen it out as if he had thoroughly considered all the ramifications of the policy change prior to approving the message.[148] Present at the meeting, in addition to the president, were Rusk, McNamara, Taylor, Gilpatrick, McGeorge Bundy, George Ball of State, Richard Helms and General Carter representing the CIA, General Krulak and the triumvirate.

After some preliminaries, the president observed that it was essential that Halberstam's reporting in the *New York Times* not be allowed unduly to influence the administration's actions. Hilsman assured him such was not the case, but in fact, the news stories coming out of Saigon had unquestionably influenced the action of Harriman, Hilsman and Forrestal. The president then added that any move to eliminate the Diem government should not be a result of *New York Times* pressure. Harriman then made an unconvincing attempt to justify the sending of the telegram as being the earliest possible moment that "we knew the situation, i.e., that the people of Vietnam had turned against the government." (Apparently, he did not elaborate on the source of this information, but almost certainly it was the *New York Times*.) Later, the president asked Taylor what chance he thought the plan as outlined in Deptel 243 had of succeeding, a revealing question in that it was an admission that this vital issue had not been probed by Kennedy prior to approving the telegram. Taylor replied that in Washington, the problem of choosing a head of state would not be turned over to the military. McNamara raised the question of what was meant by the phrase "direct support" in subparagraph (2) of the message, and Hilsman's response was a tacit admission that this essentially military matter had not been discussed with the Pentagon by the authors of the telegram. Overall, in spite of their efforts at damage control, it was a squirmy time for the triumvirate, but, in effect, Kennedy gave them a pass because to do otherwise would have been to admit his own failure. No decisions were reached at the meeting, and Kennedy concluded it by calling another meeting for the next day and specifically requesting that Nolting, who was now in Washington, attend. Knowing that Nolting would be pro–Diem, Hilsman attempted to dissuade Kennedy from including him because "his views were colored in that he was emotionally involved," but Kennedy responded, "Maybe properly."[149]

Coup Plotting

Deptel 243 accorded well with Lodge's ideas except in one respect. He believed the chances of Diem's agreeing to dispense with Nhu were virtually nil, and accordingly he had proposed and State had agreed to skip the step of first going to Diem and *go directly to the generals*.[150] Thus, a very significant fact relating to the Monday, August 26, meeting was that at Lodge's request the directions given in Deptel 243 had already been modified by State in an August 25 telegram, and that due to the 13-hour time difference between Washington and Saigon the generals *had already been contacted* by Conein, Lodge's go-between, and that at least the State Department representatives, if not Kennedy, were aware of this fact. This was particularly significant since it made pulling back from Deptel 243 much more difficult. Hilsman makes no mention of this in his account of this or later meetings.

Deptel 243 had included the plan to discredit Nhu in the media both in the U.S. and Vietnam, but in carrying it out in Saigon a snafu occurred when on August 26 Saigon time (before the first White House meeting) the Voice of America broadcast a news item, on guidance provided by Hilsman, stating that the army did not know about the police plans to raid the Buddhist pagodas and adding that Washington officials said "America may cut its aid to Vietnam if President Diem does not get rid of the police officials responsible" (meaning Nhu).[151] This press guidance was for simultaneous play in Washington and Saigon, but according to Hilsman, the last sentence about cutting aid was not in the guidance, and the Saigon broadcaster had exceeded his instructions. The next day the VOA had to broadcast a retraction of that portion. But the damage was done and the press lapped it up. The VOA broadcast, which had not been cleared by Lodge, elicited an angry message from him to State criticizing every aspect of the broadcast and saying that it enormously complicated his problems.[152] In response, Lodge got an almost groveling message from Rusk apologizing for the VOA broadcast.[153] From Kennedy on down, Lodge was always treated with the utmost deference by Washington. Where other ambassadors were instructed, Lodge was merely given suggestions for his review and comment.

When Lodge received approval on August 25 for his plan to go directly to the generals, he wasted no time. By 12:45 P.M. Monday, August 26, Saigon time (11:45 P.M. Sunday, Washington time), before the first White House meeting took place, Conein had already contacted an ARVN general perceived to be a plot ringleader. The general was told that the U.S. would provide direct support during any interim period of breakdown of the central government mechanism and that if Nhu did not go, the U.S. would not continue military and economic support of Vietnam.[154] Thus, by committing U.S. support for a coup, Lodge very quickly presented Washington with a *fait accompli* before anyone there could express second thoughts. Ironically, later that day Lodge presented his credentials to Diem and engaged in an insubstantial two-hour discussion with him.

Participants at the White House meeting on Tuesday, August 27, were essentially the same as the previous day except that the anti–Diem forces were depleted by the absence of Harriman while pro–Diem former ambassador Nolting was present. The meeting was conducted in the full knowledge that the CIA had already approached the generals. In the rather meandering discussion, Nolting was voluble in his support of Diem and affirmed that Diem and Nhu were inseparable but that Diem might be persuaded to limit Nhu's authority. Nolting also deprecated the ability of the generals to conduct a successful coup against Diem. Kennedy showed signs of wavering when he directed that Lodge and Harkins should be asked for their estimate of the prospects of a coup by the generals and whether they should proceed with the generals or wait. Nothing else of substance resulted from the meeting.

At this point a message from the Saigon CIA Station was received describing the situation in Saigon in stark, all-or-nothing terms and strongly supporting the generals. It predicted that if Diem and Nhu won the showdown with the generals, "*they* [Diem and Nhu] *would sharply reduce American presence in Vietnam.*" It concluded by saying that, if the coup failed, "it is no exaggeration to say that Vietnam runs a serious risk of being lost over the course of time."[155] Significantly, this message indicated the CIA believed not only that a reduced American presence would be contrary to Kennedy's Vietnam policy but also that Diem would never agree to an *increased* presence.

The next White House meeting was convened at noon Wednesday, August 28. Participants were expanded to include the vice president, Treasury Secretary Dillon and Attorney General Robert Kennedy, and this time, the anti–Diem forces made sure that Harriman attended. Altogether, there were 20 people in the room. Again, President Kennedy displayed indecision about the course being followed and characteristically directed that Lodge and Harkins be asked for yet another evaluation of the opposing military forces in Saigon. In crises, Kennedy always sought that perfect information on which to base his decision, something that can never be found in ambiguous and rapidly changing situations. In this the third meeting[156] on the coup crisis, for the first time the question was raised (by Nolting) of what would be the resulting government if the coup succeeded. No one could offer a carefully considered, knowledgeable response to this question, but the group apparently did not regard it as a central issue. The meandering and indecisive meeting culminated in an ad hominem attack by Harriman on Nolting whose comments had been raining on the anti–Diem parade. Kennedy called yet another meeting for 6:00 P.M. that day which resulted in still more cables to Lodge and Harkins aimed at gaining clarification of their views on the probability of success of the coup.

Lodge's response[157] to this last flurry of cables began with the often-cited statement:

> "1. We are launched on a course from which there is no respectable turning back: The overthrow of the Diem government. There is no turning back in part because US prestige is already publicly committed to this end in large measure and will become more so as facts leak out...."

If there had been any doubt in the minds of Kennedy and his advisors in Washington about the man they had as ambassador in Saigon, this message should have clarified it. First, it closed off any potential avenues of retreat for faint hearts in Washington who might get cold feet; second, it was tacit blackmail in the implicit threat of leaks by Lodge if Washington tried to reverse course. Clearly, Lodge was going to be his own man in Saigon.

Despite the definitive cable from Lodge, at the next EXCOMM meeting on the 29th, the pro–Diem forces remained squeamish about U.S. involvement in the coup plotting and argued for the retention of Diem as head of state after the elimination of Nhu from a position of influence. They urged that one last attempt be made by Lodge to persuade Diem to remove Nhu, but knowing Lodge opposed any meeting with Diem at this juncture, the president deflected this suggestion. Washington was being swept along by the coup momentum and there would be no turning back.

Following the meeting, Kennedy sent a private message to Lodge in which he cited his constitutional responsibilities as president and commander-in-chief and, accordingly, affirmed that: "*Until the very moment of the go signal for the operation by the Generals, I must reserve a contingent right to change course and reverse previous instructions.*" No message could have been more revealing of the misconceptions of Kennedy and his advisors as to their ability to control events in Saigon. In his private reply, Lodge acknowledged Kennedy's right and responsibility to change course at any time but added politely, "To be successful this operation must be essentially a Vietnamese affair" and that, "you may not be able to control it, i.e. the 'go signal' may be given by the generals."[158] Of course, this is precisely what happened when the actual coup took place November 1.

All through August 30, as tension built over an imminent coup, cables flew furiously between Washington and Saigon. But Washington's balloon was suddenly deflated by a CIA cable transmitted from Saigon at 2:39 A.M. August 31 (early afternoon August 30 in Washington) that opened with the words: "This particular coup is finished." At a meeting with the generals intended to stiffen their resolve, Harkins had been told instead that the coup was off because the generals did not feel ready and did not have sufficient balance of forces.[159]

The Interim

It must have been a very crestfallen EXCOMM (less Kennedy) that met Saturday morning, August 31, to conduct a post mortem, exactly one week after the triumvirate's drafting of the controversial Deptel 243. U.S. policy in Vietnam was now in complete disarray, aggravated by the near certainty that Diem and Nhu knew of American complicity in the generals' aborted coup. Since he had presented his credentials on August 26, Lodge had not met with Diem, so Rusk cabled him, suggesting that he now reopen discussions with Diem on the same issues, i.e., Buddhist repressions, Nhu, broadening the government, press censorship, etc., that had been exacerbating relations prior to the pagoda raids.[160] Still Lodge procrastinated, finally seeing Diem in an indecisive meeting on September 8.[161] After this, Lodge adopted a position toward Diem of cold and distant correctness, avoiding contact in a war of nerves intended to pressure Diem to come to him. Thus, the U.S. was in a position in which its ambassador in Saigon was no longer in contact with the Vietnamese chief of state, a rather unusual twist to accepted diplomatic usage governing the relationship between an ambassador and the head of the host state and government.[162]

Washington was not happy with this tactic. Rusk's deferential suggestions were having no effect on Lodge, so on September 17 the White House gave it a try in a long cable to Lodge.[163] Included was a long list of "possible helpful actions" (13 in all) on the part of the Saigon government to improve its popularity, conciliate opponents, improve press relations, etc., requiring the very face-to-face discussions with Diem that Lodge wished to avoid, but as always, deferring to Lodge's judgment. He was also informed that the president had decided to send McNamara and Taylor on a mission to evaluate the military situation while reassuring Lodge he remained in control of all political decisions. This information elicited a quick response from Lodge opposing the visit on the grounds it would upset his "policy of silence" toward Diem followed by two more cables shooting down most of the suggestions in the White House cable.[164] Even White House pressure was unable to move Lodge, who clearly intended to keep matters in his own hands and did not welcome potential interference from visitors from Washington, especially those known to be pro–Diem.

In the midst of these exchanges, Lodge astounded Rusk and McCone by asking that Lansdale be sent out to replace John Richardson as Saigon CIA station chief.[165] Lansdale was to "take charge, under my supervision, of all U.S. relationships with *a change of government* here," or in other words, to orchestrate future coup planning with the generals (emphasis added). Lodge did not trust Richardson because of his close relationship with Nhu, and Lansdale still had a powerful reputation in Vietnam as an operative. The request even got an airing in the White House, but McCone was able to quash it. When he could not get his way by this means, Lodge resorted to leaks through an October 4 *New York Times* story by Halberstam which recounted alleged State-CIA disagreement in Saigon and said: "Lodge has told Washington he wants a new chief...."[166] Thus, Lodge made Richardson's position in Saigon untenable, and he was reassigned on October 5, but Lansdale was not his replacement. And thus did Halberstam influence events in Vietnam.

Despite the disappointing outcome of the effort by the State Department's anti–Diem clique to stimulate a coup, the sentiment in Washington for one was still very much alive. Likewise, in Saigon the plotting had not ended when the generals had called off their coup on August 31. Conein, with Lodge's approval, continued to have periodic meetings with the generals which left no doubt that they were working to resolve the weaknesses in their earlier plan to overthrow Diem,[167] and Washington was being kept fully informed of these developments.

For once, Washington did not bow to Lodge's judgment, and Kennedy overrode his objections to the McNamara-Taylor mission. This caused angst among the anti–Diem clique at State because of the perceived pro–Diem tendencies at Defense, and Harriman had to be content with insinuating his protégé, Forrestal, and William Sullivan, Harriman's deputy, onto the mission team. The principal outcome of this mission was the decision by the Kennedy administration to suspend funding of the Commodity Import Program (CIP) as a means of applying pressure on Diem to obtain the political and military changes desired by the U.S. The CIP was the major USAID mechanism for generating piastre income for the government of Vietnam and thus was a vital source of funds for paying the army. The decision was taken with some trepidation because of fear that if prolonged, the suspension would affect the war with the Viet Cong, but it was projected that with the amount then in the CIP pipeline coupled with the GVN's own resources, no shortage of funds would be felt for five to six months. Thus, Washington was bluffing that Diem would cave before that point arrived, but if he did not, then the U.S. would be faced with two very unpalatable alternatives: caving itself and restoring the CIP or leaving Vietnam. In the event, the death of Diem assured that the U.S. bluff was never called, but the Vietnamese plotters in Saigon took the cutoff in aid as a clear green light.[168]

A secondary but still significant outcome of the McNamara-Taylor visit was the recommendation to reduce American military personnel in Vietnam by 1,000 by year's end. (At this point, the number was over 16,000.)[169] The reduction had been removed from the draft version of the McNamara-Taylor report because the military situation clearly did not justify it, but for PR purposes, Kennedy wanted it in, so after a private meeting of Kennedy, McNamara, and Taylor the recommendation was reinserted.[170] A statement released to the press on October 2 announced the planned reduction.[171]

On October 5, Lodge was informed of the decision on the CIP and some lesser actions being taken in U.S. support programs.[172] In a separate message sent via CIA channels, Bundy told Lodge: "*President today approved recommendation that no initiative should now be taken to give any covert encouragement to a coup. There should, however, be urgent covert effort with closest* security under broad guidance of Ambassador to identify and build contacts with possible alternative leadership as and when it appears" (emphasis added). The cable went on to stress that this effort should be totally secure and fully deniable.[173] Bundy expanded on his earlier message in an October 9 cable[174] to Lodge: "While we do not wish to stimulate coup, we also do not wish to leave impression that U.S. would thwart a change of government or deny economic and military assistance to a new regime" but Lodge was also told Washington would not consider the coup plans with any seriousness without detailed information on what was being contemplated by the plotters so that Washington could evaluate the prospects for success. Again, security and plausible deniability were stressed.

The White House position of not stimulating a coup was at total variance with the actions of Lodge and his designated representative, Conein, in maintaining and, indeed, courting contact with coup plotters and in seeking advance information on possible coups to allow an evaluation of the chances of success. While these actions may not have fallen within a narrow definition of the verb "to stimulate," there is little question that taken as a whole, U.S. actions, from the point of view of the plotters, did in fact stimulate them.

Lodge apparently sensed some vulnerability and felt the need to defend his actions to Washington. In a message to Bundy on October 25,[175] Lodge said: "We should not thwart a coup for two reasons. First, it seems at least an even bet that the next government would not bungle and stumble as much as the present one has." (Events were to prove Lodge disastrously wrong on this bet.) The message continued: "Secondly, ... Whenever we thwart attempts at a coup ... we are assuming *an undue responsibility for keeping the incumbents in office*, and in general are setting ourselves in judgment over the affairs of Vietnam" (emphasis added). This was sophistry in the extreme, as if coups were merely another form of self-determination and a legitimate means of unseating the lawful and duly constituted government of a friendly power.

Meanwhile, in contacts between Conein and General Don during the last week of October, Conein was told the coup would take place by November 2, but the plotters, fearful of security leaks, would not reveal their plans and had lingering doubts about Conein's credentials as an official U.S. spokesman. The plotters received the final assurance they needed when, in a chance meeting at the Saigon airport, General Don asked Lodge whether Conein was authorized to speak for Lodge, and Lodge confirmed that he was and added that the U.S. would not thwart a coup.[176] This meeting probably sealed the fate of the Diem regime.

Washington remained extremely nervous over the lack of information on coup plans and the resulting inability to evaluate chances for success. This feeling of insecurity was intensified by the news that instead of the 48 hours notice promised earlier, Conein had been informed by Don that the plans could be made available only four hours in advance. This intelligence was passed along to Washington by Lodge in two messages on October 29 which painted a rather uncertain picture of the balance of forces in support of the coup versus those loyal to Diem.[177] At a White House meeting that day, those of Kennedy's key advisors who had never favored a coup again surfaced their doubts, including Taylor, Robert Kennedy, and McCone. Following the pattern of the numerous White House meetings since the August 24 Deptel 243, the composition of a post-coup government, if such were to occur, was not a part of the discussion.

The upshot of the meeting was a cable[178] to Lodge expressing these reservations and asking for a combined assessment from Lodge *and* Harkins of the likely outcome of this projected coup attempt. Lodge's response[179] did not provide the requested assessment but instead attempted again to stiffen resolve in Washington for a coup. He rejected Bundy's assertion that the U.S. could still delay or discourage a coup other than by betraying it to Diem and said, "[that] would make traitors out of us." In the balance between betraying the plotters and betraying Diem, Lodge saw a higher morality in betraying Diem.

Bundy showed a certain asperity in his response, saying: "We do not accept as a basis for U.S. policy that we have no power to delay or discourage a coup." The men in the White House simply could not accept that they, the most powerful men in the world, could not control events in a small, third world nation. And Kennedy and Bundy had not yet grasped that their cables to Lodge were essentially futile. Their power to control him, short of a direct order from the president, was minimal because their directions to him always left Lodge with some wiggle room to exercise his judgment, and that judgment was unalterably committed to a coup.

The Coup

As it developed, Bundy's cable, which arrived in Saigon the morning of October 31, was the last substantive exchange between Lodge and the White House before the coup began. It was ironic that the embassy transmitted a cable[180] to State two hours after the coup started recounting Lodge's discussion with Diem that morning at the Presidential Palace in which Lodge quoted Diem as saying: "Please tell President Kennedy that I am a good and frank ally, that I would rather be frank and settle questions now than talk about them after we have lost everything.... That I take all his suggestions very seriously and wish to carry them out but it is a question of timing." Lodge added: "In effect he [Diem] said: Tell us what you want and we'll do it." It appeared a major breakthrough had occurred in the long, frustrating dialog with Diem, but it was too late. The coup began 30 minutes later.

At 1:30 P.M. the generals launched their coup, surrounding the Presidential Palace with army units commanded by the plotters, but the attack was held off by the Presidential Guard. At 4:30 P.M., Diem phoned Lodge at the embassy, and a brief conversation ensued which must go down as one of the most shameful low points in American diplomacy. The transcript needs no elaboration:

Diem: Some units have made a rebellion, and I want to know what is the attitude of the United States.

Lodge: I do not feel well-enough informed to be able to tell you. I have heard the shooting, but am not acquainted with all the facts. Also, it is 4:30 A.M. in Washington, and the U.S. government cannot possibly have a view.

Diem: But you must have some general ideas. After all, I am a chief of state. I have tried to do my duty. I want to do now what duty and good sense require. I believe in duty above all.

Lodge: You have certainly done your duty. As I told you only this morning, I admire your courage and your great contribution to your country. No one can take away from you the credit for all you have done. Now I am worried about your physical safety. I have a report that those in charge of the current activity offer you and your brother safe conduct out of the country if you resign. Had you heard this?

Diem: No. [And then, after a pause] You have my telephone number.

Lodge: Yes. If I can do anything for your physical safety, please call me.

Diem: I am trying to reestablish order.[181]

With this exchange, Diem had all the information he needed as to the attitude of the U.S. to the preservation of his regime.

As the coup progressed, cables flew between Saigon and Washington with fragmentary and sometimes inaccurate reports of developments. At 12:24 A.M. November 2 the State Department received a CIA cable informing it of the deaths of Diem and Nhu, reportedly by suicide. In the midst of a White House meeting that morning, Kennedy was handed a copy of this message. According to Taylor who was present, Kennedy rushed from the room "with a look of shock and dismay."[182] Knowing of the Ngos' devout Catholicism and as a Catholic himself, Kennedy was justifiably skeptical of the suicide story, and the next day he learned that, in fact, they had been assassinated.[183] While Kennedy had stressed from the outset that no harm should come to the brothers, his shocked reaction again reflected an ingenuous belief that he could control highly charged events in far off–Saigon.

Damage Control

The White House was, of course, extremely anxious that no hint of American complicity reach the media. As soon as reports of the coup began coming in but before the outcome was known, a State Department spokesman released a Kennedy-approved statement: "I can categorically state that the US Government was not involved in any way."[184] Then, with the knowledge that the coup had been successful in toppling Diem, the White House immediately went into a full damage-control mode. The first concern was to get the best possible treatment in the press by spinning the coup as not merely the product of a few scheming officers but as a Vietnamese "national decision," and the Washington press corps was backgrounded accordingly the evening of November 2.[185] The manner of the deaths of Diem and Nhu was causing acute discomfort in Washington since, despite the fact that by November 3 it was public information that they had been murdered, the generals had not modified their statement that the brothers had committed suicide. At this point, Lodge and Washington certainly knew they had been murdered, and at least Lodge knew that this had been done on the orders of Gen. Duong Van Minh.[186] But media reports of the manner of death of Diem and Nhu (shot and stabbed) were now reaching the U.S. public, and the ever PR-conscious administration was extremely anxious that the generals issue "a clarifying statement," i.e., a better story. Lodge received counsel from Rusk on this point,[187] and on November 6, Gen. Tran Tu Oai, information minister, issued the ludicrous statement that they had died by "accidental suicide."[188] Washington chose never to delve further into the circumstances surrounding Diem's death, but rather to avert its collective eyes from the explosive fact that the author of the deed was General Minh, the new chief of state of the Republic of Vietnam.

The New Government

During the period of plotting, the generals had indicated to the Americans that it was their intention to turn over power quickly to a civilian government, but the U.S. was not encouraged by the composition of the new government announced November 5.[189] The president and chief of state was to be Gen. Duong Van Minh, not Nguyen Ngoc Tho, Diem's vice president and thus his constitutional successor. The Americans had wanted Tho to become president to give some figment of legitimate continuity to the new regime, but instead, he was to occupy a newly created position of premier and head of government. However, executive power actually was to be exercised by the Revolutionary Military Council, a junta of 12 top generals headed by Minh. The key ministries of Defense, Security (formerly Interior) and Information were headed by generals while the remainder of the cabinet posts were filled by nonpolitical civilian technicians. U.S. officials were disillusioned that no prominent anti–Diem civilian political figure accepted an appointment in the cabinet. The constitution and the National Assembly were abolished, not to be seen again until 1967. Diem's province and district chiefs were dismissed and replaced by inexperienced new people, putting all the rural programs into a state of utter confusion.

Although the junta had announced with great fanfare the removal of restrictions on the press, by November 16, the regime was already warning that some newspapers were abusing press freedom and five days later closed two of them.[190] Further closures followed in December.

The first significant international fallout from the coup was the announcement by Prince Norodom Sihanouk, premier of Cambodia, that his country was rejecting all U.S. military and economic aid. Having seen what U.S. support had done for Ngo Dinh Diem, he was having no part of it.[191]

In sum, the U.S. had exchanged a constitutionally based, lawfully elected civilian government, albeit an authoritarian one, for a military junta. While Washington was less than pleased with the composition of the new government, Lodge recommended that the U.S. not press the generals too hard on political reforms and early elections. He urged that the U.S. be patient and give the generals a chance to get on with the war. [192] This was a far more charitable attitude than he took toward Diem in the scant 10 weeks of their acquaintance.

The Coup Revisited

While Lodge had willing accomplices in Washington, there is no question he was the prime mover in the cabal against Diem. He needed only Deptel 243 to launch him on a path from which he never deviated — the overthrow of Diem. The selection of Republican Lodge as ambassador created an unforeseen paradox for Kennedy. On the one hand, Lodge was intended to be a Republican hostage to Kennedy's policies in Vietnam, but on the other, it Lodge's appointment made the White House and State Department very hesitant to instruct Lodge since such guidance could, if things went badly, establish a record which could enable him later to say that he was merely following instructions. Thus, the Kennedy White House tacitly abdicated control to Lodge. In his memoirs, [193] Lodge practiced the art of plausible deniability so favored by the Kennedy administration by hanging his actions on the administration's policy of "not thwarting a coup," but in doing so, he also made generous use of the technique of selective omission. There is simply far too much in the record to accept Lodge's version of an essentially passive role for himself.

Diem in Perspective

What can one conclude about Ngo Dinh Diem, the man who ruled Vietnam for nine years and created the republic? First, it is clear that Diem was the indispensable man in the unstable years of 1954–55. Without him, the republic almost certainly would never have existed. That Diem was able to establish the non–Communist Republic of Vietnam fulfilled a principal U.S. objective at the time for which he was lauded in America for his courage and hailed as a political genius.

Later, Diem was indicted by State Department officials, the American media and by many scholars because his young republic did not meet their standards for liberal Western representative democracy, standards which only a handful of nations in the world could meet. While successor regimes ostensibly removed the constraints on civil liberties, the outcome, as Diem foresaw, was not constructive for the nation because of the factional proclivities of the political class in South Vietnam. The Americans who advised Diem simply did not appreciate the depth of factionalism that was characteristic of South Vietnam as illustrated by the fact that, according to Robert Shaplen, "After the overthrow of Diem ... *fifty or sixty* so-called political parties sprang up, despite efforts to limit their number...." [194]

There is much speculation among scholars as to what Kennedy would have done in Vietnam had he lived, with the Kennedy loyalists at pains to establish, on the flimsiest of evidence, that after his reelection in 1964 he would have extricated the U.S.[195] It would seem equally fair to speculate on the course that events might have followed if Diem had acquiesced to U.S. demands and remained in power, but one searches in vain for such speculation. However, on the question of deployment of large numbers of U.S. combat forces, it is safe to assume, based on better evidence than the Kennedy loyalists can advance, that Diem would never have acquiesced to the massive U.S. intervention and ultimate takeover of the conduct of the war and, effectively, the country.[196] It simply was not in his nature, as he demonstrated over and over again, to permit outsiders to exercise control over Vietnamese affairs, much to the frustration of his American advisors. Faced with the alternatives of loss of control of his country to the Americans and a negotiated settlement with North Vietnam, Diem almost certainly would have chosen the latter, and America's longest war would never have been fought.

And so, as the 1963 Buddhist crisis brought criticism of Diem to a crescendo in the U.S. media, a feckless Kennedy administration, unable to manipulate Diem and without careful consideration of what was to follow, found it expedient to sacrifice him. What did follow was chaos—a series of inept governments, continued social unrest and deterioration of the military situation such that within two years the U.S. was forced to intervene with combat troops to save the position. With the death of Diem it became America's war.

Kennedy and Vietnam

The Kennedy record on Vietnam is not a glorious one. He blundered badly in the 1961–62 Geneva negotiations which established a sham neutralization of Laos while conceding control of the eastern panhandle to North Vietnam, thus affording them the sanctuaries and supply routes so vital to the covert war they had declared on South Vietnam in 1959.

His other major blunder was in acquiescing in the Diem coup. Kennedy loyalists have maintained that it was entirely a Vietnamese affair and outside Kennedy's control, which is belied by the contemporaneous record. Instead, as a means of encouraging a coup, the generals were assured of continuing support which committed the U.S. in Vietnam more unequivocally than we had ever been under Diem. Awkward questions of morality and the composition of the resulting government were swept aside. Diem was not the only foreign leader whom the U.S. has connived to overthrow, but he is unique in being the only *leader of a friendly government* to receive such treatment. Kennedy's role in the overthrow of Diem fell rather short of his vow to "... support any friend ... to assure the survival and success of liberty."

In his public utterances and writings, Kennedy stressed over and over again his determination that South Vietnam should remain independent and free of Communist control and affirmed our willingness to aid that country in its struggle against Communist subversion and encroachment, but his actual performance reflected a pattern of vacillation, irresolution and uncertainty.

The elimination of the Diem government followed three weeks later by Kennedy's own untimely death left an extremely difficult dilemma to his successor. Kennedy had increased the U.S. military presence in Vietnam from less than one thousand to over sixteen thousand, enough to be taken as a firm commitment to the support of South Vietnam but not enough to affect the outcome of the war. Assuredly, Kennedy had put the U.S. into the Vietnam War, but his successor would have to make the Hobson's choice either to reverse the commitment of a martyred president or to continue and amplify his policy.

4

Johnson Takes Charge

In the painful three years as vice president in the Kennedy administration, Lyndon Johnson had been on the periphery of Vietnam policy-making as, for that matter, he had been on most other things. But when Kennedy sent him to Vietnam in May 1961 to demonstrate U.S. support for Ngo Dinh Diem, Johnson had developed a rapport with the Vietnamese leader, and later, in August 1963 when Washington was expectantly awaiting a coup against Diem, he disapproved, although as vice president he was impotent to influence events. In *The Vantage Point*,[1] published in 1971, Johnson said that in his judgment, Deptel 243 "was a serious blunder that launched a period of deep political confusion that lasted almost two years." This view was not just the product of eight years of hindsight for after the August coup failed to materialize, at the postmortem meeting Johnson strongly expressed his opinion that "we must reestablish ourselves and stop playing cops and robbers...."[2] In the ensuing interlude leading to the final coup, though he was not always present at the many White House meetings on the matter, he was clearly in the pro–Diem camp along with McNamara, McCone, Taylor and Harkins, but he felt that as vice president, he had, perforce, to take his lead from Kennedy.

Following the death of Diem, at Kennedy's direction McNamara convened a meeting in Honolulu on November 20–21 including Rusk, M. Bundy, Lodge, and selected subordinates to review the U.S. position with respect to Vietnam.[3] On November 24, two days after Kennedy's death, President Johnson met in the White House with the key participants in that Honolulu meeting to discuss the Vietnam situation.[4] Lodge, as the principal author of the change in government, understandably gave an optimistic report on the outlook while McCone gave a somewhat contradictory view. Johnson then stated that he was not at all sure that supporting the overthrow of Diem had been the right course, inferring that *he* would not have supported it, but that it was a fait accompli and the U.S. would now have to see that its objectives were accomplished.

Two days later, in one of his first formal actions as president, Johnson directed McGeorge Bundy to issue NSAM 273.[5] It began: "*It remains the central objective of the U.S. in South Vietnam to assist the people and Government of that country to win their contest against the externally directed and supported communist conspiracy.*" It reaffirmed the withdrawal of 1,000 military advisors by year end as announced October 2 and restated the goal of phasing out the MACV by the end of 1965, and it authorized the start of planning for covert operations against North Vietnam. It was the first formal statement on Vietnam of the new Johnson administration, and it made clear that there was to be no change in the Kennedy policy of assisting the government there in defeating the Communist conspiracy. If anything, it strengthened the commitment by underlining the need for unity at all levels within the administration in working toward that goal.

Thus, Johnson made it known that he intended to carry on with the policy set out by his predecessors as first stated by Truman and Eisenhower and reiterated by Kennedy in May 1961 in NSAM 52.[6] Throughout his presidency, as Vietnam became more and more controversial, he never ceased calling up these precedents, maintaining that he was doing nothing more than continuing a policy established by Eisenhower and Kennedy. Thus, NSAM 273 hardly qualified as a bold new initiative on his part because, as he saw it, there were many reasons to carry on and none to change. First, Vice President Johnson, while excluded from any decision-making role, had all along favored Kennedy's military buildup in Vietnam. Now, as the new president, he was acutely conscious of his lack of an electoral mandate on which to base a change in policy even if he had believed one was desirable. He knew he was deficient in foreign policy experience, making it extremely unlikely that, at least at the outset, he would reverse the policy of his predecessor nor act against the advice of the key members of his cabinet, the very ones who had devised the policy. And finally, he was temperamentally unable even remotely to consider withdrawing from Vietnam, to "turn tail and run," making him appear a weakling who had been faced down by the Communists.[7] Not only was he going to pursue Kennedy's policy but he was going to do it with the same top-level team of advisors, McNamara, Rusk and Bundy, because not to do so might be interpreted by Kennedy loyalists as a repudiation of the judgment of the martyred president. No doubt Johnson immediately began looking ahead to the 1964 elections when he hoped to obtain his own mandate and could then consider bringing in his own people, but ironically, when that time arrived he had become captive to these same advisors, and he kept them on.

Having opposed U.S. complicity in the plot to overthrow Diem, Johnson harbored some resentment against those he believed responsible, targeting Harriman, Hilsman and Forrestal, and gradually having them removed from positions of influence on Vietnam policy.[8] Lodge was a much more delicate problem. Johnson had no personal ties to Lodge, a prominent Republican and representative of the elitist Eastern Establishment, but as a Kennedy appointee, Lodge had to be handled carefully by Johnson. However, Lodge's fitness for the job, given the new situation in Saigon created by the death of Diem, was being called into question. A November 16 CIA report[9] observed that Lodge was: "running very much a vest-pocket operation and not a country team or total American effort." Following the November 20 Honolulu meeting, Bundy observed in a White House staff meeting[10] that: "There is no country team in Vietnam at the present time in any real sense ... it is not at all evident that he [Lodge] can handle the job he is now faced with." After a two-day fact-finding trip to Vietnam on December 19–20, McNamara's report to Johnson[11] had these comments on Lodge: "The Country Team is the second major weakness. It lacks leadership ... and is not working to a common plan.... My impression is that Lodge simply does not know how to conduct a coordinated administration."[12] Kennedy's too-clever appointment of Lodge was coming back to haunt Johnson. Lodge had proven himself very adept at loner-type, covert intriguing with the generals, but his deficiencies as a leader and coordinator of the U.S. Mission in Vietnam were becoming all too obvious, handing Johnson a difficult dilemma, but there was absolutely no way the administration could recall Lodge — the political fallout from such a move would be too terrible to contemplate. In the event, the administration was forced to live with Lodge until June when he did ask to be relieved. When Johnson, despite the knowledge that Lodge was not well suited to the job, appointed him in 1965 for a second tour as ambassador, he did so first, like Kennedy, to take advantage of the political cover afforded by Republican Lodge, but other factors may also have had an influence. One was that Lodge had shown himself trustworthy in Johnson's eyes because he had kept quiet about Vietnam during the 1964 campaign and had refused to support Goldwater.

Harkins' Revenge

It quickly became apparent to American officials in Saigon and Washington that the new government in Saigon was not providing the hoped-for solutions to the problems of Vietnam. While civil unrest had quieted, it had by no means disappeared as the generals learned that despite their measures to cultivate popularity, the Buddhists, students, tea house intellectuals, would-be politicians and other interest groups were still not fully appeased, and while the generals were preoccupied with essentially political affairs and struggles for power within the Military Revolutionary Council, the Viet Cong were continuing their inroads. In an atmosphere of indecision and drift, the prosecution of the war was actually less vigorous than under Diem. Following his December fact-finding trip, McNamara outlined these gloomy conditions in his report to Johnson,[13] but McNamara's public statements were more optimistic.[14] The one concrete recommendation in the report was that the planning for covert operations of sabotage and psychological warfare against North Vietnam authorized in NSAM 273 be pushed ahead without delay. Otherwise, McNamara could only recommend that the U.S. hold on and hope that the generals would soon take matters in hand.

Initially jubilant over the demise of Diem, the State Department anti–Diem clique was somewhat chastened by the adverse turn of events in Vietnam following the coup, but would never concede that it had insouciantly encouraged a change of government in complete ignorance of the composition of a successor government or the attitudes and abilities of its members. It quickly adopted the line that things had been going badly all along but that Americans in Saigon had been misled by the overly optimistic reports of their sources in the Diem government. According to Roger Hilsman, "the coup drew back the curtain," revealing what the true picture really was.[15] There was general agreement that Viet Cong successes had begun earlier, but no connection was drawn with the fact that through most of 1963 key ARVN military leaders had been preoccupied with plotting the overthrow of Diem rather than prosecuting the war.

Still, there was no getting around the disappointing performance of the Minh government, and this brought a decided shift in the Washington power balance at the expense of State and in favor of Defense that had, by and large, opposed a change in government. And thus, there was almost certainly some smoldering resentment among General Harkins and the MACV and their superiors McNamara, Taylor, and the JCS about the way Lodge and the State Department clique had, behind the back of Harkins and the MACV, conspired with the top ARVN generals in the overthrow of Diem. A demonstrated willingness by the Minh government to prosecute the war more effectively might have extinguished this resentment, but in the absence of that, Harkins and company were prepared to seek more aggressive military leadership while at the same time settling scores with State.

Another group with reason for dissatisfaction with the junta included a number of younger ARVN officers, the "Young Turks," who had become impatient with the inability of the more senior officers to provide strong leadership to the army Their leader was Maj. Gen. Nguyen Khanh, commander of I Corps (Military Region I) based in Hue. Khanh had been slow in throwing in with the anti–Diem plotters, had taken no direct role, and thus was not fully trusted by the ringleaders Generals Minh, Don, Kim and Dinh. As a result, Khanh was not included in the inner circle (the Executive Committee) of the MRC.[16] One of Khanh's key allies was Brig. Gen. Nguyen Van Thieu commanding the 5th Division of III Corps, based in the Saigon area. During the final Diem coup, Thieu's unit had taken the lead in attacking the presidential palace for which he had been rewarded by advancement from colonel to brigadier general. As will be seen, he would play a central role in the final years of the republic.

With these elements at play, little more was needed to trigger a new coup. The immediate pretext was provided by a rumor among the dissident officers that the inner circle of the MRC was covertly preparing for negotiations with the National Liberation Front with a view to the neutralization of South Vietnam. In early January Khanh so informed Col. Jasper Wilson, his military advisor, asking that Wilson sound out his MACV superiors as to the attitude of the U.S. toward the removal from positions of power of the allegedly neutralist, pro–French leaders of the MRC. For reasons described above, Harkins had no objections, so coup planning went forward, but this time liaison was conducted through Wilson, not the CIA. Early on the morning of January 29, a bloodless coup took place in which Khanh seized power, and Generals Don, Kim, Dinh and Xuan were placed under house arrest.[17] The bloodless nature of the coup is strong evidence that Khanh had the army behind him.

Was the Minh government actually planning a neutralist coup d'état? Minh stoutly maintained that he and his associates in the Executive Committee of the MRC were all patriots who were determined to carry on the war against the Communists,[18] but there is evidence to the contrary. In interviews with Professor George McT. Kahin of Cornell University in 1970 and later,[19] Nguyen Ngoc Tho, premier in the Minh government, described the strategy of the government as one of attempting "to bring the NLF out of opposition and into support of ... a government of reconciliation." He went on to say: "The NLF was overwhelmingly non–Communist, with the PRP [People's Revolutionary Party — its avowedly Communist component] still having no dominance and, indeed, only in a minor position...." Having brought the NLF out of opposition, elections would then be conducted to form a government of national reconciliation since the NLF was then "sufficiently free of Hanoi's control to have made this process quite possible." Generals Minh and Don corroborated Tho's statements.

The foregoing reveals the starkly unrealistic grasp by Tho and his associates of the realities then obtaining within the NLF. It was pure fantasy to believe that in 1964 the PRP held only a minor position in the NLF and that the NLF could be brought over except under conditions in which the PRP would dominate any resulting coalition government in Saigon. To suggest that the hard-core Communist elements of the NLF would permit it to be coopted into some *genuinely* neutralist and independent government of South Vietnam is chimerical.[20] Still, the possibility that key members of the MRC were pursuing this course would help to explain the low level of ARVN military activity during the period.

Kahin, whose sympathies are clearly with those MRC generals seeking a neutralist solution, asserted that the conduct of U.S. officers, by being "privy to the coup's planning" and "involved in its implementation" was reprehensible, and laments that "neither the military mission nor Lodge was willing to warn the South Vietnamese government to which they were accredited, and which they officially supported, of the plot to overthrow it."[21] But no such sentiments are found in Professor Kahin's account of the coup against Diem.

The Khanh Government

Reflecting the youthfulness of the group that ousted the Minh government, Maj. Gen. Nguyen Khanh was only 37 when he took control of the government of Vietnam. He had fought the Vietminh under the French and after rallying to Diem in 1954 became one of the latter's trusted younger officers. During the parachutist coup in 1960, Khanh parleyed with the rebels, allowing Diem time to bring in loyal units to put down the uprising, and Diem showed his gratitude by promoting Khanh, a non–Catholic, and giving him command of II Corps, the military region covering the middle portion of South Vietnam. Whether through disillusion with Diem or sheer ambition, Khanh joined the plotters of the abortive August 1963 coup, but for reasons that remain obscure, was slow to enlist in the successful November 1 coup and took no active part. Minh believed that Khanh, from his headquarters in Pleiku far from Saigon, played a waiting game, planning to jump to the winning side, so instead of rewarding him with a key staff or cabinet job, the junta moved him laterally to command of I Corps, even more remote from Saigon.[22]

Harkins had a high opinion of Khanh as a military leader, but in the role of chairman of the MRC, military talent would be secondary to political skills, a field in which Khanh was completely inexperienced. Harkins' favorable assessment may have been influenced by Khanh's readiness as a corps commander to accept the advice of his American military advisors, and Khanh quickly made it clear that he would be equally receptive to, indeed, he would seek out, Lodge's political advice.[23] In organizing his government, Khanh appointed himself premier, having unceremoniously fired the civilian premier Tho. General Minh accepted the figurehead role of chief of state, but Khanh would wield the real power at the head of a reconstituted MRC. In contrast to the junta in which Minh was primus inter pares with Don, Kim and Dinh, Khanh was the paramount leader of the government. The Khanh government sustained the right of freedom of association established by Minh, but the numerous political parties formed since the demise of Diem were meaningless without a functioning National Assembly.

Liking what it saw in Khanh, the Johnson administration threw its support wholeheartedly behind him.[24] The watchword was "no more coups." Johnson instructed his subordinates to end the budgetary quibbling that had been standard procedure in the Diem years and meet any reasonable request by the Saigon government that seemed likely to forward the war.

Another McNamara Mission

Impatient for progress, a scant six weeks after the Khanh coup, Johnson sent McNamara, accompanied by Taylor, McCone and William Bundy, the new assistant secretary of state for Far Eastern affairs (Hilsman had already been eased out), on yet another fact-finding mission to Saigon. Incredibly, McNamara's report[25] of his trip was drafted (and redrafted) in Washington before he left for Saigon.[26] McNamara had indeed come a long way from his first "hastily prepared" memo on Vietnam to Kennedy after the Taylor-Rostow mission of October 1961. In his March 16 report, McNamara adopted the "Goldilocks technique," something that was frequently used by Johnson's advisors in decision making on Vietnam in which three alternatives were presented: one that was "too soft," one that was "too hard" and one that was "just right." In this case, McNamara offered: A. Negotiations on the basis of neutralization (too soft); B. Initiate GVN (Government of Vietnam) and U.S. military actions against North Vietnam (too hard) and C. Initiate measures to improve the situation in South Vietnam (just right). After demolishing the straw men of Alternatives A and B, McNamara expatiated at length on Alternative C and concluded with 12 recommendations, all of which apparently were drafted before the mission left for Saigon. Eight of the 12 dealt with various military aspects, two were ringing statements in support of Vietnam and the Khanh government, one called for an increase in the fertilizer program and only one, recommending "a greatly enlarged Civil Administrative Corps for work at province, district and hamlet levels," could be construed as addressing the political aspects. At two different points in his report, McNamara stressed that the U.S. would "continue to provide all the assistance and advice required to do the job *regardless of how long it takes*" (emphasis added).

McNamara's 12th and final recommendation was: "To prepare immediately to be in a position on 72 hours' notice to ... initiate the 'retaliatory actions' against North Vietnam, and to be in a position on 30 days' notice to initiate the program of graduated overt military pressure against North Vietnam." The retaliatory actions were to be small-scale, tit-for-tat actions in reprisal for Viet Cong attacks on U.S. military personnel and installations while the graduated overt military actions" envisioned sustained air attacks against North Vietnamese military and industrial targets.

Thus, the issue of bombing the North was finally openly broached, but it would be nearly a year before sustained attacks began. Nineteen sixty-four was the year Johnson would seek his own mandate from the American people, and he was determined to avoid the appearance of taking the U.S. deeper into the war until he was safely reelected.[27] He approved all of McNamara's recommendations, including the 12th, but Johnson knew he was safe because it merely said, "prepare for," and only he could pull the trigger. The JCS and CIA director McCone argued in the National Security Council meeting that McNamara's recommendations were too little, too late and recommended strong actions against the North immediately,[28] but McNamara had known precisely what Johnson wanted to hear. The trip to Vietnam was pro forma, the report having been drafted beforehand.

National Security Action Memorandum 288

McNamara's trip report was transformed verbatim into a new NSAM on Vietnam, No. 288 of March 17, 1964.[29] In a rambling statement, it made more explicit the U.S. objective as given the previous November in NSAM 273 of a free and independent, non–Communist South Vietnam. At bottom it was an extension of the Truman Doctrine of Communist containment, recognizing the Domino Principle in stating: "Unless we can achieve this objective in South Vietnam, almost all of Southeast Asia will probably fall under Communist dominance....." It added, that "In the rest of the world ... the South Vietnam conflict is regarded as a test case of U.S. capacity to help a nation meet the Communist 'war of liberation.' Thus, purely in terms of foreign policy, the stakes are high." This was the first overt recognition in an NSAM that *the credibility of the U.S. guarantee* had become a major concern of Vietnam policy makers.

While NSAM 288 and its predecessors NSAMs 52 and 273 laid out the same political objective of containing Communism by establishing an independent and democratic South Vietnam, all failed to specify the means by which the objective would be achieved. Like Kennedy, Johnson hoped to use limited means to achieve excessive ends. As a statement of U.S. policy toward Vietnam, NSAM 288 was never officially superceded, remaining on the record to the end.

Limited Goals — Limited Actions

In looking back on March 1964 when air action against North Vietnam was first openly proposed as an option, Johnson said, " Our goals in Vietnam were *limited*, and so were our actions. I wanted to keep them that way."[30] But in fact the political goal of the U.S., a democratic and independent South Vietnam, was an unqualified commitment. It had not been hedged or limited in Kennedy's NSAM 52 nor was it in Johnson's NSAMs 273 and 288, and U.S. involvement in South Vietnam was justified to the American people on that basis. Only in the negative senses that the U.S. did *not* aim to reunite North and South Vietnam as a friendly Western-style democratic state nor threaten China were the *political* goals in Vietnam limited. So, what Johnson was really saying was that it was only U.S. *actions* that would be limited, and as it developed, against the advice of the military professionals, he adopted a strategy recommended by his civilian advisors, an incremental war in which actions were carefully, sometimes even exquisitely calibrated and hedged about with all kinds of self-imposed restraints. It was to be a "limited war" which accorded well with Johnson's wish to persuade the American people that what was happening in Vietnam was not really a "war." There would be no declaration of war, no national mobilization, and no reserve call-up. As Col. Harry G. Summers concisely put it in *On Strategy: The Vietnam War in Context*: "Stirring up the American people in support of the war would have been the surest way to insure continued congressional support, but ... this was precisely what President Johnson did not want to do."[31] The legal basis, initially, for the U.S. military presence in Vietnam was SEATO, and after August 1964, a tenuous congressional resolution which gradually lost its validity in the eyes of many members of Congress.

The U.S. had fought a limited war in Korea with the same strategic objective, Communist containment, and in the end at great cost had succeeded only in restoring the status quo ante but not in defeating the enemy. The military lesson of that war was the impossibility of defeating an enemy who operates from secure bases within an inviolable sanctuary. This lesson was lost on Johnson and his civilian advisors whose political restraints on the conduct of the war were to confer the same privileges on the Viet Cong and the People's Army of North Vietnam.

Redefining U.S. Objectives

There had been earlier signs, even before NSAM 288, that the objective of preventing Communist domination and assuring an independent and democratic South Vietnam had begun to be subordinated by some Washington officials to one centering on the integrity of the U.S. guarantee. In a draft paper of November 6, 1964, by Assistant Secretary of Defense McNaughton,[32] he gave the U.S. aims as:

(a) To protect U.S. reputation as a counter-subversive guarantor.
(b) To avoid domino effect especially in South East Asia.
(c) To keep South Vietnamese territory from Red hands.
(d) To emerge from crisis without unacceptable taint from methods."

Although this was only a draft paper, it was authored by the third ranking civilian in the Pentagon who was McNamara's chief thinker on Vietnam and, as will be seen, it portended a trend in defining U.S. objectives in Vietnam.

By the following March, in another draft for McNamara on "Proposed Course of Action,"[33] McNaughton was even able to assign percentages to the hierarchy of U.S. aims:

70 percent — To avoid a humiliating defeat (to our reputation as a guarantor).
20 percent — To keep SVN (and the adjacent territory) from Chinese hands.
10 percent — To permit the people of SVN to enjoy a better, freer way of life.
ALSO — To emerge from the crisis without unacceptable taint from methods used.
NOT — to help a friend....

It would have been extremely embarrassing to the administration had this draft leaked to the media since "to avoid a humiliating defeat" was a phrase Johnson had never used in justifying to the nation America's reasons for being in Vietnam.

By January 1966, in another draft memo to McNamara,[34] McNaughton was excluding all the other reasons for being in Vietnam when he said, "Some will say that we have defaulted if we end up ... with anything less than a Western-oriented, noncommunist, independent government, exercising sovereignty over all of South Vietnam. This is not so ... the US end is *solely to preserve our reputation as a guarantor*" (emphasis added). McNaughton had indeed distanced himself from the objectives laid down in NSAMs 52, 273 and 288. Thus McNaughton was now persuading McNamara that the final outcome in South Vietnam was not important so long as the U.S. could emerge with its reputation as a guarantor intact

Changing of the Guard

As American officials gained experience with Khanh, they continued to be impressed by his tractability, his openness to advice and his acumen, but despite these positives and free-flowing U.S. aid, going into mid–1964 Khanh had not shown a capacity to arrest the deteriorating security situation in the country. Inexperienced politically, Khanh had yet been unable to engage the Vietnamese people, and his grip on the army was uncertain. The Buddhists, under the leadership of Diem's old nemesis, Thich Tri Quang, were becoming restive, and the perennially disaffected intellectual and political classes of Saigon remained so.[35]

Meanwhile, on the American side, Lodge and Harkins were, if anything, cooler and more distant than ever. Reacting to subtle hints from Lodge, State plumped for Harkins' early replacement, but McNamara would not agree. With Harkins' retirement from the army impending July 31, McNamara, fearing rebellion in the Pentagon, could not let it appear that State had gotten Harkins' scalp.[36] But his replacement, Gen. William Westmoreland, was already in Saigon as deputy commander of the MACV. Aside from Harkins, there was still the question of Lodge. This was finally resolved when, in a June 18 telegram to Rusk, Lodge asked to be relieved.[37] And on June 20, Westmoreland officially replaced Harkins. At a June 23 press conference, Johnson announced Lodge's resignation and the appointment of Gen. Maxwell D. Taylor as his replacement. Thus, the near simultaneous announcements allowed the army and Harkins to save face.

The appointment of Taylor reflected Johnson's conviction that the problems in Vietnam were essentially military and tipped the balance of power even more in favor of Defense over State, and this was underlined by granting him full responsibility for the military effort in Vietnam,[38] something previous ambassadors had never had. State was mollified somewhat by the naming of Deputy Undersecretary for Political Affairs U. Alexis Johnson as deputy ambassador to backstop Taylor on political affairs. An amusing sidelight to Lodge's replacement was the near stampede of would-be candidates for the job — McNamara, McGeorge Bundy and Robert Kennedy. McNamara exuded modesty when, in referring to Lodge's resignation he said, "This afforded an occasion to try to strengthen the U.S. team in South Vietnam. That included, first of all, the strongest possible ambassador. Mac [Bundy], Bobby [Kennedy] and I all volunteered for the assignment."[39] Johnson's dislike of Kennedy and fear of his potential as a political opponent precluded his appointment by Johnson to any position of prominence[40] While Bundy was something of an enigma, it would be hard to imagine one more temperamentally unfitted for the job than McNamara, the quantitative analysis expert. In any case, Johnson was unwilling to spare them from their current jobs.

The Tonkin Gulf Incident

Johnson had become increasingly uneasy over not having Congress officially in bed with him on Vietnam. He believed Truman had erred seriously on Korea by never asking Congress for an expression of its support,[41] and as someone who had spent over 20 years in Congress, he was determined to avoid that error. It was no secret within the administration that at some point Johnson would ask Congress for a resolution, and in fact, drafts of such a resolution were discussed in a National Security Council meeting on May 24, 1964,[42] and again on June 15 in a meeting of Johnson's principal advisors.[43] The drafts discussed at these meetings differed, but significantly, both included an expiration date, in one case the end of fiscal year 1965, the other, January 8, 1965. The purpose of these resolutions was, of course, to cover Johnson's congressional flank where he felt badly exposed and secondarily, by drawing in Congress, to send a clear signals to the government of Vietnam and to Hanoi that the commitment of the U.S. in Vietnam had the full backing of Congress.

During the first half of 1964, the Johnson administration had found itself having to fend off frequent attacks on its Vietnam policy in the form of *New York Times* editorials, columns by the influential Walter Lippman and statements by Senators Morse and Mansfield all suggesting if not encouraging a neutralist solution to the Vietnam conflict.[44] President de Gaulle's call for neutralization of the Indochinese peninsula (excepting North Vietnam) had received worldwide attention[45] and had created further problems for the administration's policy. Proposals for a neutralist Vietnam always took in only South Vietnam and never extended to the DRV, which quite obviously would have no interest in becoming a truly neutralist state. Thus a well-armed and aggressive North would remain in place while a neutralist coalition would take power in Saigon. These proposals were aimed at a negotiated withdrawal of the U.S. from South Vietnam under the guise of neutralization, and then after the inevitable takeover by the Communists using their time-honored methods, the leftist Western proponents of this solution could always shrug it off as a "decision of the Vietnamese people."

Despite the public assurances of Johnson, Rusk and McNamara of America's seemingly unshakable commitment to a free and independent Vietnam, the continuing drumbeat of sentiment for a neutralist solution coming from influential U.S. sources compounded by de Gaulle's pronouncements was causing uncertainty among Vietnam's military and political leaders as to America's determination to stay the course.

But no action was taken to bring a resolution before Congress, because, according to Johnson,[46] he hoped "we could keep our role in Vietnam limited," but in reality, Johnson did not want to raise the profile of Vietnam in an election year and while pushing his Great Society program through Congress.⁴⁷ But the circumstances surrounding the Tonkin Gulf incident presented the ideal opportunity

On August 2, 1964, the destroyer U.S.S. *Maddox* was attacked in international waters of the Tonkin Gulf by North Vietnamese patrol boats. Two days later, North Vietnamese patrol boats allegedly launched a second attack against the destroyers *Maddox* and *C. Turner Joy* steaming near the same area, but this attack has never been fully substantiated. In any case, the U.S. ships were undamaged, and the U.S. Navy claimed to have sunk or damaged some Vietnamese patrol boats in the first attack. Volumes have been written about this episode, much of it aimed at discrediting U.S. actions by attempting to establish that the second attack, which triggered the U.S. response, actually never happened or that it was deliberately provoked. No purpose would be served by delving into these aspects which have been so thoroughly explored by others,⁴⁸ because this militarily insignificant incident draws its real importance from what followed in Washington.

Johnson was not inclined to retaliate on the basis of the first attack alone, but did so following the alleged second attack which some critics claim was entirely fabricated by the administration to create a favorable climate in Congress for the passage of what became known as the Tonkin Gulf Resolution. The circumstances of the second incident are uncertain and will probably remain so until all the pertinent U.S. documents are declassified and Hanoi opens its archives. In the event, Johnson acted on assurances from Admiral Sharp, CINCPAC, and McNamara that the incident had taken place, and having that assurance, Johnson ordered retaliatory strikes against the patrol boat bases, the first U.S. bombing of North Vietnam.⁴⁹ He would have been extremely vulnerable from the political right if it had become known that he had overridden or disregarded the assurances of McNamara and his top military leaders that an attack on U.S. naval vessels had occurred.

In fact, the entire episode was a godsend to Johnson. In the midst of the campaign for president, retaliation gave him a priceless opportunity to demonstrate to the American public that the Communists could not push Lyndon Johnson around and also to posture as calm, measured, and wise in contrast to Goldwater's bellicose "extremism."⁵⁰ But this was not pivotal to the outcome of the election. The real prize was the passage of the Southeast Asia (Tonkin Gulf) Resolution. Johnson was at pains to prepare the ground carefully by consulting and gaining the support of the key majority and minority leaders prior to submission of the draft resolution. With relatively little debate, what became the most controversial resolution in the history of Congress was quickly passed unanimously in the House and with only two dissenting votes in the Senate.⁵¹

The resolution approved and supported the determination of the president "to take all necessary measures to repel any armed attack against the forces of the United States and to prevent further aggression" and "as the President determines, to take all necessary steps, including the use of armed force, to assist any member or protocol state of the Southeast Asia Collective Defense

Treaty requesting assistance in defense of its freedom."[52] The administration had taken advantage of the uproar over alleged North Vietnamese aggressive acts to gain near blank-check powers with no expiration date, a fact that would take on huge significance as opposition to the war mounted. The resolution was, indeed, tantamount to a declaration of war.

Critics, including many in Congress, were later to accuse Johnson of deception, deceit, and chicanery in his tactics to obtain passage of a resolution giving him unprecedented powers, but the words of that brief resolution and its open-ended nature were there for all to see. But obviously, in August 1964, Congress, Johnson himself, and his key advisors all were blissfully unaware of the extent to which the resolution would be stretched as the basis for America's involvement in a long and costly war, and later, when escalation was in full swing, and despite the outrage of some indignant senators, Congress "would not deny our fighting men the tools they need to complete the job" and repeatedly voted the appropriations necessary to continue the war. Thus, Congress cannot evade responsibility for its part in "Lyndon Johnson's War."

The Decline of Khanh

Through the first six months of his administration, Khanh had continued to impress U.S. officials with his grasp of what needed to be done and his willingness to accept advice, but notwithstanding, little in the way of effective actions, either political or military, was coming out the end of the pipeline. The hoped-for turnaround in the war was not evident. Indeed, the Viet Cong continued to hold the initiative and were gaining ground against the ineffectual efforts of the ARVN. Khanh seemed unable to overcome the inertia of the Saigon bureaucracy, and the army was distracted by continued political maneuverings among the generals. The rumblings of neutralization referred to above created uncertainty and hesitancy in Saigon officialdom that undercut a total commitment to the war.

The passage of the Tonkin Gulf Resolution gave a temporary lift in morale to the regime and emboldened Khanh to move ahead with his plan to reorganize the government by promulgating a new provisional constitution drawn up by him and his military colleagues called the Vung Tau Charter. Under it, Khanh as president would head both the state and the government, and the center of power would remain the Military Revolutionary Council. The bureaucracy would continue to be headed by civilian department heads and a legislative body, largely appointive, was provided for of which 40 percent would be army officers. The net effect was not, as U.S. officials hoped, a move toward a civilian government but rather a tightening of the army's grip.

The public announcement of the charter on August 16 triggered Buddhist and student disorders as severe as any under Diem and launched a period of instability as yet unseen in South Vietnam. Challenged by the Buddhists,

Khanh lost his nerve and rescinded the Charter at a high cost to his prestige and base of power with the army. What followed was an improvised government with Khanh retaining power but with the appointment of a new High National Council of 19 civilian "notables" which was supposed to lead the way to a new constitution and civilian takeover at some future point.[53]

Taylor as Ambassador

As an experienced military officer, Maxwell Taylor understood the uses of staff and soon had the U.S. Mission organized and working as a team, something Lodge had not accomplished in his year in the job. But Taylor, whose 20 years as a general had conditioned him to expect instant obedience to his every whim, was soon frustrated by the tumultuous political situation in Saigon in which the Vietnamese leadership was sometimes unresponsive to him. As the Vietnamese persisted in their political games, Taylor's exasperation grew, and his exchanges with members of the government became increasingly testy. On October 25, in a meeting with the newly chosen chief of state, Pham Khac Suu, and others, Taylor "told them very bluntly and with some anger that we could not countenance the [High National] Council's action of last evening in which important decisions [were] taken without advising U.S. in advance. This despite our previous understanding that U.S. did not want to be surprised by actions taken by Council." As evidence of his hardening attitude, he added, "While we could overlook failure to consult in the past, we could not accept it in the future."[54] The U.S.-Vietnam relationship had indeed come a long way from a year earlier when no U.S. diplomat would have *dreamed* of addressing Diem, the Vietnamese chief of state, in such terms, and while to the Americans the deteriorating position of the government of Vietnam appeared to justify such treatment, still, it came at a price, first to the pride of the Vietnamese and second, to Taylor's longer-term effectiveness in dealing with them.

Taylor's relationship with the generals was damaged beyond repair when on December 20, the Young Turk army clique effected the abolition of the High National Council and the arrest of its members, allegedly because the council had exceeded its powers. Infuriated, Taylor summoned representatives of the Armed Forces Council (formerly the MRC) to his office where he reprimanded the three generals and an admiral like schoolboys and demanded that they reverse their action.[55] Later, in his account of this incident, Taylor seemed somewhat surprised that the officers felt humiliated.[56] The following day, in a confrontational showdown meeting,[57] Taylor challenged Khanh over the dissolution of the HNC and stated it would be difficult for the U.S. to cooperate "with such a setup" to which Khanh replied that "loyalty was a reciprocal matter and that Vietnam was not a vassal of the United States." After Taylor responded that he had lost confidence in General Khanh, Khanh's restraint fell away and he replied that "the Ambassador should keep to his place as Ambassador and, as Ambassador, it was not really appropriate for him to be dealing in this way with the Commander-in-Chief of the Armed Forces on a political matter nor was it appropriate for him to have summoned some of his Generals to the Embassy yesterday." Thus, the issue was joined between the army and Taylor. Two days later, a group of generals met and decided to propose that Taylor be declared persona non grata, something that, of course, would have been inadmissable to the U.S. and if pursued, probably would have brought an end to the U.S. effort in Vietnam. In the end, through MACV intermediaries, the full implications of such an act were pointed out to the generals who then decided to back off, and the matter was allowed to die.

Meanwhile, Rusk, who was alarmed over the potentially dangerous situation created by the intemperate remarks of his ambassador, was counseling Taylor to temporize.[58] But Taylor's demand that the HNC be reestablished was ignored although the HNC members were soon released from arrest. This episode marked the point at which Khanh, once the focus of U.S. hopes, was cut adrift from U.S. support, and Taylor, having lost the trust of the generals, lost much of his effectiveness as ambassador. But he had set a new tone in Saigon. As already related, in the "limited partnership" relationship adopted in late 1961, the U.S. believed it was entitled to prior consultation on major decisions.[59] Now Taylor seemed to be demanding prior consultation *and approval*, something that would have been totally unacceptable to Diem.

Although Taylor had gone to Vietnam with the understanding he would serve only one year, still, high Washington officialdom may have welcomed the end of his tour in mid–1965. Johnson appointed him a special consultant on diplomatic and military affairs for Vietnam, a role in which he no longer exercised significant influence on Vietnam decisions.[60]

The End of the Khanh Era

With American encouragement, a shaky civilian government had been installed in October with the Armed Forces Council, headed by Khanh, still hovering in the background. But the ambitious Khanh was not satisfied with indirect control. Using as a pretext the ongoing differences between the government headed by Prime Minister Huong and the Buddhists, in late January Khanh dismissed the civilian government and took control, presenting the Americans with another fait accompli. In one year as the strongman of Vietnam, Khanh had brought about five major political crises in Saigon.[61] A new civilian government under Prime Minister Phan Huy Quat was established, but Khanh had finally overreached. His associates on the Armed Forces Council had had enough of his ceaseless political machinations, and on February 20, after receiving a vote of no confidence from his fellow generals, Khanh was deposed as commander-in-chief and exiled as a roving ambassador,[62] leaving the Armed Forces Council without an obvious strongman, a power vacuum among the generals that could not long endure.

The Movement Toward Bombing the North

During the latter half of 1963, the U.S. Joint Chiefs of Staff had become increasingly impatient with the lack of progress in the war, and the Minh regime's failure to produce the anticipated improvements only intensified this feeling. The growing dissatisfaction of the JCS came into the open in their memo of January 22, 1964,[63] to McNamara in which they recommended the removal of self-imposed restrictions on U.S. military actions in Laos, Cambodia and Vietnam and stated that the U.S. "must make ready to conduct increasingly bolder actions in Southeast Asia...." There followed a list of 10 possible actions including taking over from the Vietnamese the direction of the war, bombing of North Vietnam and mining of ports, commitment of U.S. combat forces in South Vietnam and commitment of U.S. forces in direct actions against North Vietnam. Significantly, the memo was signed by Maxwell Taylor, chairman of the JCS who, as ambassador six months later, would assume a much less hawkish attitude. In any case, the recommendations in the memo were not taken up by McNamara.[64] By the middle of March, however, McNamara had changed his tune when, as already related, he recommended to Johnson that the U.S. prepare immediately to be able to take retaliatory actions against North Vietnam within 72 hours and to initiate graduated overt military pressure against North Vietnam on 30 days' notice.

On McNamara's next trip to Vietnam, May 12–14, 1964, General Khanh told McNamara he believed at some point South Vietnamese air strikes against the North would be desirable, but Khanh was fearful of the reaction of the DRV against a weak South Vietnam which would then have to depend on U.S. forces for protection.[65] On the other hand, Ambassador Lodge strongly supported air strikes against the North with the ambitious objectives of cutting off the flow of men and materiel to the South, destroying morale in the North and building morale in the South.[66] On McNamara's return, a National Security Council meeting was held at which the subject of air strikes against the North was discussed in generalities, but no decisions came out of this meeting.[67] Still, the concept of air strikes against military and industrial targets in the DRV by the South Vietnamese, by the U.S. under Vietnamese cover, or overtly by the U.S. had taken root. Although Johnson's advisors busied themselves drawing up scenarios to prepare the political ground for bombing and analyses of likely Soviet, PRC, DRV and world reactions, as related earlier, Johnson had no intention to begin a bombing campaign against the North in an election year if he could possibly avoid it, nor was he eager to appear to be widening the war without first having a congressional resolution.

But staff planning for retaliatory and sustained bombing was going ahead at Defense so that when Johnson did authorize retaliation for the Tonkin Gulf incidents, air strikes were mounted on very short notice. With the strikes against the torpedo boat bases and oil storage facilities, under the code name Pierce Arrow, the U.S. had crossed the threshold. The option of graduated overt military pressures against the North remained open, but concern remained that South Vietnam would not be able to resist potential DRV reactions. Thus, on August 10 in his first status report as ambassador,[68] Taylor recommended deferring such action until after January 1, 1965, to allow additional time for political stabilization of the government of Vietnam.

When Taylor took over as ambassador it was agreed that he would make periodic trips to Washington, roughly every 60 days,[69] so that Johnson and his advisors could have the benefit of face-to-face progress reports. During Taylor's first such trip September 6–10, the subject of bombing the North was discussed in a White House meeting among Johnson and his top advisors.[70] The concept of carrying the war to the North had by then become accepted — only the timing was in question due to the unstable political situation in Saigon, but for the time being, only tit-for-tat reprisals were envisioned.

As the military position continued to deteriorate through the fall of 1964, the Joint Chiefs of Staff were moved to address another memo to McNamara[71] recommending strong action "to prevent the collapse of the U.S. position in Southeast Asia." They appended a list of actions in ascending order of severity and asked for immediate authority to initiate several up to and including air strikes on lines of communications in the DRV. Other actions, e.g., mining of DRV ports, all-out air attack on the DRV and commitment of U.S. ground forces into Southeast Asia, were to be held in abeyance for later application as the situation unfolded. They specifically requested that their recommendations be put before the president, but it is not clear that McNamara actually did so.

In any case, the memo was somewhat overtaken by events a few days later when on October 31 (a few days before the American presidential election), the Viet Cong conducted a major raid against the U.S.-Vietnam air base at Bien Hoa, killing four U.S. servicemen, wounding 30 and destroying or damaging 57 aircraft.[72] At this point, with over 22,000 military personnel in Vietnam, the U.S. stance continued to be that any Viet Cong attack directly on U.S. installations and personnel was a provocation, since through some tortuous logic it was thought American forces in Vietnam were somehow immune to such attacks. Thus, this would appear to be all the pretext needed for a heavy reprisal air strike against the North which was immediately recommended to Washington by Ambassador Taylor. But despite the frequent reiteration in NSAMs and elsewhere of the determination to conduct tit-for-tat reprisals, Johnson chose to do nothing. Rusk made a weak attempt to justify inaction, telling Taylor that "we would find it hard to portray the [Bien Hoa] attack as a major act of escalation in itself," adding that "all of us here ... are negative on a tit-for-tat policy as basis for real action against the North."[73] It seemed that suddenly the tit-for-tat policy had been abandoned, but in a later telegram the same day addressed "Literally eyes only Ambassador from Secretary," Rusk admitted that the real reason no action was being taken was that the election was only a few days away.[74]

Although the Bien Hoa incident did not result in retaliation, it did inspire the White House to launch an intensive planning effort for possible later actions "to avoid any impression USG (U.S. Government) determination changing."[75] Thus, the National Security Council Working Group was formed, chaired by William Bundy and composed of officers at the assistant secretary level from JCS, CIA, Defense and the White House.[76] It was this group that developed the array of options which became the framework for the final decision to bomb the North.

At a White House meeting with the president on November 19,[77] Rusk explained the scope of the NSC Working Group's assignment, stating that the group "had focused on three broad alternatives: first, a negotiated settlement on any basis obtainable; second, a sharp increase of military pressure on North Vietnam which might perhaps lead at some future date to negotiation; and third, an in between alternative of increased pressure on North Vietnam but simultaneous efforts to keep open the channels of communication...." Rusk added that after consultations with Taylor, the group would be ready to submit its recommendations to the president by December 1. When the president asked for a restatement of the alternatives, a curious thing occurred. The three alternatives described by Rusk a few minutes earlier had mysteriously mutated into three options, all entailing bombing.[78] As outlined by William Bundy, Option A was nothing more than a reiteration of the oft-stated plan to conduct reprisals for "any further 'spectaculars' of the Bien Hoa variety." Option B, labeled the "hard/fast squeeze," envisioned air attacks of increasing intensity against the DRV during which negotiations would not be an immediate goal but could occur. Option C, the "slow, controlled squeeze," would entail a gradual increase in air operations against the North aimed at bringing about negotiations. Thus, the graduated overt military pressures concept first articulated in McNamara's March 16 report to the president reappeared under a new label, the "slow, controlled squeeze." McGeorge Bundy indicated to Johnson that Option C was the favored solution of the Working Group, but Rusk interjected that in the final deliberations the other options would not be excluded from consideration. In this connection, Johnson asked for assurance that the military (JCS) was participating fully in the planning, and McNamara assured him it was. But while the JCS was given an opportunity to respond to the NSC Working Group paper outlining the three options, its reasoned arguments against Options A and C and its recommendation[79] in favor of Option B, the hard/fast squeeze, were rejected by the civilians of the Working Group who had already settled on Option C. Thus began a period of almost four years in which the advice of the military professionals on the conduct of the air war against the DRV was consistently ignored or overridden by the Washington civilians who undertook to micromanage all aspects of the air campaign from target selection even down to the tactical approach to the target to be used by pilots.[80]

After pro forma consultation with Taylor, on December 1, the Working Group's plan was approved by Johnson. In its final form it entailed a Phase I which involved some intensification of present programs (basically Option A), while laying out specific areas for improved performance by the government of Vietnam. On evidence of GVN progress in the indicated areas, the U.S. would then be prepared to launch Phase II, Option C. Taylor so advised the GVN.[81]

The American resolve to conduct reprisals was soon tested again by the bombing of a U.S. Bachelor Officers Quarters in Saigon on Christmas Eve. After an investigation convinced Taylor that the Viet Cong had been responsible, he, CINCPAC and the JCS strongly recommended reprisal air strikes, but Rusk and McGeorge Bundy counseled Johnson against action, and no strikes were ordered.[82]

Bombing Begins

The final product of the NSC Working Group had been continued restraint from attacking the North while awaiting the long-sought political stability in South Vietnam, but instead, political turmoil and military deterioration continued into the new year. As already related, on December 20 the Young Turk generals dissolved the High National Council, this only two weeks after Taylor had delivered his list of desired improvements in effectiveness to the GVN. When on January 27 Khanh deposed the civilian government, U.S. officials began to despair that before political stability could be achieved, South Vietnam would be defeated militarily by the Viet Cong.[83]

Coincidentally, that same day, McGeorge Bundy submitted a pivotal memo to Johnson[84] giving his and McNamara's views that only a change in basic U.S. policy could save the increasingly grave military situation in Vietnam. They recommended a shift from "essentially a passive role" to the use of U.S. military power to force the Communists to desist in their effort to acquire control of South Vietnam. As a follow-up to this and in the never-ending and usually futile quest for more facts, Johnson sent Bundy to Vietnam. This would the first of only two trips there for this backstage manipulator who, as much as anyone, was responsible for U.S. escalation in Vietnam. Unexpectedly, while there Bundy got a whiff of gunsmoke when the Viet Cong attacked the U.S.-Vietnamese base at Pleiku, transforming the cool, calculating intellectual into an aggressive hawk who now backed Taylor to the hilt in recommending reprisals. Perhaps it was Bundy's weight in the balance that caused Johnson, without hesitation, to order reprisal air strikes, called Flaming Dart I, which were carried out the next day, February 7. As an indication of what was to come, target selection and the amount of force employed were controlled by civilians in Washington, not so much to inflict damage on the DRV as to send a message, and the raids were judged a weak response by CINCPAC and the JCS.[85] After the Viet Cong killed 23 Americans in an attack on the U.S. barracks at Qui Nhon on February 10, Flaming Dart II was ordered. This time, two insignificant targets were selected in a White House meeting of the president with over 20 civilian officials and one representative of the JCS. It too was not a strong reprisal.[86]

By now, the consensus of Johnson's civilian advisors was that the U.S.

could no longer afford to wait for political stability in Saigon but must launch Phase II, Option C, the slow, controlled squeeze of North Vietnam. Carried along by the weight of advice, on February 13, Johnson authorized Rolling Thunder, "a program of measured and limited air action jointly with GVN against selected military targets in DRV remaining south of the 19th parallel until further notice." It was envisioned that attacks would be launched "once or twice a week and involve two or three targets on each day...."[87] Because Rolling Thunder was to be a joint effort of the U.S. and Vietnamese air forces, the concurrence of the GVN had to be obtained, and that along with adverse weather conditions delayed the launching of the first raids until March 2, 1965.

From the outset there were fundamental differences among the key advisors as to the objectives of Rolling Thunder. In discussions and correspondence, one or more of the following objectives were cited by participants in the decision-making process: to raise morale in South Vietnam; to lower morale in North Vietnam; to break Hanoi's will to continue the fight; to interdict the flow of men and materiel from the DRV to the South; to destroy or damage the DRV's war-supporting infrastructure; to force the DRV to the negotiating table.[88] As already noted, the Washington-based authors of the plan, McNamara, the Bundys, McNaughton, et al., believed their exquisitely controlled, slowly ascending air campaign would send a message to Hanoi that would evoke dread of the future and cause the DRV to desist in its efforts to gain control of the South. This coterie of civilian intellectuals believed their highly sophisticated plan was certain to be effective against any rational adversary. The operative word was "control," and the throttle would, of course, be entirely in their hands, to increase as well as decrease the intensity in accordance with Hanoi's behavior. It was a completely novel concept in the history of warfare, and one that ran directly counter to anything in the experience of the JCS which adhered to the old-fashioned doctrine that inflicting maximum pain on the adversary to the fullest extent of one's capabilities was a key objective of war.

The air attacks triggered feverish diplomatic activity by the British and French aimed at bringing about a cessation of Rolling Thunder, activity that tended to weaken any message the bombing was intended to convey to the DRV. To counter this, Taylor, in a March 8 memo to State,[89] urged that the tempo of attacks be stepped up. He feared that to the DRV, "Rolling Thunder ... has been merely a few isolated thunderclaps." In early March, the president sent Gen. Harold Johnson, army chief of staff, to Saigon to examine what more could be done in South Vietnam to reverse the downward trend. His March 14 report[90] recommended 21 specific actions including increasing the scope and tempo of air strikes against the DRV and removal of restrictions on strikes (e.g., requirement for VNAF concurrency, denial of alternate targets, narrow geographical limits, etc).

In an April 2 memo to Rusk, McNamara, Bundy and Taylor,[91] CIA director John McCone expressed his misgivings about the "slowly ascending tempo of present Rolling Thunder operations" and the geographical restrictions on target selection, conditions which he believed indicated "restraints which will not be persuasive to the NVN and would probably be read as evidence of a U.S. desire to temporize." But aside from the removal of some restrictions requiring VNAF concurrent strikes and on the hitting of alternative targets in bad weather, the program continued as originally conceived.

Meanwhile, in anticipation of a prompt cave-in by the DRV to U.S. bombing, William Bundy busied himself preparing a position paper on negotiations. In a March 19 memo to Rusk,[92] Bundy projected a sequence of actions which in effect envisioned an abandonment by the DRV of its aspirations in the South, cessation of infiltration and organized VC guerrilla activity and nonrecognition of the NLF in return for which the U.S. would cease its air attacks on the DRV and withdraw its *combat* forces. In all, the paper was at pains to provide face-saving opportunities to Hanoi to ease their climb-down. This was indeed an idyllic scenario bordering on fantasy and one not attained after another eight years of war.

Johnson Seeks Negotiations

In a speech at Johns Hopkins University on April 7, Johnson said the U.S. was ready for unconditional discussions on Vietnam and described his vision of a postwar multinational TVA-like development project for the Mekong Valley to which the U.S. was prepared to subscribe $1 billion[93] The speech was well received everywhere except the international socialist bloc where it was derided, but it succeeded in putting Hanoi, Peking and Moscow on the defensive. By coincidence, almost simultaneously DRV premier Pham Van Dong was delivering a speech to the National Assembly in Hanoi setting forth North Vietnam's Four Points (as related in the Ho Chi Minh chapter) as the only acceptable basis for a settlement in South Vietnam.

Earlier, on April 1, a conference in Belgrade of 17 nonaligned nations drafted an appeal for a political solution to the war through negotiations of the parties without preconditions. The day after his Johns Hopkins speech Johnson replied, formally restating the willingness of the U.S. to negotiate without preconditions. On April 20 Hanoi rejected the 17-nation proposal, demanding that the war be settled in accordance with its Four Points.[94]

After the first 10 weeks of a feeble Rolling Thunder campaign, the extent of Washington's misperception of its impact on Hanoi was revealed in the first bombing pause of six days, May 12–18.[95] The plan may have been a reaction to heavy criticism the bombing was receiving both diplomatically and in the world media because in his May 10 message[96] informing Taylor of his plan, Johnson said he could use the pause "to good effect with world opinion." Johnson planned no public announcement of the pause, but it was reported by the *New York Times* on May 15 with an administration statement that it was for operational reasons. It was intended to quietly inform Moscow and Hanoi and tell them the U.S. would be watching carefully for their reactions. In the event, when a U.S. diplomat attempted to deliver the letter, the DRV embassy in Moscow at first refused to accept it, and later, after having received it, returned it ostensibly unopened.[97] Hanoi called the pause "a worn-out trick of deceit and threat." So much for the first bombing pause.[98] Obviously, the slowly ascending air campaign was not having the desired effect on Hanoi.

The Decision to Deploy Ground Combat Troops

In a February 22, 1965, telegram to the JCS,[99] General Westmoreland, MACV commander, recommended deployment of a Marine expeditionary brigade to protect the U.S. air base at Da Nang. Apparently he did not clear this with Taylor because the latter was at best lukewarm to the idea and concurred only reluctantly in the deployment of one Marine battalion landing team.[100] Taylor cited Eisenhower's warning never to commit ground forces to a land war in Asia and stated, presciently, that once the policy was breached, it would be very difficult to hold the line. In *Swords and Plowshares*, he remarked on how difficult it had been to get approval for Rolling Thunder but how relatively easy the decision to send in the marines.[101] In the event, Westmoreland prevailed when on March 8 two Marine BLTs came ashore at Da Nang followed four days later by a third BLT plus a Marine helicopter unit. As Taylor foresaw, once the policy was breached, resistance to additional deployments became progressively weaker.

Through the first half of 1965, intelligence reports indicated that Viet Cong forces were building up rapidly, raising the possibility that they could simply overwhelm the ARVN before the end of the year. General Johnson's March 14 report had recommended the immediate deployment of a U.S. Army combat division to Vietnam to stem the tide. This was endorsed in a March 20 JCS memo to McNamara[102] along with a recommendation to expand the mission of the Marines to counterinsurgency combat operations. Again, Taylor was reluctant, urging a careful analysis of the pros and cons. He cited the likely tendency of ARVN forces to turn the war over to the Americans and the danger of awakening colonialist memories among the populace by the introduction of foreign troops. Taylor believed that if introduced, U.S. combat troops should be held in coastal enclaves as a mobile strategic reserve.

At an April 1 White House meeting,[103] the president approved an earlier Westmoreland request for an 18,000–20,000-man increase in support and logistic forces, the deployment of two additional Marine battalions and a change to the mission of the marines from static defense of air bases to limited counterinsurgency combat operations, but no action was taken on the JCS proposal which had grown to two army combat divisions and a Republic of Korea (ROK) division. It was also agreed to support an increase in the ARVN of 160,000. These decisions were incorporated in NSAM 328 of April 6, the closing paragraph of which cautioned against premature publicity of the U.S. manpower increase and change in the marine mission. The final sentence said: "*The Pres-*

ident's desire is that these movements and changes should be understood as being gradual and wholly consistent with existing policy" (emphasis added). The public announcement said only that "several thousand" more troops would be sent to train South Vietnamese forces and protect U.S. installations.[104]

But Westmoreland believed even more U.S. forces would be needed during the time lag in the buildup of the ARVN, and with Washington's initial inhibitions on ground troops now overcome, he asked for more at an April 20 Honolulu meeting with McNamara, Taylor, Sharp and Wheeler. At this point, U.S. combat forces in country or approved consisted of four marine battalions, and Westmoreland was requesting an additional nine infantry battalions (three marine, six army). Following the Honolulu meeting, McNamara recommended and the president approved these further deployments, nearly doubling the authorized force level to 82,000.[105] On May 13, the *New York Times* reported U.S. strength in Vietnam had reached 46,500 from about 18,000 a year earlier. The media was unaware of the newly approved 82,000 level, and would learn only as the troops arrived. Thus, Johnson carefully metered out information on the U.S. buildup.

During the April 21 White House meeting to discuss McNamara's recommendations to the president on the increased deployments, a fundamental difference surfaced between McNamara and McCone on the conduct of Rolling Thunder. McNamara envisioned continuing the campaign at about the present tempo and providing increased pressure "by repetition and continuation" but not to intensify it by striking industrial targets in the Hanoi-Haiphong area, this in order to avoid "killing the hostage" by destroying North Vietnamese assets inside the "Hanoi do-nut." He represented this as the view of the participants in the April 20 Honolulu conference, but Admiral Sharp, CINCPAC, for one, stated explicitly in *Strategy for Defeat*, that this was, in fact, a distortion of his own view.[106] Thus, McNamara's strategy for the war was now one of low-level, harassment air attacks on the DRV while ARVN and U.S. forces carried the fight to the Viet Cong such that, over time, in perhaps six to 12 months, the Communists would become discouraged and seek negotiations. McCone expressed his opinion that such an approach of pinprick air attacks was a change from the original objective and would only stiffen the determination of the DRV and Viet Cong which would build up their forces in the South and present the U.S. "with an increasingly difficult problem requiring more and more troops." McCone's view was shared by the JCS, which was not represented at the meeting. But McCone was whistling in the wind. He had already resigned and his replacement, Adm. William F. Raborn, was announced a week later.

While the American people were generally aware that additional forces were being sent to Vietnam, no explicit statement had yet been made as to their employment in actual combat until, in response to reporters' questions, on June 8 a State Department spokesman acknowledged that U.S. forces "would be available for combat support with the Vietnamese forces as and when necessary." This was the lead story in both the *New York Times* and the *Washing-*

ton Post the next day, much to the discomfiture of the administration which was forced to issue a statement that day indicating "*there had been no change in the mission of U.S. ground combat units in Vietnam.*" This was true in the narrow sense that since U.S. forces had *already* been authorized to engage in combat, the State Department statement did not constitute a change. In carefully parsed phrases, it went on to say they were to safeguard military installations and if help was requested by ARVN forces, and "General Westmoreland also has authority ... to employ these troops in support of Vietnamese forces faced with aggressive attack ... when, in his judgment, the general military situation urgently requires it."[107] Thus, little by little, the credibility gap was opened.

Prelude to War

Johnson chose to interpret the Tonkin Gulf Resolution as granting him the open-ended authority to act in Vietnam without further reference to Congress, and after gaining his own mandate in the 1964 election, he began to exercise that power to forestall what appeared to be the impending victory of the DRV-backed Viet Cong over the U.S.-backed Republic of Vietnam. His actions in early 1965 in launching a tactical bombing campaign up to the 19th parallel and in deploying a few battalions of combat troops did not rise to the level of a full-fledged commitment, but they sketched the outlines of the policy and strategies he would follow later in conducting the war that was impending.

5

Lyndon Johnson's War

The additional troops authorized by President Johnson on April 21, 1965, and now in the pipeline to Vietnam were no help to the ARVN as it continued to be badly mauled by the Viet Cong in the northern I and II Corps Tactical Zones, prompting the fateful June 7 telegram from Westmoreland to the JCS which became known as the "forty-four battalion request."[1] In it he described the enemy's capability to mount regimental-size operations in all four corps areas and battalion-size operations in virtually every province and cited recent VC successes in what he believed was a dry season campaign to destroy government forces. He noted that elements of the North Vietnamese 325th division were now in II Corps area. Westmoreland implied that a complete ARVN military collapse was foreseeable unless reinforcements of U.S. or third-country forces were quickly made available. He therefore requested an augmentation of the previously authorized force level of 82,000 to 180,000 which would take the combat forces at his disposal from 17 (13 U.S., four third country) to 44 maneuver battalions of which thirty-four would be American and 10 third country (one Australian and nine Republic of Korea). The implications of an increase of this magnitude were not lost on Johnson and his advisors. Previous deployments had already shifted the role of the U.S. in Vietnam from purely advisory and supportive to one involving limited combat, but the then authorized level of only 13 U.S. combat battalions was far short of what could be called a major commitment. This request raised the specter of another Korea. Since logistical limitations would restrict the number of additional American troops that could be deployed through August, Johnson was determined to give the request careful deliberation before approving it. The JCS quickly endorsed Westmoreland's request,[2] but in the face of lack of unanimity among his civilian advisors, Johnson vacillated. He then asked representatives of the opposing points of view to prepare papers by July 1 for discussion.

McNamara presented his views to the president in the most hawkish memo of his entire career as secretary of defense.[3] Drafted by McNaughton, the memo was completely out of character for the usually restrained McNamara who had not been inclined to support the hawkish recommendations of the military. In his memo, he not only endorsed the deployments requested by Westmoreland and JCS but went on to support intensifying the air war in line with recommendations of the JCS and CINCPAC, including mining of harbors, destruction of railroad and highway bridges leading from China, destruction of war-making supplies and facilities in the DRV wherever they may be located, stepped up interdiction against lines of communications west and south of Hanoi and preparations to destroy MiG airfields and SAM sites as necessary. He capped all this by recommending the call-up of about 100,000 selected reserves and extending tours of duty in all services. Following these hawkish steps, McNamara proposed expanded political moves with a view to opening a dialogue with the DRV leading to a settlement in Vietnam and listed several diplomatic initiatives the U.S. should take. He closed with an evaluation of his program which predicted that only after the DRV was convinced it could not win in the South and while it was under heavy punishment from the air would it move to negotiate or effect a tacit stand down of the war.

George Ball presented the arguments for a compromise settlement[4] without spelling out exactly what this would be. He recommended holding deployments to the 72,000 in country, restricting the combat role of U.S. forces and continued bombing of the North at the current (low) levels. His political program involved a number of initiatives which the DRV, in the belief it was winning the war, would have no realistic incentive to take up.

The third paper, by William Bundy,[5] was represented as a middle way course of action. He proposed holding deployments to 85,000 in a program to *hold on* for the next 60 days. Bombing would be held at the present level and no mining or attacks on rail and road lines from China would be carried out. The objective would be "to test the military effectiveness of U.S. combat forces and the reaction of the Vietnamese army and people to the increasing U.S. role." This paper was essentially a rationale for postponing an unpleasant decision.

Not to be left out, Dean Rusk submitted a rather insipid paper[6] intended to summarize the basic issues in Vietnam but which made no contribution whatever to resolving Johnson's dilemma. Indeed, the paper may have added to Johnson's paranoia with the statement that if the U.S. commitment to Vietnamese independence became unreliable, "the communist world would draw conclusions that would lead to our ruin and almost certainly to a catastrophic war."

McGeorge Bundy's covering memo[7] submitting the four papers to Johnson provides a rare insight into the key role occupied by this manipulative insider, the degree of influence he exercised and the technique he used to subtly guide an uncertain president. It merits excerpting at length:

> The positions within the government are roughly as follows: McNamara and Ball *honestly believe in their own recommendations*, though Bob would readily accept advice *to tone down those ... which move rapidly against Hanoi by bombing and blockade.*

Dean Rusk leans towards the McNamara program, *adjusted downward in this same way.*

The second-level men in both State and Defense are not optimistic about the future prospects in Vietnam and are therefore very reluctant to see us move to a 44-battalion force with a call-up of reserves. So they would tend to cluster around the middle course suggested by my brother [William Bundy]....

The Joint chiefs of Staff are strongly in favor of going in even further than McNamara....

My hunch is that you will want to listen hard to George Ball and *then reject his proposal.* Discussion could then move to the narrower choice between my brother's course and McNamara's ... I think you may want to have pretty tight and hard analyses of some disputed questions" (emphasis added).

It is noteworthy that Bundy thought that "McNamara and Ball *honestly believe* in their own recommendations" but apparently McNamara's belief in his own was not so profound that he was not already pre-positioned to tone them down. The only group whose position was presented unequivocally was the JCS while others "lean toward" and "tend to cluster around." Bundy's dismissal of Ball's proposal is classic.

Discussion of the papers took place July 2 in a White House meeting among Johnson, Rusk, McNamara, Ball and McGeorge Bundy. The large freewheeling meetings typical of the Kennedy administration were a thing of the past as Johnson was becoming more and more secretive in formulating Vietnam decisions. Large meetings were still held, sometimes called National Security Council meetings including congressional representatives, but they were informational only. The upshot of Johnson's deliberations was to send McNamara to Saigon on yet another fact-finding mission and to send Harriman to Moscow in an effort to open a dialogue through the Soviets with the DRV. The latter mission ended in failure when Kosygin refused to act as intermediary.[8]

McNamara's party included ambassador-designate Lodge, JCS chairman Wheeler, Assistant Secretary of Defense for Public Affairs Arthur Sylvester and Leonard Unger, deputizing for William Bundy who was ill. While in Saigon, McNamara was informed by telegram that Johnson intended to approve the 44-battalion request, rendering moot that portion of McNamara's proposal.[9] This became known as the Phase I deployment. His July 20 report to Johnson[10] held to his recommendations for a reserve call-up but raised the number to 235,000 and added a recommendation to increase the regular army by 375,000 by increased recruitment, the draft and extending tours of duty. McNamara also stipulated that additional deployments of perhaps 100,000 troops would be necessary in early 1966 and that more troops could be required later, depending on developments, but his hawkish recommendations for mining of ports and intensified air attacks on North Vietnam had mysteriously disappeared. It is hard to believe that he was dissuaded from including these recommendations by any discussions he had in Saigon. Certainly, Wheeler, Westmoreland and Taylor would have endorsed them.[11] It is much more likely, as was hinted at in McGeorge Bundy's memo to Johnson cited above, that

McNamara was rather easily dissuaded by the civilian bureaucracy in State and Defense who were still wedded to the slowly ascending air campaign and the concept of avoiding "killing the hostage."

The Master Dissembler

Even though he had already indicated he would approve the 44-battalion request, Johnson elaborates in *The Vantage Point*[12] on how he agonized over McNamara's July 20 report before reaching his decision. He would escalate, giving Westmoreland the requested forces, but he would conceal from Congress and the American people the full extent of his decision, and he would not call up reserves. That would require Congress to declare a national emergency, and large appropriations would have to be voted, diverting congressional attention and money from his Great Society program and raising the profile of the war with the American public.[13] These were things Johnson was determined to avoid. Having already made his decision against calling up the reserves, in a meeting on July 27 he maneuvered congressional leaders away from that course by suggesting it was "unnecessarily provocative" and got an endorsement of his plan. He also masked the cost of his escalation by, as he put it, "giving the Congress the story now and the bill later."[14] It is significant that at the July 27 meeting, the president's power to escalate in Vietnam *without explicit congressional authorization* was never questioned by the congressional leaders. When asked by a senator if any change in policy was involved, Johnson replied: "Our fundamental policy was unchanged."[15]

Thus, at a press conference on July 28,[16] referring to Westmoreland's request for the forces needed to meet the "mounting aggression" in South Vietnam, Johnson said: "We will meet his needs." U.S. forces would be increased from 75,000 to 125,000 with additional forces to be dispatched as they were requested, this despite the fact that he had already approved the full 100,000 request.

Critics of U.S. involvement in Vietnam point to Johnson's July 27 decision to escalate as a monumental mistake, the crossing of the Rubicon, which put the U.S. on the slippery slope that led to the ultimate debacle, but this judgment is usually made with the benefit of years of hindsight. *At the time*, Johnson and his principal advisors saw the decision as a stark choice between escalation and the loss of Vietnam to the Communists. Containment of Communism had been *the* national imperative since it was first enunciated by Truman in 1947. The Domino Principle was still an article of faith as it had been for some 15 years, and the effect of an American defeat in Vietnam on the reliability of our guarantee was being described in apocalyptic terms by high administration officials as well as highly respected nongovernmental figures such as former President Eisenhower, Dean Acheson, Robert Lovett, John J. McCloy, and others. Given the bipartisan policy of containment pursued by the three preceding administrations and the weight of advice he was receiving, it is grossly unrealistic to expect that Johnson would have acted other-

wise.[17] Thus, the focus of criticism should not be on the decision to escalate but on the manner in which he chose to implement it:
- It would be a "limited war" with U.S. military actions circumscribed by crippling political restraints.
- To a degree wholly unprecedented in American history, military strategy would be dictated by Washington civilians.
- A "slowly ascending tempo" strategy would be pursued in the air campaign against the DRV, and the flow of combat troops for the ground war would be metered very carefully by Johnson and the Washington civilian bureaucracy.
- There would be no "call to arms," no arousal of the nation, no mobilization, no reserve call-up so as not to distract Congress and the people as Johnson led the nation toward the Great Society. On the contrary, he would conceal from the nation as long as possible the full extent of American involvement.
- Johnson would pursue a guns-and-butter policy to avoid leveling with the American people as to the cost of the war and would fail to take timely and prudent fiscal measures to pay for the war, thus planting the seeds of a ruinous inflation which was not checked for 15 years.[18]

Thus did Lyndon Johnson set the stage for America's defeat in its longest war and for his own political destruction.

Westmoreland

William C. Westmoreland, a West Point class of 1936 graduate, had been on the army's fast track, regularly moving up in grade ahead of his contemporaries. He had a good combat record in World War II as an artillery officer, but after the war he opted for airborne. Airborne generals Ridgway, Taylor and Gavin came out of the war covered with glory and clearly were going places fast, and Westmoreland thought it opportune to align himself with them, becoming a protégé of Taylor. He commanded the 187th Airborne Regimental Combat Team in Korea, was the Army's youngest major general in 1956 and got the 101st Airborne (Taylor's old division) in 1958. He commanded the XVIII Airborne Corps when named in early 1964 as Harkins' deputy, taking over the MACV June 20, 1964, and getting a fourth star with it.

By late 1963 the U.S. Army in its advisory role to the Army of the Republic of Vietnam had become thoroughly frustrated with the ARVN's ineptitude and was spoiling to enter the fight itself. Thus, Maxwell Taylor, chairman of the JCS, and Gen. Earle G. "Bus" Wheeler, army chief of staff, were intent on selecting a successor to Harkins who would be capable of leading the major U.S. military action they saw developing in Vietnam. Whom better than Westmoreland, an airborne man and Taylor protégé? Already, in January and October 1964 the JCS had made several very hawkish recommendations to McNamara which left no doubt the JCS was itching to exchange the American advisory role for one of active involvement in if not direction of the war. There is no question Westmoreland, as COMUSMACV, shared these aspirations, but it took a civilian, McGeorge Bundy, to make the breakthrough when, as already related, in January 1965 with McNamara's concurrence, he recommended to Johnson the use of U.S. military power to force a change in Communist policy. And in February 1965 when, after careful groundwork within the Pentagon, Westmoreland's first request for combat troops was approved by the president, there must have been a degree of grim satisfaction within the JCS. The door had been forced open, and within a year, U.S. forces in Vietnam numbered over 200,000.

A Strategy Is Chosen

The decision to intervene directly with combat forces required the JCS and Westmoreland to settle on a ground-war strategy, within the parameters laid down by Johnson and his civilian advisors, that would defeat North Vietnam and its NLF surrogate. The limited war strategy being pursued by Washington civilian officialdom entailing tight control of the size of U.S. ground forces in Vietnam and the prohibition on attacking into the enemy's sanctuaries in Laos, Cambodia and across the DMZ dictated that the ground war would be fought entirely within South Vietnam, so three alternatives were open to Westmoreland: attrition of Communist forces through a search-and-destroy strategy; a clear-and-hold strategy; or an enclave strategy. Since army doctrine taught that the objective of war was to meet and destroy the enemy's army in the field, and only search-and-destroy held out that possibility, there was little debate when Westmoreland chose it. He could not foresee that this choice foredoomed the U.S. to a very costly, drawn-out, and ultimately stalemated ground war in Vietnam.

While they were not happy with the restraints placed on the air and ground strategies, the military leadership had no reason to doubt that even with a less-than-ideal strategy, overwhelming U.S. power would prevail, leading North Vietnam to recognize the futility of its efforts and to negotiate peace or at a minimum to effect a tacit stand down of the war and thus achieve the U.S. objective of an independent and democratic South Vietnam free of insurgency.

Westmoreland's plan envisioned three phases.[19] The first phase, beginning in mid-1965 as troops became available, involved the use of American combat forces in a "fire brigade" role to stave off what appeared to be the impending military defeat of the ARVN. By the spring of 1966, this had been accomplished, and with the nearly 50 U.S. and third-country maneuver battalions now in hand and more on the way, he would be ready to launch Phase II, "search-and-destroy" operations against VC and PAVN main force units in four high-priority areas of South Vietnam. This would be conventional warfare, the only kind Westmoreland knew how to fight, in which large enemy units would be found, fixed and destroyed by overwhelming American firepower. The objective of Phase II was to cause the attrition rate on the enemy to exceed his capacity to replace casualties (the crossover point). Westmoreland avoided predicting a specific terminal date for Phase II, but when that point was reached, Phase III was projected to require another year and a half to destroy or drive out the remaining enemy forces. In the event, of course, Phase III was never reached in the Vietnam War, but Westmoreland pursued Phase II until he was succeeded by Gen. Creighton Abrams in mid–1968. At that point the Tet offensives had changed the nature of the war.

The Failure of Search-and-Destroy

Westmoreland's search-and-destroy strategy was fundamentally flawed because Viet Cong and PAVN forces always held the initiative as to when and where to give battle and could withdraw to the safety of their sanctuaries if the tactical situation so indicated. Thus, while the U.S. held the *tactical* offensive (search-and-destroy), the Communists always held the *strategic* offensive, allowing them to modulate the rate of attrition and preserve their forces while inflicting continuing losses on the Americans and avoiding climactic, large-unit battles which, with their superior firepower, the Americans were sure to win. In the event, most large-unit search-and-destroy operations were conducted in remote, less-populated areas of Vietnam under conditions that almost always favored the Communists, creating mounting U.S. casualties.

The U.S. forces required to reach the attrition crossover point were indeterminate, depending on the readiness and capacity of North Vietnam to escalate to meet the American escalation, so Westmoreland was cautious in estimating the number of troops required or how long it would take, but even though as many as 10 or more Communist fighters were dying to one American, it was the absolute number of *American* casualties, not the ratio, that influenced public opinion in the U.S. In the end, the U.S. grossly miscalculated Hanoi's patient willingness to match American escalation and to absorb appalling casualties so that when Westmoreland returned from Vietnam to a war-weary America in July 1968, ironically, it was he who had been "attrited" by North Vietnam.

By mid–1966 if not earlier, Westmoreland and the JCS had grasped the essential truth that search-and-destroy and Rolling Thunder (as it was being conducted) were having little impact on the core war-fighting capability of North Vietnam. It was then that they began urging a move into Laos to set up a blocking position that would cut the Ho Chi Minh Trail, deny the use of Laotian sanctuaries and draw the PAVN into a decisive battle, but Johnson, McNamara and later Clark Clifford, McNamara's successor, rejected this strategy.[20] Through the rest of Johnson's term the American ground-war strategy continued as before, and though Rolling Thunder was gradually intensified, the combination of search-and-destroy and the air campaign could not force a decision in the war.

In the years following the war, arguments were advanced by several wartime military leaders and others[21] that a U.S. move in force into Laos to block the Ho Chi Minh Trail could have been decisive in bringing an end to the war on terms that would have achieved U.S. objectives in Vietnam. In *On Strategy: A Critical Analysis of the Vietnam War*, Col. Harry G. Summers made the case for that strategy as the only one likely to succeed. This influential book was considered revisionist by the orthodox school, but lacking credentials to refute it on military grounds, adherents of that school have relied principally on the very dubious argument that an American move into Laos would have brought Chinese intervention, the same argument used by President Johnson to deny this strategy to the military. The orthodox version is that an American breach of the 1962 Laos Accords "would restart the great power crisis the Laos Accords were meant to resolve."[22] Exactly what form the "great power crisis" would take is not specified, but it is strongly implied that China would have intervened, and the word "Armageddon" is used.[23] The argument goes that North Vietnam could violate the Laos Accords with impunity but that somehow the U.S. could violate them by bombing but not with ground troops.

But a China that in 1966 and 1967 was thoroughly preoccupied with Mao's chaotic Great Proletarian Cultural Revolution and rising tensions with the Soviet Union was in no position to launch another Korean-type venture, especially since, unlike Korea, this time China itself might not be spared from attack. It seems highly unlikely that China would have been inclined to start a war with the U.S. when its territory was not threatened by events taking place over 400 miles from its borders. It is hardly credible that the Johnson administration could have so badly misread Chinese intentions. At bottom, Johnson's opposition to the strategy was probably based less on a genuine fear of Chinese intervention or respect for Laotian neutrality than on his desire to avoid opening himself to accusations of widening the war and further antagonizing domestic antiwar groups. Throughout, domestic political considerations were always the overriding factors in Johnson's decision-making on the war,[24] and thus, the only ground-war strategy likely to achieve U.S. objectives was forgone.

American Takeover of the Ground War

Having chosen a strategy, Westmoreland conducted his war of attrition against the enemy almost exclusively with U.S. and third-country forces, and in doing so he took control of the war out of the hands of the Vietnamese Joint General Staff. Some elite ARVN ranger, marine and airborne units were used with American troops in search-and-destroy operations, and responsibility for Tactical Zone (Military Region) IV, the Mekong Delta area, remained with the ARVN, but the bulk of the South Vietnamese Army was relegated to pacification and static, defensive roles.[25]

While Washington civilians believed they were competent to micromanage the Rolling Thunder air campaign, in the matter of the ground war, for the most part they confined themselves to analyzing, massaging and second-guessing Westmoreland's troop requests while refraining from interfering in his conduct of actual tactical operations within South Vietnam. For their part, the Joint Chiefs of Staff were invariably supportive of Westmoreland's requests for more troops, but they too, in keeping with the tradition of allowing the operational commander great latitude to exercise his judgment, were reluctant to question his relegation of the ARVN to a secondary role. Postwar, some American military leaders have cited political restraints imposed by Washington civilian officialdom as a major cause of U.S. defeat, but the takeover of the ground war was a serious mistake for which the military cannot blame the civilians.

With the Americans focused on fighting the Communists, little progress was made in upgrading the ARVN with better training and equipment. The less competent ARVN commanders were only too willing to allow the U.S. to take over the heavy fighting while the few able ARVN generals chafed at being relegated to less important roles in the defense of their own country, and ARVN morale suffered. In 1969 when the crash "Vietnamization" program was launched to reequip and retrain the ARVN to take over the war, nearly four precious year had already been dissipated.

The Missing Political Strategy

Aside from the military aspects, a winning strategy in Vietnam demanded an effective political program aimed at countering the Viet Cong in the villages of South Vietnam, but in the period from Diem's overthrow to late 1967 the U.S. failed to give adequate recognition to this crucial need. Thus, pacification, as it came to be called, took a back seat. From the American side, pacification was a stepchild with neither the military nor the U.S. Mission accountable,[26] and in the absence of energetic American leadership, the Vietnamese had not been able to mount a successful program. As will be seen, this changed with the appointment of Robert Komer in 1967.

To succeed, pacification required the supporting military strategy of clear-and-hold. Westmoreland's plan was for the ARVN to conduct clear-and-hold in the villages leaving U.S. forces free for his big-unit search-and-destroy operations against enemy main force units in the more remote areas, but he stated that, "In reality ... more American troops were usually engaged ... supporting the pacification process, than were engaged in the big fights."[27] This may have been so, but the effort was not well coordinated and lacked effective political follow-up so that through his tenure as COMUSMACV, pacification made little progress.

This raises the question: would early implementation of an effective clear-and-hold–pacification strategy instead of search-and-destroy have changed the outcome of the war? As will be seen, experience with the clear-and-hold/pacification program implemented after Tet showed that a well-coordinated military-political program in the villages could, indeed, roll back the Viet Cong, achieving a degree of security not seen since the late 1950s, but this was after the VC had been seriously weakened by losses in the Tet offensive. Still, early employment of large numbers of American and ARVN troops in well-conducted clear-and-hold operations followed up by effective political measures in the villages would undoubtedly have suppressed the Viet Cong in the more populated rural areas by cutting off their food supply and sources of recruits. But it also would have left North Vietnam regular forces intact, and given the steely determination of Hanoi to gain control of the South, a trial of arms through an invasion of the South would almost surely have taken place as it did in 1972 and after the withdrawal of American forces.

The Enclave Strategy

An alternative enclave strategy was proposed by Lt. Gen. (ret.) James M. Gavin in a January 1966 *Harper's* magazine article. A highly decorated general, Gavin enjoyed considerable credibility and was invited by Senator William Fulbright to testify before the Senate Foreign Relations Committee in February 1966, much to the irritation of Johnson.[28] Gavin's proposal came at a critical decision point when the Phase II escalation was being debated, and it captured the interest of some dovish senators. In this strategy, U.S. forces would remain within defensive coastal enclaves containing the bulk of the population, acting as a strategic reserve and leaving the war in the hinterlands in the hands of the ARVN. The objective was not to destroy the VC-NLF but simply to deny them victory, create a stalemate and thus bring about a negotiated peace between the GVN and the NLF. In a memo to McNamara, the JCS provided a strong rebuttal to Gavin's *Harper's* article,[29] and the administration never seriously considered his proposal.[30]

Gavin was not the first to suggest this strategy. In early 1965, Gen. Maxwell Taylor, then ambassador to Vietnam, had proposed it, and Taylor only concurred in the initial deployment of marines with the understanding they would be held in coastal enclaves. By April, however, Johnson had already authorized offensive operations by the Marines up to 50 miles inland,[31] and in June the enclave strategy was effectively abandoned in favor of employment of U.S. forces wherever they were needed although Johnson did his best to conceal this from the public.[32]

The enclave strategy would have brought far lower U.S. casualties, but it is highly doubtful that it would have induced North Vietnam to negotiate an end to the war. Instead, it probably would have created a de facto partition of South Vietnam in which control of substantial areas of South Vietnam would have been conceded to the Communists, and with DRV forces largely intact, an invasion like the one in 1975 would have been inevitable. To forestall this would have required an indefinite stay by significant U.S. forces as in Korea.

The Ground-War Strategy Summarized

Of the strategies discussed above, clear-and-hold and enclave would have impacted on the Viet Cong, but would have left the PAVN essentially intact, and as long as this condition prevailed the threat of invasion would hang over South Vietnam. Only the continued presence of substantial American forces might have forestalled it. As to search-and-destroy, it proved a costly failure because in the 1966–67 period when it could have been decisive, American ground forces were not allowed to block the Ho Chi Minh Trail and attack the Laotian sanctuaries, and thus the PAVN never needed to risk a general engagement with U.S. forces.

In *America in Vietnam*, Guenter Lewy said, "The war, in the final analysis, had to be won in South Vietnam,"[33] but this is facile as are similar assertions in the works of other writers. Certainly, the military-political war against the VC-NLF had to be fought in South Vietnam, but to create conditions for real, lasting peace would have required the decisive defeat of the People's Army of Vietnam, and as long as the ground war was restricted to South Vietnam, such a defeat was very unlikely. It may be argued that the PAVN was, in fact, defeated in South Vietnam in the 1972 Easter Offensive, but that defeat was not decisive, leaving the PAVN in control of valuable strategic ground in South Vietnam from which the final 1975 offensive was mounted.

The Antiwar Movement

During the Eisenhower and Kennedy presidencies, there was no organized opposition to U.S. policy in Vietnam for two principal reasons: first, from the signing of the Geneva Accords in July 1954 until early 1961, the U.S. policy of nation building in South Vietnam had the support of the media and the general public; and second, the U.S. commitment was small — the number of U.S. military personnel assigned to South Vietnam as advisors never officially exceeded 685, all military professionals who were prohibited from engaging in combat. President Kennedy expanded the U.S. role in Vietnam so that by late 1963 some of the over 16,000 advisors were involved in direct support of Vietnamese forces in combat, but even then his policy remained noncontroversial because America's increased role was not fully revealed to the public, the Laos and Cuban missile crises overshadowed Vietnam, and Kennedy was an extremely popular president, particularly with idealistic college-age young people. But with the death of Kennedy, the shield afforded by his charisma fell away, and the same policy in the hands of a much-less-popular Lyndon Johnson would have to stand on its own merits. Though his Great Society was the most liberal legislative program since the New Deal, Johnson was regarded as a devious southern politician by the liberal wing of the Democratic Party which was never as comfortable with him as it had been with John Kennedy.

In the early months of 1964, Senator Wayne Morse of Oregon was a lone voice repeatedly opposing the U.S. policy on the Senate floor,[34] but no significant organized opposition had yet appeared in the country. A straw in the wind appeared when Radio Hanoi announced that a group calling itself the May 2 Committee had been formed in March at a Yale University conference of student delegations from 20 elite colleges to collect funds for medical supplies for the Viet Cong. The committee planned to conduct demonstrations on May 2 in New York, Chicago and San Francisco against the "U.S. imperialist intervention" and call for the withdrawal of U.S. forces.[35]

In the buildup to the 1964 election, Republicans supported American objectives in Vietnam but criticized Johnson's policy as indecisive and ineffectual until the Tonkin Gulf incident brought a temporary closing of ranks behind the president. Only Senators Morse and Gruening of Alaska opposed the Tonkin Gulf Resolution, Morse calling it a "declaration of war."[36] The day the resolution was passed, demonstrations were held in New York opposing U.S. policy; however, during the political campaign, leftist and liberal groups, anxious to avoid anything helpful to Goldwater, were fairly restrained in their criticism of Johnson.

Senate support for Johnson held up well into 1965 with only Senators Morse and Gruening voicing open opposition, but it had begun to dawn on other senators, as they watched the U.S. buildup taking place in Vietnam, that through the Tonkin Gulf Resolution they had granted extraordinary war-making powers to Johnson without further need to consult Congress.[37] This was particularly galling to Senator William Fulbright, chairman of the Senate Foreign Relations Committee, who had steered the resolution through the Senate and who believed that his position entitled him to be consulted in the decision-making processes regarding strategy, bombing and peace negotiations. When Johnson, over Fulbright's opposition, resumed Rolling Thunder on February 1, 1966, after the 37-day Christmas pause, Fulbright was furious and announced his intention to hold open hearings on the administration's Vietnam policy.[38] In nationally televised sessions, retired Gen. James Gavin and retired diplomat George F. Kennan questioned the strategic importance of Vietnam to the U.S., warned of the danger of Chinese intervention and recommended the U.S. adopt an enclave strategy and wait for a political solution.[39] In rebuttal, the administration called on Ambassador and retired general Maxwell Taylor and Secretary Rusk to neutralize Gavin and Kennan respectively.[40] Fulbright used the hearings as a personal forum from which to criticize U.S. policy, but he was disappointed in the outcome for the hearings had little effect on the attitudes of the senators and the general public. When Morse offered an amendment to kill the Tonkin Gulf Resolution in March, it was tabled (killed) 92–5, but Fulbright was one of the five.[41] Henceforth, Fulbright would be an implacable critic of Johnson's and later Nixon's Vietnam policies.

Although his defection angered Johnson, Fulbright posed no serious personal political threat to Johnson, but after the first few days of the hearings, the individual viewed by Johnson as his most dangerous rival within the Democratic Party, Senator Robert Kennedy, also broke with administration policy, suggesting that the U.S. offer the NLF a share of power in South Vietnam as a means of achieving a political solution.[42] Kennedy's statement signaled his loyal political following that it was now all right to oppose Johnson's Vietnam policy, and dutifully they followed him into opposition. The *New York Times* quickly backed Kennedy's proposal in a front-page editorial on February 22. Perhaps justifiably, Johnson seethed at what he saw as an opportunistic shift by Kennedy away from a policy crafted by the previous administration of which Kennedy had been an influential member.[43] Compared to Fulbright, however, Kennedy initially was fairly restrained in his criticism of Johnson's Vietnam policy.

During 1966 and 1967 more senators were feeling the need to make public statements on the war. The hard-core antiwar group of Morse, Gruening and Fulbright was joined by a growing number expressing opposition to Johnson's policies including Senate Democrats R. F. Kennedy, Eugene McCarthy, McGovern, Church, Clark, Pell, and Hartke. Liberal Republican Senators Percy, Hatfield and Javits were making dovish noises calling for an end to the bombing and negotiations.[44] In November 1967, Senator McCarthy publicly committed himself to trying to persuade the Democratic Party to repudiate Johnson's policies before the 1968 election.[45]

Prior to February 1965, opposition to the Vietnam policy had failed to gain much traction with the public because the U.S. had not yet begun bombing the North and no combat troops had been committed. The focus of criticism was still on political aspects—U.S. interference in what was alleged by the left to be a civil war between the American-supported "illegitimate" Saigon regime and the National Liberation Front which allegedly represented the true aspirations of the South Vietnamese people. At antiwar demonstrations, participants often numbered less than 100 and seldom exceeded a few hundred. When bombing of the North began in February, the emphasis quickly shifted to a "stop the bombing" campaign and the numbers and volume rose markedly. Liberal and leftist groups that previously had said little were now heard from, including the Nonviolent Action Committee, Students for a Democratic Society, World Council of Churches, Women Strike for Peace, Youth Against War and Fascism, National Committee for a Sane Nuclear Policy (SANE) and others, which made statements, held vigils, fasted or demonstrated against U.S. policy. Much of the opposition agitation began to emanate from elite colleges and universities where the technique of teach-ins by militant, left-leaning faculty was adopted to radicalize students in opposition to the war.[46] Until the final U.S. withdrawal from Vietnam in early 1973, the *New York Times* chronicled antiwar activities in excruciating detail. It seemed no demonstration or vigil, however small, nor opposition statement from whatever source went unreported in its pages.

While various left-wing parties, front organizations and individual radicals, parroting the international socialist bloc line, had opposed American involvement in Vietnam from the early 1950s, these groups generally were shunned by mainstream American public opinion and media and thus, by themselves, would never have been able to marshal a significant antiwar following. It was only after the antiwar movement took root on college campuses in 1965 that it gained legitimacy with the media and with an important segment of American society.

It happened that America's involvement in Vietnam came at a time when radical changes were taking place in Western society, changes which were unrelated to the war in Vietnam. With the coming of age of the baby-boomers, the mid–1960s into the mid–1970s was a time of dissent unlike anything ever experienced in America and Western Europe as young people, primarily college students, displayed their alienation with "the system," that is, the way the Establishment had been running things. The 1960s saw the birth of the New Left and the launch of movements across a wide spectrum of causes with civil rights, feminism and environmentalism foremost among them along with the sexual revolution, the discovery of hallucinatory drugs, hippies, dropouts, and communes. The ferment and turmoil were not unique to America for a similar thing was occurring in Europe indicating that the war in Vietnam was not the sole or even necessarily the primary source of alienation. But in America, the war was the catalyst that focused and channeled the alienation, serving as a rallying point where all the causes could unite.

Clearly, there was seething disaffection on college campuses in the '60s, but it is unlikely that it would have resulted in the antiwar explosion that occurred absent some guiding influences. All this has remained controversial, but it seems safe to say there were several contributing factors. First, there was unquestionably a concerted effort by the left to proselytize on the campuses with the aim to radicalize and mobilize impressionable students by appealing to their idealism in support of the antiwar position. An example of this was the teach-in technique. This found fertile ground with many young college-age people who are naturally receptive to such appeals. This is not to say that all antiwar college students were brought to the movement by left-wing proselytizing. Many were moved by genuine personal idealism and opposition to all war and joined spontaneously. And certainly, an indeterminate portion of the protesters participated simply because it was the trendy thing to do.

Another influencing factor playing off youthful idealism had its roots in the military draft. Until modified in late 1969, educational deferments enabled hundreds of thousands of college-age men to avoid military service during a war.[47] Thus it was the source of a deep sense of guilt among many idealistic young men who, as they watched less-privileged blue-collar men volunteering and being drafted, recognized within their private inner selves that their elite position in society as college students was shielding them from a civic duty that others were performing, but this did not deter them from stretching their college years to the maximum extent possible. (The graduate schools had never been so full.) But if the Vietnam War were morally wrong, then they would be able to rationalize the moral ambiguity of their position, and this went far to explain the almost religious fervor evident in some of the young protesters. In effect, they became conscientious objectors who reserved the right to choose which wars they would object to.

The essential falseness of much of the moral indignation on college campuses is revealed when one notes that as the likelihood of being drafted and sent to Vietnam was reduced by Nixon's changes in the draft law and his troop withdrawals beginning in 1969, so too did the enthusiasm among male students to crusade against the war.[48]

Ironically, educational deferments not only stimulated the antiwar movement but deprived the military services of a prime source of officer material. Peer disapproval deterred many young men from enrolling in ROTC, and violent campus opposition forced the withdrawal of ROTC programs at some private colleges and universities and even a few public institutions.

As coordination improved, the antiwar movement gained momentum in the fall of 1965. A new National Coordinating Committee to End the War in Vietnam[49] organized nationwide demonstrations for the weekend of October 15–16 and succeeded in mobilizing thousands of students. This was the first major show of opposition to the war and got page one coverage in the *New York Times* under the headline: "Mass Demonstrations Continue."[50] In the spring of 1966 the committee showed its growing effectiveness by organizing and coordinating a three-day International Days of Protest in several cities in late March.[51] The steady drumbeat on college campuses of opposition to the war continued through 1966.

In the fall election campaigns, Republican candidates generally supported the war, and liberal Democrats who might have wanted to criticize Johnson's war policy were wary that such criticism could backfire on them. Thus, with a few exceptions, the war played little part in the campaigns although Republican gains of three Senate and 47 House seats and eight governorships probably exceeded what might be considered normal off-year political gains by the opposition party.

Figures such as Dr. Benjamin Spock, Dr. Martin Luther King, Jr., and Norman Mailer were early leaders of the antiwar movement. Spock was cochairman of the leftist National Committee for a Sane Nuclear Policy. King's involvement signaled his shift from purely a civil rights leader to a closer alignment with left-wing political groups.[52] By 1967, Dr. King, leader of the Southern Christian Leadership Conference, supported by Floyd McKissick of the Congress on Racial Equality and Stokely Carmichael of the Student Nonviolent Coordinating Committee, was calling for all civil rights group to support the antiwar movement,[53] but the National Association for the Advancement of Colored People and the Urban League chose to continue to focus on civil rights and remain aloof from involvement in other causes.[54] King was taking a steadily more radical position against the war, leading an April 15, 1967, New York march of 125,000 (King claimed 200,000) antiwar demonstrators organized by the Spring Mobilization Committee. Dr. Spock and Harry Belafonte were co-leaders.[55] Simultaneously in San Francisco Mrs. King was addressing an antiwar rally of 50,000.[56] In the most violent confrontation yet, on October 21 thousands of antiwar demonstrators attempted to storm the Pentagon after a peaceful rally at the Lincoln Memorial of about 50,000 organized by the National Mobilization Committee.[57]

Through 1967 however, the war continued to receive support from major segments of American society, especially the AFL-CIO and veterans organizations, and there were counterdemonstrations by students on some campuses, but public confidence in Johnson's handling of the war continued to slip in the polls. Although supporters of the war were more numerous, the opposition was more vocal. The antiwar forces sustained a cacophony of cries for negotiations to end the war while they ignored the repeated statements by Hanoi that the DRV was inflexibly committed to a settlement that would be strictly in accordance with its Four Points and that it was not prepared to negotiate on any other basis.[58] And periodically, through statements in the press, broadcasts over state-controlled radio and letters, Hanoi expressed its appreciation to the antiwar forces in the U.S.

As 1967 ended, an embattled Johnson appeared unintimidated by the rising chorus of protest and seemed determined to continue the war, but this would soon change in the pivotal year of 1968.

Political Changes

Vietnam had had a period of wobbly civilian control since late February 1965 when Khanh had been deposed by his fellow generals, and Premier Phan Huy Quat had formed a government. In May Quat had even succeeded in persuading the generals to disband the Armed Forces Council, but Quat was viewed as too pro–Buddhist by the powerful Catholic political leaders in Saigon. In early June, as Catholic demonstrations against his government mounted and believing his position was hopeless, Quat resigned and turned the government back over to the military. The power vacuum among the generals which had existed from the ouster of Khanh was then filled by Gen. Nguyen Van Thieu's assuming power as head of a new National Leadership Committee of 10 generals with Gen. Nguyen Cao Ky as premier over a government made up of civilians.[59] Thieu and Ky represented the Young Turk faction which had by now largely cleansed the army of the old guard. As it developed, the Thieu-Ky combination ended the 18 months of revolving-door governments since the death of Diem and gave continuity to the Vietnamese government into 1967 when Thieu was elected president. Thieu was to lead South Vietnam until the final defeat in 1975, a tenure exceeding the nine years of Diem.

As related earlier, despite manifest evidence that Lodge had not been effective in managing the U.S. country team during his first tour, Johnson could not resist the seductive political cover afforded by Republican Lodge as a replacement for Taylor. A subtle, secondary consideration was Lodge's close relationship with Eisenhower. Johnson was concerned that Eisenhower, whose prestige with the American people was unmatched, might publicly criticize his Vietnam policy, so he consistently sought to coopt the ex-president by flattering him with frequent consultations,[60] and the Lodge appointment would help to keep Eisenhower on board.[61] To offset Lodge's deficiencies as a manager, it was planned to give him not one but two deputies. And in a surprise move, it was announced that Edward Lansdale would be going to Vietnam to work for Lodge on rural development (pacification).[62]

More Peace Efforts

With every White House decision to augment forces in Vietnam came further exhortations to State to leave no stone unturned in efforts to open a dialogue with Hanoi. There is no doubt that U.S. eagerness for talks had to be unmistakably clear to Hanoi, but these overtures were being ignored because the DRV believed it was winning, a collapse of the Saigon regime was imminent, and U.S. staying power would wilt. The latter belief was encouraged by the growing antiwar agitation in the U.S. in the forms of demonstrations and editorial criticism of administration policy in leading newspapers. This overeagerness to negotiate was opposed by Taylor and then Lodge as premature, potentially demoralizing to South Vietnam and weakening U.S. efforts to convince Hanoi of American determination to prevail.[63] In a September 15 telegram to State,[64] Lodge astutely observed that the Communists would enter negotiations only with the aim of winning at the conference table what had eluded them on the battlefield, and that there was no hope of negotiating them out of anything they held on the ground. Events were to bear out the accuracy of these comments.

The pattern of public diplomacy in pursuit of peace talks was criticized as naive and lacking in subtlety. In his 1970 book,[65] Chester Cooper, former White House National Security aide, said, "Where finely tooled instruments were required, we used a sledgehammer ... we proceeded with the subtlety of a Fourth of July parade...." Such facile hindsight criticism ignored the simple truth that U.S. peace initiatives in the 1965–1967 period, naive and lacking in subtlety as they may have been, were not successful because Hanoi had no incentive to negotiate. The Communists believed they were winning and would reject any offer for talks which did not include the key concessions of prior acceptance of the Four Points and unconditional cessation of bombing, and no amount of subtlety would have changed that. Had these "clumsy and fumbling" efforts included these concessions (which would have been tantamount to capitulation), they would have been taken up instantly by Hanoi. During this period, the U.S. overrated the value of its key bargaining chip, cessation of bombing, because the slowly ascending tempo of the air campaign had not begun to apply real pressure on the DRV.

The Christmas Bombing Pause

Despite evidence that Rolling Thunder as it had been conducted to that point was not having the desired effect on the DRV, sentiment began building in early fall 1965 among the Washington civilian bureaucracy to push the key bargaining chip out on the table in the form of another bombing pause.

McGeorge Bundy took up the idea in an October 22 draft,[66] and McNamara weighed in on November 3 in a draft memo to Johnson[67] recommending a four-week bombing pause. In the likely event that this did not move Hanoi to negotiate, the pause would be followed by an evolving or stepped-up Rolling Thunder in a further effort to induce negotiations which, if unproductive, would in turn be followed in 1966 by Phase II deployment of 155,000 to 185,000 troops, bringing the total to 380,000 or more.

In a November 9 memo to Johnson,[68] Rusk recommended against a pause if the quid pro quo were only the initiation of negotiations. He argued that bombing was "our only bargaining counter" and it was, therefore, important that "we carefully preserve it and play the card ... only at the optimum point...." This was especially true since Hanoi had not shown a willingness to negotiate, and therefore, the U.S. risked playing its only card without receiving anything substantial in return. Lodge shared Rusk's opposition to a pause as did McNamara's military subordinates, the JCS, CINCPAC and Westmoreland.[69]

With his advisors split, Johnson was in a dilemma. In the event, he never made a decision for or against an extended pause, instead slipping into it beginning with a two-day Christmas pause and extending it in increments of a few days for 37 days through January 30. During this period, Johnson unleashed an intensive worldwide diplomatic campaign to get negotiations started using every available channel but to no avail.[70] Hanoi remained obdurate in its demands for prior acceptance of the Four Points, cessation of bombing and U.S. withdrawal.

Bundy Leaves

The foreign policy team so carefully constructed by Kennedy five years earlier began to break up when on November 19, 1965, Bundy informed Johnson that he had decided to accept a position heading the Ford Foundation, and on December 4 he submitted his resignation to Johnson, but no announcement was made.[71] He agreed to remain until the end of February. Bundy's biographer, Kai Bird, attributes his decision to a growing distaste for the Johnson persona. "If it had been Jack Kennedy's war, he would have remained, but he didn't want to fight Lyndon Johnson's war."[72] Another likely motivating factor was a foreboding about Vietnam. Bundy had his fingerprints all over that situation, and he may have realized, as he watched his Eastern Establishment friends turn dovish, that he needed to get out now to salvage whatever reputation he could from the impending debacle. Given the unpopularity of the Vietnam War in academia, it was unlikely he would be welcomed back there. Perhaps his Establishment friends, seeing his plight, had thrown him a life ring.

Many of the documents bearing his signature were covering memos to the president of proposals and recommendations from other top advisors in which Bundy acted as the honest broker, laying out both sides of the argument, but it is hardly credible that Bundy, who had unrivaled access to the president, did not exercise great, perhaps decisive influence on both Kennedy and Johnson in backstage discussions. Throughout Bundy's tenure, presidential actions on Vietnam formed an unbroken sequence of decisions to escalate, lending credence to the charge that he, no less than McNamara, performed a role as instigator of the deepening U.S. involvement, and at the same time he was one of the civilian dilettantes who crafted the disastrous strategy of gradualism which was a major contributor to the eventual American defeat in Vietnam. But unlike McNamara and others who mutated into doves while still in the administration or shortly thereafter, Bundy for a time remained a supporter of the war and Johnson continued to seek his advice.[73] Walt Rostow, a resolute hawk, served as national security advisor through the rest of Johnson's term.

Escalation — Phase II

On November 28–29, 1965, McNamara made his seventh trip to Vietnam where he met with Lodge, Westmoreland and Sharp. In his November 30 recommendations to Johnson[74] from this trip he reiterated his November 3 proposal for a bombing pause, the principal purpose of which would be to gain favorable PR for the U.S. as a base for the next stage of escalation. In view of the buildup of VC and PAVN (North Vietnamese) forces, McNamara believed the originally contemplated Phase II deployment of 28 more battalions would be inadequate and now recommended this be raised to 40 which along with logistical support, additional air forces, etc., would bring total U.S. personnel to about 400,000 by the end of 1966. He stated additional deployments could be needed in 1967. He further recommended that Rolling Thunder be stepped up over the next six months to include at the end of the period attacks on petroleum storage facilities, power plants and the mining of harbors. Thus, McNamara sustained the hawkish approach projected in his recommendations from his previous trip four months earlier.

From his first request in February 1965 for two marine battalions to guard the air base at Da Nang, General Westmoreland had at his disposal in February 1966 35 maneuver battalions of U.S. troops plus 10 battalions of third-country forces (one Australian and nine South Korean). When Phase I was completed in early 1966, total U.S. strength in country was about 220,000 plus third-country forces. The resumption of bombing on January 31, 1966, opened the way for final discussions on Phase II deployments which concluded in early April with Johnson's approval to increase U.S. forces to 383,500 by year's end 1966. Westmoreland's actual request to McNamara had been for a total strength of 459,000 by the end of 1966[75] but was whittled down in Washington because the troops were not available without seriously depleting the strategic reserve. For political reasons, Johnson again rejected proposals by McNamara and the JCS for a reserve call-up, and the ports were never mined during the Johnson administration.

The McNamara Shift

When McNamara next visited Vietnam in October 1966, the authorized troop level at year's end had crept up to 400,000, but it was not the same hawkish McNamara of the previous year. In his October 14 report to Johnson,[76] he recommended stabilizing U.S. forces in 1967 at 470,000 although Westmoreland had asked for 570,000. He gave as a reason the need to avoid exacerbating inflation in South Vietnam, but it was clear he wished to avoid "the specter of apparently endless escalation of U.S. deployments." He also recommended stabilizing Rolling Thunder at the present level of intensity and targeting, citing the low "marginal utility" of added strikes. Even though the bombing had caused enormous difficulties for the DRV, he deprecated the effectiveness of the campaign in interdicting the flow of materiel from the DRV to the Viet Cong and implied that the air campaign had value only as a bargaining chip in negotiations. In effect, he was proposing abandoning the slowly ascending tempo strategy. This stabilization of troops and bombing, according to McNamara, would remove factors "complicating our political posture and distracting from the main job of pacification in South Vietnam." Pacification was now the long-overdue focus of McNamara's concerns, after five years in which it had been a stepchild of U.S. efforts in Vietnam. Finally the matter was being surfaced at high levels, and in early 1967, for the first time, Washington gave pacification a high priority

Although Westmoreland's large-unit operations were inflicting heavy losses on Communist forces, the general knew that he would need more than the 470,000 troops then authorized to reach the point at which VC losses would exceed their ability to recruit and infiltrate additional men. In messages on March 18 and 28, 1967, he made a new request in the form of 80,576 additional troops by not later than July 1, 1968, to achieve a "minimum essential force" of 555,741 which would contain the enemy and allow the U.S. to retain the initiative, and an additional 118,441 for later deployment which would bring U.S. forces in Vietnam to an "optimum force" of 678,248 and would enable him to defeat the enemy in two years.[77] The request was quickly endorsed by the JCS, including his proposal to attack into the sanctuaries in Cambodia and Laos, and the JCS added its recommendations for expanding the bombing, mining the ports and a reserve call-up without which the full request for troops could not be met. This request went directly counter to McNamara's plan to stabilize the U.S. effort in 1967, and launched a wide-ranging review of the U.S. position and objectives in Vietnam in which the differences between the civilian and military sides of the Pentagon were brought into sharp relief. In responding to Westmoreland and the JCS, McNamara went well beyond his stabilization recommendations of the previous fall. In a draft presidential memorandum of May 19,[78] representing the consensus of civilian opinion in the Pentagon, he recommended an increase of no more than 30,000 troops and an end to bombing north of the 20th parallel. But the most significant part of this memo was his attempt to rephrase American objectives in Vietnam from the uncompromising wording of NSAM 288 of March 1964 to a more ambiguous formulation that effectively would act as a cover to a compromise political settlement in South Vietnam and enable a swift disengagement by the U.S. (ostensibly with our guarantee intact). He said, "The time has come to eliminate the ambiguities from the minimum objectives — our commitments — in Vietnam. Specifically, two principles must be articulated, and policies and actions brought in line with them: (1) Our commitment is only to see that the people of South Vietnam are permitted to determine their own future. (2) This commitment ceases if the country ceases to help itself." McNamara's statement glided by the fact that it was never the objectives of the NSAMs that were ambiguous — it was the means by which the objectives would be achieved. The memo urged Johnson to issue a new NSAM incorporating McNamara's wording so as to supersede NSAM 288 which was proving an awkward impediment for the Pentagon civilian doves since, as official U.S. policy, it provided the rationale for the hawkish, victory-seeking JCS.

Thus, from the eager hawk on intervention in 1965, McNamara's mutation was unmistakable, and from this point his influence with Johnson steadily diminished. Johnson did not buy in on the recommendations in McNamara's memo, but he needed no encouragement from McNamara to veto the reserve call-up, and without it, the JCS had no alternative but to pare down Westmoreland's request. Although McNamara wanted to hold the increase to 30,000,[79] at a White House meeting on July 13, 1967, he reported to Johnson that there was "complete accord" on an increase of 19 or 20 maneuver battalions for a total of 50,000, raising the authorized ceiling to 525,000 for June 30, 1968, and this level was approved by Johnson.[80]

The McNamara Line

Included in McNamara's October 1966 recommendations was a new item— *install an infiltration barrier*—an idea that had been floating around Defense for five years but now had a powerful sponsor. The origin of the idea is difficult to pinpoint but according to Halberstam,[81] as told by Lansdale, when Lansdale was a member of the 1961 Taylor-Rostow mission to Vietnam, he had been assigned by Taylor to look into "the possibility and cost of erecting a huge fence which would run the length of the country and stop infiltration." This may have been merely a red herring by Taylor to occupy the troublesome Lansdale and keep him from meddling in high matters of state in Saigon. In any case, nothing came of it. The idea then submerged to reemerge in a January 1966 memo from McNaughton to McNamara entitled "A Barrier Strategy."[82] McNaughton proposed that a barrier of barbed wire, walls, ditches and military strong points flanked by defoliated areas be built paralleling the DMZ from the sea and extending to the Mekong, a distance of 160 miles! The memo did not take up the technical feasibility and cost of the idea, but apparently the concept was passed along to the JCS for comment. JCS chief General Wheeler recommended against construction of a barrier in an

April 18 memo to McNamara,[83] but this failed to kill the idea and may have only served to trigger the next event in its evolution. This was a convocation instigated by McNamara of some 40 distinguished scientists under the auspices of the Defense Department's Institute for Defense Analyses to study ways in which technology could be brought to bear on the war. They received a nine-day briefing from military and civilian officials and then split into four groups to study various aspects of the war. The barrier concept was one of the four areas of study.[84]

In its August 1966 report the Jason Summer Study Group, as it came to be called, concluded that Rolling Thunder was almost completely ineffectual in achieving its objectives of interdicting DRV support of the VC-NLF and in its effect on morale in North Vietnam. It recommended the construction of an air-supported anti-infiltration barrier along the DMZ extending into Laos to cut the Ho Chi Minh Trail and included a fairly detailed description of the technical aspects. The cost was estimated at $1 billion to build and $800 million per year to maintain. Having passed the proposal along to the JCS but prior to receiving the reaction, McNamara instructed Lt. Gen. Alfred D. Starbird of the U.S. Corps of Engineers to take charge, proceed with the project and *have it installed by September 15, 1967*.[85] Admiral Sharp, CINCPAC, had already gone on record September 13 to the JCS[86] strongly opposing the concept as ineffective and likely to divert air power and manpower away from more critical needs, but in their September 17 memo to McNamara, the JCS gave rather guarded support to the idea, *provided* that "logistical support for the barrier be of a scale that precludes diverting critical munitions and strike forces from other combat operations." Knowing that the barrier had become McNamara's thing and that he had already ordered the project to begin, the JCS most likely believed, based on experience, that their objections would be disregarded anyway. McNamara later admitted to Johnson[87] that "the military leaders, with the possible exception of Westmoreland and Wheeler, are opposed to it because philosophically they are opposed to static defense ... and they use the analogy of the Maginot Line." He added that some were opposed because "it might ... reduce the arguments in favor of bombing of North Vietnam."

The reservations and outright opposition of his military advisors did not deter McNamara from including construction of the barrier in his recommendations to Johnson. In their October 14 response to McNamara's recommendations,[88] the JCS noted their reservations concerning the barrier's effectiveness and that the effort "must not be permitted to impair current military programs." Westmoreland told him, "It would be difficult to build and even more difficult to defend."[89] In the event, of course, North Vietnam was not prepared to stand aside passively and allow the barrier to be built. The Seabee construction crews came under fire from PAVN artillery and snipers, and only a few miles of the eastern end were cleared before work was stopped. The idea of a physical barrier was then abandoned in favor of a barrier of air-dropped electronic sensors.

In his book *In Retrospect*, McNamara devoted only a brief paragraph to the barrier project,[90] concluding with the statement: "Once put in place, the barrier was intended to increase infiltration losses. And it did." But not by any significant amount. It was characteristic of the mindset of McNamara who, on a matter which was essentially military, would accept the judgment of a group of academics over that of his military advisors.

McNamara Leaves

McNamara had followed up his hawkish July 1, 1965, recommendations with an equally strong proposal on November 3 to remove restraints from Rolling Thunder after a bombing pause intended to test Hanoi's willingness to negotiate. In what may have been a straw in the wind, in that memo McNamara for the first time raised the thought of a compromise settlement in South Vietnam but then quickly drew back from it.[91] Between his Vietnam visit of November 1965 and his next visit in October 1966 he grew increasingly reluctant to support escalation in any form, leading to his stabilization recommendations following the latter visit, to his strong opposition to Westmoreland's spring 1967 request for more troops to his May 1967 recommendation to stop bombing north of the 20th parallel.

A telling clue to this trend was his decision in June 1967 to have his staff begin secretly compiling documents on the history of U.S. involvement in Vietnam in what was to become the Pentagon Papers. At this juncture, he said: "By now it was clear to me that our policies and programs in Indochina had evolved in ways we had neither anticipated nor intended, and that the costs—human, political, social and economic—had grown far greater than anyone had imagined. *We had failed.*[92] (emphasis added). If this was his conviction in June 1967, as the chief civilian in charge of prosecuting the war, the honorable course of action would have been an offer of resignation, but none was forthcoming. At a minimum, he owed Johnson a forthright statement of his position since this state of mind would certainly raise questions as to his fitness to continue as secretary of defense, but McNamara hoped to work from within to change Johnson's Vietnam policy.

Finally, on November 1, 1967, he submitted a set of recommendations to Johnson that left no doubt as to his attitude to the war.[93] First, he recommended that the U.S. *announce* it was stabilizing the war at present levels of forces and air attacks. Second, that bombing of the North be *unconditionally* halted before the end of 1967, and third, that measures be taken to place greater responsibility for ground fighting on the South Vietnamese. McNamara's proposals were circulated by Johnson among his advisors for comment including Rusk, Rostow, Taylor, Abe Fortas, Clark Clifford, Nicholas Katzenbach, Westmoreland and Ellsworth Bunker, the new ambassador to Vietnam.[94] While there were mixed reactions on stabilizing Rolling Thunder, no one supported an unconditional halt to bombing nor did anyone agree to *announcing* that U.S. ground forces would not be increased beyond presently authorized levels although all hoped no additional forces would be necessary. No one had difficulty agreeing to shift greater responsibility to South Vietnam as and when that was feasible. A hawkish Clifford strongly rejected McNamara's proposals and accurately characterized them as "a resigned and discouraged effort to find a way out of a conflict for which we had lost our will and determination."[95] Johnson accepted the consensus, and thus McNamara's position in the administration became untenable. A month later Johnson announced McNamara's election as president of the World Bank and his departure from Defense at an unspecified date.[96] McNamara claims not to know if he resigned or was fired,[97] and Johnson's account of his departure does little to clarify the matter, but there is no doubt Johnson knew it was time for McNamara to go.[98]

McNamara's transformation was inevitable. His closest friend in Washington was Robert Kennedy, who had turned against the war in 1966 and had taken all of McNamara's other Camelot friends with him. McNaughton[99] too had turned against the war, and when he was killed in a plane crash in July 1967, he was replaced by Paul Warnke, another strong opponent of Johnson's policy in Vietnam. It seemed there were no hawks left among the Pentagon civilians. Johnson sensed McNamara's guilt-racked agonies, but although their relationship cooled, Johnson eased his exit by generously awarding him the prized World Bank job where he would be able to salve his conscience in humanitarian works for the next 13 years.

Rolling Thunder

No aspect of the Vietnam War was more divisive within the Johnson administration than the bombing of North Vietnam. The strategy of the slowly ascending tempo had been conceived in its entirety by the civilian bureaucracy and had been accepted only grudgingly by Johnson's military advisors. The chief critic of the strategy was Adm. U.S. Grant Sharp, CINCPAC in Honolulu, the theater commander exercising only nominal authority over Westmoreland and the ground war but with full operational control of Rolling Thunder within the restrictions laid down by the civilians in Washington.[100] Raids were carried out from U.S. Navy carriers in the South China Sea and by the U.S. Air Force from bases in South Vietnam and Thailand.

When begun in March 1965, Rolling Thunder air attacks were restricted to the area of North Vietnam below the 19th parallel, but the limit was soon moved to the 20th parallel which is about 60 nautical miles south of Hanoi. Attacks were of two types: those directed against specific fixed targets designated by Washington and armed reconnaissance against targets of opportunity in which the kinds of targets to be attacked, e.g., railroad rolling stock, trucks, radar sites, etc., were specified in the pilot's orders. The process of target selection did not change materially over the course of the Johnson administration. A list of targets was submitted by CINCPAC to the JCS for their review after which it passed through several layers of Defense and State civilian bureaucracies for comment before it reached the secretary of defense. The final decisions on targets were made at Tuesday luncheons in the White House attended by the president, McNamara, Rusk and the national security advisor (McG. Bundy or Rostow), but no professional military man attended until September 1967 when, after Johnson had lost confidence in McNamara, Wheeler was included in the luncheons. This group not only selected the targets and the number of sorties to be allowed but, incredibly, *sometimes even dictated the tactics to be used by the pilots.*[101] In his memoirs, Rusk said, "At these luncheons we selected strictly military targets; *the overriding criterion was the avoidance of civilian casualties.* The Tuesday lunch group also determined the direction of attack for aircraft ... to attack targets by more heavily defended routes which would reduce the risk of civilian casualties. We did this knowing American lives would be lost"[102] (emphasis added). Such a targeting process, that is, complete civilian control to the exclusion of military professionals with the overriding criterion being the avoidance of civilian casualties by placing at increased risk one's own air crews has no precedent in the history of modern warfare.

While the application of restraints intended to avoid civilian casualties was indeed laudable from a humanitarian aspect, an underlying and cynical motivation was an attempt to disarm domestic opponents of the bombing campaign, and in this it failed. No amount of restraint would have forestalled Hanoi from mounting what became a very successful propaganda campaign playing off alleged massive civilian casualties which was echoed by the liberal Western news media. Also, while the U.S. armed services are constitutionally subject to civilian control, never before had this control been exercised at this level of detail, yet the military leadership supinely acquiesced in this. After the war, some of the generals and admirals expressed various degrees of outrage, but not one was prepared to risk his career in protest against this overreaching by the civilian bureaucracy in what should have been a civilian-military partnership.[103]

At the outset, a prohibited zone having a 10-nautical-mile radius was established around Hanoi inside a restricted zone with a radius of 30 miles, and similarly, four-mile prohibited and 10-mile restricted zones were established for Haiphong. In addition, a 30-mile prohibited buffer zone was created along the North Vietnam side of the border with China.[104] These zones did not come into play as long as bombing was restricted to below the 20th parallel, however as high-value targets were exhausted in that area, most of the remaining lucrative fixed targets were concentrated in the Hanoi-Haiphong complex and to the northeast in the area called the northeast quadrant. Beginning in the fall of 1965, bombing was gradually extended to the area northwest of Hanoi, but the restricted zones and the northeast quadrant remained off limits. Armed reconnaissance was not permitted in the northeast quadrant until April 1966. Attacks against SAM sites in the restricted zones were permitted in late 1965 but *only after* they were observed firing on U.S. aircraft.[105] Johnson even prohibited attacks on North Vietnamese airfields and SAM sites while under construction for fear that casualties among Russian or Chinese technicians might trigger intervention.[106]

Having already backed away from his July 1, 1965, recommendation for intensifying the air campaign against the North and mining the ports, in a July 30, 1965, memo,[107] McNamara gave Johnson an evaluation of the first five months of the bombing campaign against North Vietnam. He began by reviewing the objectives of Rolling Thunder: to promote a settlement, interdict infiltration, demonstrate the U.S. commitment, and raise morale in South Vietnam. To this list he tellingly added a new one not previously mentioned: "to reduce criticism of the Administration from advocates of a bombing program." In summarizing results with respect to North Vietnam, McNamara observed that obviously the campaign had not induced a settlement and admitted it had been ineffectual in interdicting infiltration. It had temporarily raised morale in South Vietnam but the effect had been short-lived. As to criticism of the administration, Rolling Thunder had accomplished nothing since one body of opinion (hawks) continued to criticize because of the self-imposed limitations on the conduct of the campaign while a whole new group of vociferous critics (doves) had been created by the very existence of the campaign.

In this evaluation as in other discussions of Rolling Thunder, McNamara played on Johnson's fear of China despite intelligence analyses by the CIA and other groups[108] which consistently minimized the likelihood of overt Chinese intervention unless its borders were physically threatened. This may have been a defensive tactic by McNamara and his civilian aides against JCS recommendations for stronger air attacks. Playing the China card was intended to stiffen Johnson's resistance to these proposals and avoid any erosion of the civilian concept of the "slowly ascending tempo." Thus, while conceding the campaign was not accomplishing its objectives, McNamara was able to deflect discussion of stronger measures.

In his discussion of the future of the program, he highlighted three aims: continued emphasis on the *threat* of future destruction, i.e., the "don't kill the hostage" concept; the need to minimize DRV loss of face, i.e., to make it politically easy for the DRV to capitulate; and finally, "to optimize interdiction vs. political costs." This last was a veiled argument against bombing Hanoi and mining the ports so as "to minimize the political repercussions." He went on to say: "Physically, it makes no difference whether a rifle is interdicted on its way into North Vietnam, on its way out of North Vietnam, in Laos or in South Vietnam." This statement is ludicrous on its face when one considers the relative ease with which the ports could have been closed and the immense difficulties that would have been created for North Vietnam as compared to the challenge of interdicting war materiel once it was dispersed within North Vietnam. Ominously, the first downing of a U.S. aircraft over North Vietnam by a Soviet SAM missile occurred July 24, six days before McNamara submitted his evaluation to Johnson.[109]

The two most controversial issues between the civilians and CINCPAC and JCS were the bombing of petroleum, oil and lubricants (POL) targets and the closing of the ports. While air attacks on the port of Haiphong rightfully could be judged politically sensitive because of the presence of neutral shipping, the striking of POL storage facilities was entirely a self-imposed restriction because of their locations within the restricted and prohibited zones. Still, elements within the civilian bureaucracy (chiefly the State Department) were able to forestall POL attacks by raising the specter of Chinese or Soviet intervention which somehow might be triggered by such attacks.[110] Finally, in late June 1966, Johnson grudgingly granted authority to attack POL, but before the raids could be launched, the plans were leaked to the press, making the raids more hazardous to the attacking planes.[111] After the successful attacks on June 30 the *New York Times* characterized them as "marking an important escalation of U.S. effort."

This characterization by the *Times* illustrated perfectly the trap the administration had constructed for itself by the bombing strategy of the slowly ascending tempo. After over a year of what had been rather ineffectual attacks on relatively low-value targets, any attempt to raise the level of pain on the DRV would now be interpreted as an escalation in the liberal media, not to mention the propaganda mills of Hanoi and its socialist patrons. In an administration which was hypersensitive to criticism, the fallacy of the strategy was that each new bombing increment in the slowly ascending tempo was labeled a new escalation, effectively drawing out and intensifying over time the drumbeat of criticism. Bombing the POL a year earlier as advised by CINCPAC and the JCS would not have avoided an outcry, but it would have been more difficult to label subsequent attacks on Hanoi and Haiphong as escalation.

Aside from the propaganda advantage, the slowly ascending bombing strategy had another very direct advantage to Hanoi in telegraphing U.S. intentions. From the beginning, the U.S. made no secret of the existence of and the area covered by the prohibited and restricted zones. And given the slowly ascending tempo, any rational adversary would take all prudent measures to protect, disperse or conceal whatever vital materiel and installations it could against the likelihood of future attacks. This the DRV did, and when Rolling Thunder finally began attacks in the latter part of 1966 in the vital Hanoi-Haiphong sector, it met with the most intense antiaircraft defense ever faced by an attacking air force in any war.[112] Over the course of Rolling Thunder, the U.S. lost 928 aircraft over North Vietnam.[113]

That Hanoi would take these measures must have been transparent to the civilian authors of the bombing strategy, but they believed, as it developed, erroneously, that the strategy of holding hostage the industrial heartland of the DRV was a bargaining chip that would bring Hanoi to the negotiating table. But where Hanoi earlier had demanded prior acceptance of its Four Points as the basis for negotiations, it now added a new requirement — an unconditional end to the bombing.

Overall, the advocates of the slowly ascending tempo made two fundamental miscalculations. First, they were wildly overoptimistic as to the immediate impact of Rolling Thunder on the DRV leadership, actually believing that the feeble level of pinprick attacks mounted in the first few weeks against low-value targets below the 20th parallel would bring Hanoi to the negotiating table.

Growing out of this error, they then failed to foresee that in the resultant drawing out of Rolling Thunder over three and one-half years, Hanoi and the international socialist bloc would mobilize all the left-liberals of the world (including the liberal media and much of American academia) in a very effective campaign against the bombing. In an April 2, 1965, memo[114] (one month after the start of Rolling Thunder) addressed to McNamara, Rusk, McG. Bundy and Taylor, CIA director John McCone warned presciently: "We must look with care to our position under a program of slowly ascending tempo.... With the passage of each day and each week, we can expect increasing pressure to stop the bombing.... Therefore *time will run against us in this operation* and I think the North Vietnamese are counting on this" (emphasis added). McCone went on to recommend jettisoning the slowly ascending tempo strategy and hitting them harder. "A bridge here and there will not do the job. We must strike their airfields, their petroleum resources, power stations and their military compounds. This ... must be done promptly and with minimum restraint." Of the four addressees, only Taylor was likely to concur in any degree at all. McCone may as well have been shouting to the wind in addressing his concerns to McNamara, Rusk and Bundy who would most assuredly not pass them on to Johnson. McCone's advice eventually was followed after Rolling Thunder had been going for almost 30 months, but as he predicted, by then time had run out.

In mid–April 1967, Johnson approved an expansion of the bombing program including destruction of thermal power plants in the Hanoi-Haiphong industrial complex.[115] This intensification of Rolling Thunder during the second quarter was met by heavy antiaircraft and MiG opposition, but, despite repeated appeals from Admiral Sharp, authority was withheld to hit the main MiG air base, Phuc Yen, until October 24, 1967, two and one-half years after the start of Rolling Thunder.[116] Rolling Thunder was now hurting the DRV very badly, but strangely enough, in Washington the attacks unleashed a flurry of proposals to ease off on bombing in the Hanoi-Haiphong-northeast quadrant in favor of concentrating on interdiction south of the 20th parallel.[117] In response, Johnson compromised, halting strikes within the prohibited areas of Hanoi and Haiphong but allowing them to continue in the northeast quadrant. At the urging of the military the ban was lifted for two weeks in August but was reimposed on August 24 when what seemed a promising opening for possible peace talks materialized through French intermediaries. This quickly came to nothing when Hanoi rejected the overture.[118]

The proposals from Rostow and McNamara to concentrate Rolling Thunder on areas south of the 20th parallel were debated within the administration through the second and third quarters of 1967, but Johnson, fearful of the reaction among powerful hawks in the Senate, temporized. Thus, the bombing north of the 20th parallel continued, with restrictions, until Johnson's March 31, 1968, speech in which he announced that bombing would be confined to the area south of the 20th parallel. In practice, no bombing took place north of the 19th parallel until Johnson's October 31 announcement of a total halt to the bombing of North Vietnam.

What did the three years of Rolling Thunder accomplish? Intelligence estimates of damage to the DRV's economy and the effect on Hanoi's ability to supply the Viet Cong are controversial and highly speculative. For example, the Jason Summer Study Group's second evaluation of Rolling Thunder in December 1967 concluded that Rolling Thunder had actually *increased* the war-fighting ability of the DRV because the bombing had forced Hanoi to take measures to create added redundancy in their transportation systems.[119] One can extrapolate these dubious findings to conclude that Rolling Thunder was actually *helpful* to the DRV and that, for example, the estimated 500,000 people at work repairing bomb damage to lines of communications[120] were making a net contribution to the gross domestic product. Logically, therefore, one can assume that *increased* bombing would have helped North Vietnam even more. In any case, by the end of 1967 one could question the objectivity of any such evaluation by a group of academics, given the virulent opposition to the war in the faculties of the elite eastern universities.

There is no disputing that Rolling Thunder was unable to interdict the relatively small amounts of supplies needed to sustain what was initially a guerrilla war, but as the DRV began deploying regular PAVN units to the South, the logistical requirements increased. When in late 1967 Johnson began to lift the restraints on strategic targets (steel mills, generating plants, etc.) within the restricted areas, North Vietnam was by then almost entirely dependent on imported materiel to carry on the war, and destruction of these targets had almost no effect on its war-fighting ability. The port of Haiphong and the railroads from China had been from the outset the targets with by far the highest payback, but due to the perceived political risks, they were never closed off during the Johnson administration.

So, was Rolling Thunder bombing north of the 20th parallel worth the loss of pilots and planes? Most civilian analysts believe it was a costly failure.[121] The military leaders responsible for carrying it out believe it was only a qualified success due to the restraints imposed, chief of which was the slowly ascending tempo which deprived it of any shock value and made it far more costly than necessary in air crews and aircraft.[122] As will be seen, when bombing was resumed by Nixon in April 1972 in response to the DRV's Easter Offensive, the air attacks (Linebacker I) were conducted with few restraints other than the need to minimize civilian casualties. Linebacker II, the so-called Christmas bombing, was largely carried out by B-52s and brought about the final negotiations that effectively ended U.S. involvement in the war. Many air force and naval aviation leaders believe the two Linebacker campaigns demonstrated what could have been done in Rolling Thunder had these measures been applied at the outset.[123]

Mining the Ports

Contrary to McNamara's specious theory that "it makes no difference whether a rifle is interdicted on its way into North Vietnam, on its way out..., in Laos or in South Vietnam,"[124] no amount of armed reconnaissance was likely to cut off the flow once the materiel had passed through the choke points represented by Haiphong and Hanoi and become dispersed within North Vietnam. The obvious solution was to interdict the entry of imported war materiel by closing the port of Haiphong through which an estimated 85 percent of the sea shipments passed and other lesser ports and by cutting the two rail lines from China. While this would not have closed off all avenues of entry, it would have increased Hanoi's problems enormously. Bombing Haiphong was politically sensitive because of the presence of neutral shipping, but mining could be used by notifying mariners of the presence of mines and allowing ships in port an interval to depart before the mines were activated. Nixon ordered the ports mined at the start of Linebacker I in May 1972.

The effectiveness of mining was borne out by the fact that when Linebacker I was ended October 23, 1972, North Vietnam had depleted most of its stocks of antiaircraft ammunition and SAM missiles and had not been able to replace this imported materiel. Also, it was consuming more POL in its offensive in the South than it was able to bring in overland from China.[125]

Johnson's military advisors repeatedly recommended mining Haiphong, and even McNamara himself endorsed it in his July 1, 1965, recommendations although he backed away from it three weeks later. The idea was discussed at White House meetings and frequently appeared as an option in various papers but was always put in abeyance or "held for possible later action."[126] Johnson's civilian advisors, including McNamara, initially were opposed to mining because they believed their slowly ascending tempo strategy would make it unnecessary, and when in 1966 they concluded that their strategy was not working, continued to oppose mining because they had shifted to the mode of stabilizing the air war, and they characterized mining as an escalation. And they never ceased playing on Johnson's fear of triggering Chinese intervention to keep the issue of mining off the table. In his May 6, 1967, memo to Johnson,[127] Rostow examined the alternative of "closing the top of the funnel," i.e., mining Haiphong, but rejected it because of the perceived political risks in favor of concentrating south of the 20th parallel.[128] On May 19, 1967, McNamara weighed in with a draft presidential memorandum[129] in which he set up the straw man alternative of mining Haiphong and then quickly disposed of it by raising an array of possible reactions (some rather far-fetched) by China and the USSR which he knew would unnerve Johnson. Massive amounts of vital war supplies from the USSR continued to pour through Haiphong until May 1972 when Nixon authorized mining, and the flow resumed after the mines were cleared following the Paris agreement.

A Linebacker I-type air offensive along with blocking the Ho Chi Minh Trail were the two actions best calculated to force the DRV to reconsider its war aims, especially if those actions were conducted simultaneously. The orthodox school has much greater difficulty in attempting to discredit the mining strategy than the ground invasion of Laos, and as a result, the subject receives only perfunctory treatment.[130] It is difficult to claim closure of the ports would trigger Chinese intervention since the ports were mined in 1972, and China did nothing. The argument then goes that had that action been taken before Nixon's 1971 trip to Beijing, the Chinese reaction would have been more belligerent, but it is tenuous to maintain that China would have risked war with the U.S. over the closure of DRV ports when mine warfare, an essentially passive activity, was nonthreatening to Chinese territorial integrity.

Pacification

Stimulated by McNamara's recommendations from his October 1966 trip, in the spring of 1967 Johnson took action to turn around the ineffectual U.S. effort on pacification by assigning all responsibility for the U.S. role in pacification to Westmoreland and naming Robert W. Komer as his deputy to head a new unified team in Saigon.[131] The U.S. support of pacification had been fragmented between the civilian Office of Civilian Operations (OCO) run from the embassy and the MACV's support of the ARVN's Revolutionary Development Support (RDS) program. Komer's new group, Civil Operations and Revolutionary (later Rural) Development Support (CORDS), fused the civilian and military programs. To assure that he had the necessary muscle, Komer was given the rank of ambassador, reporting directly to Westmoreland. With this status and authority, Komer put an end to the infighting, built an effective team and got the pacification program moving after several years of futility,[132] but CORDS received a major setback from the 1968 Tet and mini-Tet offensives which diverted it from pacification to aiding with the refugee problem and the reconstruction of villages damaged in the fighting. Thus, it was late 1968 before CORDS was able to focus on its original task.

The 1968 Tet Offensive

In his 1966 work, *Viet Cong: The Organization and Techniques of the National Liberation Front of South Vietnam*, Douglas Pike wrote: "The initial doctrine of the NLF was *Khoi Nghia*, or the General Uprising.... Essentially it consisted of the belief that the NLF could develop the revolutionary consciousness of the Vietnamese in the nation's 2500 villages to such a pitch that at some golden moment there would come a spontaneous uprising, and the people would seize political power, led of course by the NLF."[133] In the late spring of 1967, the Politburo of the DRV decided that that golden moment had arrived and ordered the planning to begin for a general offensive–general uprising to take place in early 1968. While it would be conducted by the Viet Cong, it was the Hanoi Politburo that made the decision, underlining again the subservice of the NLF to its masters in Hanoi.[134]

From its founding, the NLF held to the doctrine that the revolutionary war would be ended by a successful general uprising even though Giap's doctrine held that the third and final phase of the war would be, as it was in the First Indochina War, the defeat of enemy main force units by those of the revolutionary forces. By early 1965, the Viet Cong was well into Giap's third phase as their main force units were everywhere challenging and defeating the ARVN, and it appeared the war might be won without a general uprising through the collapse of the government of South Vietnam or forced negotiations on Communist terms. The intervention of U.S. combat troops in 1965 ended the hopes of the DRV and the NLF for an early victory, and from late 1965 into early 1967, the Viet Cong were badly bloodied whenever they chose to challenge the Americans. Sometime in the second quarter of 1967 the DRV Politburo concluded that while they may not have been losing the war, they certainly were no longer winning, and the likelihood of a military victory over the Americans was slight.[135] On the other hand, the leaders in Hanoi believed they were still winning the political war in the villages and that the continuing Buddhist-led disturbances in South Vietnam reflected widespread dissatisfaction with the Thieu regime. The apparent military stalemate along with the perceived political vulnerability of the Thieu government led Hanoi to believe that conditions were doctrinally correct for the general offensive–general uprising aimed at toppling the Saigon government or forcing it to the negotiating table under unfavorable conditions.[136]

The doctrine of the general offensive–general uprising called for simultaneous and coordinated attacks throughout South Vietnam by guerrilla units, usually in battalion size or smaller, to sow confusion and panic in the countryside, cities and towns. Through a proselytizing program of agitation and propaganda within the ARVN, the army's will to resist would be sapped, mutinies would break out, government officials would be assassinated, the masses led by the workers would take to the streets, and the war would be brought to an end either through the disintegration of the GVN or a negotiated political takeover by the NLF. Significantly, with the exception of some PAVN attacks on U.S. forces near the DMZ, the Tet offensive was conducted exclusively by the Viet Cong.[137] U.S. military forces were not primary targets because the Politburo believed a successful general uprising would bring an end to American intervention in South Vietnam without costly battles to defeat the U.S. military forces.

Much has been written on the Tet Offensive,[138] so no purpose would be served here in recounting in detail the fighting that took place over several weeks[139] following the initial attacks of January 30, 1968. While there are substantial differences among writers as to the interpretation of events that occurred over the 25 years of U.S. involvement in Vietnam, there is unanimity on one point: *the Tet Offensive was the turning point of the war.* But the significance of Tet lies not so much in the actual events of those weeks as in how they were interpreted by the political and military leaders on both sides, by the media and by the American people, and in the actions that flowed in the aftermath of Tet.

While there is unanimity that Tet was the turning point, controversy continues over the question of who won if in fact there was a winner. In this regard, there are some generally accepted facts. Obviously, no general uprising took place, the government did not collapse, the ARVN did not disintegrate, and indeed, fought well overall. Although the Viet Cong succeeded in temporarily overrunning some areas of the countryside previously under GVN control, they were dislodged fairly quickly. Pacification was temporarily set back, but following Tet a resurgent CORDS program began making spectacular gains in the villages, at least partially due to heavy Tet losses of VC cadre.[140]

The MACV estimated the Communists' losses during the course of the February 1968 Tet offensive at some 45,000 killed and captured of a total of 84,000 employed in the offensive.[141] While the 45,000 figure has been disputed, there is no doubt Communist losses (almost all VC) were disastrous. To this has to be added the losses in the mini–Tets that followed. Gen. Phillip Davidson, intelligence chief of the MACV, put it succinctly: "The Tet offensive for all practical purposes destroyed the Viet Cong."[142] After Tet, VC morale never fully recovered, the political infrastructure in the villages was never rebuilt to its former level, and with recruitment of southerners now more difficult, the indigenous nature of the VC was drastically reduced as depleted VC ranks had to be filled by infiltrated northerners. After 1968, the burden of the war was carried by PAVN regulars and VC units loaded with inexperienced northern recruits. But most damaging to the VC was the loss of its hitherto unchallenged mystique of omnipotence. The South Vietnamese people were eyewitnesses as ARVN and U.S. forces destroyed the attackers, and in the immediate aftermath of Tet, the Thieu government was never stronger. The decimation of the VC destroyed any remaining veneer of insurgency — it was now a straightforward war between north and south.

Yet despite the decisive military defeat of the Viet Cong, most accounts of the Tet offensive record it as a Communist political victory because of the putative negative shift it brought about in American public opinion toward the war, but as will be seen, the negative shift occurred primarily among the civilian Washington bureaucrats and opinion makers in the news media, not among the general public. Ironically, this impact on the bureaucrats and opinion makers came about not through the clever machinations of the Machiavellian leaders in Hanoi who ostensibly orchestrated Tet precisely to bring about this result. No, even in hindsight they did not make this claim.[143] Instead, in an impressive demonstration of the power of live TV backed by print journalism, the Western media created a victory for the DRV where none existed by their interpretation of Tet as a humiliating defeat for the U.S It is not credible that the Politburo could possibly have foreseen how favorable to them the media's treatment of Tet would be. For Hanoi it was sweet serendipity.

Beginning in the final years of the Ngo Dinh Diem regime in the early 1960s, the attitude of American media representatives in Saigon had grown increasingly skeptical tending to adverseness to the Vietnam War. While many Saigon correspondents reacted to all MACV statements with skepticism if not derision, their editors were usually somewhat more reserved. Thus, when the Communists launched 84,000 men into coordinated attacks throughout South Vietnam, the reaction of the correspondents was: "See, I told you they [MACV] were lying," and of the editors one of shock and indignation that they had been "misled" by official statements. These attitudes set the stage for the subsequent reporting of Tet.

The story line as seen by the news media had several parts: 1) that the size of the attack was *prima facie* evidence that the Johnson administration and Westmoreland had been deliberately misleading the American people about progress in the war; 2) that the Communists inflicted a military defeat on U.S. and ARVN forces; 3) that the tactical surprise achieved by the Viet Cong was a failure of intelligence comparable to Pearl Harbor; 4) that American tactics in reacting to the attacks were responsible for widespread destruction, civilian deaths and massive numbers of refugees; and 5) that Khe Sanh, the American base in northwest Vietnam near the DMZ, would be overwhelmed by PAVN forces, inflicting a catastrophic defeat comparable to Dien Bien Phu.

(1) In the fall of 1967, Johnson was conducting a "progress campaign," a PR effort to bolster public support for the war. In November he asked Westmoreland, Ambassador Bunker and Komer to come to Washington ostensibly to confer on McNamara's recommendations from his July trip to Vietnam, but Westmoreland knew that in reality Johnson wanted him in Washington to be point man for his PR campaign.[144] Knowing that he was being used, Westmoreland was a good soldier and gave the desired upbeat statements in a television interview, before House and Senate committees and in a National Press Club speech, saying that the U.S. was now entering Phase Three of the war, and he thought Phase Four, gradual troop withdrawal, could begin in about two years.[145] Naturally, these statements received heavy coverage, but the qualifications he attached were downplayed or ignored by the news media.[146] Later, when the Tet Offensive began, his earlier comments were the basis for an avalanche of criticism. Critics questioned his professional competency and his integrity, and the more extreme antiwar elements held him up to ridicule. Did Westmoreland really believe his own optimistic statements or was he merely playing the role assigned him by Johnson? It is fair to say that when the situation in late fall 1967 was compared to that of early 1965, Westmoreland had good reason to believe that progress had been made,[147] but from the intelligence at his disposal in Saigon, he knew the VC were by no means defeated and that much heavy fighting lay ahead against both the VC and PAVN regular units before his Phase Four could begin. He believed in what he said, but he erred in allowing himself to be subtlely manipulated by Johnson so that to please his commander, he stressed progress but downplayed some unpleasant realities. Thus, Westmoreland's credibility, already shaky with the Saigon correspondents,[148] was shredded by the Tet offensive. Although his prediction that in less than two years the U.S. would begin troop withdrawals from Vietnam proved correct, the decision for withdrawal flowed more from political than military considerations.

(2) On January 19, 1968, there were already 464[149] accredited news correspondents in Vietnam and by the end of February this had climbed to 627, the

highest number reached during the war.[150] Thus, there was no shortage of reporters to cover the Tet Offensive, yet what resulted was both narrow in scope and misleading in content as borne out by nearly every objective postmortem of those events.[151] That the focus was narrow is understandable since the largely Saigon-based press and TV were not able to witness the VC attacks on the many provincial and district capitals where in most cases the VC had been quickly defeated by ARVN forces. Thus, print and TV reports reaching America were overwhelmingly devoted to U.S. forces fighting in Saigon and Hue and the Khe Sanh siege.[152] Though ARVN forces did most of the fighting and took most of the casualties in turning back the Tet Offensive, the reports coming from Vietnam gave the American people the impression the U.S. was doing all the fighting, and when the ARVN was mentioned, it was usually disparagingly. Since almost none of the press corps had experience covering battle in urban areas, they found it very difficult to process much less evaluate the devastation, thunderous explosions, blazing buildings, fleeing refugees, and general chaos that were taking place in Saigon. The result was, "from the standpoint of the average reporter over there, it was the acorn that fell on the chicken's head and it said 'The sky is falling!'"[153]

The tone of coverage was set on the first day by the reporting of the unsuccessful assault by 19 VC sappers on the U.S. Embassy. Though the VC never gained entry to the building, initial news reports stated that they had taken over the building, and some correspondents persisted in this inaccurate report despite the on-the-spot denial by Westmoreland.[154] Once they realized the scale of the offensive, the shocked correspondents' first reaction was to report it as, *per se*, a defeat if not a disaster for the U.S. and its GVN ally. Statements in early February by Westmoreland, Bunker and MACV spokesmen in Saigon and Johnson in Washington that the offensive had been contained and then defeated at huge cost to the VC were met with utter skepticism and disbelief by the media representatives.[155] But gradually, toward the end of February the more responsible print media began to realize that what they were being told was essentially true and to report that indeed, Tet had *not* been a military victory for the VC. However, unlike the earlier front-page stories trumpeting disaster, these reports were relegated to interior pages. Meanwhile, the American public was receiving a daily dose of lurid television images of the fighting in Saigon and Hue with dramatic if not apocalyptic commentary that left the impression that U.S. forces were fighting with their backs to the wall and were facing defeat. The climax of CBS' coverage occurred February 27 when Walter Cronkite, the oracle of American TV news, abandoned his previous supportive position on the war and closed his half-hour presentation by calling for negotiations as "the only rational way out."[156]

Unlike most of the print media, which had begun to inject some degree of balance into their Tet stories, from the outset the major networks treated Tet as a defeat for the U.S. and its Vietnamese allies, and the emergence of facts contradicting this view was never allowed to catch up with the original story line.[157]

Initial opinion polls after the onset of Tet showed a closing of ranks among Americans in support of the war but a further erosion in President Johnson's already dwindling approval rating of his handling of the war, slipping from 39 percent in January to 35 percent.[158] The Tet Offensive had focused public resentment on the Johnson credibility gap and intensified the feeling in the country that the White House had no strategy for ending the war, but the polls failed to show a massive shift in public opinion against the war. In fact, those who considered themselves hawks rose to 61 percent from 56 percent in January and 52 percent in December, and those in favor of continuing the bombing of the North rose to 70 percent from 63 percent in October.[159]

Senator Eugene McCarthy's strong showing in the March 12 New Hampshire presidential primary (42.2 percent of the Democratic vote) was interpreted by the dovish media as an antiwar vote, but later analyses showed it was probably as much an anti–Johnson as an antiwar vote.[160] In any case, these results caused Senator Robert Kennedy, who up to then had declined to challenge Johnson, to declare his candidacy for the Democratic nomination and to use media reports on Tet to criticize the administration's policies on Vietnam.[161]

In hindsight, it is apparent that despite the avalanche of doomsday media reporting of Tet, the general public handled the crisis more calmly than the State and Defense Department civilian bureaucracy, already liberally sprinkled with antiwar officials in key positions.[162] But there is no doubt that absent the dramatic crisis reporting by the news media, the Tet Offensive would still have forced a reexamination of the conduct of the war and U.S. objectives in Vietnam by both hawks and doves, but more accurate and dispassionate handling by the media would have allowed that reexamination to take place under more sanguine conditions.

(3) In *A Soldier Reports*,[163] Westmoreland tells of the many indications picked up by U.S. intelligence in the months preceding the Tet Offensive that the enemy were planning something big for early 1968 and how he acted to prepare for the impending attack. While some may discount this as pure hindsight in a self-serving memoir, in fact he is able to document the warnings he gave the JCS, his troop commanders and the ARVN Joint General Staff and the changes he made in the disposition of his forces in the weeks preceding Tet. In the last week of January, he and his intelligence staff pinpointed Tet, January 30, as a highly likely time for the start of whatever the Communists were planning, and accordingly, all leaves were canceled and U.S. forces put on full alert, but he was not successful in convincing the ARVN Joint General Staff of the gravity of the situation. While ARVN forces were alerted, up to 50 percent of the troops in many units were nevertheless granted leave for the Asian New Year Tet holiday.

Westmoreland's assessment was that the main enemy effort would be by PAVN forces in the northern I Corps Tactical Zone along the DMZ coordinated with diversionary VC attacks elsewhere.[164] As it developed, that assessment was wrong; the PAVN forces were held back, and the main effort was conducted almost entirely by the Viet Cong against population centers countrywide. Thus, there was no massive intelligence failure, but both Westmoreland and his intelligence chief conceded that the Viet Cong achieved nearly complete tactical surprise and that MACV was not prepared for the size and extent of the coordinated VC attacks.

A far greater intelligence failure lay with Hanoi and the NLF in believing their own propaganda that the South was ripe for a general uprising, but this fact was lost on the American news media at the time and remains so many years after the event.

(4) Prior to Tet, the VC had had small successes in repeated attempts to seize individual population centers varying in size from small district capitals to remote provincial capitals, requiring ARVN and U.S. forces to retake them and eject the Communists. But during Tet, the VC simultaneously attacked 36 of the 44 provincial capitals, 64 of 242 district capitals, five of the six autonomous cities and were even able to insert several battalions into Saigon itself, not with any expectation of taking the city by force of arms but with the intent to create conditions conducive to the chimerical general uprising[165] These tactics were intended to generate an exodus of refugees that would be disruptive to the GVN and to use the civilian populace as a shield. Television images of the fighting in Saigon invariably showed destruction, debris, burning buildings and fleeing refugees, implying that the whole country was in flames and in some cases stating flatly that the U.S. used excessive force to dislodge the VC, causing unnecessary civilian casualties and destruction of property and disregarding the fact that it was the same VC who by their presence put the civilians at risk.[166] After the shock of the first attacks, some perspective began to filter into the print news with the *New York Times* reporting on February 11 that Saigon had escaped general or widespread destruction despite almost two weeks of fighting, noting there were 16 relatively small areas of heavy destruction, primarily in Cholon and the suburbs. However, these facts never caught up with the TV coverage. The networks, insatiable for dramatic and lurid scenes, merely moved on to Hue and Khe Sanh when the fighting ended in Saigon.

(5) "More drivel has been written and televised about the siege of Khe Sanh than about any other episode of Indochina War II"[167] was how General Davidson described the media coverage of this event that began January 20 and ended April 6 when ground contact was reestablished with the base. While Khe Sanh was actually an entirely separate and distinct military event from the Tet Offensive, the siege fitted well with the news media's ongoing doomsday crisis reporting on Vietnam, so it was treated as if it was a continuance of Tet. By late February when the fighting had ended in Saigon and Hue, the networks shifted their attention to Khe Sanh, providing an ongoing series of gloomy reports and commentaries that almost always included the words "Dien Bien Phu" and much pessimistic speculation that Khe Sanh would end for the U.S. as Dien Bien Phu had for the French 14 years earlier. Every correspondent with any aspirations to a Pulitzer Prize had to get his ticket punched by at least one visit to the besieged base, and every pundit newspaper columnist and TV

news commentator felt the need to provide his own lugubrious "analysis" of the situation. Johnson himself began to believe the doomsday press coverage, so much so that he demanded that a special White House Khe Sanh Situation Room be set up where he received daily briefings on the siege.[168] Without going into the tactical details which have been thoroughly described by others,[169] it is enough here to say in retrospect that the outcome of the siege made the analogy with Dien Bien Phu ludicrous. American casualties totaled 205 killed in action and 852 wounded of the four Marine battalions reinforced by one ARVN Ranger battalion that made up the 6,000-man garrison while PAVN losses from Marine and ARVN resistance and from the niagara of bombs and shells from B-52s, tactical aviation and long-range artillery were estimated by U.S. intelligence at 10,000 to 15,000.[170] When his losses exceeded those at Dien Bien Phu, even Giap, with his cold-blooded willingness to accept appalling casualties to achieve a key objective, lost his enthusiasm for Khe Sanh.

Thus did the American news media interpret the events of the Tet Offensive and Khe Sanh to the American public. The media coverage of Tet was well summarized by reporter Peter Braestrup: "Rarely has contemporary crisis-journalism turned out, in retrospect, to have veered so wildly from reality."[171]

The Consequences of Tet

Westmoreland was confident that U.S. and ARVN forces would be able to defeat the Tet Offensive with the troops already available in Vietnam and so informed the JCS, but JCS chief General Wheeler apparently did not fully share Westmoreland's confidence. Reacting to the near panic pervading the White House and Pentagon civilians from early press and TV reports, in early February Wheeler practically invited Westmoreland to ask for reinforcements, and the latter, like any general when offered more troops by his superior, did so on February 12.[172] Nevertheless, when Johnson immediately approved the sending of 11,000 additional combat troops,[173] it was treated in the press as a response to Westmoreland's "emergency" request.[174]

At this point, the U.S. was scraping the bottom of the strategic reserve barrel for combat units for Vietnam, again raising the issue of a reserve call-up. An indication of Johnson's determination to avoid, evade, duck and dodge this decision is given in *The Vantage Point* when he said: "Why, I asked, is it necessary to call up reserve units at this time?"[175] as if the answer could not have been more obvious. To forestall the need for an immediate decision, Johnson sent General Wheeler to Saigon for consultations with Westmoreland and Bunker, a trip that would prove momentous in influencing the future course of U.S. strategy in Vietnam.

As chairman of the JCS and the top U.S. military figure, Wheeler believed, rightly, it was his duty to assure the preparedness of U.S. armed forces to meet not only the demands of Vietnam but also those brought about by the Cold

War in other theaters, and he and the service chiefs were becoming increasingly alarmed at the drawdown of the strategic reserve and the resulting perilous position of the U.S. should the Soviet Union launch a challenge in Europe or elsewhere. Thus, Wheeler privately decided to use his trip to Saigon as a pretext for rebuilding the strategic reserve by forcing Johnson's hand on a major reserve call-up.[176]

In Saigon, he and Westmoreland talked in terms of taking the strategic offensive which could entail drives into the Laotian and Cambodian sanctuaries and perhaps even an amphibious operation against North Vietnam. To do this, a figure of 206,756 additional troops was jointly arrived at, 108,000 to be deployed still in 1968 with the remainder to be held for possible later deployment and to replenish the strategic reserve.[177] But when he presented his report to Johnson on February 28, Wheeler emphasized the uncertainties of the situation in Vietnam, implying that Westmoreland needed reinforcements to *hold off* the enemy and downplaying the strategic offensive that he and Westmoreland had discussed.[178] (Actually, the request was for about the same number of troops as in Westmoreland's "minimum essential and optimum" forces request of the previous March which resulted in his getting 50,000.) Wheeler's report triggered an intensive review of the entire U.S. position, as he knew it would, but the outcome would not be as Wheeler envisioned.

The president named Clark Clifford, who would replace McNamara on March 1, to head the review. Prior to his being appointed defense secretary, Clifford had been an unofficial advisor to Johnson, and his reliably hawkish position on Vietnam was undoubtedly a factor in Johnson's selecting him as McNamara's successor, but as will be seen, Clifford's attitude on Vietnam was to undergo a mysterious metamorphosis. This was not immediately apparent in the Clifford group's first report on March 4 which recommended "an immediate decision to send approximately 23,000 ... men...; early approval of a reserve call-up of about 245,000 men; and reserving judgment on the 205,000 package and examination of requirements 'week by week.'" Opinions were divided on what to do about Rolling Thunder.[179] At the March 4 meeting Johnson instructed Wheeler to "Tell him [Westmoreland] to forget the 100,000 ... 22,000 is all we can give at the moment."[180]

Johnson said in *The Vantage Point* that at a meeting four days later when the original proposal for 205,000 was raised, he made it clear to the group that he did not favor that proposal or anything approaching it.[181] Two days later, on March 10, Johnson was infuriated when the *New York Times* broke the story that Westmoreland had requested approximately 206,000 more troops. Believing that the information had been deliberately leaked to embarrass him, Johnson expressed serious doubts "about the integrity, judgment and reliability of some lower-level officials in my administration."[182] It is not clear if Johnson's definition of "lower-level" extended up to assistant and deputy secretaries, but in fact there were some dedicated doves at those levels in Defense who strongly opposed the war and were probably *Times* sources.[183]

By March 8, the Clifford group had raised the troop number from 23,000 to 33,000, subject to the call-up of selected reserves, but with the unpleasant issue of a reserve call-up still cropping up, Johnson asked for further study. By March 15, the number had dropped to 30,000, still contingent on a significant reserve call-up.[184] Finally, on March 22, the figure was settled at a token 13,500 support troops which, when added to the "emergency" reinforcement of 11,000 combat troops approved February 13 raised authorized strength in Vietnam from 525,000 to its peak of 549,500.

The scaling down of the troop deployment allowed a parallel downward massaging by Pentagon civilians of the reserve call-up. From the March 4 recommendation for a reserve call-up of 245,000, by March 15 the figure had been whittled to 98,000[185] and by March 22 had been further refined to 62,000,[186] much to Johnson's satisfaction, but this number was never called up. Ultimately, only 22,600 reservists in small specialist units and as individuals were called of which only 11,000 served in Vietnam.[187]

Twenty-four thousand five hundred troops was truly a long way from 206,000 as were 22,600 reservists from 245,000, but Johnson was quick to justify this "further scaling down of our plans" with four specious reasons: (1) another massive Communist attack was increasingly unlikely (temporarily true); (2) the ARVN was improving (but not very fast); (3) Congress had not passed a tax bill and we faced a large budgetary deficit (the guns-and-butter syndrome); and finally, (4) the public was discouraged by the Tet Offensive and the way it had been presented in newspapers and TV (Johnson had made no strong effort to rally the public since Tet).[188] Having arrived at these minimalist numbers, Johnson, the always careful politician, wanted to ensure that no recalcitrant general would jump the traces and make embarrassing revelations to the news media, so he sent Wheeler, who by then had been stripped of any illusions, on a mission to explain the realities to Westmoreland and to assure he was on board. As it happened, on March 22, the day before Wheeler and Westmoreland met, Johnson announced that Westmoreland would become army chief of staff at midyear and though his successor was not announced, everyone assumed correctly that it would be his deputy, Gen. Creighton Abrams. Although Wheeler and Westmoreland knew that the manpower decisions just taken had put a definitive end to any hope of a winning strategy in Vietnam, a complaisant Westmoreland agreed that *the 13,500 support troops were all he required to balance out his forces.*[189]

Clark Clifford

Wheeler had made his plan to reconstitute the strategic reserve and enable a winning strategy in Vietnam in the belief that Clark Clifford, the incoming defense secretary, would support him, but to Wheeler's dismay, it was this same Clifford who was largely responsible for derailing the plan. Clifford's rapid mutation from hawk to dove is one of the great enigmas of the Vietnam War.

Clifford, a close confidant of Johnson and a kind of minister without portfolio, was a prominent Washington lawyer and Democratic Party insider. In mid–1945, a friend who had been appointed President Truman's naval aide brought Lt. Clifford, USNR, to the White House to act as his assistant. By April 1946, Captain Clifford[190] was naval aide and by mid–1946 had become civilian special counsel to Truman, remaining in that post until the end of 1949 when he resigned to establish his Washington law practice. During his years in the Truman White House, Clifford became extremely well connected within the liberal wing of the Democratic Party, and during the Eisenhower years he was never far from the center of Democratic Party politics. He was an informal advisor to Kennedy during the 1960 campaign and headed Kennedy's transition team after the election. After the Bay of Pigs in 1961, when Kennedy established the President's Foreign Intelligence Advisory Board, Clifford was one of the original members, becoming chairman in 1963. Though Clifford had no special qualifications in the area of intelligence, this appointment gave him official standing in the White House.

There is no question but that Clifford was a Johnson White House insider from the very start and was consulted by the president on major decisions. Prior to his appointment as defense secretary he was one of the "Wise Men," a group of prominent private citizens convened periodically by Johnson to get their views on the conduct of the war.[191] When called together in November 1967, the Wise Men were fully briefed by representatives of Defense, State and the CIA and then invited to give their views and recommendations. In general, they were very supportive of the president's handling of the war but recommended a greater effort to get a better understanding by the public, the media and academia of the issues involved. Clifford joined the nearly unanimous view.[192] In reality, these eminent citizens were merely being used by Johnson as window dressing in his "progress campaign" because he knew from ongoing contacts with the most influential members of the panel that it would be supportive, or he would not have risked consulting them.

So when McNamara had to be replaced, Johnson naturally turned to Clifford as one who had been supportive, who had been privy to many of Johnson's decisions on Vietnam and thus was well up on the learning curve. But even before he took office he gave signs of how he would operate later as defense secretary when during his Senate confirmation hearings, he provided a new interpretation of the San Antonio Formula[193] that had not been cleared by Johnson or State. He may already have been harboring secret doubts about Vietnam when the president offered him the job in January although he failed to voice them, but the Tet Offensive was almost certainly the most telling factor in changing his attitude. In any case, while secretary-designate during February he was in close contact with lame-duck Secretary McNamara whose influence on Clifford would have been towards deescalation. And during the critical March 1968 when the pivotal decisions were made, Clifford was of course working closely with civilian officials in the Pentagon who had been selected by McNamara, were loyal to him and shared his attitude to the war.[194] Thus, the balance within the Pentagon was heavily weighted against Wheeler and Westmoreland.[195]

In his memoirs,[196] Clifford recounts with evident pride his backstage machinations to undercut Johnson's Vietnam policy. In the days of late March leading up to the final decisions on troop deployment and the future of Rolling Thunder, Clifford was using all his guile to influence Johnson toward deescalation. At Clifford's suggestion, Johnson reconvened the Wise Men. Clifford had already taken precautionary soundings around Washington and on Wall Street and knew that Dean Acheson, probably the most influential voice among the Wise Men, had shifted to a position favoring disengagement and that others were wavering. To be doubly sure of getting the outcome he wanted, Clifford probably subtly stage-managed the briefings to create an air of gloom, for the outcome was just what he sought — the majority recommended that Johnson adopt a policy of disengagement and seek to negotiate a way out.[197] Although Johnson suspected someone had "poisoned the well,"[198] he was nonetheless impressed by the shift in attitudes that had taken place since the previous November, and undoubtedly this contributed to the three crucial decisions he announced on March 31.

The Bombing Halt

In addition to the issue of additional troops, the matter of announcing another bombing pause was the subject of intense debate within the administration during March. The more dovish elements in the Pentagon supported a complete and unconditional bombing halt as a means of bringing the DRV to the negotiating table, but Johnson refused to consider this because of the threat of PAVN attacks on U.S. forces from across the DMZ. Dean Rusk, who at this point was the most influential of Johnson's advisors, recommended a bombing pause above the 20th parallel. His logic was, first, it would position Johnson favorably as seeking peace and thus would help to rebuild public support for his conduct of the war, and second, the military cost would be negligible because monsoon weather in the coming months would make bombing of the north ineffectual anyway, and if there was no response from the DRV, bombing could begin again when weather permitted. From his close position of trust, Rusk knew by mid–March that Johnson was going to follow his suggestion.[199]

The March 31 Speech

The president determined in late February that recent events in Vietnam along with domestic political developments (the New Hampshire primary and Robert Kennedy's entry into the presidential race) made it desirable that he address the nation, so a speech was scheduled for the evening of March 31. This triggered a struggle within the administration to influence the content and tone of the president's remarks pertaining to the war, especially with respect to a bombing pause. Fearing leaks, Johnson held his cards closely though, as Rusk predicted, he had already decided privately in favor of Rusk's pause above the 20th parallel.

In the event, Clifford and his allies did influence the speech toward a more conciliatory tone by persuading Johnson to drop the conditions he had attached in the San Antonio formula so that even though he offered only a partial bombing halt, Hanoi would be able to interpret it as unconditional.

But only a very few of Johnson's closest confidants knew he planned to add a startling conclusion to his speech: "I shall not seek, and I will not accept, the nomination of my Party for another term as your President." In *The Vantage Point*,[200] he said, "I felt I should make it clear that my decision [the bombing-halt peace initiative] had been made without political consideration.... The most persuasive way to get this across, I believed, would be to couple my announcement of a bombing halt with the statement I would not be a candidate for reelection."

It is not clear whom Johnson was trying to persuade, and one would have to question if subsequent actions by Hanoi were influenced in any way by his withdrawal from the presidential race. In any case, this was the gloss that Johnson chose to put on his decision, but in reality, there was a deeper motivation. Johnson knew that he had hit the stops—that he no longer had the standing, the credibility to rally the American people around a war that he had no strategy to win or end.[201]

Johnson's March 31 bombing pause initiative is credited with opening the door to the negotiations that eventually enabled the U.S. to disengage from Vietnam, but in fact, this initiative differed from previous pauses only in its slightly more conciliatory tone. At bottom, Rusk's plan was a cynical one — to gain favorable PR for the president while giving up nothing militarily and with the full intention of resuming the bombing once Hanoi had rejected the overture as it was expected to do.

For Hanoi's part, the speech offered some interesting insights and possibilities. First, the token nature of new troop deployments announced by Johnson indicated to Hanoi that American escalation of the war was probably at an end, and perhaps this was a more important signal to them than the bombing pause. It meant the U.S. had given up attempting to break the military stalemate to achieve victory, and that therefore Washington was now resigned that negotiations were inevitable to end the war. Second, as mentioned above, the removal of conditions attached to previous offers to end the bombing allowed the DRV to regard Johnson's offer as unconditional, thereby allowing Hanoi to accept without loss of face. Johnson's comments with respect to shifting more responsibility for the war to the South Vietnamese may have actually been welcomed in Hanoi.

Coming when it did, the speech may have dovetailed well with Hanoi's planning. Having taken appalling losses in the Tet Offensive and around Khe

Sanh, it offered the opportunity to move to a talk-and-fight strategy while they rebuilt their forces, and a talk-and-fight strategy could be even more effective in testing American staying power, given the Communists' ability to draw out talks indefinitely.

Thus, on April 3, Washington received a message from Hanoi stating that the DRV was prepared to meet with U.S. representatives "to decide ... the *unconditional cessation of bombing* and all other war acts against the DRV *so that talks could begin*"[202] (emphasis added). This was greeted in Washington with jubilation — we had finally brought the DRV to the negotiating table, but in doing so Johnson had unilaterally conceded a major bargaining trump, the bombing north of the 20th parallel,[203] without an advance quid pro quo by Hanoi to reciprocate *in any way*. In pocketing Johnson's concession, Hanoi had agreed only to discuss ending the bombing altogether.

The Campaign

While Johnson's withdrawal from the presidential race and the partial bombing halt temporarily cooled the antiwar movement, its leaders were not appeased and soon were making plans to disrupt the Democratic National Convention in Chicago in August. The results were violent confrontations over several days between the Chicago police supported by National Guard troops and thousands of youthful demonstrators exhorted by a battery of leftist organizers and speakers. In the weeks following, antiwar activity actually diminished as the chief spokesmen for the antiwar movement focused their energies on trying to win the media debate over who was to blame for the Chicago violence. Ironically, during the campaign the liberal Humphrey, as a member of the Johnson administration, was subjected to more heckling and disturbances from antiwar groups than Nixon. The liberal wing of the Democratic Party, angered and frustrated by Humphrey's refusal to break with Johnson's Vietnam policy, was sitting out the campaign until Humphrey, on September 30, shifted his ground and called for a full bombing halt and "de–Americanization" of the war. Meanwhile, Richard Nixon, in speeches and interviews, said he had a plan to end the war but refused to reveal specifics on the grounds that to do so would limit his freedom of maneuver.[204]

In the aftermath of the Democratic convention, Gallup showed Humphrey trailing Nixon in the polls by 12 points, 43 percent to 31 percent,[205] but over the course of the campaign, Humphrey slowly eroded Nixon's lead so that the final count was Nixon 43.3 percent, Humphrey 42.6 percent and Wallace 13.5 percent. (Wallace was a hawk on the war.) Television coverage of the tendentious and disorderly Democratic convention compounded by lurid images of the antiwar riots outside the convention hall produced an impression of disunity and rancor in the party that Humphrey was never able to overcome. Thus did the antiwar movement contribute to the election of the liberals' bête noir, Richard Nixon.

Peace Talks

Johnson named Averell Harriman as chief negotiator, but aware of the latter's reputation for overeagerness to compromise with Communists, he sent Cyrus Vance as his assistant to hold Harriman in check.[206] When the talks began May 14 in Paris, the U.S. side may have thought it was entering peace talks, but the DRV, as stated in its April 3 message, was interested in discussing only one subject — the unconditional cessation of bombing. The U.S. negotiating position included three major points: in return for a cessation of bombing, 1) the DRV would agree to begin substantive peace negotiations promptly (within two weeks) and South Vietnam would join the talks; 2) Hanoi would not violate the DMZ nor fire artillery from or across it; and 3) VC and North Vietnam forces would cease large-scale attacks on the ground or by rockets on South Vietnam's major cities.[207] Talks in Paris dragged on inconclusively for about five months until the impending U.S. elections brought the first movement.

For its part, Hanoi believed the election of liberal Democrat Hubert Humphrey, who was now endorsing an unconditional bombing halt, would be distinctly preferable to that of the enigmatic conservative Republican Richard Nixon. Thus, in the days leading up to the election, Hanoi probably calculated that the Democratic administration, in an effort to influence the election in favor of Humphrey, would be inclined to make concessions to show progress in ending the war. For their parts, Harriman and Clifford were of course more than willing to fall in with this in a desperate effort to keep Nixon out of the White House.[208] Events showed that Hanoi had calculated correctly for on October 31, Johnson conceded what remained of the United States' principal bargaining trump and announced the complete cessation of the bombing of North Vietnam. What the U.S. actually got in return for ending the bombing was one explicit "concession"— an agreement to allow South Vietnam to join the talks, but to gain this the U.S. conceded the presence of the NLF on the other side, thus tacitly recognizing the NLF over the strenuous objections of South Vietnam. On the other two points of the American negotiating position, Harriman got a "wink and a nod" from the Communist negotiators, which he persuaded President Johnson to interpret as their agreement.[209]

Clifford, who always thought primarily in domestic partisan political terms, believed Johnson made a grievous error when, given his decision to withdraw from the presidential race, he had not at the same time announced a complete cessation of bombing.[210] Between March 31 and October 31 when Johnson did announce an end to the bombing, Clifford and Harriman were the principal advocates of the bombing halt in the illusory belief that it would quickly lead to successful negotiations and an end to the war and thus thwart a Republican victory in November.[211] While Harriman hated the war, he hated Richard Nixon even more.[212]

There is little question but that both parties attempted to play the Paris negotiations for political advantage, the administration to pull off a dramatic "breakthrough" just prior to the election while the Republicans sought to deny Humphrey the political boost such a development would give him. Indeed, Nixon had legitimate reasons to wish to retain the bombing card should he be elected rather than see it played in the dying days of an outgoing administration. A number of writers have provided versions of the events of the last two weeks of October leading up to Johnson's announcement on October 31, much of it speculative,[213] alleging that the Nixon camp used Mrs. Anna Chennault, the widow of Gen. Claire Chennault and a Republican activist, as an intermediary through whom Thieu was encouraged to stall in accepting the deal Harriman had worked out with the DRV negotiators. As the story goes, the Democrats had proof of this channel but could not expose it because they had obtained their information through illegal wiretaps. But it should not be surprising that Thieu, with or without the encouragement of the Nixon camp, would be unwilling to endorse an agreement that granted the NLF a status in the negotiations equal to that of the government of South Vietnam and conceded a major negotiating trump, the bombing, in return for some ephemeral, unwritten commitments by the DRV. In the end, Thieu refused to endorse the Harriman-Clifford deal, forcing Washington to go it alone. For this he earned the undying hatred of Clifford who was absolutely certain that Thieu's recalcitrance delayed Johnson's announcement just enough to cost the Democrats the election.[214] Larry Berman's version in *No Peace, No Honor* is the most explicit (and speculative) in which he goes so far as to imply at several points that Nixon's unswerving loyalty to Thieu through Nixon's first term was because he believed he owed his election to Thieu and that this had the effect of needlessly prolonging the war another four years.[215]

In fact, it is a myth that there was ever any explicit agreement by the Communist side to points two and three, and VC and PAVN forces never ceased to violate the DMZ nor to attack South Vietnamese cities with rockets and ground forces. Before Johnson's October 31 announcement, he had secured General Abrams' agreement that a complete bombing halt of the North would not be detrimental militarily, but Abrams conditioned this *on the enemy's meeting the stipulated commitments*.[216] Clifford and Harriman knew very well that if the Communists defaulted on their "commitments," the U.S. would have little recourse because a resumption of the bombing would not be politically feasible if Humphrey were elected, but they nevertheless urged Johnson to go ahead with the announcement. Nor did substantive peace talks begin promptly. During the remainder of Johnson's term, the Paris talks were given over entirely to protocol issues such as the shape of the table to accommodate the two new participants.

Lyndon B. Johnson and Vietnam

While Lyndon Johnson has been heavily criticized by the antiwar political left for taking the United States into the Vietnam War, in all fairness even his severest critics must acknowledge that America's prestige and guarantee had already been engaged there by Eisenhower and then more deeply by Kennedy. The latter's loyalists maintain that he would have extricated the U.S. from Vietnam after his reelection, but for obvious reasons Kennedy could not announce his purported intentions to a public (or to Lyndon Johnson) that had heard nothing but Kennedy's avowals to remain steadfast in support of South Vietnam. So even if Johnson had been inclined to disengage, he was trapped by the rhetoric and actions of his predecessor. Thus, even though it happened on Johnson's watch, Kennedy must be tagged with a heavy share of the responsibility for taking America into the shooting war in Vietnam. But responsibility for the conduct of three and one-half years of costly war without a strategy for victory must remain entirely with Lyndon Johnson.

It was America's fate to have as the constitutional successor to an assassinated president a man whose education, experience and character made him woefully ill-equipped to lead the nation through a major war which had complex and ambiguous political and diplomatic aspects unlike any America had ever experienced. International relations had never been a subject of particular interest to Lyndon Johnson, whose consuming interest was always domestic legislation. His grasp of foreign policy did not extend much beyond simplistic references to the "lesson of Munich"[217] nor did his years in the House and Senate enrich his background in that area. His first real exposure to the world outside the U.S. was when Kennedy, needing to find something to occupy his underemployed vice president, sent him on 11 separate foreign trips to 33 countries[218] but never on one with any real substance. So when Kennedy's death placed a stunned Lyndon Johnson in the Oval Office, his insecurity in foreign affairs was palpable, and he grasped like a drowning man for the support of men like McGeorge Bundy, Dean Rusk, and Robert McNamara who could help him with what had become a critical foreign policy issue, Vietnam. That these were Kennedy's men was all the more reason for Johnson to want, to need their counsel — because they carried that aura of brilliance that came with the New Frontier and because they were connected to the indispensable eastern foreign policy establishment, but most importantly because as Kennedy's men they would confer legitimacy on his conduct of foreign policy until he could acquire a mandate in his own right. And after he was elected, he kept them on, Bundy for two years, McNamara for over three years, while Rusk remained to the end.

And did they serve him well? An uncertain Johnson was terribly impressed by the coterie of intellectuals (he thought McNamara was the smartest man he ever met[219]) with which Kennedy had filled his administration. The man from the hill country of Texas was impressed by their facility to produce on demand persuasive policy papers filled with delicately nuanced options, and in the end, with his approval, Pentagon and State Department civilians arrogated control over the military strategy and conduct of a war to a degree unprecedented in American history. Military leaders were largely denied a voice in the high councils, and their recommendations as filtered through

McNamara were rejected, pared down or ignored by Johnson and his civilian advisors. And it was these civilians who persuaded Johnson that the U.S. could fight a war in increments in which our actions were carefully, sometimes exquisitely metered and hedged about with all kinds of limitations and restraints. It was a strategy of gradualism to which Johnson was receptive for it fitted well with his imperative to fight a low-key war while he pushed his Great Society program, but it was a fundamentally flawed strategy of waging war that had no chance to defeat a determined adversary or force him to negotiate. And thus Johnson, bereft of foreign policy experience, was led into a grave error because, unlike an Eisenhower, a Kennedy or a Nixon, he had no basis independently to evaluate the advice of his counselors other than its impact on his domestic legislative program.

Even before the fateful decisions for intervention of early 1965, Johnson had begun to fall into another error when he decided to hold his Vietnam cards closely and to keep all the levers in his own hands just as he had as Senate majority leader. Through this he believed he could conceal from the American people what he was doing in Vietnam while he led them toward the promised land of the Great Society. Thus, Congress and the American people were to be lulled into believing that Vietnam was really only a limited war, and to prove it, the country was not going to be asked to sacrifice any of its material comforts, its butter, for the guns. And early on, even before his election in 1964, he was assuring the people "that American boys should not have to do the fighting that Asian boys should do for themselves"[220] when he had already authorized planning for U.S. air attacks on North Vietnam. Again and again Johnson dissembled, revealing only piecemeal and unwillingly the extent of his decisions on troop deployments, on authorizing Americans to engage in combat, on bombing the North, and on the war costs, but the news reaching the public through the media belied his pious assurances, creating a growing credibility gap. Public approval of his handling of the war steadily declined, reaching 28 percent in October 1967, reflecting disapproval from both hawks and doves. The American people realized that Johnson had no strategy for ending what had become a terribly costly war that was tearing the country apart. It was then, in the fall of 1967, that Johnson, sensing that he could no longer rally the public to his policies, began contemplating leaving office at the end of his term.[221] And thus it was not, as many believe, the Tet Offensive that drove Johnson from office, although that was the final catalyst. Rather, it was the deep inner knowledge that he could not unify a badly divided nation because he had forfeited his credibility with the American people.

6

Richard Nixon's Peace

When Lyndon Johnson was sworn in Dallas on that fateful November 22, the U.S. had 16,700 military professionals in Vietnam as advisors to the South Vietnamese armed forces, and fewer than 200 Americans had lost their lives in what was then purely a guerrilla war. Then, the American people were only dimly conscious of events there but had been supportive of the Kennedy administration's efforts to assist that small country in defeating a Communist insurgency. There was no significant protest movement. Ngo Dinh Diem, South Vietnam's leader since the founding of the nation in 1954, had been assassinated only three weeks earlier in a military coup conducted with Kennedy's knowledge and tacit support, and Washington officialdom was just beginning to grasp the full implications of this event on America's commitment to Vietnam.

Vice President Johnson had had no part in the Kennedy administration's policy-making, so Johnson's fingerprints were not on the policy being pursued in Vietnam. The pullback of 1,000 advisors announced by Kennedy in October 1963 might have given Johnson the pretext to assert that the Kennedy policy had been one of gradual disengagement, and he could have continued on that course. But Johnson, for reasons that he thought compelling, followed the advice of the counselors he had inherited from Kennedy, and as we have seen, after he had been securely reelected, chose to escalate.

When Richard Nixon took office in January 1969, he was confronted with an enormously more complicated situation than that of five years earlier. Over 36,000 Americans had died in Vietnam during Johnson's presidency with almost half, 16,589, occurring in 1968.[1] United States forces in Vietnam were leveling off near their peak of about 545,000 with the ranks full of draftees, and having declared a moratorium on bombing the North, Johnson had reluctantly conceded that there could be no military victory, and negotiations had begun with North Vietnam while fighting continued. Beginning in 1965, antiwar protests had become increasingly widespread and disorderly with highly alienated college students in the vanguard, the influential media had largely turned against the war, and the country was badly divided. And now, with their nemesis Richard Nixon in the White House, the liberal left would find it even easier to oppose a war that was the product of the policies of the two liberal administrations that had preceded him. But the most telling factor facing Nixon was the diminishing support of mainstream America after four years of direct U.S. involvement in an inconclusive war. Sensing this, many moderate congressmen and senators, now less fearful of a voter backlash, were emboldened to adopt an antiwar position. It was in this difficult environment that Nixon would have to decide what to do in Vietnam.

The Nixon Foreign Policy Team

In contrast to Johnson who had entered the White House with a deep feeling of insecurity in foreign affairs, a confident Nixon had chosen that area as the arena in which he planned to leave a lasting imprint, and thus he intended to conduct foreign policy from the Oval Office.[2] To do this he would need a national security advisor he could trust to implement his initiatives, and he quickly settled on Harvard professor Henry A. Kissinger, whose writings had established his bona fides as a deep thinker on foreign policy. During the Kennedy and Johnson administrations, Kissinger had functioned briefly in a consulting capacity, and in 1967, he had served as an ad hoc intermediary in one of Johnson's fruitless efforts to establish contact with Hanoi. More recently he had been associated with liberal Republican Nelson Rockefeller as his foreign affairs advisor. Still, it would be a giant leap to put aside his reflexive Harvard anti–Nixon bias and actually join the Nixon administration. Attracted by the power and influence he would have at the very center of foreign policy formulation, the ambitious Kissinger swallowed any reservations he may have had and accepted.[3] Though their relationship was never easy, Nixon and Kissinger complemented each other well, and together they launched some of the boldest and most successful foreign policy initiatives in recent history.

With all major foreign policy matters to be controlled from the White House, experience in that field was not a prerequisite in Nixon's choice of secretary of state. He chose William P. Rogers, a friend who had been attorney general in the Eisenhower administration. An experienced Washington hand, Rogers brought the strong administrative talents Nixon believed would be needed to handle the State Department bureaucracy. Nixon and Kissinger did their best to keep Rogers out of Vietnam peace negotiations and relations with Russia and China, but they were not always successful. The irrepressible Rogers, to the fury of Kissinger, occasionally made off-the-cuff public statements which unwittingly upset some of Kissinger's carefully crafted negotiating strategies.[4]

The third key slot, secretary of defense, went to Melvin Laird, a congressman from Wisconsin with 17 years in the House where he wielded considerable influence. A professional politician, Laird had specialized in defense budgetary affairs, a critical area for any administration. He proved to be his own man, advising against some of Nixon's military initiatives in Vietnam, but when overruled he was always publicly supportive of Nixon's decisions.

To head the delegation to the Paris peace talks, Nixon chose Henry Cabot Lodge whose years of diplomatic experience in Vietnam were unmatched. Lodge endured almost a year of Communist stonewalling during which no substantive negotiations took place between the delegations. He resigned for personal reasons in November 1969 and was replaced by David K.E. Bruce.

In Search of a New Policy

Johnson's war-fighting strategy of gradualism had not produced military victory, and the start of the Paris negotiations had permitted the Communists to shift to a talk-and-fight strategy aimed at consuming that crucial element, time, to out wait the U.S. The four years of fighting by American forces in Vietnam now equaled the duration of World War II for the U.S., and the country wanted it ended. Mainstream America still yearned for victory, but that could come only through a major escalation, and the country was now too divided to make that even remotely feasible. With military victory no longer a realistic option, Nixon knew that his first imperative was to develop a strategy to extricate the U.S. from Vietnam and end the war, so during the honeymoon period traditionally enjoyed by newly inaugurated presidents he and Kissinger focused on that problem.[5] At that point, extreme antiwar factions were demanding immediate, unilateral, and unconditional withdrawal, an action that would be difficult to disguise to the nation and the world as anything less than utter defeat. While they were sick of the war, Americans, firm in the belief that the country had never lost a war, were not ready in 1969 to accept defeat at the hands of a small Asian power. And certainly, the sacrifices of the 36,000 who had already died could not be lightly dismissed. Aside from these essentially domestic considerations, there remained the need to protect the integrity of the U.S. guarantee in the eyes of our allies and the world's uncommitted nations. Nixon believed the only acceptable solution would be a negotiated peace and withdrawal that would be judged honorable by the American people while also preserving the validity of the U.S. guarantee wherever and whenever it was given.[6] But he knew his main constraint would be that of time — how much time did he have before he would be overwhelmed by opponents of the war in Congress and in the streets?

Negotiations, therefore, were the only honorable way out, but Nixon knew that Hanoi, only too aware of the divisions wracking America, might simply out wait him. The strategy, then, had to be one that would permit the U.S. an honorable disengagement in the briefest practical period of time but would also leave a South Vietnam capable of defending itself after the U.S. departure. Out of these two conditions followed ineluctably the strategy of strengthening the Vietnamese armed forces, "Vietnamization," while gradually withdrawing U.S. forces, the objective being, within the indeterminate interval Nixon had at his disposal, to reach the point at which a complete American withdrawal would coincide with a South Vietnam fully capable of defending itself.[7] Meanwhile, the U.S. would negotiate in Paris in an effort to resolve the military and political issues and end the war while preserving an independent non–Communist South Vietnam. Thus Nixon's strategy would be two-track; Vietnamization and negotiations, but he would be forced to conduct this strategy against an adversary who was free of the pressures of time and of public opinion. In the event, the negotiations became a battle of wills between the Hanoi Politburo, which had never wavered from its objective of gaining political control of the South, and Nixon, whose objective of preserving the integrity of the American guarantee required the maintenance of a non–Communist regime in Saigon. Thus, the military aspects of the negotiations were always secondary to the central issue, i.e., the nature of the regime in Saigon that would survive the war, and it was this that took four years to resolve.

Negotiations I

In the waning days of the Johnson administration, the Paris talks had been able to resolve only the protocol issues, but this allowed the negotiations to begin in earnest after Nixon's inauguration. Between the start of talks in May 1968 and the resolution of the protocol issues the following January, about 8,000 American servicemen had been killed in Vietnam,[8] a grim insight into North Vietnam's strategy. At the time of Nixon's inauguration, the U.S. negotiating position for peace in Vietnam was still the 1966 "Manila formula" which called for North Vietnam to withdraw its forces and cease infiltration, and as the level of violence subsided, U.S. forces would be withdrawn as soon as possible and not later than six months afterward.[9] The other side, however, had already gained one of its main demands, an end to bombing of the DRV, while conceding nothing of substance.[10] Hanoi's other principal demands remained total, unconditional, and unilateral U.S. withdrawal and the dismantling of the Thieu government, to be replaced by one acceptable to the DRV.

With no movement on either side in the first months of 1969, the Communist delegation used the plenary sessions in Paris as a propaganda forum until early May when the National Liberation Front advanced a "new" 10-point peace program. Containing no concessions, the program merely provided window dressing for a restatement of the Communists' principal demands, but as a "peace plan" it brought cooing from doves in Congress and the media.[11] In response, Nixon, in a May 14 speech,[12] counterproposed an eight-point program which abandoned the Manila formula by agreeing to simultaneous withdrawals— the North Vietnamese withdrawal could be de facto, without explicit agreement, since the DRV continued to deny that any PAVN troops were even in South Vietnam. He also offered cease-fires under international supervision and to set a timetable for U.S. withdrawal. The plan made a key political concession in agreeing to NLF participation in the political life of South Vietnam, but it failed to meet the DRV's demands with respect to unconditional U.S. withdrawal and replacement of the South Vietnamese government. Nixon's speech was well received on Capitol Hill, but the *New York Times* gave it a lukewarm reading, saying it did not go far enough on the political side.[13] North Vietnam, however, remained obdurate, no counterproposals were advanced and the stalemate continued.

Prior to announcing his peace plan, Nixon had already decided to begin troop withdrawals, subject to three conditions: the ability of South Vietnam to defend itself; progress in the Paris talks; and the level of enemy activity. He and Kissinger believed some token initial withdrawals would win public support and buy the all-important element of *time* and thus might give Hanoi an incentive to negotiate. Reluctantly, the JCS agreed, seeing it as the beginning of a rear-guard action and an end to any residual hopes they harbored for military victory.[14] A meeting was arranged for June 8 on Midway Island with South Vietnamese president Thieu to gain his concurrence to the first withdrawal of 25,000 troops. Having no alternative, Thieu obliged, and the withdrawal was announced then and there.[15] The U.S. negotiating position continued to call for simultaneous withdrawals, but Nixon hoped that if Vietnamization were well executed, he might gradually end American involvement even without withdrawals by Hanoi.

Nixon immediately began to ignore his own stipulations governing withdrawals as he began announcing a new and larger withdrawal as the previous one was completed despite the complete lack of progress in the talks and in the face of continuing enemy activity. (The ability of South Vietnam to defend itself may have begun to show marginal improvement.) In reality, these withdrawals were being driven solely by the need to undercut domestic criticism.

On September 16, Nixon announced another withdrawal, this one of 35,000 troops by December 15. The *New York Times* said the reduction was "a timid move in the right direction but not a 'significant' step toward peace."[16] North Vietnam denounced it as a "perfidious trick."[17] The withdrawals enabled Secretary Laird to announce sharp reductions in the draft for the remainder of the year and restriction of draft calls to 19-year olds. The administration asked Congress for a draft lottery law which would eliminate almost all educational deferments, and Nixon signed this into law November 26.[18] On December 15, Nixon made a third withdrawal announcement, this time of 50,000 by April 15, but to his domestic critics, these withdrawals had become, as Kissinger put it, like "salted peanuts,"[19] because the more troops he withdrew, the more would be demanded. Liberal Democratic politicians and various antiwar groups were frustrated by Nixon's refusal to be tied down to a specific schedule and began calling for withdrawals to be completed by the end of 1970[20] while the more radical elements demanded immediate and total withdrawal.

The exchange of peace plans and the first troop withdrawals set the pattern for the next three years. Under intense domestic pressure to break the negotiating stalemate and end the war, Nixon and Kissinger slowly gave ground, making new concessions and restating previous concessions with new phrasing intended to be sufficiently ambiguous to gain Communist agreement, all the while unilaterally withdrawing troops. Each new concession and withdrawal was briefly applauded by Nixon's domestic political and media critics, but soon the same critics were labeling them as inadequate and demanding new concessions to "show our good faith" and to get the talks moving. Rarely was lack of progress in the peace talks attributed to the Communists. Meanwhile, North Vietnam never made a reciprocal concession nor wavered from its basic position.

When Lodge resigned in November 1969, Nixon decided to delay his replacement to indicate to the Communist side Washington's displeasure at the lack of progress in the talks. Fearing that Nixon was downgrading the Paris talks, which would undercut their talk-and-fight strategy, the Communists demanded that Lodge be replaced, but Nixon took his time. David Bruce took over as head of the U.S. delegation in July 1970.[21]

The "Secret" Bombing of Cambodia

Nixon had been in office less than 60 days when he took his first major action in ordering the bombing of Viet Cong and PAVN sanctuaries in Cambodia, reversing one of the crippling political restraints imposed by Johnson.

Prince Norodom Sihanouk, the Cambodian chief of state, had been a prickly problem for U.S. diplomacy. From his vantage point in Phnom Penh, Sihanouk, aware of American complicity in the coup that ended the life of Diem, concluded that the presence of American advisors could be hazardous to the health of heads of small Southeast Asian states. Accordingly, in late 1963 he put an end to U.S. economic and military aid to his country and expelled American aid personnel. In the years following, while maintaining a façade of neutrality, Sihanouk, convinced that Communist China would be the inevitable winner in the contest then underway in Southeast Asia and taking as a pretext some minor American bombing incidents along the Vietnam-Cambodia border, broke off diplomatic relations with the U.S. in May 1965 and moved closer to China.[22]

In the late 1950s, the Viet Cong already were using the sparsely populated border areas of Cambodia as bases and sanctuaries, but at that point these forces were largely self-sufficient. Sihanouk was aware of their presence but chose to do nothing because Cambodian relations with Saigon were then decidedly unfriendly. And beginning in 1965, Sihanouk tacitly acquiesced in the use of the Cambodian port of Sihanoukville by North Vietnam for shipments of arms to the Viet Cong in the border areas, allowing a major buildup in Communist forces threatening Saigon and the Mekong Delta. Arms offloaded in Sihanoukville and rice purchased on the Cambodian open market were shipped in Cambodian army and commercial trucks to Viet Cong bases in the border areas.[23]

But in the late 1960s, Sihanouk began to have second thoughts. He objected to the presence of North Vietnamese regular army units on Cambodian territory, and he was becoming fearful that the indigenous Communist Khmer Rouge could threaten his regime. He publicly expressed indifference should the U.S. bomb Communist bases in Cambodian border areas, saying that so long as no Cambodians were killed, he would regard it as a nonincident.[24] This was how the incoming Nixon administration found the situation in January 1969.

Although the DRV had ostensibly agreed to desist from attacks on South Vietnam cities in return for a bombing moratorium, in early 1969 the MACV detected a buildup of enemy forces, indicating that the Communists planned to lose no time in testing the new administration. Since bombing of North Vietnam was now closed off, General Abrams proposed to retaliate by bombing the Cambodian sanctuaries, and when the Communists launched the anticipated offensive on February 23, Nixon approved the first B-52 raid which was carried out March 18.[25] This and subsequent raids in what became a regular bombing program by B-52s against Viet Cong and PAVN bases in Cambodia were never publicly acknowledged by the administration for two reasons: first, such an acknowledgment would have given Sihanouk little alternative but to protest and demand an end to the raids; and second, the administration hoped to avert the public outcry such an announcement was certain to generate. Inevitably, the fact of the raids became known when an article appeared May 9 on page one of the *New York Times* in which unidentified Nixon administration sources (leaks) said that B-52s in recent weeks had raided several enemy supply areas and base camps in Cambodia for the first time but that Cambodia had made no protests. Articles appeared in several other print media over the next two months, but Sihanouk chose to keep silent. Instead, he elected to pursue rapprochement with the U.S., and diplomatic relations were reestablished in July.[26] Ironically, Hanoi could say nothing because to do so would be an admission that PAVN forces were present on Cambodian territory. As expected, the press reports raised a furor among the antiwar activists who were outraged that Nixon was "widening the war" and the U.S. was "attacking" a small, neutral country. This act by the "madman" in the White House was especially infuriating to the antiwar forces because it indicated he might be impervious to their pressures, and the Cambodian bombings were added to the liberals' already extensive collection of anti–Nixon lore under the pejorative "secret" label.[27] But the administration was unmoved, the raids continued, and Hanoi had learned its first lesson on the personality differences between Johnson and Nixon.

Vietnamization

Along with cessation of bombing north of the 20th parallel and leveling off of U.S. ground forces, the other major decision that came out of the March 1968 review of the war strategy by the Clifford task force was to "de–Americanize" the war by shifting an increasing share of the responsibility to the Vietnamese armed forces. The term "Vietnamization" was strongly resented by the South Vietnamese who, in considering the death and destruction that had been visited upon their country over the previous 10 years, believed the war had been "Vietnamized" from the outset. In fact, from 1955 when the U.S. assumed responsibility from the French for the training and equipping of the South Vietnamese armed forces until 1965 when deployment of U.S. combat troops began, the objective of the U.S. military presence all along had been "Vietnamization," i.e., to prepare the republic to defend itself from North Vietnam.

In early 1966, with over 200,000 American troops in country, Westmoreland assumed the tactical offensive in large-unit, search-and-destroy operations and the MACV effectively took control of the ground war. From this point until mid–1968 when General Abrams was instructed to restart the upgrading of the ARVN, the training and equipping of South Vietnamese forces had been decidedly secondary to the war being fought by the Americans. Although the MACV had continued to assign military advisors to ARVN units, the heavy needs of U.S. forces for equipment and logistical support brought a downgrading of priorities for the ARVN. The two armies, separate in all things, were in effect competing for resources which though plentiful, were still finite, and the ARVN always came out second best. Thus, three years of what might be called benign neglect had passed when the Johnson administration, seeking a way to disengage, adopted the new strategy of rebuilding the ARVN.

In his memoirs, Westmoreland referred to his efforts to improve ARVN capabilities through joint operations with American units, but the nature of his comments leads one to conclude that he did not place high importance on this activity. He attributed the shortage of equipment for the ARVN to "the President's policy of guns and butter — but mainly butter" and stated it was well into 1968 before new items were available in any quantity for the ARVN.[28] By the end of March 1968 President Johnson had concluded that "de–Americanizing" the war was a good idea, but though Clifford told President Thieu very bluntly in July 1968 that this was now American policy,[29] through the remainder of Johnson's term little was done beyond lip service to formally implement such a policy. According to Westmoreland, Deputy Secretary of Defense Paul Nitze acting for Clifford "vetoed the engineer and logistical troops and their equipment that were essential if the ARVN was to ... support itself."[30]

With the first months of the incoming Nixon administration devoted to evaluating policy options, it was not until May 1969 that Vietnamization was formally adopted as policy, and Thieu was so informed by Nixon at the June 8 Midway Island meeting when the first troop withdrawals were also announced.[31] In July, General Abrams, the successor to Westmoreland, received a new mission statement from Washington, effective August 15, which focused on strengthening the Vietnamese armed forces, supporting pacification efforts and reducing the flow of supplies to the enemy. Significantly, defeating the enemy and forcing his withdrawal from South Vietnam were not a part of the new statement.[32]

An illustration of the state of the ARVN in mid–1969 was the fact that all but one of its regular infantry divisions were still equipped with M-1 rifles and carbines of World War II vintage while it had to engage the VC which had superior firepower from modern AK-47 assault rifles.[33] (By 1967 all U.S. forces were equipped with the new M-16 assault rifle.) While Westmoreland implies otherwise, it appears no ARVN infantry divisions were equipped with M-16s before the Tet Offensive.[34]

As late as mid–1962 the Republic of Vietnam Armed Forces (RVNAF), including the ARVN plus small naval and air forces numbered only 150,000, a figure limited by the funds the U.S. was willing to make available. This strength was augmented by the poorly armed and organized militia, i.e., the Civil Guard and the Self Defense Corps. After McNamara approved an increase in financial support, by the fall of 1964 the RVNAF had grown to 230,000 with some 270,000 in the province-level Regional Forces and village-level Popular Forces, the new names for the Civil Guard and Self Defense Corps. At that point, all Vietnamese males between the ages of 20 and 45 were eligible for military service.[35]

Three years later, at the end of 1967, South Vietnamese regular forces had climbed to 343,000 with 300,000 in the Regional and Popular Forces.[36] By then the militia (Regional and Popular Forces) were uniformed, and with better training and arms, some RF and PF units fought very effectively during Tet.

The Tet Offensive had the effect of rallying the South Vietnamese people behind the government to the extent that Thieu was able to decree general mobilization, a step that he had hitherto shied away from for political reasons. Draft age was lowered from 20 to 18 and Thieu announced an increase of 135,000 men to the armed forces.[37] Even more significant was his decision to arm the civilian population in the newly created People's Self Defense Forces which by 1969 numbered some 400,000. The RVNAF by this time had reached about 400,000.[38] Thus by 1970, South Vietnam had over 1 million men under arms.

Prior to Vietnamization, ARVN divisions were essentially lightly armed infantry forces without the full depth of supporting arms that are normally an integral part of U.S. infantry divisions, so in addition to the basics like M-16s, the ARVN would need additional artillery, armored cavalry, signal, engineer, medical and other support units and the training to use the new equipment, and all of this had to be supplied on a crash basis beginning in mid–1969. As U.S. troops were withdrawn, new equipment became available for the ARVN, but training was the most critical problem, considering that it had to be conducted in the midst of a war which usually did not permit taking units out of the line. Those wasted years were coming back to haunt the Americans.

General Creighton W. Abrams

After four years as COMUSMACV, Westmoreland was due for a move, but when President Johnson announced his recall to Washington as army chief of staff, there was gleeful murmuring in the media that he was being kicked upstairs because of Tet. Although he had persistently attempted to cultivate the media, perhaps for that reason Westmoreland was never popular with the Saigon press corps, but even worse, he had no credibility with them[39]. In this respect, the contrast between Westmoreland and his successor Abrams could hardly have been greater. Where the cool, precise Westmoreland was ever conscious of projecting a certain image, the volatile and ebullient Abrams was completely indifferent to media reactions to his persona. He did not cultivate the press, and as usually happens, they admired him for it. Also, the media approved of the changes Abrams made in the way the U.S. fought the war, giving credit which under careful analysis was not always due him. Thus, in contrast to Westmoreland, Abrams received generally favorable treatment from the Saigon press corps and retrospectively from most post–Vietnam writers.[40]

Like Westmoreland, Abrams was a West Pointer, class of 1936, but where Westmoreland chose artillery, Abrams chose cavalry and when that branch was phased out, he fought World War II in Patton's armored forces, coming out of the war as one of the army's most highly decorated officers. He had no combat command in Korea, serving there in 1954 as a corps chief of staff. Like Westmoreland, he was on the army's fast track, but Westmoreland always got his stars a little ahead of Abrams. In early 1964, Lieutenant General Abrams had been on the short list along with Westmoreland to replace General Harkins in Saigon, but Abrams, through his outspoken dislike of paratroopers, had created a critical disadvantage for himself — Gen. Maxwell Taylor, chairman of the JCS and an airborne man, was doing the picking. Abrams became a full general and army vice chief of staff in September 1964, a few months after Westmoreland had reached that level as COMUSMACV. Once Westmoreland had been selected, both Wheeler and McNamara pushed Abrams for the job of deputy COMUSMACV, but Westmoreland had other ideas and was allowed his choice.[41] Later, in May 1967 when Abrams was sent out as his deputy, Westmoreland was given little choice in the matter, but he was not pleased for it was obvious that Abrams was to be his successor, and no one cares to have his successor looking over his shoulder.[42]

While Abrams, as noted above, has received almost universally favorable treatment from writers in contrast to the generally critical treatment given Westmoreland, in fairness to the latter, it should be pointed out that when Abrams took over in June 1968, the circumstances of the war, both political and military, had changed dramatically over the previous six months. First, it was clear that there would be no further escalation in the U.S. commitment in Vietnam. While Westmoreland knew that to achieve the original goal of clearing the Viet Cong and PAVN from South Vietnam would require the additional forces that he had consistently requested, Abrams now knew that those additional forces would not be made available, making it highly unlikely that he could ever go over to the strategic offensive. He also knew that the U.S. hoped to negotiate its way out of Vietnam in the Paris talks which had begun the previous month and that a political compromise was a likely outcome of the war. And he knew that South Vietnam would have to assume greater responsibility for the war. Also, he took over at a point when the Viet Cong had largely shot their bolt in the 1968 Tet and mini–Tet offensives and would never again be the threat they once were. These were conditions that had not obtained through Westmoreland's tenure.

Within a year of Abrams' mid-1968 takeover of the MACV, the new Nixon administration made explicit a policy of pacification, Vietnamization, unilateral withdrawal of troops and negotiating a political settlement, leaving nothing ambiguous in the strategy Abrams would need to follow in contrast to Westmoreland who consistently received mixed signals from Washington.

Westmoreland had hardly been gone from Saigon a week before Abrams gave the order to close the Khe Sanh outpost. The swiftness of the decision strongly implied a basic difference between the two over the usefulness of that base and portended other changes to come in the way Abrams would run the war.[43] A major change was the shift away from conducting large-unit search-and-destroy operations to small-unit patrolling nearer the more populated areas. His admirers credit Abrams with making a deliberate decision to adopt these tactics when in reality it was in response to a change in Communist tactics. The abortive February–March 1969 offensive, coming after the disastrous losses in 1968 from Tet and the mini–Tets, had caused Hanoi to reevaluate its strategy. The heavy losses combined with Nixon's June 1969 announcement of the first troop withdrawals brought a decision by Hanoi to go over to guerrilla warfare, preserve and reequip its forces and wait.[44] Accordingly, Communist main force units were largely withdrawn to the sanctuaries in Cambodia and Laos, and with no main force units to engage, Abrams shifted to small-unit tactics with emphasis on support of pacification.

An indication that Abrams' changes were more form than substance was the fighting in May 1969 in the A Shau Valley in the northern border area near Laos. In this battle, known infamously as the Battle of Hamburger Hill, six battalions of the 101st Airborne, in several days of fighting, were able to take a PAVN position (Hill 937) with losses in the engagement of 56 killed to 610 of the enemy. After holding the position briefly, the U.S. forces were withdrawn, leaving the impression that the objective had no real value and setting off a furor in Congress and among antiwar groups.[45] As will be seen, Abrams was also a strong advocate of the Cambodian incursion in 1970. So, although his admirers in the media and elsewhere credit Abrams with sweeping changes from Westmoreland's approach, in fact Abrams, while he still had adequate combat forces at his disposal, was quite prepared to slug it out with Viet Cong and PAVN main forces in tactics that were much the same as Westmoreland's,[46] and as a result, American deaths in Abrams' first full year as MACV (1969) were about the same as they were in Westmoreland's last full year (1967).[47] But as troops available to him dwindled, by the end of 1970 Abrams' discretionary ability to launch aggressive attacks on main force enemy units had become limited.

Thus, as Westmoreland presided over the American buildup in Vietnam, so Abrams presided over the drawdown. In the last major fighting while Abrams was COMUSMACV, the 1972 North Vietnamese Easter Offensive, few American combat troops remained in Vietnam, and the ARVN bore the brunt of the fighting.

Pacification

Ngo Dinh Diem knew precisely what he was doing when in the spring of 1962 he launched the strategic hamlet program aimed at seizing the political initiative from the Viet Cong in the villages while providing security to the rural population. The resident western journalists and other "experts" failed to grasp the rightness and timeliness of Diem's concept and derided the program as inappropriate for Vietnam and another example of the alleged incompetence of the Diem regime. With Diem's death, the "tyrant's" program was quickly dismantled, but over the next three and a half years, successive governments were never able to devise anything else which had the promise of strategic hamlets. Instead, there was a chaotic succession of new programs: New Life Hamlets, Hop Tac, Peoples Action Teams, Census-Grievance teams, Armed Propaganda Teams, and more, but through it all, pacification remained a stepchild of the government of Vietnam, the MACV and the embassy. All this would change with the entry on the scene of Robert Komer.

As described earlier, Robert W. Komer was sent to Vietnam by Johnson in the spring of 1967 to head a new pacification organization called Civil Operations and Revolutionary Development Support (CORDS) which consolidated under the MACV the previously fragmented American efforts in this area. Probably no American who played a major role in Vietnam was more controversial than the abrasive Komer, known as "Blowtorch" for his aggressive, hard-driving style. From March 1967 until he returned to the U.S. in November 1968 he had as his deputy William Colby of the CIA. The bespectacled, pipe-smoking Colby, whose air of a college professor contrasted sharply with Komer, was a CIA professional who had been station chief in Saigon from 1959 to 1962. Succeeding Komer, Colby served as CORDS head until he returned to the U.S. in early 1971.[48]

Westmoreland had always paid lip service to the importance of pacification, but until the program was placed under his control in 1967, he had done little to support American civilian efforts in that area. President Johnson's sudden interest in pacification as evidenced by his dispatching of Komer, his hand-picked special assistant, to be Westmoreland's deputy indicated to the latter that it would be expedient to make sure Komer got the backing he needed from MACV. Going in, Komer understood that security was the prerequisite to the success of pacification, and thus he arranged for CORDS to assume responsibility for the support and training of the Regional and Popular Forces and launched a program to upgrade their training and arms.[49] Later, after Tet, when Thieu created the People's Self Defense Forces, CORDS also assisted in arming and training it.

By the end of 1967, Komer had created and staffed a mixed organization of senior U.S. military and foreign service officers as senior provincial advisors and more junior district advisors as counterparts to the Vietnamese province chiefs and district chiefs respectively. Eventually CORDS had a staff of 6,000 Americans.[50] A Hamlet Evaluation System (HES) devised earlier by the CIA was used to rate the degree of Communist penetration in each of the roughly 2,500 hamlets, and this was used as a guide to direct the efforts of the district teams in coordination with the Regional and Popular Forces.[51]

Komer had hardly gotten his organization in place and functioning when the Viet Cong launched the Tet Offensive, bringing widespread chaos and destruction and creating a flood of refugees. It was a major setback for CORDS as its teams and resources had to be diverted to aiding the refugees and rebuilding the damage wrought by the fighting. Thus, pacification was at a standstill through most of 1968, but Komer and Colby, realizing the Viet Cong's political infrastructure had been badly weakened by Tet casualties, saw an opportunity to make major gains in pacification. This was the genesis of the Accelerated Pacification Campaign, a three-month blitz launched November 1 to bring 1,000 hamlets from an HES rating of "contested" to a relatively "secure" state with priority given to the Mekong Delta.[52] It succeeded, and following the APC, pacification finally began to make progress.

Overall, CORDS was probably the best example in the years of American involvement in South Vietnam of successful cooperation between Americans and Vietnamese. In the heavily populated Mekong Delta region (Military Region IV) where beginning as early as 1959 one could not travel the main roads without an armed escort, by late 1970 the situation had been almost completely reversed.[53] The same could be said of MR III north of Saigon while in the more thinly populated northern regions (MRs II and I) nearer the DMZ, the Viet Cong influence remained fairly strong. When he left Vietnam in 1971, Colby believed with good reason that the pacification battle had been all but won.

The Phoenix Program

The most controversial aspect of Colby's work with CORDS was the Phoenix Program. The program, initiated by a Thieu decree in late 1967 but set aside by the Tet Offensive, was reactivated by Colby as part of the APC.[54] Phoenix was essentially an intelligence program to identify members of the Viet Cong Infrastructure (VCI) and then to encourage them to rally to the government, to capture them or as a last resort, to use force to eliminate them. Colby provided U.S. military advisors at the district level to train and advise Phoenix teams made up entirely of Vietnamese police, military personnel and civilians. By pooling intelligence from a variety of South Vietnamese agencies, Phoenix succeeded in identifying and eliminating thousands of VCI cadres. Colby stated in testimony before a congressional committee in 1971 that since mid–1968 Phoenix "had brought about the capture of some 28,978 Communist leaders in the VCI, that some 17,717 had taken advantage of the amnesty program, and that some 20,587 had been reported as killed."[55]

The effectiveness of any program conducted against the Communists could always be measured by the volume and shrillness of the outcry it generated among the left-wing antiwar elements in the U.S. who took their cue from the international socialist bloc. Thus, only the bombing of the north outstripped the Phoenix Program in the intensity of the propaganda effort to get it stopped, usually through allegations of American complicity in corruption, brutality, blackmail and murder.[56] Many Americans were persuaded by this line including some journalists who discounted the effectiveness of Phoenix, but in interviews after the war, North Vietnamese officials made no secret of the severe damage inflicted on the VCI by Phoenix.[57]

The Raids into the Cambodian Sanctuaries

Though the U.S. had never been happy with Sihanouk's dalliance with Communist China, Kissinger regarded Sihanouk's delicately balanced neutrality as "the best attainable situation" for Cambodia.[58] Sihanouk resented the presence of PAVN and Viet Cong forces on his territory but did not have the military strength to expel them, and he had not objected to the U.S. bombing which was continuing. After the restoration of U.S.-Cambodian diplomatic relations in July 1969, a small mission was established in Phnom Penh, but largely at the request of Senator Mansfield, no CIA personnel were assigned to it.[59]

Thus, when Sihanouk departed in January 1970 for Europe for his biennial cure, leaving Prime Minister Gen. Lon Nol in charge, neither Sihanouk nor the U.S. had any inkling of the dramatic events that would soon upset the precarious equilibrium that had prevailed in Cambodia. In early March, after nationalist student demonstrations in Phnom Penh against North Vietnam and the Viet Cong, including the sacking of their embassies, the Cambodian parliament announced the suspension of a trade agreement with North Vietnam and a 10,000-man expansion of the Cambodian army, and the Cambodian Foreign Ministry notified the North Vietnamese and Viet Cong embassies that their armed forces were to be out of Cambodia by March 15.[60] Clearly, Sihanouk's modus vivendi with the Communists was being dismantled in his absence.

Meanwhile, in Paris, Sihanouk, instead of returning directly to Phnom Penh to reassert control, announced he would return via Moscow and Peking where, ostensibly, he would attempt to enlist the support of the two governments in obtaining the departure of the Communist forces from his territory. But while in Moscow, on March 18 Sihanouk was deposed by the Cambodian parliament. A figurehead chief of state was named, but real power was held by Prime Minister Lon Nol, who continued in office. Sihanouk continued on to Beijing where he took up residence. The Nixon administration denied it had any role whatever in these events, and though at the time some skeptics doubted this, with the passage of over 30 years, no one has yet produced evidence of U.S. involvement. Notwithstanding, Sihanouk, from his perch in Beijing, turned violently against the U.S., blaming the CIA for his overthrow and aligning himself with the DRV, which pledged its support to overthrow the Lon Nol regime.[61] Almost immediately the new Lon Nol government closed the port of Sihanoukville to the Communists. In early April, the Communist forces in the base areas of eastern Cambodia began a drive west toward Phnom Penh against an overmatched Cambodian army, and very quickly the Communists occupied all of eastern Cambodia and were threatening Phnom Penh.[62] The political and logistical advantages to the Communists from a victory in Cambodia would almost certainly bring about the collapse of South Vietnam. Nixon memoed Kissinger on April 22: "We must do something symbolic to help him [Lon Nol] survive."[63]

In the event, Nixon's actions were more than symbolic. Against the advice of Laird and Rogers but with the support of Kissinger, Helms (CIA), Abrams, Bunker and Thieu, he approved ground attacks into the Cambodian sanctuaries by U.S. and ARVN troops. On April 29, ARVN forces moved into the Parrot's Beak, an area of Cambodia that projected to within 32 miles of Saigon, followed two days later by a joint U.S.-ARVN attack into the Fish Hook area north of Parrot's Beak. Resistance was not heavy, and by May 3 the enemy had retreated west, abandoning his bunkers and stockpiles of supplies to the Allies. Vast amounts of materiel were captured: 23,000 individual weapons, 2,500 crew-served weapons, over 16 million rounds of small-arms ammunition, 7,000 tons of rice and much more along with tons of enemy documents. In an operation that lasted two months, the U.S. lost 338 killed and 1,525 wounded, a lower casualty rate than earlier major search-and-destroy operations, while total Communist losses were estimated at some 13,000 killed or captured.[64]

No single operation of the entire war dealt the Communists a more devastating blow than the raids into the Cambodian sanctuaries. The capture of huge quantities of materiel and rice and the destruction of facilities coupled with the closing off of the port of Sihanoukville (renamed Kompong Som), were a disaster for the Communists which set back the North Vietnamese offensive timetable by at least 12 and possibly as much as 24 months.[65] The time gained was vital to the Vietnamization program. The Allied attacks on what was in effect the rear areas of the Communist drive toward Phnom Penh lessened the pressure on the Cambodian Army, giving it time to regroup. The raids shocked the Communists who were confident, based on Johnson's policies, that their sanctuaries were immune from attack, and it demonstrated again the disturbing unpredictability of the new man in the White House.

Nixon's decision to launch the Cambodian incursions was a courageous one, made in the full knowledge that it would trigger a huge uproar from domestic antiwar groups. When the news broke on April 29 that ARVN forces had entered Cambodia the clamor began with dovish senators demanding that Nixon disavow South Vietnam's action, but it reached new heights of fury with his speech on April 30 announcing U.S. participation in the incursions. The liberal media quickly labeled it an "escalation" and a "widening of the war"[66] in the reasoning that it was acceptable for the PAVN and Viet Cong to use neutral Cambodia as a sanctuary but not acceptable to enter Cambodia to attack those same forces there. But what was most galling to the antiwar elements was that they had not been able to intimidate Nixon as they had Johnson.

On April 20 Nixon had announced the largest troop withdrawal yet, 150,000 over the next year. These withdrawal announcements had been undercutting support for the antiwar movement,[67] but the Cambodian crisis gave it new life, and the tragic event of May 4 at Kent State University when four students were killed by panicked National Guardsmen became forever linked with Nixon's decision to invade Cambodia. The domestic crisis reached such proportions that in an attempt to calm it, Nixon announced limitations in the depth and duration of the Cambodian operation to 30 kilometers and a withdrawal of U.S. forces by June 30.[68]

The Cambodian incursion also triggered some of the first serious attempts in the Senate to legislate U.S. policy on Indochina. The Cooper-Church amendment, proposing to prohibit the extension of military aid to and U.S. military activities in Cambodia after June 30, was approved by a 58–37 vote but failed of passage in the House. This was followed by the more sweeping McGovern-Hatfield amendment which would have ended U.S. involvement in the Indochina war altogether simply by cutting off funds after December 31, 1971. It was eventually defeated 55–39.[69] While these early legislative efforts failed, by dramatizing U.S. political disunity they encouraged Communist negotiating intransigence.

The Raid into Laos

At the end of 1970, U.S. troop withdrawals had reached 200,000 with another 60,000 scheduled to leave in the next four months. From a peak of about 545,000 in early 1969, by April 1971 nearly half would have been withdrawn, and following his practice of announcing a new withdrawal as the last one was completed, Nixon was preparing another announcement for April. (On April 7, 1971, he announced that another 100,000 would leave by December 1, leaving 184,000 in Vietnam.[70]) In the 18 months since its formal launch, Vietnamization had made good progress, but just how much progress was about to be tested by a major operation in 1971. The Cambodian incursions of 1970 had put the Viet Cong and PAVN forces in the Cambodian border areas in serious disarray and had bought months of respite from major Communist attacks in the southern Military Regions III and IV. In the Central Highlands of MR II and MR I along the DMZ, however, where Communist supply lines were shorter and pacification had been less successful, the military situation remained threatening. The Rolling Thunder air campaign had ended November 1, 1968, and while the U.S. had never ceased air attacks on the Laotian infiltration trails, they had not succeeded in interdicting the flow of men and equipment, and thus the Communists had been able to build large stockpiles of materiel in Laos adjoining MRs I and II and across the DMZ.

Kissinger and his staff in Washington and the MACV in Saigon believed these conditions made a major Communist offensive into northern South Vietnam inevitable in early 1972. Given the success of the Cambodian raids, American civilian and military planners concluded that a similar raid into Laos in 1971 could preempt the anticipated Communist offensive, disrupt the Ho Chi Minh Trail which, since the closure of the port of Sihanoukville, was now North Vietnam's sole means of supplying its forces in the South, and give Vietnamization precious additional time. The one major difference from the 1970 Cambodian raids was that Congressional action had now barred the use of U.S. ground forces in Laos and Cambodia so that the operation, called Lam Son 719, would have to be conducted solely by the ARVN with U.S. air support. The plan that evolved was in two phases: in Phase I, U.S. and ARVN troops would drive west along Route 9 paralleling the DMZ to reopen the old Khe Sanh base in the northwest corner of South Vietnam. This would be the jumping-off point for Phase II in which ARVN troops would attack into Laos along the axis of Route 9 with the objective of disrupting the enemy's lines of communications and destroying stockpiles of materiel centering around the town of Tchepone, an important junction of the Ho Chi Minh Trail about 38 kilometers inside Laos. It was intended that the attack be a protracted raid with ARVN forces remaining in Laos for perhaps up to three months, but there was no intention to occupy this area of Laos permanently. In the event, ARVN forces were in Laos for 44 days, reaching Tchepone which they held briefly, but the capture and destruction of Communist stockpiles never approached the successes of the 1970 Cambodian operation.[71]

It is not necessary here to describe the tactical details of what proved to be a highly controversial and less than successful operation. In *The White House Years*,[72] Kissinger assumed the role of military expert in his criticism of the planning and execution of the operation, claiming that he foresaw the weaknesses which the JCS and MACV allegedly overlooked and viewing it as a semi-disaster. In *A Better War*,[73] Lewis Sorley, who does have a military background and was clearly not inclined to criticize Abrams, gave a more favorable judgment but did not claim the operation met its objectives. Though no longer chief U.S. intelligence officer in Vietnam at the time of Lam Son 719, Gen. Phillip Davidson was well qualified to critique the operation. His analysis, in *Vietnam at War*,[74] concluded that the operation was badly conceived, even more poorly executed and was little short of a military disaster. As outlined in these sources, there were several reasons for the failure. First, security was so poor that tactical surprise was completely lost. A news embargo clamped on Phase I in Saigon was so riddled with leaks that a page one *New York Times* article on February 1 stated that State and Defense Department officials had refused for the third consecutive day to comment on speculation that an allied attack across the Laotian border was imminent or under way and reported a Viet Cong radio announcement that South Vietnamese troops were about to invade Laos. Similar speculative articles continued to appear through the first week of February until Phase II was actually launched on February 8.[75]

Aside from extremely poor security prior to the operation, a more fundamental weakness was that the ARVN forces, totaling about 17,000 of Thieu's best troops, were not strong enough for the task at hand. Lam Son 719 was a thrust into North Vietnam's vital logistical lifeline for the entire war, so unlike Cambodia, resistance in Laos was fierce from four PAVN infantry divisions, a reinforced tank regiment, several regiments of artillery and other forces that were available in the general area, altogether totaling 40,000 troops.[76] A 1967 MACV plan (never approved by Johnson) for an operation into the same area of Laos called for the use of *four American* divisions.[77]

The official U.S. Army After-Action Report showed enemy killed in action at 19,360 and combined ARVN and American casualties at 9,065 (215 U.S. and 1,764 ARVN killed in action).[78] The ARVN, in its first major offensive operation without U.S. advisors, showed it had indeed progressed, considering that two years earlier the MACV would never have dreamed of attempting such an operation with ARVN troops alone. Still, in the judgment of American military observers, Lam Son 719 demonstrated that the ARVN in 1971, even with plentiful U.S. air support, was not ready to take on the PAVN. While the Laotian operation may have temporarily disrupted Communist logistical arrangements, it did not forestall the Easter Offensive one year later.

On February 3, before the operation had even started, *The New York Times* was already editorializing against it: "South Vietnamese drive into Laos would have profound implications for future of war, none of them encouraging for prospect of American disengagement.... Vietnamizing Cambodia and Laos will not speed the withdrawal of American troops from Vietnam ... best hope for restoring neutrality of Cambodia and Laos lies in moving more positively than Nixon Administration has yet done toward political solution in South Vietnam...."[79] Of course, the *Times* and Nixon's other critics were completely oblivious to the ongoing secret negotiations between Kissinger and Le Duc Tho.

Negotiations II

Convinced that the plenary sessions of the Paris peace talks had little prospect for real progress in achieving a settlement, in June 1969 Kissinger invited the North Vietnamese to begin private and secret talks in Paris.[80] His initiative was accepted by the DRV, and the first private meeting took place in Paris on August 4, 1969, between Kissinger and Xuan Thuy, a representative of the DRV foreign ministry who Kissinger soon realized was a functionary with no negotiating authority. Although the meeting was inconclusive, it did open a channel for future communications through the U.S. defense attaché in Paris, Gen. Vernon Walters. Within the administration, knowledge of the existence of the private talks was held to a very small group.

In late November, Kissinger instructed Walters to request another meeting which after considerable delay was granted by Hanoi for February 21, 1970, but this time Kissinger's interlocutor would be Le Duc Tho, a veteran Communist and close ally of Le Duan in the DRV Politburo. Thus began the long series of secret meetings between Kissinger and Le Duc Tho which culminated in the 1973 cease-fire agreement. The February 21 meeting was followed by others on March 16 and April 4 in which Tho never wavered from the position of demanding total and unconditional U.S. withdrawal from Vietnam and replacement of the Thieu regime by one acceptable to the Communists. This first series of talks ended with Tho's statement that unless the U.S. *changed its position*, there was nothing more to discuss.[81]

From the very beginning of the drawn-out negotiations that continued through Nixon's first term, the underlying sticking point was his refusal to acquiesce in the Communists' demand to replace the Thieu regime with one acceptable to them. If early in the negotiations Nixon had opted to sell out Thieu, given that a U.S. military withdrawal was already underway, a peace agreement might have been reached perhaps as early as 1970, and certainly, there was no lack of encouragement from the liberal left (Clifford, Harriman, et al.) to do exactly that. But Nixon believed that preserving American prestige and the integrity of our guarantee and preserving a non–Communist regime in Saigon were not separable, and to acquiesce in dismantling a government we had supported for so long or to force South Vietnam to accept a role for Hanoi's surrogates in a "compromise" coalition would be read by the non–Communist world as a clear defeat for America.[82] In this, Nixon's analysis was undoubtedly correct.

The indefatigable Kissinger asked for another meeting which was held September 7 with Xuan Thuy, indicating that the DRV would have nothing new to offer. At this meeting Kissinger reiterated the earlier offer for withdrawal, this time stating that "no residual forces, bases *or advisors* would be left behind"[83] (emphasis added). This was an entirely gratuitous concession for which the U.S. received nothing in return, and thus what would have been an extremely valuable bargaining chip in later stages was thrown away. Following the pattern of these negotiations, it was pocketed by the Communists without reciprocation. At this point, the U.S. was still calling for mutual withdrawals, but the ongoing unilateral U.S. withdrawals were making this position meaningless.

Another meeting was set for September 27, but before it was held, on September 17 Madame Nguyen Thi Binh, "foreign minister" of the Provisional Revolutionary Government (PRG),[84] made public a new eight-point peace program. It called for complete U.S. withdrawal by June 30, 1971, at which point the Thieu government would be replaced by a provisional coalition acceptable to the Communists which would then negotiate a final settlement with the PRG. Only with the acceptance of this proposal by the U.S. would Hanoi then be prepared to discuss the release of U.S. prisoners of wars, and a separate U.S.-Hanoi cease-fire would take effect only after the U.S. had agreed to these conditions.[85] Domestic antiwar elements were quick to criticize the Nixon administration for not taking up this program which they regarded as quite reasonable. After a fruitless September 27 meeting, no further secret talks took place until the following May.

Nixon responded in an October 7 speech in which he proposed a standstill cease-fire, an end to U.S. bombing throughout Indochina and an international conference to bring peace to all of Indochina and promised to abide by the outcome of the agreed political process to determine the future government of South Vietnam. The speech was well received on all sides in the U.S., but the next day Xuan Thuy publicly rejected the Nixon proposals.[86] Unfazed by North Vietnam's intransigence, Nixon's critics quickly began demanding new concessions to Hanoi including a preposterous *unilateral* cease-fire by the U.S.,[87] but in Hanoi, where public opinion did not weigh in the balance, the government had only to wait patiently for the American political process to do its work.

Kissinger, for his part, did not have the luxury of waiting. With Nixon's approval, he prepared a new seven-point proposal[88] which he presented to Xuan Thuy as a "final offer" on May 31, 1971. In this proposal the U. S. made a key concession by stating its willingness to set a terminal date for withdrawal but not explicitly requiring *mutual* withdrawals. Instead, it proposed that the Indochinese people should discuss among themselves the withdrawal of "all other outside forces." It proposed a cease-fire in place under international supervision to be effective when final U.S. withdrawal began and no further infiltration of outside forces into the countries of Indochina. And it stipulated that the release of POWs would be completed at least two months before the completion of final U.S. withdrawal. The May 31 proposal was a major concession in that it did not require the withdrawal of North Vietnamese forces from South Vietnam while agreeing to the complete withdrawal of U.S. forces. For the first time, the U.S. proposal was not rejected out of hand, and the fact that Tho would attend the next meeting on June 26 indicated possible interest on the part of the DRV.

Two events occurred in June which impinged indirectly on the negotiations, one with potentially positive implications, the other with clearly negative effects. The first was the receipt on June 2 of the definitive Chinese invitation for Kissinger to make his secret trip to Peking in July which led to Nixon's triumphal visit to China the following February.[89] The other was the publication of the Pentagon Papers, which amplified dissension in America over the Vietnam War and certainly did nothing to discourage Hanoi from its strategy of waiting until U.S. domestic pressures forced a cave-in to its demands.

In the first hopeful sign that some progress was being made, at the June 26 meeting Le Duc Tho introduced a new nine-point proposal.[90] The points pertaining to the military side, i.e., U.S. withdrawal, cease-fire in place, return of POWs, either matched U.S. proposals or where differences existed, Kissinger believed they were negotiable, but on the political side, Hanoi's wording was either very ambiguous or outright unacceptable. Still, Kissinger regarded the proposal as a major step forward and planned as a next step to work toward a merger of the two documents. But again the Americans failed to reckon on the duplicity of their adversary for on July 1 Madame Binh made public a new seven-point proposal which was only partly congruent with Tho's secret proposal of a week earlier.[91] Madame Binh then granted interviews to antiwar journalists and legislators, including Senator George McGovern, creating a clamor in the media and Congress that Nixon should seize the offer of the Binh proposal.[92] (But Nixon's critics on the left were thoroughly deflated by his July 15 speech announcing his planned visit to China, growing out of Kissinger's secret trip there.) The Binh proposal crystallized a belief that had been growing with Kissinger that the secret nature of his talks with Tho was working to the disadvantage of the U.S. While he pursued negotiations in good faith with Tho unbeknownst to the media and the administration's antiwar critics, Hanoi was whipsawing Nixon and Kissinger with its public proposals designed to create domestic pressure on Nixon, but Nixon and Kissinger agreed for the time being to continue on the track of secret talks[93]

Further meetings were held with Tho on July 12 and 26 at which seven of Hanoi's nine points were effectively merged with the U.S. proposal, but in the end, the talks ran up against the key Communist political demand that the U.S. throw over the Thieu regime, a point which Kissinger firmly rejected. Thus, this series of talks ended with peace no closer, and no further private meetings were held until the following May.[94]

In the meantime, Congress was edging closer to legislating the U.S. withdrawal from Vietnam. The Senate was regularly passing variations of such amendments, but the House continued to reject them, albeit by steadily diminishing margins. Finally, on November 5, a Senate-House conference committee agreed on wording for the Mansfield Amendment which had previously passed the Senate in various versions. The agreed language stated it was the policy of the U.S. to require a termination of military operations and a prompt withdrawal from Indochina, subject to the release of all American POWs. Without giving deadlines, the amendment urged the president to set a date and negotiate a phased withdrawal tied to a phased release of the POWs.[95] In essence, this would be a withdrawal-for-prisoners deal which Le Duc Tho had already turned down, but given the secret nature of the negotiations Congress was unaware of this. The principal effect of the amendment was to encourage Hanoi's intransigence.

These events were the final straws that brought Nixon and Kissinger to recognize that going into an election year, they had to establish that the administration had done everything it could to negotiate a peace in Vietnam, and that therefore the record of the secret negotiations must be made public. This was done in a speech by Nixon on January 25, 1972, in which he also described a new U.S. proposal for a political settlement involving internationally supervised free elections with Communist participation and revealed Thieu's willingness to step down a month before the election.[96] Nixon's speech was well received by the media and temporarily silenced his stunned critics who would no longer be able to concoct "new" formulas for ending the war that had already been rejected by Hanoi, but in a matter of days, they were carping that Hanoi's rejection of U.S. proposals had been entirely the fault of the U.S. Harriman and Clifford had long cited Thieu as the principal obstacle to peace, and now others joined them in calling for the U.S. to dump the Thieu government as a means of meeting Hanoi's demands and reaching a settlement.[97]

Here matters stood as the U.S. entered the final year of its direct involvement in the Vietnam War.

The Easter Offensive

The previous major Communist offensive had begun in February 1969, a month after Nixon's inauguration, to test the new administration. Centered on Danang and Saigon, it had been fairly easily contained by U.S. and ARVN forces which inflicted heavy casualties on the main force VC units involved. If nothing else, the February 1969 offensive served to destroy any illusions in Washington that the Communists would show restraint based on the alleged understandings of the previous October when Johnson had halted the bombing of the North. The VC and PAVN forces had now conducted four major offensives since the beginning of 1968, and all had been turned back at a high cost in Communist casualties. Knowing they could not continue to absorb these losses, in mid–1969 the Politburo, as related earlier, shifted from a strategy of main force engagements to one of protracted warfare, reverting to the small-unit tactics of an earlier time and aimed at preserving their forces while continuing to inflict losses on the Americans.[98] With the Paris peace talks having started in January, this strategy meshed with their plan to draw out the negotiations, out-wait the Americans, and allow domestic antiwar pressures to force the U.S. to withdraw. In the meantime, North Vietnam could now build stockpiles of war materiel along the DMZ in complete security from American bombing attacks.

Thus, by the end of 1971, the Communist buildup had been going on for two and one-half years, and with the unceasing influx of Chinese and Soviet materiel, it was a certainty that the PAVN was now prepared for a major offensive. Unlike Tet and the other offensives of 1968–69, this one would be conducted almost entirely by regular North Vietnamese Army (PAVN) forces. It would be aimed at inflicting a decisive defeat on ARVN, thus revealing the failure of Vietnamization. Also, Hanoi had always tied military moves closely to political objectives, and given the stalemate in the Paris talks, U.S. troop withdrawals, and the impending American elections, 1972 would be the year for a final throw of the dice in a maximum effort at military victory that would defeat the ARVN, force the U.S. out of Vietnam, and enable the DRV to impose a settlement. Hanoi was counting on domestic opposition to tie Nixon's hands in responding to the offensive.

Ironically, in the same period of Communist buildup, the U.S. had been drawing down. Nixon's January 13 announcement of the withdrawal of another 70,000 troops by May 1 would leave about 69,000 aviation personnel and logistical troops. In early 1972 the last American combat battalion had left Vietnam.[99] Clearly, when the blow landed, it would have to be dealt with on the ground by ARVN forces, but U.S. tactical air, helicopters and B-52s would still be available. In fact, in anticipation of the Communist offensive, in January the U.S. began deploying additional air force tactical and B-52 aircraft and up to four navy aircraft carriers would be available in the South China Sea along with additional surface ships.[100]

By early 1972, Vietnamization had strengthened the ARVN so that it now fielded 11 infantry divisions, totaling 120 battalions, plus 58 artillery battalions, 19 armored battalions and the appropriate engineer, signal and other supporting arms. An airborne and a marine division and 21 ranger battalions formed the general reserve.[101] While this seemed a formidable army, it was spread thinly across the four military regions, and in an emergency it was very difficult to move an ARVN infantry division from its established operational area to another region due to the presence of dependents with the troops. In contrast, the PAVN had the classic military advantages of concentration of forces and tactical surprise from its jungle-covered sanctuaries in Laos and Cambodia and across the DMZ and was unencumbered by dependents.

On March 30 the anticipated offensive began with attacks across the DMZ and from Laos into northern Quang Tri Province. This was followed a day later by an attack into the Central Highlands of Military Region II and the next day by a third drive into Military Region III north of Saigon. Attacks were preceded by heavy artillery fire and employed large numbers of tanks. In straightforward conventional warfare, the fighting was the heaviest to date of the entire war, continuing into September.[102]

In Washington, the question of what should be the American response was debated among Nixon's top advisors. At this point, preparations were underway for a Nixon-Brezhnev summit scheduled for late May in Moscow, and key figures in the administration believed a strong U.S. military reaction to the offensive by Moscow's client state could jeopardize the summit. Nixon wanted the summit badly for its potential to improve U.S.–Soviet relations and to achieve his personal goal of being the first American president in Moscow. For their part, the Soviets had been badly nettled by Nixon's stunning visit to Peking in February and were now determined on having their own countervailing summit with the American president. Some of Nixon's advisors counseled caution, that nothing should jeopardize the summit, that the U.S. had done all it could in Vietnam, and that the outcome should now be left to a contest between North and South Vietnam. Nixon, however, believed that if Hanoi, a Soviet client state using Soviet-supplied arms, were allowed to impose its will on the U.S.-backed South, he could not ratify that humiliation of the U.S. by attending a summit in the Kremlin. Therefore, he was determined to use every means at his disposal short of reintroducing ground troops to help South Vietnam defeat the offensive, and if this caused the

Soviets to cancel the summit, so be it. Accordingly, he ordered massive reinforcements of U.S. air and naval forces in Southeast Asia.[103]

Meanwhile, Kissinger made sure Moscow was only too aware of U.S. anger over the Russian-supplied arms that had made the offensive possible, thus raising Soviet concern over the potential impact of the offensive on their much-desired summit. Hoping to smooth ruffled American feathers, they invited Nixon to send Kissinger on a secret trip to Moscow from April 20–24, ostensibly as a preliminary to the summit, but Nixon instructed Kissinger to use the trip to pressure the Soviets to make their client desist in its offensive. In *The White House Years*, Kissinger implies that he was able to influence Brezhnev et al. toward Nixon's purpose, but as events later showed, Moscow did little if anything to persuade Hanoi to rein in the offensive, and the USSR continued as the DRV's chief arms supplier through the end of the war.[104]

Before the Easter Offensive began, Kissinger had been engaged in exchanges with Hanoi over another secret meeting, but the other side delayed, and after it launched its offensive, the reason for the delay was transparent—Hanoi wanted the meeting to occur *while* it was conducting what it thought would be a decisive offensive. The Communist attack gave the U.S. all the pretext it needed to cancel the meeting, but Nixon wanted the onus for cancellation to be on Hanoi, and after further exchanges on a date, Le Duc Tho and Kissinger met in Paris on May 2. With the Communist offensive an apparent success, Tho was at his truculent worst, and the meeting accomplished nothing.[105]

This inconclusive and unpleasant meeting triggered Nixon's final decision to retaliate. In a May 8 speech to the American people he condemned the Communist offensive, cited American willingness to negotiate as evidenced by Kissinger's Moscow trip and the May 2 meeting, and announced, in view of the foregoing, his decision to renew bombing of military targets in the North and to mine the ports. He demanded an internationally supervised cease-fire in place (which would allow the Communists to hold on to areas they had gained by their offensive) and a return of U.S. prisoners after which the remaining 70,000 U.S. forces would be withdrawn within four months.[106] Hanoi had gambled that domestic antiwar pressures would prevent Nixon from renewing the bombing, and they expected even less that he would mine the ports, an action Johnson had repeatedly vetoed. The gamble against the unpredictable Nixon had not paid off.

In early April, Nixon had authorized tactical air strikes up to the 19th parallel, then later to the 20th parallel. His May 8 announcement was the beginning of the Operation Linebacker air campaign against North Vietnam which continued until progress in the negotiations brought a halt on October 23, 1972, to all air operations north of the 20th parallel. Linebacker was conducted with far fewer restrictions than Rolling Thunder, and since the end of Rolling Thunder, the U.S. had developed the smart bomb, making Linebacker far more effective with lower aircraft losses. But it was the mining that created the greatest problems for the DRV, and naturally, caused the greatest uproar among the antiwar elements in the U.S.[107]

Nixon's May 8 speech was greeted with outrage by the congressional doves and on college campuses and met almost universal disapproval in the influential media which were certain that Nixon's actions risked a major U.S.–Soviet confrontation and were sure to torpedo the impending summit. A May 10 *New York Times* editorial[108] said: "Nixon's decision on closing land and sea routes to N. Vietnam is a 'desperate gamble' that alters the nature of war ... and runs counter to Congressional mandate and the 'will and conscience' of a large segment of the American public; ... mining harbors poses a direct challenge to the USSR; ... peace offer included in Nixon's speech has a 'specious ring to it....'" But a Harris poll showed 59 percent of the American people supported Nixon's decision to mine North Vietnamese ports.[109] Nixon's critics were confounded when the USSR registered only a relatively mild protest and within a few days removed all doubt that it wanted the summit to go ahead.[110] Beijing's reaction was similarly restrained.[111] Hanoi was shocked when its patrons in Moscow and Beijing failed to exact a diplomatic and political price from Nixon for his "reescalation" of the war.[112]

Each of the three Communist drives was initially successful, forcing the ARVN to give ground, but each in turn ran out of momentum, and everywhere, when the Communists regrouped for a new attack, they were pounded by B-52s and tactical air strikes as daily sorties of U.S. Air Force and Navy aircraft reached the highest levels of the entire war. With ARVN forces resisting tenaciously, tenuous Communist logistics were not capable of sustaining simultaneous drives in three widely separated locations, accounting for the spasmodic nature of the offensive, and thus as each new attack developed, South Vietnam, with interior lines, was able to move its general reserves to meet the threat. By mid–June, the PAVN offensive had clearly been contained.[113]

South Vietnam lost more than 8,000 killed in action and triple that in wounded while two of its infantry divisions had been completely shattered, and 40,000 troops had deserted, but it had stopped the Communist offensive. Vietnamization had been vindicated, but doubts remained that the outcome would have been the same without the decisive intervention of American air power. PAVN casualties were estimated at over 100,000 plus heavy losses in tanks and artillery.[114] It would be nearly three years before the North was capable of another offensive.

Despite the heavy losses of men and materiel, Hanoi followed its usual practice after a defeat of adjusting the objectives to fit the results obtained. Although it had set out to inflict a heavy if not decisive defeat on the ARVN and destabilize if not topple the Thieu regime, when these things did not happen, this did not deter Hanoi and its sympathizers from claiming victory. Thus, Gareth Porter, in *A Peace Denied*, cut North Vietnam's strategy to fit the results and then said; "If this was indeed the strategy of the offensive, it was an unqualified success...." An indication of Porter's political persuasion is that in his account of the offensive, nowhere did he use the term People's Army of Vietnam (PAVN), always referring to the Communist forces as People's Liberation Armed Forces (PLAF), the accepted term for Viet Cong main force units,[115] this to perpetuate the myth that in 1972 the Viet Cong was still the main force conducting the war against the Thieu government when in fact the PLAF played no significant role in the Easter Offensive while North Vietnam committed 14 of its 15 regular infantry divisions and 26 separate regiments.[116]

The Easter Offensive had been masterminded by General Giap, and its failure ended his long-time dominance of North Vietnamese military strategy and the beginning of his fall from grace. While Giap remained defense minister, Gen. Van Tien Dung, who became chief of staff and a Politburo member, led the North Vietnamese armed forces through the end of the war. In 1982, Le Duan removed Giap from the Politburo, and he slipped into obscurity.[117]

Compared to the Tet Offensive, the media treatment of the Easter Offensive was far more accurate and objective. While the renewal of the bombing of the North and the mining of ports brought the expected outcry in the liberal media, Nixon, unlike Johnson, was not cowed, and the polls showed a majority supported him.[118]

However, one outcome favorable to Hanoi was that Communist forces were able to hold some areas they had occupied in the offensive along the western end of the DMZ as well as parts of other provinces in northwestern and western Vietnam. Communist control of these areas was not only strategically advantageous but also buttressed claims of legitimacy by the Provisional Revolutionary Government which could now assert it governed part of South Vietnam.

Negotiations III

Over the years, patient and artful Communist negotiators have repeatedly been able to win at the bargaining table what they have not been able to win on the battlefield, but in four years of Paris talks, while Hanoi had gained major concessions on military issues, it had not broken through the American determination to preserve a non–Communist government in South Vietnam. Thus, the underlying objective of the 1972 offensive was to break the negotiating impasse or in Communist terms, to change the "objective conditions" in their favor, allowing them to dictate a political settlement. Nixon and Kissinger believed the offensive was Hanoi's last throw of the dice, and whatever the outcome, it would end the war. If it succeeded, the Thieu regime would not survive, but if it failed, Hanoi would then negotiate an end to the war.

With the failure of its offensive, Hanoi knew there could be no military solution in the short term so it had no choice but to return to the bargaining table, but it had a terrible dilemma: should it stall in the hope that perhaps a liberal dove would defeat Nixon in November, or on the other hand, if it appeared Nixon would be reelected, would it be wise to push for an agreement before the election gave him a new mandate? In the event, in mid–July the Democrats did nominate a liberal dove, George McGovern, who favored an immediate and total end to *all* US involvement in Indochina *without* a prior agreement on return of prisoners, terms that were even more favorable to Hanoi than those Hanoi was already offering.[119] But Hanoi's hopes on that front were quickly dispelled by the polls that showed McGovern had little chance of defeating Nixon,[120] bringing the Politburo to conclude that a settlement *before* Nixon was reelected was in its best interests.

Nixon, for his part, was riding a crest of public approval from the trip to Peking, a successful Moscow summit, the bombing and mining, and the defeat of the Easter Offensive, but he was by no means free of pressures. Hardly a week went by without an attempt in the House or Senate to legislate the U.S. out of the war by another end-the-war amendment, usually involving better terms for the Communists than their side was already offering. Nixon knew that with the Democrats in control of both houses and little prospect of this changing in November, when the new Congress convened in January it was almost certain to deny or severely restrict new appropriations for the war as a means of getting the U.S. out of Vietnam.[121] So, like the Communists, Nixon too had a time constraint. If a settlement was not reached by year's end, the main complication in Nixon's calculations would become the new Congress that would be seated on January 3, 1973.

Meanwhile, in Saigon there were signs that Thieu was balking at the trend of the negotiations. In mid–1972, Thieu's reading of the situation was no different from that of the Americans—that North Vietnam was now prepared to settle on the best terms obtainable, and after four years of stalemated negotiations, an agreement could be imminent.[122] This would mean that the Americans would soon go home, and he would be left to face the Communists alone. He was looking into an abyss, and he was frightened by what he saw. Having fought the Communists for 25 years, he knew an agreement would be only a tactical pause in North Vietnam's drive to conquer the South, and realizing an agreement was near, the terms being negotiated took on a terrible immediacy for him. His fears were exacerbated by the secret nature of the negotiations being conducted on behalf of South Vietnam by Kissinger, whom he did not trust,[123] and although ostensibly Thieu was being consulted at each step, he was afraid that suddenly he might be confronted with a fait accompli negotiated over his head.

Thieu recognized the right of the U.S. to negotiate the military aspects pertaining to the cease-fire, its own withdrawal and the return of prisoners, but he was not prepared to concede to Kissinger the unilateral right to negotiate the military situation on the ground *after* the U.S. withdrawal. He objected to the standstill cease-fire on the grounds that it would permit PAVN troops to remain in South Vietnam with the sanction of an international agreement.[124] Kissinger thought Thieu had concurred in this as far back as October 1970 when Nixon had first proposed a standstill cease-fire and implicitly abandoned the requirement for mutual withdrawal, but then, Thieu had been less confident, and he had at least tacitly agreed, believing that it was the price for continued American support and that the proposals would be rejected by the

Communists anyway.[125] Now, with the collapse of the Easter Offensive, a more confident Thieu thought he had the upper hand militarily and that *as long as he had the support of American air power*, the Communists could never defeat him.[126] The U.S. proposal for a standstill cease-fire under international supervision included a provision prohibiting infiltration of personnel which Kissinger believed would cause any PAVN troops remaining in the South "to atrophy owing to normal attrition,"[127] but Thieu knew from the 1954 Geneva Accords and the 1962 Laos agreement that international supervision would never be effective in assuring Communist compliance.

While he was gravely concerned with the military issues being negotiated, Thieu strongly resented Kissinger's negotiation of the political aspects outside the presence of a representative of South Vietnam. He felt that this made his government appear as the puppet of the U.S., which as later events were to demonstrate was definitely not the case. And he knew it was on the political side where the real danger lay that the Communists could snatch the victory they had been unable to gain on the battlefield by outmaneuvering a well-meaning but naive Kissinger. So in mid-1972, Thieu saw no real advantage to South Vietnam in a peace agreement that would leave PAVN troops in South Vietnam, ratify the standing of the Viet Cong (Provisional Revolutionary Government) and bring about the departure of the Americans.[128]

When in early June it was clear North Vietnam's offensive had run out of steam, Nixon and Kissinger agreed the U.S. was now in a strong position to resume the negotiations which effectively had been stalled since the previous October, and accordingly the U.S. proposed another meeting. After several exchanges, July 13 was agreed upon. In the meantime, at the end of June, Nixon announced another withdrawal, bringing U.S. forces down to only 39,000.[129]

At a July 19 meeting Kissinger put forward Nixon's proposals from his May 8 speech to which Hanoi had never responded: a standstill cease-fire under international supervision, release of prisoners and total American withdrawal within four months. The proposals would have left the Thieu government intact, and this was unacceptable to Hanoi. It was rejected by Le Duc Tho. The two agreed to meet again on August 1.[130]

It was at the August 1 meeting that the Communist side showed the first signs of movement, an indication that they were reading the presidential election polls that showed Nixon far ahead of McGovern. There is no need here to detail all the intricacies of the negotiations as the reader can find full expositions in Kissinger's *The White House Years*[131] and in Porter's *A Peace Denied*, from the points of view of the U.S. and the DRV, respectively. Overall, the period beginning with the July 19 meeting was marked by an obvious urgency on the part of the Communists to conclude an agreement before November 7, the U.S. election day, as shown by their unprecedented negotiating flexibility and by their advancement of a succession of new proposals. Where previously Kissinger had usually taken the initiative in requesting negotiating meetings, it was now an eager Le Duc Tho who pressed for a compressed schedule of meetings which were held August 14, September 15, 26 and 27. In this series of meetings, the military issues were largely settled and the Communist emphasis shifted to the political side in the form of a succession of proposals that would have given the PRG a juridical role in governing South Vietnam in a coalition "Government of National Concord." The Communists continued to insist that Thieu could have no role in a future government. These proposals were rejected by Kissinger on the not unreasonable grounds that they would have given the PRG, which controlled at most 20 percent of the land and people of South Vietnam, a grossly disproportionate role in the government without an electoral test of any kind. Kissinger's counterproposal to this was a Committee of National Reconciliation which would include the PRG but would be limited to supervising elections.

At the September 27 meeting, Le Duc Tho proposed that a negotiating schedule be drawn up that would produce a settlement within a month, targeting October 31 for the signing of an agreement. In agreeing to this proposal, Kissinger committed a serious tactical error. The Communists were already working against the self-imposed deadline of the impending elections. Where the urgency was entirely on the Communist side, by establishing an agreed-upon, arbitrary schedule, they were able subtly to draw the U.S. into sharing that urgency when it was not necessarily in the interests of the U.S. to do so. In fact, Nixon felt no urgency whatever to settle before the elections which he believed he was sure to win.[132] At the same meeting, Le Duc Tho proposed a three-day "decisive" negotiating session which was agreed would begin October 8.[133]

Meanwhile, in Saigon, there was growing recalcitrance on the part of Thieu which gave the lie to any suggestion that he was a U.S. puppet. For the Nixon administration, the overriding objective of the negotiations was to disengage with honor, but whatever the outcome in Vietnam, the survival of America was not threatened. But for Thieu, the very survival of his nation depended on the negotiations being conducted on his behalf by Kissinger, and Thieu was not at all sure that he and Kissinger shared the same imperatives. For Kissinger, the essence of negotiation was compromise, but for Thieu, Kissinger's compromises could only give legitimacy to the PRG, sanction Communist control of part of South Vietnam and undermine the sovereignty of his government, so perhaps justifiably, he did not trust Kissinger. Thus, in discussions with Kissinger aide Maj. Gen. Alexander Haig on October 2–4, Thieu rejected almost all of the American negotiating position as it stood following the September 27 meeting. Nevertheless, Nixon and Kissinger decided to proceed in the expectation that Thieu could be brought around.[134]

The negotiating sessions beginning October 8 proved to be the pivotal breakthrough. In their drive for an agreement, the Communists continued their retreat from what had been, for four years, an inflexible negotiating position. The demand for a Government of National Concord coalition was dropped, and the two "administrations" (the GVN and the PRG) would simply coexist and would administer the areas each controlled with its own army.

Kissinger's proposal for a "National Council of National Reconciliation and Concord" was accepted along with an ambiguous description of its functions which Kissinger believed ruled out any inference that it was a governing body. The demand for the replacement of the Saigon government, first enunciated in 1965 by Phan Van Dong in the "Four Points," was dropped, and thus the Thieu regime would continue in place. In discussions that extended over four days, almost all the military and political issues were resolved, and on October 12 a jubilant Kissinger returned to Washington to report to Nixon that an agreement was all but complete.[135]

But it still remained to convince the reluctant Thieu for which Kissinger traveled to Saigon on October 18. Anxious to avoid a blowup with Saigon which might alienate the hawks, Nixon told Kissinger that if Thieu balked, Kissinger was to back off, and the U.S. would wait until after the election to conclude the agreement.[136] However, Kissinger feared that any delay would prompt Hanoi to publish the agreement and charge the U.S. with reneging, providing the liberal media with an opening to embarrass the administration,[137] so Kissinger resolved to push ahead. But after four days of tortuous meetings in Saigon, Thieu rejected the entire agreement, and it was only then that Kissinger realized that "Thieu objected not to specific terms but to the *fact* of an agreement.... The South Vietnamese ... simply did not feel ready to confront Hanoi without our direct involvement."[138]

It was a bitter pill for Kissinger who deluded himself in believing he had bested an implacable adversary in over three years of intense negotiations and had emerged with an excellent agreement that met the goals of the U.S. and was in the best interests of South Vietnam. Thieu's rejection of his handiwork aroused strong feelings of anger and frustration in Kissinger who had become captive to his own negotiations and saw the agreement as a masterful personal achievement that was being wrecked by pettiness in Saigon. In his eagerness for a settlement, Kissinger might well have been prepared to sacrifice Thieu had it not been for the stiffening provided by Nixon who counseled patience. In a message from Nixon, Hanoi was informed that "difficulties in Saigon have proved somewhat more complex than originally anticipated," but that "The U.S. side reaffirms its commitment to the substance and basic principles of the draft agreement."[139] As a sop to Hanoi for the failure to obtain South Vietnam's agreement, Kissinger proposed to end all bombing of the North, but Nixon, recalling Johnson's bombing cessation announcement just prior to the 1968 elections, agreed only to cease bombing above the 20th parallel beginning October 23.[140]

Back in Washington, Kissinger had to hold the agreement together while he tried to persuade Hanoi to discuss the changes demanded by Thieu. Just as he feared, on October 26 Hanoi Radio went public with the agreement and placed the blame squarely on the U.S. for failing to meet the agreed-upon target date for signature of October 31. Kissinger blamed Hanoi's "impossible" schedule for triggering the brouhaha,[141] but it was now clear that his tactical error in agreeing to the schedule had come back to haunt him. In fact, at this point the agreement was a slapdash work, far from ready for signing. The necessary protocols to implement the agreement were not complete, and the South Vietnamese objected violently to some of the wording of the Vietnamese language version of the agreement.

Hanoi's action forced a U.S. response which was delivered by Kissinger the same day at a nationally televised press conference. It was in his opening remarks that he uttered the fateful phrase: "We believe that *peace is at hand*. We believe that an agreement is within sight...."[142] This most unfortunate phrasing proved to be another major tactical error by Kissinger which he aggravated by affirming that only one more negotiating session would be needed. While creating premature expectations in the U.S., Kissinger had "seriously eroded his bargaining position with the North Vietnamese and made dealing with South Vietnamese objections more difficult.[143] In an attempt to overcome Thieu's objections, Nixon wrote him November 14: "You have my absolute assurance that if Hanoi fails to abide by the terms of this agreement it is my intention to take swift and severe retaliatory action," but even this failed to move Thieu.[144]

After several exchanges, the two sides agreed to renew talks in Paris on November 20, but Hanoi warned it intended to stick by the original agreement. At the first meeting, Kissinger introduced 64 changes demanded by the South Vietnamese, most of which were trivial, but a few were substantive. In his haste for an agreement Kissinger had been less than meticulous on the wording of some key points, and now it would be very difficult to gain agreement on revised wording. Thus began a series of 19 Kissinger-Tho meetings ending December 13 with a breakdown in negotiations. The forthcoming and cooperative Tho of September and October was replaced by the obdurate Tho of old. The urgency so apparent before Nixon's reelection was gone, replaced by an unhurried willingness to draw out the negotiations indefinitely. Viewing the divisions within the U.S., the differences between Washington and Saigon, and the likelihood of some form of congressional action in January to end U.S. involvement, Hanoi believed it held a winning hand, and it was now Nixon who was cornered.[145] But again they misread their adversary.

The Christmas Bombing and the Final Agreement

Nixon and Kissinger believed they had two alternatives: renew talks in January, recognizing that Hanoi, with no incentive to change its strategy, could continue to draw out the negotiations, or apply a massive shock that would cause Hanoi to alter its strategy and end the war quickly. Nixon, Alexander Haig, now acting as the president's military advisor, and Kissinger chose the second alternative with Laird opposed for domestic political reasons. Kissinger, initially uncertain as to what form the military response should take, quickly concurred with Nixon and Haig on renewing the bombing of Hanoi and Haiphong using B-52s over these targets for the first time, and remining the harbors.[146] After the secret bombing of Cambodian border areas in 1969, the incursions into the sanctuaries in 1970, and the renewed bombing of the North in May 1972, Nixon was again knowingly making a decision that would bring down on him all the fury of his domestic critics, but he gave the order to launch Linebacker II, and bombing began December 18. Predictably, this triggered the greatest outcry in the entire eight years of direct American involvement in the Second Indochina War, orchestrated by Hanoi and amplified by the liberal U.S. media. Critics settled on the charge of "indiscriminate carpet bombing of heavily populated areas,"[147] and the press echoed Hanoi's claims of massive civilian casualties.[148] But the relatively mild reaction of its Russian and Chinese patrons to the bombing must have been disappointing to Hanoi.[149]

On December 18, the day the bombing started, the U.S. sent a message to Hanoi proposing a basis for the renewal of talks and suggesting a date anytime after December 26. After additional exchanges, Hanoi affirmed that technical talks could resume as soon as the bombing stopped and that Le Duc Tho could be available on January 8. On December 27, the U.S. agreed to stop the bombing within 36 hours of Hanoi's acceptance of the U.S. proposal of December 18 which Hanoi confirmed on December 28. Bombing was stopped at 7:00 P.M. Washington time December 29 and announced publicly on December 30.[150]

What did the Christmas bombing accomplish? Linebacker II, with an intensity far exceeding anything previously experienced by the DRV, unquestionably sent shockwaves through the Politburo which was understandably eager for it to be stopped. Over the course of the raids, antiaircraft opposition grew progressively weaker as the DRV exhausted its stock of SAMs so that at the end, North Vietnam was nearly defenseless to B-52s.[151] According to Kissinger, it brought the DRV back to the table in a more conciliatory frame of mind, as evidenced by the speed with which a final agreement was concluded. But according to Gareth Porter,[152] the unexpected military reverses over Hanoi (the downing of fifteen B-52s) was the crucial factor in defeating Nixon's efforts to rewrite the agreement ... (his) bargaining hand had been greatly weakened.... Far more than in the October or November–December rounds, the DRV was in a position to reject American demands." To attribute the resumption of negotiations to the loss of 15 B-52s seems a bit of a stretch, but Porter is correct that in the resumed negotiations Kissinger was not able to obtain all the changes to the agreement that he wanted. Hanoi had gotten the bombing stopped in exchange for a renewal of talks, however, Linebacker II had demonstrated again that it was unwise to test the unpredictable Nixon. Thus the Politburo had a real incentive to reach an agreement without delay.

Beginning on January 8, Kissinger and Le Duc Tho quickly settled the outstanding issues, and an agreement with the necessary protocols was completed by January 13. It now only remained to bring Thieu on board. Nixon, more so than Kissinger, had been understanding of Thieu's dilemma and had repeatedly assured him in writing, most recently in a January 5 letter, "We will respond with full force should the settlement be violated by North Vietnam."[153] But after January 13, Thieu had exhausted his credit with Nixon who was now prepared to issue an ultimatum. In a letter delivered to Thieu by Haig on January 16, Nixon said: "I have therefore irrevocably decided to proceed to initial the Agreement on January 23, 1973, and to sign it on January 27, 1973, in Paris. I will do so, if necessary, alone...."[154] After some face-saving demands for further changes to the text which were flatly rejected by Nixon, Thieu caved in and agreed to sign. Nixon was inaugurated on January 20, the agreement was initialed by Kissinger and Tho on January 23 and on January 27, Secretary of State William P. Rogers and the foreign ministers of the DRV, the PRG and the Republic of Vietnam signed the Agreement On Ending The War And Restoring The Peace In Vietnam.[155] America's longest war was over.

7

The Aftermath

Though America's war was over, the Paris Agreement did not end the war between North and South Vietnam. The DRV never wavered from its goal of bringing South Vietnam under its control, preferably by political means but failing that, by military conquest. Initially, it hoped to use the political provisions of the agreement to achieve a coalition government in Saigon which would include the PRG. Knowing that the Thieu regime would obstruct this avenue, the Communists would work to undermine and destabilize the Saigon government, and when conditions were proper, overthrow it in a general uprising of the masses.[1] But while it worked for a political solution, at the same time, the DRV would prepare for a military solution which could be pursued if it judged the balance of forces was sufficiently in its favor. Thus it began immediately to prepare for another invasion of South Vietnam at some point in the future. The American bombers and reconnaissance aircraft having departed, the DRV could enhance its base areas in northwest South Vietnam, Laos and Cambodia in almost complete security. Thousands of miles of the Ho Chi Minh Trail were upgraded to all-weather roads with spurs reaching in to South Vietnam at several points, and the fuel pipeline was extended. The former American bastion at Khe Sanh became a principal PAVN logistics base.[2]

The drastic asymmetry of the peace agreement now began to make itself felt. First, and most critical, North Vietnam was not required to withdraw its forces from the areas it held in South Vietnam. (North Vietnam had never even acknowledged the presence of its regular forces in the South.) The terms (Chapter 2, Article 7) specified that no new war materiel could be introduced into *South Vietnam* by either party except to replace worn-out, damaged or destroyed materiel. Thus, the agreement barred the U.S. from increasing the armaments of South Vietnam[3] while the DRV was not restricted in any way from importing war materiel which continued to flow in large amounts into the North from the USSR and China. No sooner had the agreement been signed than the DRV began to violate it by moving men and materiel into the South across the DMZ and through Laos.

The asymmetry was, of course, obvious to Nixon, Kissinger and Thieu and would certainly explain the latter's deep reluctance to accept the agreement, but not having driven the PAVN forces out, Thieu could hardly expect that Kissinger would be able to negotiate them out. Thieu's alternative to the cease-fire was continued American involvement in a fight to the finish, something that was no longer feasible in the U.S.

Domestic pressure to end U.S. involvement pushed Nixon into signing an agreement that was clearly disadvantageous militarily to South Vietnam, but it was done on the strength of his determination to enforce the agreement by retaliating with American air power for DRV violations.[4] In the end, Thieu had no choice but to accept Nixon's assurances. In January 1973 no one could foresee the devastation that Watergate would bring to the Nixon presidency, stripping him of the power to make good on his commitments in Vietnam.

Effectively, the cease-fire in place provisions of the agreement never came into force. Both sides had used the preagreement period of late 1972 to attempt to expand areas under their control with the more aggressive South Vietnamese making marginal gains, probably because the PAVN forces in South Vietnam were still recovering from the heavy losses from the failed Easter Offensive, but the fighting did not stop with the signing of the agreement. A COSVN report of the period estimated that the amount of land under its control was reduced to no more than 20 percent containing 12 percent of the population of South Vietnam.[5] Even this may have been an exaggeration.

Thieu's refusal to compromise with the Communists was embodied in his program of "four nos": 1) no abandonment of territory; 2) no coalition; 3) no negotiations; and 4) no Communist or neutralist activities in South Vietnam.[6] The PRG (Provisional Revolutionary Government), in line with the strategy dictated by Hanoi, was pursuing a relatively passive stance while they watched and waited to see if a coalition government would materialize in Saigon in line with their interpretation of the agreement. Also, a major Communist concern was to avoid provocations that could invite American air power to reenter the conflict. They planned to raise the level of conflict gradually, all the while testing the American response.

As to the U.S., while the final withdrawal of U.S. forces and the repatriation of POWs were still underway, Kissinger visited Hanoi beginning February 10 to discuss observance of the Paris Agreement, normalization of relations and economic reconstruction. Only two weeks after the signing of the agreement, the U.S. had incontrovertible proof of 200 major military violations by the DRV through the movement of men and materiel across the DMZ. When Kissinger raised the matter, he was stonewalled by his DRV interlocutors. Nor was the DRV anxious to normalize relations, even at a level below actual diplomatic recognition. With respect to U.S. financial aid for reconstruction, Pham Van Dong found it unacceptable that it would first be subject to strict compliance by the DRV to the terms of the agreement and then must be appropriated by Congress. Dong charged the U.S. with attaching political conditions when financial aid must be unconditional.[7] Kissinger had no illusions on the prospects for real peace in Indochina, but after his visit to Hanoi, he had even more reason to be pessimistic.

During a state visit to the U.S. by Thieu in April, Nixon again assured him of his determination to retaliate for gross breaches of the agreement by the DRV,[8] but already, Nixon was being distracted by the burgeoning Watergate scandal which was beginning to drain away not only his power but his will to act. A series of strong U.S. notes to Hanoi in March protested continued DRV movement of men and materiel across the DMZ and through Laos into South Vietnam and warned of grave consequences, but in April when Kissinger recommended B-52 strikes on PAVN concentrations in northern South Vietnam, Nixon vacillated. The strikes were never conducted, the notes were empty threats, and Hanoi began to sense how badly Nixon had been emasculated by Watergate.[9]

The Border Campaigns

With growing boldness, in November the DRV launched a division-strength attack in the Central Highlands against ARVN border posts, and when the U.S. failed to react, pressure for a quick military solution began to grow in the Politburo. In the spring and summer of 1974, the DRV cautiously stepped up its attacks, always with one eye cocked on a possible U.S. reaction which never came. Nixon's resignation in August led the DRV to conclude, correctly, that there was now very little likelihood of renewed U.S. intervention in Vietnam.[10] Accordingly, the Politburo approved plans for a limited offensive in South Vietnam's Military Region III in Phuoc Long province north of Saigon, and by January 7, 1975, that strategically located province was entirely in Communist hands.[11] This successful testing of the ARVN in the border regions and with no U.S. reaction led the Politburo to approve a second offensive to the north in Military Region II. This was launched on March 10 by three PAVN divisions which quickly overran the meager ARVN forces defending the Darlac provincial capital of Ban Me Thuot in the Central Highlands, thus outflanking on the south the key ARVN strongpoints of Pleiku and Kontum which North Vietnam had failed to take in the 1972 Easter Offensive. This brought about the decision by Thieu to withdraw from the Central Highlands to a more defensible line farther south and east, but the poorly conducted withdrawal turned into a disorderly rout and most of the ARVN forces defending the Central Highlands were lost. In keeping with his "four nos" campaign, Thieu had feared that contingency planning for withdrawals would have given rise to defeatist attitudes among his generals.[12]

In another replay of the Easter Offensive, the Communists next launched a strong attack across the DMZ into Quang Tri province defended by ARVN's crack 1st Infantry Division. PAVN forces quickly drove the division back on Hue and then cut it off from the south. Unable to evacuate by sea, the division attempted to withdraw along the coast but was destroyed. The demoralized ARVN forces withdrew into an enclave around Danang, but this last bastion in the north fell on March 29. PAVN forces drove south, rolling up the coastal cities against little opposition.[13]

The Ho Chi Minh Campaign

The success of the offensive had far exceeded the expectations of the Politburo which now saw an opportunity to decisively crush the remaining the ARVN forces and conclude the conquest of South Vietnam. Gen. Van Tien Dung, the PAVN commander, was ordered to regroup his army for a final offensive, the Ho Chi Minh Campaign, that would capture Saigon and end the war. At this point, Thieu had lost half his army. Though his remaining forces put up a valiant holding action on a defensive line north and east of Saigon, in four weeks of hard fighting they were overwhelmed by the more powerful North Vietnamese forces, which entered Saigon on April 30.

After the disastrous reverses in the north, it was obvious to the South Vietnamese leadership that the military situation was hopeless, so during the final battle for Saigon, peace feelers went out to the DRV, but it was too late for that. Knowing that victory was near, the Communists had no interest in negotiating with the despised Thieu regime. In a desperate attempt to find someone with whom the Communists would negotiate, the Saigon peace faction pressured Thieu to resign on April 21 but was unable to find an acceptable sacrificial lamb until the 27th when Gen. Duong Van Minh was appointed president by the National Assembly. In a gesture to the Communists that had more form than substance, Minh ordered all U.S. personnel out of Vietnam within 24 hours, but the U.S. evacuation was already well advanced. His appeal for a cease-fire was contemptuously rejected, and in the end, his final service to Vietnam was to order his troops to lay down their arms on April 30. The Second Indochina War was over.[14]

America's Final Role

In the 25 months between the U.S. withdrawal and the dénouement in Saigon, the war faded from the front pages and from the consciousness of the average American, displaced by Watergate. Knowing they no longer risked a voter backlash, congressmen and senators who had previously been supportive now joined those who had opposed the war in moving, through legislation and budgetary limitations, to restrict the president's power to act. No sooner had the Paris Agreement been signed than the president's alleged secret commitments to Thieu were challenged as illegal by opponents of the war. To the radicals, any resort to force to enforce the agreement was unthinkable, although the U.S. had maintained substantial forces in South Korea for over 20 years to enforce the peace there. The antiwar forces now pushed to abandon the Thieu regime to its fate and were willing to accept, in fact, some would even welcome, an eventual Communist victory despite the terrible price in lives paid by their nation to achieve the independence of South Vietnam.[15]

In June 1973, Congress passed a supplemental appropriations bill that prohibited any U.S. military operations in or over Cambodia and Laos. Nixon vetoed the bill, but recognizing that Watergate was rapidly diminishing his ability to govern, he agreed to a compromise that would prohibit military operations in or over Laos, Cambodia and *North and South Vietnam* after August 15.[16] Thus, he would have to seek congressional approval to conduct *any* military action to enforce the agreement, an approval that was almost certain to be denied. Believing that in the course of the Vietnam War the executive branch had grossly exceeded its constitutional war-making powers, Congress passed the War Powers Act, and after overriding Nixon's veto, that controversial piece of legislation became law on November 7, 1973. The act would severely restrict the power of the commander-in-chief to deploy U.S. armed forces without the approval of Congress.[17] Needless to say, North Vietnam watched these developments with great interest.

Having obviated the possibility of renewed U.S. intervention, Congress now acted to deny South Vietnam the military and economic aid it had been assured it would receive after the U.S. pullout. For fiscal year 1975 (beginning July 1, 1974) Congress reduced the administration's request for $1.6 billion in military aid for Vietnam by one-third despite knowledge of a blatant large-scale North Vietnamese buildup in northern South Vietnam, Cambodia and Laos. The South Vietnamese armed forces quickly began to feel the cuts in shortages of spare parts, fuel and ammunition. In Saigon there was a growing sense of betrayal, but in the U.S. Congress, the liberals were exulting in their newfound dominance. They were not receptive to President Gerald Ford's pleas in February 1975 for emergency aid to Vietnam to hold off the Communist offensive, but at that point, morale in South Vietnam was so badly shattered by America's seeming indifference that it is doubtful that any amount of emergency aid could have saved the dispirited South Vietnamese.[18]

It was not America's finest hour, but in the death throes of the South Vietnamese republic in the last days of April, the U.S. redeemed some of its honor by conducting a massive air and sealift that evacuated some 58,000 of the South Vietnamese military personnel and government officials and their dependents who would be most compromised by their support of the U.S.-backed Thieu regime.[19]

* * *

Postwar Vietnam

In the postwar years, the DRV grew even closer to the Soviet Union and more distant from China. In the closing years of the war the Russians had gained a clear ascendancy over China within the DRV, and Chinese-Vietnamese relations cooled as the traditional animosity between the two peoples began to reassert itself. This trend was exacerbated by the Chinese decision to seek an opening with the U.S. Postwar, the DRV became an undisguised Soviet satellite and in 1978 a member of COMECON. Amidst the demands of reconstruction, the continued maintenance of large military forces and the counterproductive collectivization of the South Vietnamese economy, the nation was able to survive only through continuous infusions of Soviet economic aid.

From the creation of the republic in 1955, South Vietnam had fought the Communists for 20 years, but in the end had been overwhelmed, peace had come, and the people of South Vietnam now awaited the changes the victors would impose by right of conquest. Initially, the DRV installed a military government in Ho Chi Minh City (formerly Saigon) called the Military Management Committee which after a few months was dismantled in favor of a Provisional Revolutionary Government, but actual power was exercised from Hanoi. The DRV was not about to entrust its hard-won victory to members of the Provisional Revolutionary Government it had created primarily as a negotiating tactic. Hanoi quickly decided to abandon any pretense of a separate government in Saigon, and in July 1976 North and South were unified as the new Socialist Republic of Vietnam (SRV) with its capital in Hanoi. In December, the Vietnamese Workers Party and its adjunct in the South, the People's Revolutionary Party, were integrated into a new Vietnamese Communist Party.[20]

While there were undoubtedly some executions of highly compromised individuals, the bloodbath predicted by some in the West did not occur. Instead, those closely identified with the Thieu regime, government officials, military officers and private individuals thought loyal to the old regime, numbering well over 1 million, were required to register with authorities and several hundred thousand were sent to reeducation camps, i.e., concentration camps, where they were held for varying periods, sometimes years, until it was felt they had been rendered harmless to the regime.[21]

A second measure intended to siphon off the large numbers of unemployed in the cities and to remove others whose loyalty was questionable was the New Economic Zones program under which additional hundreds of thousands were sent to resettlement zones on uncultivated land in remote underpopulated areas. This program had all the earmarks of Stalin's gulag system in which political prisoners, deportees and criminals were sent to remote locations in the Siberian taiga and ordered to build their camps from scratch, the principal difference being that the South Vietnamese would not freeze to death. As with the gulags, many of the Vietnamese settlers lacked the necessary skills to make such a program successful, and this was compounded by the failure of the government to provide adequate support in the form of seeds, tools and equipment. By the end of 1975, 500,000 had been settled in the NEZs.[22] The program may have helped superficially to resolve the unemployment problem but created in its stead a seething discontent among those unfortunate enough to be sent to a resettlement center.

Following the Communist takeover, the majority of everyday South Vietnamese, without a strong ideological bias either for or against Communism, were prepared to wait and see what life would be like under the new regime and thus had no immediate reason to wish to leave the country. As the nature of life under the SRV brand of Communism, the severe economic problems, food shortages, the reeducation centers, the resettlement zones and the generally harsh, repressive character of the regime was gradually revealed to the populace, more and more people of all classes sought to flee South Vietnam. Between 1975 and 1980 an estimated 1.5 million became refugees or "boat people," many choosing to risk their lives in small boats to escape a life that had become intolerable.[23] While the voluntary departure of so many "political unreliables" may have been considered beneficial by the regime, still Hanoi and the international socialist bloc were humiliated by worldwide media coverage of this massive flight from a socialist people's democratic republic. It recalled 1954 when nearly 900,000 had fled the North for the South, but this time the much larger exodus was entirely spontaneous and took place without official assistance of any kind, much like the ongoing flight from Castro's Cuba.

Imposition of Socialism on the South

With the reunification of Vietnam, Le Duan, the hard-line general secretary of the party, and his Politburo colleagues set about to install socialism in the South that mirrored the Stalinist model already implanted in the North. To these old-guard Stalinist disciples of Ho Chi Minh, any deviation from this line would have been unconscionable. Initially the Communists chose to take a gradual approach. Major industries were nationalized but private commerce was left alone for the time being. An exception was the merchant class of "comprador bourgeoisie" made up largely of overseas Chinese who controlled major commercial enterprises which were confiscated.[24] Partly for fear that abrupt collectivization of agriculture would disrupt the already tenuous food situation, private farming was allowed to continue, but typical socialist disincentives created by price controls and new regulations inevitably led the peasants to grow only what they needed for themselves.[25] After a period of gradualism in which the South Vietnamese economy fell steadily into deeper chaos and the food situation worsened, Hanoi decided the correct Marxist-Leninist solution was to accelerate the transition to a collectivized economy, and this was done beginning in 1978 with the abolition of all private trade and the launch of collectivization of agriculture.[26]

This rigid, doctrinaire approach only exaggerated the defects inherent in the socialist centralized system, and by Le Duan's death in 1986 the national economy was on the point of collapse.[27] Meanwhile, from the aspect of individual civil liberties, the grim totalitarian Hanoi regime had remained frozen in the Stalinist mode of 1950 while it maintained one of the largest armies in the world. Hanoi's problems were not limited to the South. After the years of unremitting labor and privation during the war, continuing food shortages and the lack of consumer goods were causing restiveness in the North as well[28].

The War in Cambodia

Going back to the founding of the Indochinese Communist Party in 1930, the Vietnamese Communists had nursed the concept of an Indochinese Federation of Laos, Cambodia and Vietnam, dominated, of course, by Vietnam. The formation of separate Communist parties for Laos and Cambodia in 1951 did nothing to diminish this ideal in the minds of Hanoi's leadership.[29] Of the two other states of Indochina, Laos was brought safely under the influence of Hanoi when a puppet Pathet Lao government was installed there in early 1975, but Cambodia was another story. When Sihanouk was overthrown in 1970, the Khmer Rouge had been a small Communist guerrilla movement in the jungles of eastern Cambodia which North Vietnam then undertook to organize, arm and train as its surrogate in the war to oust the Lon Nol government. But North Vietnam's efforts to control the movement were resisted by the independent-minded Khmer Rouge leader, Pol Pot, who was determined that Cambodia would not become a satellite of Hanoi.[30] Following their capture of Phnom Penh and takeover of the country in 1975, the Khmer Rouge began attacks along the border with Vietnam arising from long-standing differences over the location of the demarcation line.[31] These differences had been aggravated by the years of Vietminh and Viet Cong use of Cambodian border areas as bases and sanctuaries. While the DRV-SRV regarded itself as the aggrieved party, in reality, it may have welcomed these provocations as providing a pretext for fulfilling its long-held dream of establishing an Indochinese federation under its hegemony. In any case, in December 1978, the Vietnamese regular army invaded Cambodia. In a brief campaign, the Khmer Rouge forces were forced to flee to the jungles of western Cambodia, and the Vietnamese installed a friendly puppet government.[32] Suddenly Vietnam, whose status as underdog during the war with the Americans had brought international sympathy and support, now found itself identified in the UN General Assembly as an aggressor with expansionist ambitions and shunned in its efforts to establish relations with nonsocialist governments. At this point the U.S. and China declared embargoes on trade with the SRV, and Japan and several Western Europeans countries cut off aid programs.

The ill-starred invasion of Cambodia not only created international diplomatic complications for Hanoi but also brought a complete break in relations with China which had been a sponsor of the Khmer Rouge. Aside from differences over Cambodia, China and Vietnam each claimed the Paracel and Spratly Islands in the South China Sea, and the Hanoi regime's harsh treatment of ethnic Chinese in South Vietnam had become a contentious issue.[33] Taking as a pretext some rather minor differences over their common border China invaded the SRV in early 1979 with the intent to punish the upstart Vietnamese, but after a brief and shallow penetration, the Chinese withdrew. Meanwhile, in Cambodia, low-level fighting continued through the 1980s, and it was only through the presence of its occupying army that Vietnam was able to maintain its puppet government in power. In 1989 new leadership in Hanoi ended the Cambodian adventure, and the SRV forces were withdrawn. In 1991 a UN treaty ended the fighting, and in 1993 a neutralist coalition government was formed with Sihanouk restored as king.

Reform Begins

With the death of Le Duan in 1986, reformers gained control of the party and Politburo at the Sixth Party Congress in December. Nguyen Van Linh was elected general secretary of the Vietnamese Communist Party, and the process was begun of liberalizing some of the more disastrous economic policies of the old guard.[34] Although the country was taking small, grudging steps toward a limited market economy, the SRV as a client of the Soviet Union continued to be rewarded for its political loyalty with annual infusions of vital economic aid until the USSR itself broke up in 1991.[35] The loss of this aid was a heavy blow. While economic reforms gradually improved the material well being of the Vietnamese people, Hanoi resisted the political liberalization that occurred in the late 1980s and the 1990s throughout the international socialist bloc (with the exception of Cuba and North Korea) and remained a monolithic one-party state in which political dissent was not permitted. In 1989, 14 years after the end of the war, the SRV announced its intention to demobilize half of its 1 million-man army.[36]

In response to postwar overtures by the Carter administration aimed at establishing diplomatic and commercial relations, Hanoi laid down conditions with respect to the payment by the U.S. of war reparations which the U.S. found unacceptable, and the negotiations failed.[37] In any case, the invasion of Cambodia by the SRV in 1978 and the short war with China ended any chance for rapprochement with the U.S. About 20 years would pass before diplomatic relations at the ambassadorial level were established in 1994 by the Clinton administration.

The Price

When Vietnam at the start of the new millennium is compared to the Asian tigers of South Korea, Taiwan, Hong Kong, Singapore, Malaysia and Thailand, the magnitude of the terrible wrong perpetrated by the Communist leadership on their long-suffering people is clear. When the economic takeoff of the Asian Tigers began in the 1980s, the pool of educated and industrious low-cost labor represented by the rapidly growing population of Vietnam[38] would have been just as attractive to high-tech entrepreneurs as that of, say, Thailand, but given the choice of investing in open-market economies and a totalitarian one steeped in doctrinaire socialism, naturally they chose to invest in the free market. Vietnam remains one of the poorest states in Asia.

But the enduring poverty inflicted by the disastrous economic policies of the successors of Ho Chi Minh was nothing compared to the tyranny perpetrated on the people of Vietnam by that group of superannuated revolutionaries in Hanoi who, in perpetuating a fossilized Stalinist-style totalitarian regime, denied the people the basic human freedoms of speech, association, press and the right to choose their own leaders.

Although the true nature of the Ho Chi Minh regime was always evident, those in America who so vocally supported North Vietnam in its "war of national liberation" on the South have averted their gaze from the result and have been remarkably silent.

8

Conclusion

The reasons for the U.S. presence in Vietnam and the goals we hoped to achieve there have been amply set forth in the body of this work and so will not be enumerated again. Rather, this concluding chapter will focus on the reasons for America's defeat and will briefly summarize the consequences of that defeat.

With the launch of the Second Indochina War through Resolution 15 in early 1959, the DRV recognized the crucial importance of unfettered access to the infiltration routes through eastern Laos to the successful prosecution of operations against South Vietnam. The ensuing Laos crisis of 1961 was, if not a direct, at least an indirect result of the DRV's push to secure this corridor. At the Geneva Conference on Laos, Kennedy, in allowing the U.S. to be maneuvered out of Laos, effectively wrote off that country, having determined to make his stand in Vietnam — this despite repeated warnings from his military and civilian advisors that Vietnam would be almost impossible to defend if the DRV controlled eastern Laos. Thus, the failure to intervene in Laos in 1961–62 was a serious mistake which Johnson had the means to repair, but it became a fatal one when he failed to do so.

Of all the mistakes we made in Vietnam, encouraging the overthrow of Diem may well have been the most disastrous because one can speculate that had he lived, he would have resisted the massive American military buildup and takeover of the war and our intrusion into every aspect of his government, and thus, America's war in Vietnam would not have followed the tragic path that it did. With the departure of the French, Diem was simply not about to accept a new protectorate. He would have continued the struggle against the insurgency with his own forces, and America's role would have remained one of military aid and advice and only nominal combat support. In the latter half of 1963, however, it appeared he was losing the struggle, and whether, with his back to the wall, he would have continued to reject direct U.S. intervention or would in the end have negotiated a settlement with the NLF is something we cannot know. In any case, with the ill-considered Kennedy White House decision to withdraw support from Diem, heedless of who and what would follow, the U.S. assumed a new commitment that transcended any prior relationship. Our guarantee had taken on a new moral dimension that would be even more difficult to revoke. We were locked in to the Vietnam War.

Johnson's February 1965 decisions to begin Rolling Thunder and to insert the first combat units, taken at a point when the alternative was the likely collapse of South Vietnam, were far more consequential than any that his predecessors Truman, Eisenhower and Kennedy had ever had to make on Vietnam, but it was their decisions, cumulatively, that had put U.S. prestige in play and pledged its guarantee in the struggle to preserve South Vietnam as a non–Communist state. Johnson, who had not created these circumstances, was faced with a choice among three alternatives: 1) withdraw, repudiate the U.S. guarantee, and abandon South Vietnam to its fate, which would have been a near-immediate Communist takeover; 2) opt for a negotiated sham neutralization of Vietnam in an attempt to save face, as Kennedy had done in Laos, which would have been merely a prelude to an eventual Communist takeover; or 3) intervene to save the position, protect the integrity of the U.S. guarantee, and adhere to a policy of Communist containment consistent with that of his predecessors. Knowing that the nation would not accept a Cold War defeat by the international Communist bloc, Johnson chose the third alternative. Thus it is unjust to criticize him for his decision to intervene in Vietnam, but there are more than ample grounds to criticize the way in which he conducted that intervention.

At bottom, Johnson's failure to achieve victory in Vietnam can be traced to his decision to conduct a limited war. This gave rise to several fundamental errors in U.S. strategy.

That the Ho Chi Minh Trail and the related Laotian and Cambodian sanctuaries were central to North Vietnam's successful prosecution of the war was a fact well understood by the military leaders of both sides, but within the constraints of Johnson's limited war, American troops were never authorized to enter Laos and Cambodia in force, thus affording the Viet Cong and PAVN inviolable sanctuaries in which to rest, reform and launch new attacks. His stated reasons for this were his sanctimonious wish to respect Laotian "neutrality" and to avoid "widening the war," but his unstated reasons were his unreasoning dread of China and his fear of the reaction of the domestic antiwar movement. His political restraints on the ground war caused the U.S. to pursue a costly and futile search-and-destroy strategy within South Vietnam while at the same time he hypocritically violated Laotian neutrality by authorizing an unacknowledged eight-year tactical bombing campaign in Laos against the Ho Chi Minh Trail.

Such a move into Laos to interdict the Ho Chi Minh Trail should have been made no later than the latter half of 1966, but Westmoreland's requests for authorization and the necessary troops were rejected by Johnson and his civilian advisors, and thus the only ground-war strategy likely to succeed was forgone.

A second mistake growing out of the limited war concept was the "slowly ascending tempo" of the Rolling Thunder air campaign that was the product of Johnson's civilian strategists contrary to the advice of the military professionals. North Vietnam, with its relatively primitive industrial economy, could sustain the war only through the importation of arms and ammunition, petroleum products and food from its Communist bloc patrons. Thus, the obvious strategy was to close off this influx by denying the DRV the use of its ports and rail connections to China. Instead of the feeble pinprick attacks of the early Rolling Thunder, an air campaign like Linebacker I should have been conducted with minimum restraint, as recommended by the JCS and Director of Central Intelligence John McCone. Had this been done in 1965, or at the latest 1966, and if coordinated with ground attacks on the Ho Chi Minh Trail and sanctuaries, it would have created enormous and perhaps insurmountable difficulties for the DRV. Linebacker I, when actually conducted six years later in response to the 1972 DRV Easter Offensive, succeeded in the six months of its operation in putting the DRV into a severe supply crisis, something which Rolling Thunder never produced in its three-year duration.

The limited war also fitted well with Johnson's wish to avoid arousing the public while he pushed his Great Society program legislation. Thus he failed to mobilize the nation and refused to call up reserves. His guns-and-butter policy backfired because by not requiring shared wartime material sacrifices from the people, they were not drawn together in a cohesive spirit in support of the war. He was deceptive in his communications on the war with the American people, thereby opening the notorious credibility gap which led eventually to his decision not to seek another term.

Finally, a major error beginning in the Eisenhower years and continuing through Kennedy and Johnson into early 1967 was the failure to assign adequate priority to contesting the NLF politically in the villages, something only the South Vietnamese could do. For too long we failed to support the Saigon government in effectively addressing this critical need.

It is the nature of a democracy to have a low tolerance for long wars, particularly those like Korea and Vietnam where we were defending the principle of freedom for other peoples even though our own freedom was not immediately threatened. Thus it was imperative that the war in Vietnam *not become drawn out*, but that was precisely the result of Johnson's limited war strategy so that after four years of futility, the tolerance of our democracy for the war was exhausted. It was then manifestly clear that the U.S. must disengage from Vietnam and that there would be no military victory despite the gross disparities in the military power of the two adversaries.

Instead, once the decision was taken to intervene, the U.S. should have brought to bear overwhelming force with minimum restraint (except for the lives of noncombatants) to bring the war to a close as quickly as possible, certainly no later than mid–1967. Indeed, this was a principal lesson taken from the Vietnam experience by our military leaders and applied, for example, in the 1991 Persian Gulf War.

The Lost Peace

For a time after the conclusion of the cease-fire agreement the U.S. made good on its commitments to provide material support to Saigon, but as the burgeoning Watergate scandal stripped Nixon of his prestige and authority, the antiwar elements in Congress were emboldened to repudiate those undertakings which were moral rather than legal. America's guarantee to a small ally of 20 years standing effectively was voided.

The Paris agreement contained the seeds of the eventual outcome. It was flawed, and Nixon and Kissinger knew it was flawed, so did they "lose the peace" in Vietnam? They did indeed accept a flawed agreement, believing, correctly, that it was the best they could get without an indefinite prolongation of American involvement, something that Congress and the American people would not support, but Nixon was determined to hold the DRV to the agreement, if necessary through the use of American air power. It will never be known if, absent Watergate, he would have made good on his assurances to Thieu that U.S. air power would reenter the conflict in the event North Vietnam attacked the South. Watergate intervened to shroud these questions in ambiguity.

So how *was* the peace lost in Vietnam? After the signing of the cease-fire agreement, many factors combined to bring about the ultimate Communist victory and the final defeat of America's objectives there, but the most determinative one was the duplicity of the DRV, which never intended to abide by the agreement and began gross violations immediately fed by a stepped-up flow of Soviet-supplied arms.

On the part of the U.S. and South Vietnam, these factors were:

• Continued pressure by antiwar elements outside and within the U.S. government to end American support for South Vietnam in any form whatever.

• Loss of will to persist, apathy, antipathy to the South Vietnamese government within an important segment of the political class and bureaucracy in Washington which failed to grasp or would willfully disregard the full consequences of withdrawing the U.S. guarantee from a small ally.

• Growing war-weariness on the part of mainstream America — an intolerance for further involvement even in the face of grave breaches of the agreement by the North.

• Demoralization, internal weaknesses in the government of South Vietnam.

• Watergate, which destroyed the Nixon presidency and with it any chance that America's guarantee to South Vietnam would be sustained.

In the period following the signing of the cease-fire these factors were all too obvious to the leaders in Hanoi who did not hesitate to seize the main chance and end the war in a decisive victory. Admirers of the DRV explain its victory over the much more powerful U.S. by citing the "indomitable will of the Vietnamese people" which has enabled the nation to prevail throughout its history, and indeed it was Johnson's flawed strategies that allowed the war to become a drawn-out test of wills. But in modern warfare, will alone without the necessary arms cannot win battles against a determined adversary. With the 1965 decision of the Soviet Union to transform the struggle in Vietnam into a Cold War proxy came the arms that enabled a small nation in Southeast Asia to outlast a far more powerful adversary whose will had faltered.

The Consequences

The war for the survival of South Vietnam as a non–Communist state became a challenge to America's prestige and a test of the validity of America's guarantee in the eyes of the uncommitted nations of the world. Were these mere abstractions that could be conceded at little cost to America as argued by opponents of the war or were they vital anchors to the U.S. position as leader of the free world, as maintained by six presidents and endorsed by Congress. The answer came when, after Watergate stripped Nixon of the power to govern, the liberal left opponents of the war prevailed, and despite the awful sacrifice of lives and treasure, the American guarantee was allowed to lapse, whatever the ultimate cost to America's prestige and position.

That America's prestige and guarantee were more than abstractions was soon evident from the reactions of many of the uncommitted nations of Africa and the Middle East which had watched with bemusement the collapse of American will at the hands of international Communism and concluded that perhaps the Soviets did indeed hold the winning cards in the Cold War. With the U.S. recoiling from the Vietnam experience, the Soviets met few obstacles to their adventurism in Africa and the Middle East. That the way was clear for Communist inroads was all too obvious when even Cuba felt free to send expeditionary forces to Angola and Ethiopia in support of Communist-led movements while Congress prohibited any counteraction by the U.S. Soviet arms and advisors poured into Africa and the Middle East, and leftist regimes took power in Afghanistan, Angola, Ethiopia, Yemen, Mozambique and Somalia. Soviet imperialism followed the Brezhnev Doctrine that held that Communist gains were irreversible and would be defended by the Soviet Union. In 1979, when a Soviet-backed regime in Afghanistan was threatened by a rival, an arrogant Brezhnev invoked the doctrine and invaded to keep that country securely in the Soviet orbit. The destabilizing effect of unconscionably large Soviet arms sales and grants in the third world continued to be felt into the 1991 Persian Gulf War and in subsequent events in Iraq.

Whether as fallout from Vietnam or Watergate, the 1976 presidential election brought a naive and inexperienced Carter to the White House where he conducted a feckless and ineffectual administration. While focusing on disarmament, he proved incapable of containing the aggressive Soviet geopolitical strategy. And after the successful triangular diplomacy and rapprochement brought about by Nixon, China was badly disconcerted by the lack of firmness in U.S. foreign policy against Soviet aggressiveness. The CIA came in for special scapegoating in sensational public hearings before the Church Committee of the Senate which resulted in legislation weakening the operations of that agency such that it was unable to detect and cope with the growing terrorist threat beginning in the 1990s.

While the Soviets were busy in Africa and the Middle East, their surrogate Cuba was not idle in the Western Hemisphere where Cuban-supported Communist movements gained strong footholds in Nicaragua and El Salvador. U.S. countermeasures were strenuously opposed by the same elements of the Senate that had opposed the Vietnam War.

That Western democracy paid a heavy price for the degradation of U.S. prestige and the integrity of its guarantee can hardly be debated, and the aftereffects of the lapse in Vietnam were aggravated by what seemed an almost willful disregard of the consequences on the part of those in Washington most responsible in the first instance. With the election of Ronald Reagan in 1980, the U.S. began the long road back despite continued opposition at almost every turn from those same elements, and ultimately, the Cold War ended when the USSR disintegrated in 1991.

There are some who would argue, in perfect hindsight, that there was no real penalty to America's perceived lack of will to contest Soviet imperialism in the proxy war in Vietnam and elsewhere because, by encouraging them to overreach, it brought about the ultimate collapse and dissolution of the Soviet Union. But this was certainly not the view in Washington in 1979 as the Soviets invaded Afghanistan, and while overreaching clearly contributed to the demise, the collapse was actually brought about by a calculated and deliberately implemented American policy beginning in 1981 that was far different from that pursued in the years following America's retreat from Vietnam.

And even though America did win the Cold War, at this writing some 30 years after Vietnam, the U.S. is still paying a price to repair the damage wrought by our lapse in Vietnam and its aftermath.

Notes

Chapter 1

1. William J. Duiker, *Ho Chi Minh: A Life* (New York: Hyperion, 2000), 17, 22–39.
2. *Ibid.*, 44. From this point until some time in 1918, the story of Ho's movements and activities is entirely as told by him many years later. It may be true, partly true or a total fabrication.
3. William J. Duiker, *The Communist Road to Power in Vietnam* (Boulder, CO: Westview, 1981), 16.
4. *Ibid.*
5. Duiker, *Ho Chi Minh*, 90–92
6. Henceforth, the short Vietnamese forms of the names of political organizations will be used.
7. Duiker, *Communist Road*, 17–19.
8. *Ibid.* 24.
9. Phuc Quoc had as its symbolic leader Prince Cuong De, a descendant of former emperor Gia Long of Vietnam but its effective leader was Phan Boi Chau, a Vietnamese patriot generally regarded as the grand old man of Vietnamese revolutionaries. An opponent of French rule, he fled Vietnam in 1904 for Tokyo where he was granted asylum, and was joined there by Cuong De in 1906. Expelled from Japan in 1911, Chau took Canton as his base where he later came under the influence of the Kuomintang. During World War II, the Japanese briefly toyed with the idea of deposing Bao Dai and placing the pro–Japanese Cuong De on the throne. Dennis J. Duncanson, *Government and Revolution in Vietnam* (London: Oxford University Press, 1968), 123–25, 149; Joseph Buttinger, *The Smaller Dragon: A Political History of Vietnam* (New York: Praeger, 1958), 425–29, 433–34.
10. A comprehensive summary of Vietnamese political parties based on OSS and State Department files is provided in Archimedes L. Patti, *Why Viet Nam?* (Berkeley, CA: University of California Press, 1980), Appendix III, 498–534. Patti provides an insight into the degree of factionalism in Vietnamese politics in the prewar and early postwar periods. Also, see Douglas Pike, *Viet Cong: The Organization and Techniques of the National Liberation Front of South Vietnam* (Cambridge, MA: M.I.T. Press, 1966),18–26.
11. Jean Lacouture, *Ho Chi Minh: A Political Biography* (New York: Random House, 1968), 51.
12. Alan Bullock, *Hitler and Stalin: Parallel Lives* (New York: Knopf, 1992), 211, 214; Duiker, *Communist Road*, 30.
13. Lacouture, 52.
14. Duiker, *Communist Road*, 30–33.
15. Duiker, *Ho Chi Minh*, 171–72.
16. Bernard B. Fall, *The Two Viet-Nams* (New York: Praeger, 1963), 96.
17. Duiker, *Communist Road*, 33–43.
18. Duiker, *Ho Chi Minh*, 200–210. Fall, 97, raised the possibility that Ho bought his freedom from the British by agreeing to act as a double agent. If he did, there has never been any evidence that he followed through on his commitment. Also, the fact that the leftist Ramsay MacDonald Labour government was in power in Britain at the time of Ho's arrest may have accounted for his lenient treatment in Hong Kong.
19. Duiker, *Communist Road*, 48.
20. Duiker, *Ho Chi Minh*, 223–25.
21. Duiker, *Communist Road*, 51, 63. Le Hong Phong was captured by the French in November 1940 while traveling from Hanoi to Saigon on a party mission. He was either executed or died in prison.
22. *Ibid.*, 50–55
23. *Ibid.*, 58–61.

24. Robert Shaplen, *The Lost Revolution* (New York: Harper & Row, 1965), 39–40, stated that in the period 1933–41, Ho traveled widely for the Comintern and spent an unspecified part of this period in Indochina, but no dates are given, and he cites no authority for this. He is almost certainly wrong as Ho's authoritative biographers, Duiker and Lacouture, indicate Ho spent the period in Moscow.
25. Duiker, *Ho Chi Minh*, 229–32.
26. Ibid., 240.
27. There are conflicting accounts as to where and when this front was established, but all agree it had Kuomintang sponsorship. See Duiker, *Communist Road*, 67, and *Ho Chi Minh*, 245; Patti, 505; Ellen Hammer, *The Struggle for Indochina, 1940–1955* (Stanford, CA: Stanford University Press, 1966), 95. Neither Lacouture nor Fall mentions this front.
28. Duiker, *Communist Road*, 68, *Ho Chi Minh*, 251–57; Patti, 524; Lacouture, 74; Fall, 62.
29. As will be seen, in the fall of 1945, Ho ostensibly disbanded the ICP, but the clandestine party never ceased to exist.
30. Duiker, *Communist Road*, 77.
31. Duiker, *Ho Chi Minh*, 271–72
32. Duiker, *Communist Road*, 78–79.
33. Ibid., 79.
34. Duiker, Ho Chi Minh, 276–82.
35. Ibid., 295–96, and *Communist Road*, 82.
36. *On August 14, 1945, Japan declared Cochinchina independent and joined it to Annam and Tonkin. Thus, until August 28 when Bao Dai abdicated under the pressure of the Vietminh, Vietnam was briefly united for the first time since 1867 when the French colonized Cochinchina.* Hammer, 52.
37. Ibid., 97.
38. Duiker, *Communist Road*, 80.
39. Ibid., 91–100.
40. Hammer, 101; Duncanson, 159.
41. Fall, 63–64. Fall's figure for the strength of the British-Indian force is 1,400 men of the 20th Indian Division.
42. Duncanson,158; Patti, 381, made the hardly credible claim that Ho's dissolution of the ICP was in response to vague statements by the U.S. favoring self-determination for colonized peoples.
43. Duncanson, 160–61; Duiker, *Communist Road*, 110–11.
44. Duiker, *Communist Road*, 113–17.
45. Fall, 72–3. It was several months later than the agreed-upon date before all Chinese troops were out of Vietnam.
46. Duiker, *Communist Road*, 117–20.
47. Duiker, *Ho Chi Minh*, 379–80.
48. Again, there are discrepancies in the record with respect to the establishment of this front organization. Hammer stated,175, that the Lien Viet was set up in May 1946. Fall, in *Two Viet-Nams*, 179, agreed but stated correctly that the Lien Viet and Vietminh coexisted until 1951 when the Vietminh was merged into the Lien Viet. Duiker, in both *Communist Road*, 143, and *Ho Chi Minh*, 438, stated that in 1951 the Vietminh Front was renamed the Lien Viet Front but said nothing about the prior existence of Lien Viet.
49. Fall,130; Pike, 43–44; Duiker, *Communist Road*, 121.
50. Patti, 525 and 529. Examples were the Viet Nam Democratic Party and the Viet Nam Socialist Party which held seats in the DRV National Assembly but never at any time formed an opposition to Ho's Communist regime.
51. Duiker, *Communist Road*, 122–25; *Ho Chi Minh*, 395–99.
52. Duiker, *Communist Road*, 135.
53. Patti, 129; Fall,70.
54. Duiker, *Communist Road*, 139–40.
55. Duiker, *Ho Chi Minh*, 429.
56. Ibid., 438–39.
57. Ibid., 474. In 1955, the Lien Viet Front in turn was subsumed by the newly created Fatherland Front which was intended to attract sympathetic elements in South Vietnam to a program of unification of North and South. The impetus for the creation of the Fatherland Front was probably preparation for the reunification referendum then scheduled for 1956.
58. Duiker, *Ho Chi Minh*, 437–41.
59. Ibid., 414, 438–39. After World War II, nationalist groups in Laos and Cambodia created the Lao Issara and Khmer Issarak, respectively, to lead the fight for independence. With the onset of the First Indochina War, these groups came under the influence of Vietminh cadres and were in effect subsumed into the Indochinese Communist Party which had been, in theory, dissolved by Ho Chi Minh in 1945 but in practice was still functioning. With the formation of the Vietnamese Worker's Party in 1951, the Indochinese Communist Party ceased to exist, and Laotian and Cambodian groups were emancipated, that is, allowed to form separate parties, but always under the close guidance of VWP cadres. These new parties became the Pathet Lao (Land of Lao) and the Khmer Rouge (Red Khmer).
60. Duiker, *Communist Road*, 113–17, 138, 174.
61. Duiker, 147–51.
62. Duncanson, 197–200
63. Duiker, *Communist Road*, 155; George McT. Kahin, *Intervention: How America Became Involved in Vietnam* (New York: Knopf, 1986), 39. Jules Roy, *The Battle of Dien Bien Phu* (New York: Pyramid, 1966), 26, gave the figure as 375,000 but this may not include paramilitary units.
64. The figure of 300,000 is generally agreed as the size of Giap's total forces, made up of 125,000 to 150,000 People's Army of Vietnam

regulars, 75,000 regional troops and 150,000 guerrillas. Stanley Karnow, *Vietnam: A History* (New York: Penguin, 1983), 184; Roy, 26.
65. Duiker, *Ho Chi Minh*, 453–55; Bernard B. Fall, *Hell In a Very Small Place* (Philadelphia: Lippincott, 1966), 487.
66. Duiker, *Ho Chi Minh*, 458.
67. *Ibid.*, 460.
68. For the texts of the Agreement and Final Declaration, see Richard N. Goodwin, *Triumph or Tragedy: Reflections on Vietnam* (New York: Vintage, 1966), 68–95.
69. Duiker, *Ho Chi Minh*, 438. This was pursuant to the Chinese model.
70. Duncanson, 173–74.
71. *Ibid.* It was later admitted by the official DRV government newspaper, *Nhan Dan*, that 30 percent of persons liquidated as landowners did not own any land.
72. Bernard B. Fall, *Viet-Nam Witness: 1953–1966* (New York: Praeger, 1966), 96–104, 124; *Two Viet-Nams*, 155–58; Duiker, who draws heavily on DRV sources, did not give specific numbers but in *Ho Chi Minh*, 474–88, implied a much lower level of victims than Fall, and in *Communist Road*, 153–54, he glided over the unsavory aspects of this episode in DRV history. Frances Fitzgerald, *Fire in the Lake: The Vietnamese and the Americans in Vietnam.* (New York, Vintage, 1972), 299–300, cites D. Gareth Porter, a leftist American scholar, who asserted that the number of deaths was grossly exaggerated by "devious Diemist officials" who " ... mistranslated, misinterpreted, or actually falsified" DRV documents and that the death toll "could not have been above 2,500 and may have been as low as 800." Fitzgerald made no mention whatever of the Nghe An uprising. But even Lacouture, who was not given to criticism of Ho and the DRV, says in *Ho Chi Minh*, 204, "a savage and hastily implemented land-reform policy brought the DRV to the brink of catastrophe." And, 210, "in 1955 and 1956, the land reform campaign was applied so harshly that ... his [Ho's] own native province of Nghe Tinh ... rose in rebellion.... The repression that followed was extremely harsh...." The weight of evidence tends to support a high number of victims.
73. Duiker, *Ho Chi Minh*, 484–86.
74. *Ibid.* 497–99, *Communist Road*, 179–80; Fall, *Two Viet-Nams*, 360–61.
75. Fitzgerald,119,195–201.
76. Duiker, *Ho Chi Minh*, 499. In September 1960 at the Third National Congress of the VWP, Le Duan was formally elected first secretary of the party, 524. He retained that position until his death in 1986.
77. *Ibid.*, 505.
78. *Ibid.*, 492.
79. Jean Lacouture, *Between Two Truces* (New York, Random House, 1966), 28–31, 35, 52, 53, 67, 68. Duiker, *Ho Chi Minh*, 511–13.

80. Duiker, *Ho Chi Minh*, 513–14.
81. *Ibid.*, 482, 504–5, 508, 572. Certain Western writers have contributed to Ho's cult. Lacouture even set him above all others when, in *Ho Chi Minh*, 209, he said, "In fact, no other leader in the world today is viewed by his followers as being both inventor and protector, source and guide, theory and practice, nation and revolution, yogi and commissar, good-natured uncle and great war leader."
82. Duiker, *Communist Road*, 195–99; Pike, Chapter 4.
83. Pike, 74–84. Pike stated, 82, that the NLF "was formally organized by a group of about ten persons representing specific organizations and approximately fifty others attending as individuals" but did not name the organizations represented. One can assume, for example, that the Cao Dai was represented, but it never formally aligned itself the NLF. Also, see Helms memo to McNamara, *Foreign Relations of the US, 1964–1968, Vol. IV, Vietnam 1966*. (Washington, DC: USGPO, 1998), Doc. 65, 205, which describes the managing hierarchy of the NLF.
84. Pike,110.
85. *Ibid.*, Chapter 10.
86. *Ibid.*, 76–77.
87. *Vietnam: Between Two Truces*, 54–55. Emphasis added.
88. *Ibid.*, 56. Emphasis added.
89. Fall, *Two Viet-Nams*, 439–43; Goodwin, 103–10.
90. Pike, 139–40.
91. *Ibid.*, 137.
92. *FRUS, 1964–1968, Vol. II, Vietnam, January–June 1965*, Doc. 245, 543. North Vietnamese premier Pham Van Dong announced the Four Points in an address before the United National Assembly in Hanoi on April 8, 1965. For the full text see Goodwin, 103–10.
93. Duiker, *Ho Chi Min*, 534
94. *Ibid.*, 536–38, 542. Significantly, Ho was not included in this mission. He was being increasingly marginalized by the hard-liners who distrusted his compromising tendencies and believed he was becoming increasingly addled.
95. *Ibid.* 544.
96. Kai Bird, *The Color of Truth* (New York: Simon & Schuster, 1998), 305–8. *FRUS, 1964–1968, Vol. II, Vietnam, January–June 1965*, Doc. 80, 166. Four army barracks were targeted for the reprisals, three to be hit by U.S. aircraft and one by the South Vietnamese Air Force. Two U.S. targets and the one Vietnam target were weathered in and not hit. No follow-up strikes were conducted.
97. Duiker, *Ho Chi Minh*, 555–56.
98. *Ibid.*, 557–59.
99. This dates the beginning of Ho's struggle to 1924 when he joined the Communist International.

100. As related earlier, Le Hong Phong and others who led the party within Vietnam during the 1930s and who ran the greatest personal risks were largely eliminated by the Sûreté.
101. Duiker, *Ho Chi Minh*, 566.

Chapter 2

1. Samuel Eliot Morison, *History of United States Naval Operations in World War II, Volume 3, The Rising Sun in the Pacific: 1931–April 1942* (Boston: Little, Brown, 1963), 58–63; Dean Acheson, *Present at the Creation*. (New York: Norton, 1969), 23–27.
2. Morison, 79.
3. Barbara W. Tuchman, *Stilwell and the American Experience in China: 1911–45.* (New York: Bantam, 1972), 525.
4. *New York Times*, March 29, 1945.
5. Duiker, *Ho Chi Minh*, 282–283, 286–292; Patti, 57–58.
6. Duiker, *Ho Chi Minh*, 291–294
7. *Ibid.*, 284–85.
8. *Ibid.*
9. Patti, 76, 85, 90–93, 242. France, her colonial policies and the French representatives with whom Patti came in contact in China and Vietnam were generally presented unsympathetically throughout.
10. Patti, 83–88.
11. *Ibid.*, 127–29. Patti did not specify the total number of Americans on this team nor the quantities and types of arms furnished. Nor is it clear what training in guerrilla tactics the Americans were able to provide since the Vietminh allegedly had been conducting guerrilla warfare against the Japanese and French colonials for over two years.
12. Neil Sheehan, *A Bright Shining Lie: John Paul Vann and America in Vietnam* (New York: Random House, 1988), 46, stated the OSS provided thousands of carbines, submachine guns, and other equipment to arm the original Vietminh formations. He gave no source for this information.
13. Patti, 231–32, 350.
14. *Ibid.*,199, 220, 231, 300, 348, 366.
15. *Ibid.*, 203, 246, 295; Duiker, *Ho Chi Minh*, 331.
16. Patti, 249.
17. *Ibid.*, 238.
18. *Ibid.*, 365.
19. *Ibid.*, 341.
20. *Ibid.*, 360.
21. 1 *Ibid.*, 462.
22. *Ibid.*, 271–272
23. *Ibid.*, 317, 320–321; *New York Times*, Sept. 28.
24. Russell H. Fifield, *Americans in Southeast Asia: The Roots of Commitment* (New York: Crowell, 1973), 179.
25. James R. Arnold, *The First Domino: Eisenhower, The Military, and America's Intervention in Vietnam* (New York: William Morrow, 1991), 70.
26. *Ibid.*, 186, 308.
27. Kahin, 5–6.
28. Fifield, 57.
29. Kahin, 5–7; Arnold, 51–53; Robert D. Schulzinger, *The United States and Vietnam, 1941–1975* (New York: Oxford University Press, 1997), 19–22.
30. Fifield, 122–23.
31. Similarly, after the Communist victory in China, the Democrats in the U.S. would come to appreciate the uncomfortable consequences of being on the wrong side of the "Who lost China?" question.
32. Kahin, 21–23.
33. Patti, 29, 53, 232, 350, 380; Fifield, 109–11; Schulzinger, 18; Robert A. Mann, *A Grand Delusion* (New York: Basic Books, 2000), 724; Shaplen, 27–35.
34. Fall, *Viet-Nam Witness*, 7; Karnow, 136; Patti, 392–93.
35. Duiker, *Ho Chi Minh*, 390–392; Patti, 203, 246.
36. Duiker, *The Communist Road* , 19–23.
37. Duiker, probably the leading American scholar on Ho Chi Minh, in *Ho Chi Minh*, 573–574, gave a closely reasoned analysis which supports this point of view.
38. Acheson 203, 305.
39. Fifield, 126.
40. Fifield, 84–85.
41. Acheson, 671–75.
42. *New York Times*, March 17, 1954; Kahin, 42.
43. See Kahin, Chapter II, "To the Brink of War in Support of France," which has throughout an underlying tone of criticism of U.S. policy.
44. To name just three: the Berlin blockade, the Russian atomic bomb, and the fall of China to Communism.
45. Mann, 68–69; Fifield, 174
46. The actual decision to become involved in the First Indochina War was made on April 24, 1950, when Truman approved NSC-64 which stated, "It is important to United States security interests that all practicable measures be taken to prevent further Communist expansion in Southeast Asia." The underlying logic of NSC-64 was the Domino Theory. Note that this *preceded* the start of the Korean War. William Conrad Gibbons, *The U.S. Government and the Vietnam War, Part I, 1945–1961.* (Washington, D.C.: USGPO, 1984), 66–67. NSC-64 was superceded in June 1952 by NSC-124/2 which took an even stronger position with respect to Indochina and called for "military action against

China itself if necessary to save Southeast Asia." Gibbons, 105.
47. Acheson, 671–72.
48. Ibid., 373–77.
49. Gibbons, 71–73.
50. Ibid., 66–68.
51. Ronald McGlothlen, *Controlling the Waves: Dean Acheson and U.S. Foreign Policy in Asia* (New York: Norton, 1993), 195. In May 1950, Secretary of State Dean Acheson was informed flatly by Foreign Minister Robert Schuman that the rearming of Germany would require the maintenance of countervailing French military strength in Europe, and that in view of its heavy commitments in Indochina, France must have full U.S. military support there.
52. *New York Times*, August 31, 1954.
53. McGlothlen, 199–200.
54. Fifield, 209.
55. Gibbons, 250–56.
56. Anthony Eden, *Full Circle: The Memoirs of Anthony Eden*, (Boston: Houghton Mifflin, 1960), 149. Gibbons, 252.
57. Gibbons, 271–76.
58. *New York Times*, August 17, 21, and October 25, 1954.
59. Gibbons, 267–71. The U.S. position vis-a-vis Indochina following the Geneva Accords was defined in NSC-5429 of August 12, 1954, the provisions of which foreshadowed the supplanting of France by the U.S. in the dominant role in non-Communist Indochina.
60. Lansdale's initial cover in Saigon was as assistant air attache. He is alleged to be the model for "Colonel Hillandale" in the Lederer and Burdick novel *The Ugly American* and for "Pyle" in Graham Greene's *The Quiet American*.
61. *The Pentagon Papers* — as published by the *New York Times* (New York: New York Times, Bantam Books, 1971), 54.
62. Ibid., 53–66.
63. Gibbons, 289.
64. Ibid., 287–299.
65. Ibid., 305.
66. Fitzgerald, 102; Kahin, 76–77; Fall, *Two Viet-Nams*, 153–54, agreed that a psychological warfare operation was conducted by American agents but stated," The Tonkinese Catholics fled because they had long experience of persecution at the hands of their non-Catholic fellow citizens." The American agents in North Vietnam were part of Lansdale's Saigon Military Mission. Edward G. Lansdale, *In the Midst of Wars* (New York: Harper & Row, 1972), 168.
67. Fall,*Two Viet-Nams*, 59, stated, "The northern Catholics were facing political annihilation when the French, in the process of the contraction of the delta defenses into a tighter perimeter ... decided to abandon 600,000 (Catholics) to the advancing Viet Minh."
68. Fall, *Viet-Nam Witness*, 76, said 5,000–6,000 while Duiker, *Communist Road*, 173, said 10,000 to 15,000. The usually accepted figure is 5,000.
69. Karnow, 222.
70. Fall provided the best account of the showdown between Diem and the sects in *Viet-Nam Witness,* Chapter 11. Also see *New York Times*, March, 5, 30; April 1, 29, 30; May 1, 2; July 7.
71. Fall, *Two Viet-Nams*, 256–58; *New York Times*, October 19, 24, 27, 1955. While there were charges of vote rigging in the referendum , there is little doubt Diem would have won easily in any case.
72. For a detailed account of Diem's transformation of South Vietnam from monarchy to republic, see Robert Scigliano, *South Vietnam: Nation Under Stress*. (Boston: Houghton Mifflin, 1963), Chapters 1 and 2, 13–31.
73. Fall, *Two Viet-Nams*, 77. *New York Times*, February 22, March 24, 1956.
74. Scigliano, 134; Duiker, *Ho Chi Minh*, 469–72.
75. Goodwin, 93.
76. Scigliano, 41–43, 45, 98–100.
77. Shaplen, 121–23; Kahin, 82–84.
78. See *New York Times*, May 7 through 20, 1957, for a continuing account of his visit.
79. Ibid., May 7, 1959.
80. Ibid., July 7, 1959.
81. Fall, *Viet-Nam Witness*, 238–39.
82. Gibbons, 311. In the spring of 1956,Wolf Ladejinsky supplanted Lansdale as personal advisor to Diem.
83. Scigliano, 164, 201–6.
84. As noted above, Lansdale's replacement was Wolf Ladejinsky, the leading U.S. expert on agrarian reform in developing countries.
85. Scigliano, 199–200.
86. The foregoing description of Diem's land reform program is drawn from Scigliano, 121–24 and Duncanson, 244–46.
87. George C. Herring, *America's Longest War*, 2d ed., (New York: Knopf, 1986), 57.
88. Gibbons, 288–89.
89. Ronald H. Spector, *Advice and Support: The Early Years, 1941–1960* (Washington, D. C.: Center of Military History, U.S. Army, 1983), 360–361; *The Pentagon Papers* , 120.
90. Spector, 278.
91. Ibid., 263–264.
92. Ibid., 296–99.
93. *FRUS, 1958–1960, Vol. I, Vietnam*, Doc. 104, 283.
94. Spector, 349–52.
95. Ibid., 365.
96. *The Pentagon Papers*, 131–32.
97. *FRUS, 1955–1957, Vol. 1, Vietnam* (USGPO, Washington, D.C., 1985), 16. From seven divisions and a large number of independent battalions when the truce was signed, by early 1955 it had risen to 11 divisions, an in-

crease in regulars from 145,000 to 230,000, and its firepower was being increased by large amounts of artillery and other equipment from Communist bloc sources.

98. Herring, 59.
99. *FRUS, 1958–1960, Vol. I, Vietnam*, Doc. 97, 259.
100. *Ibid.*, Doc. 112, 302.
101. Fall, *Two Viet-Nams*, 271–72.
102. *Ibid.*, 272.
103. *FRUS, 1958–1960, Vol. 1, Vietnam*, Doc. 178, 512.
104. *Ibid.*, Doc. 214, 626 and Doc. 253, 694.
105. William Colby, *Lost Victory* (Chicago: Contemporary Books, 1989), 73–76. Colby was CIA station chief in Saigon, 1959–1961.
106. *FRUS, 1958–1960, Vol. I, Vietnam*, Doc. 87, 222; Doc. 88, 229; Doc. 89, 230.
107. Karnow, 235, describes Durbrow as a "chubby figure with a Rotarian manner."
108. Spector, 367–68n.
109. *The Pentagon Papers*, 120–21.
110. Scigliano, 215–16.

Chapter 3

1. *New York Times*, January 21, 1961
2. *Ibid.*
3. Kai Bird, *The Color of Truth: McGeorge Bundy and William Bundy, Brothers in Arms: A Biography* (New York: Simon & Schuster, 1998), 79–80.
4. *Ibid.*, 119.
5. *Ibid.*, 109. In 1951, when Bundy was recommended for tenure in Harvard's government department, Harvard president James B. Conant was shocked to learn that Bundy had never taken either an undergraduate or graduate course in government, but he still approved the appointment.
6. Arthur M. Schlesinger, Jr., *A Thousand Days: John F. Kennedy in the White House* (Cambridge, MA: Riverside Press), 139–40.
7. David Halberstam, *The Best and the Brightest* (New York: Random House, 1972), 36–37, 315–17; Schlesinger, 432–36, 1017.
8. Schlesinger, 131.
9. Robert S. McNamara, *In Retrospect: The Tragedy and Lessons of Vietnam* (New York: Times Books, 1995), 3–10.
10. Halberstam, 224–40.
11. Schlesinger, 545; Halberstam, 213–14.
12. Schlesinger, 45–57, 705–7.
13. Halberstam, 492–95, 629.
14. Bird, 16, 73.
15. Halberstam, 362–66.
16. *Ibid.*, 190.
17. William C. Gibbons, *The U.S. Government and the Vietnam War, Part II 1961–1964*, (Princeton, NJ: Princeton University Press, 1986), 17, 106, 139.
18. Rudy Abramson, *Spanning the Century: The Life of W. Averell Harriman, 1891–1986* (New York: Morrow, 1992), 152.
19. Abramson, 123, 152–53, 582–83; Halberstam, 75.
20. Halberstam, 156–62.
21. Laos is a thinly populated country by Southeast Asian standards with a population density in 1961 of about 20 people per square mile compared to about 200 in South Vietnam and 72 in Cambodia. Moreover, the population is concentrated in the Mekong valley, leaving the rest of the country even more sparsely populated. *Life Pictorial Atlas*. (New York: Time, 1961), 363.
22. Duiker, *Communist Road*, 142.
23. Fifield, 121; The Elysée Agreement of July 19, 1949.
24. Schlesinger, 324.
25. John F. Cady, *The History of Post-War Southeast Asia* (Athens, Ohio: Ohio University Press, 1974), 366.
26. *Ibid.*, 367–69.
27. Schlesinger, 323–29.
28. Cady, 377–78, 412–14. The Pathet Lao were drawn largely from non–Buddhist Meo tribesmen who populated the mountainous northern provinces of Laos adjoining Tonkin and who were ethnically distinct from the Lao of the Mekong Valley. Pathet Lao forces were trained by North Vietnamese cadres, and Vietnamese regulars often spearheaded attacks on a Laotian national army that was no match for the fierce, disciplined North Vietnamese fighters. From the early 1960s onward, North Vietnam maintained 40,000 to 50,000 troops in Laos, and by the late 1960s only about a third of Laos was under the Vientiane government's control.
29. Schlesinger, 163–64; Gibbons, Part II, 9.
30. *New York Times*, January 26, 1961.
31. Gibbons, Part II, 18–23.
32. *Ibid.*, 22–23, 31. Much of the discussion in Washington and with other SEATO members on intervention entailed implementation of SEATO Plan 5, which was a contingency plan for the deployment of a major SEATO force to defend Thailand, Laos, Cambodia and South Vietnam from positions on the Mekong River. *FRUS, 1961–1963, Vol. XXIV, Laos Crisis.* (Washington: USGPO, 1994), Doc. 163, 371.
33. Charles A. Stevenson, *The End of Nowhere: American Policy Toward Laos Since 1954.* (Boston: Beacon Press, 1972), 150. Gibbons, Part II, 27.
34. Schlesinger, 337.
35. *Ibid.*, 340.
36. Gibbons, Part II, 33
37. *Ibid.*, 49; Abramson, 584.
38. Abramson, 585–86.

39. *Ibid.* 586.
40. *FRUS, 1961–1963, Vol. XXIV, Laos Crisis*, 497.
41. Stevenson, 191. In April 1963, after Harriman had been named undersecretary of state, he was sent to Moscow by Kennedy to remind Khrushchev of his pledge to insure the compliance of the Communist signatories with the 1962 Geneva Accords. Khrushchev indicated he could no longer restrain the DRV or Pathet Lao forces in Laos and would not try to do so.
42. *Ibid.*, 165. The so-called Pushkin agreement was strictly an oral understanding between Harriman, Pushkin and the British. It was not a part of the final accords nor was it made public at the time.
43. *Ibid.*
44. Abramson, 587.
45. *Ibid.* The Ho Chi Minh Trail was later labeled the Harriman Highway by American troops in South Vietnam.
46. To appreciate the full depth of Kennedy administration ingenuousness on the matter of policing the accords, one need only read Acting Secretary of State George Ball's June 28, 1962, memo to Kennedy, *FRUS, 1961–1963, Vol. XXIV, Laos Crisis*, Doc. 405, 856. The section on policing the accords begins: "The principal way the agreements can be policed is through action by the Soviet Union in its capacity as co–Chairman." A slim reed, indeed, on which to place the faith of the U.S. that the accords would be honored.
47. Gibbons, Part II, 49.
48. Schlesinger, 516.
49. Abramson, 588.
50. *FRUS, 1961–1963, Vol. XXIV, Laos Crisis*, 485–88.
51. *Ibid.*, 557n. Economic aid to the Royal Laotian Government provided funds to pay the army.
52. *FRUS, Laos Crisis*, 363. Renunciation of SEATO protection was the result of a prior agreement between Harriman and Pushkin, another Harriman compromise.
53. Abramson, 582–91; Schlesinger, 512–18; John F. Newman, *JFK and Vietnam: The Tragedy and Lessons of Vietnam* (New York: Time Books, 1995), 476–91.
54. Newman, 268. The 10,000 number was an estimate of Vietnamese forces believed to be operating with the Pathet Lao and did not include those holding the eastern infiltration trails.
55. Schlesinger, 517.
56. Cady, 397.
57. Gibbons, Part II, 375.
58. Henry Kissinger, *Years of Upheaval* (London: Weidenfeld and Nicholson and Michael Joseph, 1982), 21–23.
59. Gibbons, Part II, 26, 28, 49, 60, 117.
60. *Ibid.*,121

61. Major Kennedy biographers Schlesinger, Richard Reeves, *President Kennedy: Profile of Power* (New York: Simon & Schuster,1993), and Robert Dallek, *An Unfinished Life: John F. Kennedy, 1917–1963* (Boston: Little, Brown, 2003) are consistent in not acknowledging Kennedy's failure in the 1961–62 Laos crisis and in ignoring its disastrous consequences in the Second Indochina War. While Schlesinger, writing in 1965 may have had some excuse, Reeves and Dallek had the benefit of full hindsight.
62. *FRUS, 1961–1963, Vol. I, Vietnam, 1961* (Washington, DC: USGPO,1985), Doc. 5, 19.
63. *Ibid*, 12; Halberstam, 127.
64. Gibbons, 11–13.
65. *FRUS 1961–1963, Vol. I, Vietnam, 1961*, 46, note 2.
66. Schlesinger, 548.
67. Gibbons, Part II, 41–43.
68. *FRUS 1961–1963, Vol. I, Vietnam, 1961*, Doc.1, p.1.
69. Gibbons, Part II, 35–36.
70. *The Pentagon Papers*, 120.
71. *FRUS, 1961–1963, Vol. I, Vietnam*, 132–34.
72. Gibbons, Part II, 49–50. With respect to the "selected elements" phrase, Diem stated this would necessitate a "considerable expansion" of the MAAG, which at that time numbered 685, but the word "considerable" was never defined. An October request by Diem's defense minister for "combat-trainer units" is misleadingly headlined in *The Pentagon Papers*, 140, as "1961 Request by South Vietnam for U.S. Combat Forces" but envisioned only token, symbolic numbers.
73. *FRUS, 1961–1963, Vol. I, Vietnam*, 133.
74. Gibbons, Part II, 70.
75. Maxwell D. Taylor, *Swords and Plowshares* (New York, Norton, 1972), 225–26.
76. New York, Harper & Bros., 1960.
77. Schlesinger, 297, 341.
78. Taylor, 252.
79. *FRUS 1961–1963, Vol. I, Vietnam*, 481
80. Halberstam, 169.
81. *FRUS 1961–1963, Vol. I, Vietnam*, 493.
82. *The Pentagon Papers*, 143.
83. Gibbons, Part II, 86–87; McNamara, 38–39, characterized his memo as "hastily prepared" and a "bad idea."
84. Gibbons, Part II, 89–91.
85. Gibbons, Part II, 92n43; McNamara, 39.
86. Gibbons, Part II, 99–100, 102–3; *The Pentagon Papers*, 107–9.
87. Schlesinger, 545; Newman, 146.
88. Gibbons, Part II, 384–86.
89. *New York Times*, February 9 through 18, 1962.
90. *Ibid.*, February 14, 1962.
91. Gibbons, Part II, 71.

92. *FRUS, 1961–1963, Vol. II, Vietnam, 1962,* Doc. 248, 546. During the meeting, McNamara asked Harkins how long before the VC could be eliminated as a disturbing force. Harkins estimated about one year from the time that the ARVN, the Civil Guard and the Self Defense Corps were fully operational and really pressing the VC in all areas. From this response, McNamara instantly extrapolated that it would require approximately three years to bring the VC under control and thus established the goal of winding down U.S. military involvement by the end of 1965.
93. McNamara, 48–49.
94. Schlesinger, *Robert Kennedy*, 742–43.
95. *The Pentagon Papers,* 112
96. *Ibid.,* 110.
97. Schlesinger, *Robert Kennedy,* 741–45; Newman, 324; and Kahin, 146–47. This assertion by Kennedy loyalists reveals a deeply cynical side of Kennedy's character which they probably would prefer remain hidden. In 1978, when told of the alleged statement to Mansfield, Dean Rusk discounted it. In *As I Saw It.* (New York: Norton, 1990), 441, Rusk said: "Had he [Kennedy] decided in 1963 on a 1965 withdrawal, he would have left Americans in a combat zone for domestic political purposes, and no president can do that." McNamara, 95–97, speculated loosely that he felt Kennedy would have pulled out of Vietnam. Schlesinger is the foremost advocate of the thesis that Kennedy intended to pull out of Vietnam after his reelection. He implied this in *A Thousand Days,* but in *Robert Kennedy,* 741–45, written 13 years later, he flatly asserted that this was the case, based largely on the same conversation with Mansfield that others have cited, and while conceding that it was a political calculation, he does not address the question of the morality of it.
98. *FRUS, 1961–1963, Volume III, Vietnam, January 1963–August 1963,* 185.
99. Fall, *Viet-Nam Witness,* 279.
100. *FRUS, 1958–1960, Vol. I, Vietnam,* Doc. 169, 485; Doc. 213, 623; Scigliano, 180–81. The agroville project failed, principally because of peasant resistance to being relocated from their traditional village and lands. Announced in mid-1959, it was halted in early 1961.
101. Fall, *Viet-Nam Witness,* 272–73; Fitzgerald, 165; Karnow, 256; George C. Herring, *America's Longest War — 1950–1975* (New York: Wiley 1979), 89; and others accepted the thesis that the program was modeled on the Malayan experience and was therefore inapplicable to Vietnam. Respected Vietnam experts Pike and Scigliano made no mention of the Malayan experience as the origin of the strategic hamlet program. With regard to Thompson's role in Vietnam, William Colby, *Lost Victory* (Chicago: Contemporary Books, 1989), 100, said, "Sir Robert Thompson certainly influenced the process, but Nhu stressed that the security of the hamlet should begin within it and gradually build the necessary defenses around that essentially political core. Thompson's Malayan experience suggested essentially an administrative action, surrounding the community with security so that its inhabitants could be controlled and their links to the guerrillas outside severed. I shared Nhu's view I ... so this difference between Thompson and myself persisted for years...."
102. Colby, Chapter 6, "Roads to Strategic Hamlets," 82–103.
103. Duncanson, 313–16. As a member of the Thompson Advisory Mission to Vietnam from 1961 to 1965, Duncanson was in a position to know the origins of the strategic hamlet program.
104. Pike, 116–17.
105. *Ibid.,* 158–59.
106. *Ibid.,* 143.
107. *Ibid.* Examples are, 141, point two of the 10-point program of the PRP, and 353, point one of the NLF's first post–Diem policy statement which referred to strategic hamlets as "disguised concentration camps." These references failed to note that the residents of these "concentration camps" had guns.
108. *Ibid.*
109. Duncanson, 363–64.
110. That the Kennedy administration was hypersensitive to adverse material on Vietnam in the influential press is shown by the frequency with which newspaper articles were cited in official correspondence. In *FRUS, 1961–1963, Vietnam, Vol. IV, August–December, 1963,* the index has 17 citations for the *New York Times,* three for the *Washington Post* and two for the *Washington Times.* Often, these were messages requiring a response in the form of an explanation or a rebuttal from Saigon embassy staff and leaving the distinct impression that the administration was being media driven.
111. Neil Sheehan, *A Bright Shining Lie* (New York: Random House, 1988), 203–65.
112. *FRUS 1961–1963, Vol. III, Vietnam, January–August, 1963* has numerous references to the press relations problem in Vietnam.
113. Robert Manning, editor-in-chief, et al., *The Vietnam Experience: America Takes Over, 1965–67.* (Boston: Boston, 1982), 70.
114. This description of the events in Hue is drawn from Duncanson, 327–30, which is the most insightful and balanced account of the episode found by the author.
115. Colby, 29.
116. Even such an anti–Diem figure as Roger Hilsman admitted that the crisis was not caused by religious persecution and that there was not really any significant amount of persecution of the Buddhist religion in Vietnam. *To Move a Nation.* (Garden City, NY: Doubleday, 1967), 470.

117. *New York Times*, May 19, 1963. In a February 24, 1964, news article buried on page 28, the *Times* reported that a letter by Senator Dodd accompanying the report of the UN fact-finding mission stated that the report showed persecution of Buddhists was either nonexistent or vastly exaggerated and that agitation was mainly political.
118. *FRUS, 1961–1963, Vol. III, Vietnam*, 381.
119. *New York Times*, July 3.
120. Sheehan, 334–35.
121. Duncanson, 335 and 335n.; In South Vietnam, the Buddhist lay following, consisting of about 1 million registered, practicing Buddhists, was confined to Saigon and the towns. Unregistered Buddhists brought the total to about 3 million. The Cao Dai and Hoa Hao sects together exceeded this number. Of the peasantry not affiliated with Catholicism or the sects, few regarded themselves as having a professed religion, Buddhist or otherwise, but usually reverted to Buddhist consecration rites for important occasions.
122. *New York Times*, June 14, 1963.
123. *FRUS 1961–1963, Vol. III, Vietnam, January–August 1963*, 60–61.
124. *Ibid.*, 97.
125. Henry Cabot Lodge, Jr., *The Storm Has Many Eyes: A Personal Narrative* (New York: Norton,1973), 20–23.
126. Schlesinger, *A Thousand Days*, 988–89; Rusk, 524. Rusk did not state explicitly that it was his idea to appoint Lodge, only that he *sent* Lodge to Vietnam. If the idea actually originated in State, it may have been suggested by Harriman, who was much more a political animal than Rusk.
127. *FRUS 1961–1963, Vol. III, Vietnam, January–August 1963*, 473.
128. Gibbons, Part II, 141–43. Gibbons elaborated on Diem's loss of support among influential Kennedy supporters in 1963 and stated: "This, together with the lack of progress being made on the military front in Vietnam provided the ingredients for the decision to 'drop Diem,' which was made during the period between May and August 1963 ... in meetings of the Special Group (CI)." This lent support to the thesis that there was consensus in Washington for the removal of Diem many months in advance of the event, a thesis that is almost certainly false. Some of the most influential members of the Special Group (CI) including Maxwell Taylor, chairman, John McCone, CIA director; and Attorney General Robert Kennedy, opposed the removal of Diem, as did McNamara, and in any case, such a decision was not within the authority of that group. While the Harriman clique did make such a decision, that did not constitute a Washington consensus. At this time there probably was a consensus among liberal intellectuals like John Kenneth Galbraith and Hans Morgenthau, liberal journalists like Theordore White and American correspondents in Saigon that Diem had to go.
129. Diem had been the object of two previous coup attempts, in 1960 and 1962, which failed because neither had the backing of the army's top officers.
130. Duncanson, 336.
131. Following the raid on Xa Loi, Thich Tri Quang was granted political asylum in the U.S. Embassy by Lodge.
132. Halberstam and Sheehan claimed to be witnesses to the Xa Loi raid. In *The Best and the Brightest*, 261, Halberstam stated that the raiding party was made up of Nhu's Special Forces *disguised* in ARVN uniforms to shift blame to the army, but Sheehan in *A Bright Shining Lie*, 355, contradicted Halberstam in stating that the shoulder patches of the raiders identified them as Special Forces.
133. Aug. 23, 28, and 30, 1963.
134. *FRUS, 1961–1963, Volume IV, Vietnam, August–December 1963.* (Washington, DC: USGPO, 1991), Doc. 80, 146. The Saigon CIA Station reported on September 10 that it now concluded that general officers were themselves also involved in responsibility for the pagoda raids, but this intelligence was never made public by the administration since it contradicted the scenario it had already propagated. *New York Times*, August 27, 29.
135. *FRUS III*, Doc. 274, 613, and *Ibid.*, Doc. 275, 614 have two contradictory accounts by ARVN Generals Kim and Don of the event leading up to the pagoda raids with Kim's maintaining the army's noninvolvement while Don's admits that the army recommended and had foreknowledge of the actions taken by Diem and Nhu. The greater detail provided by Don makes his account more credible.
136. Abramson, 617.
137. Gibbons, 148. Gibbons persisted in the erroneous view that the actions of Harriman, Hilsman and Forrestal were in accordance with some previously agreed-upon plan when in fact no such plan existed and the entire crisis from Deptel 243 to the final coup on Nov. 1 was handled by the administration entirely on an ad hoc basis.
138. Schlesinger, 990–91, stated that Lodge, confronted with the chaotic situation in Saigon, cabled Washington for instructions and that Deptel 243 was in response to this request, yet no such cable has been produced by supporters of this thesis. It is almost certain that Deptel 243 was entirely at the initiative of Harriman, Hilsman and Forrestal.
139. *FRUS 1961–1963, Vol. III, Vietnam, January–August 1963*, Doc. 278, 625.
140. *Ibid.*, Doc. 280, 627.
141. Hilsman, 85–89, gave his version of this

event in which he made it appear that nothing unusual or irregular was done in the drafting and clearing of Deptel 243. What he omitted from his account is that Rusk, Gilpatrick and Helms were told that Kennedy had already approved the cable. Halberstam's sympathies were clearly with the triumvirate, and thus, his account in *The Best and the Brightest*, 263, written five years after Hilsman's, followed Hilsman's version very closely. Halberstam even added a special fillip by making the unsupported assertion that the cable was drafted *at the President's suggestion*, a claim found nowhere else by this author.

142. Rusk, 437.
143. Taylor, 292.
144. *Ibid.*
145. Karnow, 287.
146. *FRUS 1961–1963, Vol. III, Vietnam, January–August 1963*, Doc. 281, 628.
147. Schlesinger, *A Thousand Days*, 991; Taylor, 292–93.
148. According to Hilsman, 491 and Halberstam, 264, in the August 27 EXCOMM meeting Kennedy moved to close off dissent ("backtracking" is Halberstam's word) over Deptel 243 among his advisors by asking each of the principals around the table if he agreed to the course being followed. In Halberstam's account, none of the principals had the fortitude to dissent openly. Reeves, 567–68, gave the same account but placed it on the 26th. Neither provided sources, but Reeves, who published well after Hilsman and Halberstam, probably used the earlier books as his source. In Krulak's for-the-record memo of the August 26 meeting (*FRUS 1961–1963, Vol. III, Vietnam, January–August 1963*, Doc. 289, 638) and in the minutes of the August 27 meeting, *Ibid.*, Doc. 303, 659, there is no hint that any such exchange occurred. It was not until the August 29 meeting, *FRUS 1961–1963, Vol. IV*, Vietnam, *August–December 1963*, Doc. 15, 26, that anything even remotely resembling their accounts occurred when the president asked the general question if anyone had any reservations about the course of action being followed.
149. *FRUS, 1961–1963, Vol. III, Vietnam, January–August 1963*, Doc. 289, 638. This account of the meeting is based on General Krulak's contemporaneous for-the-record memo.
150. *Ibid.*, Doc. 285, 634.
151. *Ibid.*, Doc. 287, 636
152. *Ibid.*, Doc. 288, 636.
153. *Ibid.*, 637, note 5.
154. *Ibid.*, Docs. 290 and 291, 642 and 643.
155. *Ibid.*, Doc. 307, 671.
156. *FRUS 1961–1963, Vol. IV, Vietnam, August–December, 1963*, Doc.1, p.1.
157. *Ibid.*, Doc. 12, 20.
158. *Ibid.*, Doc. 18, 35 and note 2, 36.
159. *Ibid.*, Doc. 32, 64.
160. *Ibid.*, Doc. 70, 128.
161. *Ibid.*, Doc. 77, 140.
162. *Ibid*, Doc. 130, 260.
163. *Ibid.*, Doc. 125, 252.
164. *Ibid.*, Doc. 126, 255, Doc. 130, 260 and Doc. 131, 262.
165. *Ibid.*, Doc. 104, 205 and note 4.
166. *Ibid.*, Doc. 176, 364 and note 2.
167. *Ibid.*, Doc. 119, 239; Doc. 171, 354; Doc. 177, 365.
168. Gibbons, Part II, 187.
169. The end of 1965 had become the stated goal of the administration but it was not yet a decision. The withdrawal of 1,000 men is taken by some as proof that Kennedy had already decided to withdraw from Vietnam after he was reelected in 1964, as related earlier.
170. Schlesinger, *Robert Kennedy*, 749. Reeves, 613, Taylor, 298–99, and McNamara, 79–80, all omitted to mention the controversy within the McNamara-Taylor mission over the inclusion of this recommendation. McNamara did say that in the National Security Council meeting to discuss the recommendations, there was "heated debate" over the withdrawal recommendation.
171. *FRUS, 1961–1963, Vol. IV, Vietnam, August–December 1963*, Doc. 170, 353.
172. *Ibid.*, Doc. 181, 371.
173. *Ibid.*, Doc. 182, 379.
174. *Ibid.*, Doc. 192, 393. This message was cleared by Kennedy.
175. *Ibid.*, Doc. 216, 434.
176. *Ibid.*, Doc. 224, 449.
177. *Ibid.*, Doc. 225, 450.
178. *Ibid.*, Doc. 236, 473.
179. *Ibid.*, Doc. 242, 484.
180. *Ibid.*, Doc. 262, 516.
181. Transcripts or partial transcripts are given in almost every book on Vietnam covering this period. See *FRUS, 1961–1963, Vol. IV, Vietnam, August–December 1963*, Doc. 259, 513, *The Pentagon Papers*, 232; Karnow, 307.
182. Taylor, 301. For the reaction within the CIA to Kennedy's reaction, see Gibbons, Part II, 201.
183. *FRUS 1961–1963, Vol. IV, Vietnam, August–December 1963*, Doc. 283, 545.
184. Reeves, 647.
185. *Ibid.*, 648.
186. Karnow, 310–11, and *FRUS 1961–1963, Vol. IV, Vietnam, August–December 1963*, Doc. 273, 531. There is general agreement that the military detail ordered to go to Cholon on the morning of November 2 to pick up Diem and Nhu was under the command of Gen. Mai Huu Xuan, and that at his direction, Maj. Duong Huu Nghia and a Captain Nhung who was Minh's personal bodyguard, assassinated the brothers inside an armored personnel carrier en route from Cholon to JGS headquarters. According to Karnow, when the detail arrived back

at JGS, Xuan reported to Minh: "Mission accomplished."
187. *FRUS, 1961–1963, Vol. IV, Vietnam, August–December 1963*, Doc. 286, 550.
188. Ibid., Doc. 301, 574n5.
189. Ibid., Doc. 296, 567.
190. *New York Times*, November 17, and November 22.
191. Gibbons, 209n5.
192. *FRUS 1961–1963, Vol. IV, Vietnam, August–December 1963*, Doc. 321, 611.
193. Lodge, 206–13.
194. Robert Shaplen, *The Road From War: Vietnam, 1965–1970* (New York: Harper and Row, 1970), 126. This situation only deteriorated with the passage of time. Later, in material dated April 12, 1969, Shaplen stated, 272, "In South Vietnam today, there are some fifty registered political parties and nearly one hundred unregistered ones.... Despite the dire need for a two or three-party system, fragmentation, mistrust, ambition and competition still run so deep in Vietnam that the efforts of the National Assembly to write a new political law that would limit the number of parties have so far proved fruitless...."
195. McNamara, 95–96; Halberstam, 300; Rusk, 44
196. See note 86.

Chapter 4

1. Lyndon B. Johnson, *The Vantage Point: Perspectives of the Presidency 1963–1969*. (New York: Holt, Rinehart and Winston, 1971), 61.
2. *FRUS, 1961–1963, Vol. IV, Vietnam, August–December, 1963*, Doc. 37, 69.
3. McNamara, 85–86.
4. *FRUS, 1961–1963, Vol. IV, Vietnam, August–December, 1963*, Doc. 330, 635.
5. Ibid., Doc. 331, 637. There was now no going back on the 1,000-man withdrawal plan, despite the adverse military situation, and accordingly, the withdrawal was ordered, but it was purely a bookkeeping exercise since normal personnel rotations, medical evacuations, etc., accounted for well over a 1,000 returnees per month. Still, the American people were left with the distinct impression that the U.S. was reducing its commitments in Vietnam.
6. Earlier policy statements with respect to U.S. involvement in Vietnam were NSC 64 of April 1950 and NSC 124/2 of June 1952 by Truman and NSC 5405 of January 1954 by Eisenhower. These NSCs are referenced in the chapter "Origins of U.S. Involvement." In *The Vantage Point*, 46–61, Johnson was at pains to cite supportive statements on Vietnam involvement by Presidents Truman and Eisenhower, John Foster Dulles, President Kennedy, Robert Kennedy, Senator William Fulbright and others going back to 1950 to buttress Johnson's position that he was only continuing a well-established bipartisan policy.
7. Doris Kearns Goodwin, *Lyndon Johnson and the American Dream* (New York: Signet, 1976), 264–65.
8. Over the course of the Kennedy and Johnson administrations, Harriman moved through a series of jobs in which his influence on Southeast Asian policy rose to a peak and then fell to near zero. After he masterminded Deptel 243 which set in motion Diem's demise, he was never trusted by Rusk and Johnson and was deflected from significant influence on Vietnam policy. In February 1965, Johnson named him ambassador-at-large in charge of Johnson's "peace shop" where for three years he conducted unavailing peace overtures toward Hanoi but had no role in policy formulation. Finally, he headed the U.S. delegation to the Paris peace talks until the end of Johnson's term, a role in which he was kept under very tight rein by Johnson and Rusk. Roger Hilsman, who as assistant secretary for Far Eastern affairs was coauthor of Deptel 243, was fired by Rusk in early 1964. In mid-1964, Forrestal was moved out of his White House job as a national security assistant to a staff job in State from which he resigned in January 1965. Abramson, 632–35.
9. *FRUS, 1961–1963, Vol. IV, Vietnam, August–December 1963*, Doc. 318, 602.
10. Ibid., Doc. 322, 625.
11. Ibid., Doc. 374, 732.
12. Lodge, 213. McNamara believed his communications would never become public, but his memo to Johnson with disparaging remarks about Lodge was revealed in the Pentagon Papers. In a June 23, 1971, note he tried to smooth Lodge's feathers.
13. *FRUS, 1961–1963, Vol. IV, Vietnam, Aug.–Dec. 1963*, Doc. 374, 732.
14. McNamara,105.
15. Hilsman, 522.
16. William C. Westmoreland, *A Soldier Reports* (Garden City, NY: Doubleday, 1976) 62.
17. *FRUS. 1964–1968, Vol. 1, Vietnam, 1964*, Doc. 75, 135. Gibbons, 218.
18. *Ibid.*
19. Kahin, 185–94.
20. See Pike, 136–50.
21. Kahin, 198, 202.
22. Westmoreland, 61.
23. Gibbons, Part II, 229, 247.
24. McNamara, 112; Taylor, 309.
25. *FRUS, 1964–1968, Vol. I, Vietnam, 1964*, Doc. 84, 153.
26. Ibid., note 1. The draft was prepared by

William Bundy the weekend of February 29–March 1 as an "overall vehicle for thought and also designed by Secretary McNamara to serve as a vehicle for his report on his return." The final report as submitted to Johnson did not differ materially from the pre-trip draft.

27. Kearns, 206.
28. Johnson, 119.
29. *The Pentagon Papers*, Doc. No. 64, 283
30. Johnson 19 (emphasis added).
31. Col. Harry G. Summers, *On Strategy: The Vietnam War in Context* (Carlisle Barracks, PA: Strategic Studies Institute, U.S. Army War College, 1981),16.
32. *The Pentagon Papers*, 365.
33. *Ibid.*, 432.
34. *Ibid.*, 491.
35. Westmoreland, 71–74, 90.
36. *FRUS, 1964–1968, Vol. I, Vietnam,* Doc. 100, 199.
37. *Ibid.*, Doc. 218, 521.
38. *Ibid.*, Doc. 228, 538.
39. McNamara, 123. McNamara also related that Johnson asked him in 1964 to accept the nomination as his vice president. McNamara said he turned down the offer. *Ibid.* Also, see *FRUS 1964–1968, Vol. I, Vietnam, 1964,* Doc. 204, 472, memo from Bundy to Johnson listing candidates including himself and giving their pros and cons. He and Robert Kennedy came out on top. In *The Vantage Point* there is no mention of the volunteers for the ambassadorship nor of Johnson's offer to McNamara. Also, see Schlesinger, *Robert Kennedy,* 761, for Kennedy's application to Johnson for the job.
40. Kearns, 271.
41. Johnson, 115.
42. *FRUS, 1964–1968, Vol. I, Vietnam, 1964,* Doc. 169, 356.
43. *Ibid.*, Doc. 214, 500.
44. *New York Times,* February 1; March 5; March 21; June 1; July 11; *FRUS, 1964–1968, Vol. I, Vietnam, 1964,* 8–15, 67, 400–402, 1009–12.
45. *New York Times,* February. 1.
46. Johnson, 119.
47. Kearns, 206, 263.
48. See Karnow, 364–76; Kahin, 219–27; Johnson, 112–18; McNamara,129–39; and U.S. Grant Sharp, *Strategy For Defeat: Vietnam in Retrospect* (San Rafael, CA: Presidio Press, 1978), 39–46, to cite only five.
49. Sharp, 39–45. In *In Retrospect,* 127–43, published in 1995, McNamara continued to deny there was any provocation on the part of the U.S. or that there was deception in the manner in which the incident was presented to Congress.
50. Goodwin, 207.
51. Johnson, 118–19.
52. *New York Times,* August 8. Gibbons, Part II, 302–3.
53. Taylor, 318–22.
54. *FRUS, 1964–1968, Vol. I, Vietnam, 1964,* Doc. 387, 845.
55. *Ibid.*, Doc. 451, 1014. The Vietnamese officers were Generals Ky (VNAF), Thieu (IV Corps), and Thi (I Corps) and Admiral Cang, chief of naval operations.
56. Taylor, 330–331.
57. *FRUS, 1964–1968, Vol. I, Vietnam, 1964,* Doc. 454, 1021.
58. *Ibid.*, Doc. 463, 1035 and Doc. 465, 1036.
59. Gibbons, Part II, 102–3. *The Pentagon Papers,* 109. As already related, following the Taylor-Rostow mission in the fall of 1961, Diem rejected the U.S. attempt to participate in the decision-making of his government, and the U.S. had to settle for a "close partnership."
60. Taylor, 359.
61. *FRUS, 1964–1968, Vol. II, Vietnam, January–June 1965.* (Washington, DC: USGPO, 1996), Doc. 40, 91.
62. *Ibid.* Doc. 148, 339.
63. Gibbons, Part II, 229–31.
64. McNamara, 108–9.
65. *Ibid.* 117–18.
66. *FRUS, 1964–1968, Vol. I, Vietnam, 1964,* Doc. 154, 322.
67. *Ibid.*, Doc. 156, 328.
68. *Ibid.*, Doc. 306, 656.
69. Taylor, 320.
70. *FRUS, 1964–1968, Vol. I, Vietnam, 1964,* Doc. 343, 749.
71. *Ibid.*, Doc. 388, 847.
72. Sharp, 48.
73. *FRUS, 1964–1968, Vol. I, Vietnam, 1964,* Doc. 396, 876.
74. *Ibid.*, Doc. 397, 878.
75. *Ibid.*, Doc. 400, 881.
76. *Ibid.*, Doc. 403, 886.
77. *Ibid.*, Doc. 417, 914 and Doc. 418, 916.
78. *Ibid.* Rusk's first alternative, a negotiated settlement on any basis obtainable, now labeled the "devil's advocate" exercise, had obviously been rejected out of hand by the Working Group, but to provide the appearance of even-handedness, George Ball, the administration's pet dove, had been assigned to prepare a case for that alternative. It never received serious consideration.
79. *FRUS, 1964–1968, Vol. I, Vietnam, 1964,* Doc. 420, 932.
80. On November 1, 1968, Johnson discontinued bombing north of the DMZ. Nixon continued the moratorium during the Paris peace talks until, in response to the DRV's 1972 spring offensive in the South, air attacks were restarted along with mining of the ports.
81. *The Pentagon Papers,* 373–78. Gibbons, 375–76, 379–81.
82. Gibbons, 382–83.
83. Taylor 334–35.
84. *FRUS, 1964–1968, Vol. II, Vietnam, January–June 1965,* Doc. 42, 95.

85. Sharp, 57.
86. *Ibid.*, 59.
87. *FRUS, 1964–1968, Vol. II, Vietnam, January–June, 1965,* Doc. 115, 263.
88. McNamara, 171–72; Sharp, 60–61, 72, 74–75, 79; Taylor, 350; Johnson, 129; Bird, 308.
89. *Ibid.*, Doc. 187, 412.
90. *Ibid.*, Doc. 197, 438.
91. *Ibid.*, Doc. 234, 521. This memo was sent to the president April 28. Doc. 279, 614.
92. *Ibid.*, Doc. 207, 460.
93. Johnson, 132–34.
94. *Ibid.*
95. *Ibid.*, 136–37. Johnson said nothing as to the origin of the idea but McNamara, 185, stated that he asked John McNaughton to draft a one-week bombing pause proposal.
96. *FRUS, 1964–1968, Vol. II, Vietnam, January–June 1965,* Doc. 288, 629.
97. *Ibid.*, Doc. 298, 647.
98. Johnson, 233.
99. *Ibid.*, Doc. 153, note 3, 347.
100. *Ibid.*, Doc. 153, 347.
101. Taylor, 338.
102. *FRUS, 1964–1968, Vol. II, Vietnam, January–June 1965,* Doc. 208, 465.
103. *Ibid.*, Doc. 230, 512.
104. *New York Times,* April 3, 1965.
105. *FRUS, 1964–1968, Vol. II, Vietnam, January–June 1965,* Doc. 265, 574.
106. Sharp, 80. Sharp had been from the outset a proponent of Option B, "the hard, fast squeeze." He learned from experience that in most conferences with McNamara, the "consensus" as later described in McNamara's reports reflected McNamara's own views and not necessarily those of the other participants.
107. *FRUS, 1964–1968, Vol. II, Vietnam, January–June 1965,* Doc. 339, 738.

Chapter 5

1. *FRUS, 1964–1968, Vol. II, Vietnam, January–June 1965,* Doc. 337, 733.
2. *Ibid.*, Doc. 346, 754.
3. *FRUS, 1964–1968, Vol. III, Vietnam, June–December 1965,* Doc. 38, 97.
4. *Ibid.*, Doc. 40, 106.
5. *Ibid.*, Doc. 41, 113.
6. *Ibid.*, Doc. 39, 104.
7. *Ibid.*, Doc. 43, 117.
8. Abramson, 638–39.
9. Westmoreland, 143.
10. *FRUS, 1964–1968, Vol. III, Vietnam, June–December 1965,* Doc. 67, 171.
11. In *Swords and Plowshares,* 350, Taylor said with respect to the discussions in Saigon, "I favored any combination of the three (increasing the rate of attack, the intensity of attack, or the territorial limits) which would convince Hanoi that we meant business and that we would progressively and inexorably destroy everything of war-sustaining value if the aggression against the South continued."
12. 146–50.
13. *FRUS, 1964–1968, Vol. III, Vietnam, June–December 1965,* Doc. 93, 263n9.
14. Johnson, 150.
15. *Ibid.*
16. *FRUS, 1964–1968, Vol. III, Vietnam, June–December, 1965,* Doc. 97, 273.
17. Regarding Johnson's initial decision to escalate, Doris Kearns Goodwin, 416, had this to say: "Indeed, given the momentum, the necessity of choice—since not choosing would have meant turning South Vietnam over to the Communists—and the consistency of advice from almost every corner, it is easy to imagine many other Presidents, acting under very different internal compulsions, making the same decision."
18. In *The Vantage Point,* Johnson understandably had little to say about this aspect until after inflation had clearly taken root, and he pictured his administration in late 1967 as struggling with a recalcitrant Congress to rein it in. Chapter 19.
19. Westmoreland, 142.
20. When Westmoreland made his 1967 request for the "minimum essential" and "optimum" numbers of troops and following Tet when he and Wheeler requested 206,000 additional troops, it was his intention to use these forces in a move into Laos.
21. To name a few: Gen. Bruce Palmer, *The 25-Year War: America's Military Role in Vietnam* (Lexington: University of Kentucky Press, 1984); Michael Charlton and Anthony Moncrief, *Many Reasons Why: The American Involvement in Vietnam* (New York: Hill and Wang, 1978; Michael Lind, *Vietnam: The Necessary War* (New York: The Free Press, 1999). See also Westmoreland, 148, and Summers, 76.
22. Marc Jason Gilbert, ed., *Why the North Won the Vietnam War* (New York: Palgrave, 2002), 15.
23. *Ibid.* The orthodox argument for predicting Chinese intervention apparently rests on assertions by "Ridgway [retired army general] and others" who "*had long since established* that any major American military operation that was perceived by China as a violation of the territorial integrity of its former tributary states, Laos or Vietnam, would trigger a Chinese intervention." How and where this opinion had become "long since established" is not clarified, nor is it brought out that other high military and intelligence officers with excellent credentials and with direct involvement in the war thought otherwise.
24. We have already seen how, in 1964 when American involvement was still small, Johnson

avoided raising the profile of the war until he was safely elected. Beginning in 1965 as U.S. involvement grew rapidly, he tried to conceal the cost and the extent of the U.S. commitment from Congress and the public to allow his Great Society program to continue. Goodwin, 416.

25. Westmoreland, 146.
26. Herring, 158–59; Gibbons, Part II, 58–61, 355, 468–78. In his second tour as ambassador, Lodge brought Lansdale back to Vietnam as the U.S. Mission spokesman on pacification to the government of Vietnam, but he was never given real clout so accomplished almost nothing.
27. Westmoreland, 146.
28. *FRUS, 1964–1968, Vol. IV, Vietnam, 1966*, Doc. 64, 204.
29. *Ibid.*, Doc. 61, 198.
30. In March 1968, as the Clifford Task Force was formulating its recommendations to Johnson, several civilian Pentagon officials tried to press a modified enclave strategy on Clifford, but it was not adopted. Karnow, 554.
31. Westmoreland, 131.
32. *Ibid.*, 135, 141; Johnson, 143.
33. Guenter Lewy, *America in Vietnam* (New York: Oxford University Press, 1978), 438.
34. *New York Times*, March 5, 31, April 3.
35. *Ibid.*, April 4.
36. *Ibid.*, August 6.
37. William C. Gibbons, *The U.S. Government and the Vietnam War, Part IV* (Princeton, NJ: Princeton University Press, 1995), 40–42. Ironically, it was not Vietnam but Johnson's handling of the crisis in the Dominican Republic that brought several Democratic senators, including William Fulbright, to break with Johnson in the fall of 1965.
38. *Ibid.*, 223–24.
39. *Ibid.*, 239–42; *New York Times*, February 9 and February 11.
40. Gibbons, Part IV, 242–46; *New York Times*, February 18 and February 19.
41. Gibbons, Part IV, 251–58; *New York Times*, March 2. Senators voting to keep the amendment alive were Morse, Gruening, Fulbright, Eugene McCarthy and Young (Ohio), all Democrats. Many senators viewed the vote as a reaffirmation of the Tonkin Gulf Resolution.
42. Gibbons, Part IV, 254; *New York Times*, February 20.
43. Goodwin, 271.
44. Gibbons, 671.
45. *New York Times*, Nov. 3.
46. *Ibid.*, April 8.
47. Gibbons, Part IV, 697. In the spring of 1967, there were 2 million male students deferred from the draft.
48. Kissinger, 1305. Campus protests were effectively ended by Nixon's announcement at the end of June 1972 that no more draftees would be sent to Vietnam unless they volunteered.

49. Gibbons, Part IV, 27 and 27n80. In late 1966, this organization mutated into the Spring Mobilization Committee to End the War in Vietnam which in the fall 1967 became the National Mobilization Committee to End the War in Vietnam, called the Mobe. After Nixon's election it became the New Mobilization to End the War in Vietnam, and it became defunct in the spring of 1970.
50. *New York Times*, October 17. .
51. *Ibid.*, March 27.
52. *Ibid.*, August 11, 1965.
53. Gibbons, Part IV, 693.
54. *Ibid.*, 693n61.
55. *New York Times*, April 16, 1967.
56. *Ibid.*
57. *Ibid.*, October 22, 1967. Gibbons, Part IV, 867–68. The tactics of the demonstrators proved counterproductive. A Harris poll on Dec. 18, 1967, showed a firming of public support for Johnson's Vietnam policy.
58. *Ibid.*, April 26, 1966, and August 8, 1966.
59. Taylor, 343, 345.
60. *FRUS, 1964–1968, Vol. III, Vietnam, June–December 1965*, Doc. 104, 291; Doc. 118, 325; Doc. 180, 485. Also, McNamara, 172.
61. *FRUS, 1964–1968, Vol. III, Vietnam, June–December 1965*, Doc. 118, 325 for Lodge meeting with Eisenhower at Johnson's request.
62. *New York Times*, September 1.
63. *FRUS, 1964–1968, Vol. III, Vietnam, June–December 1965*, Doc. 50, 128; 174n3; Doc. 131, 363.
64. *Ibid.*, Doc. 143, 391.
65. Chester L. Cooper, *The Lost Crusade: America in Vietnam* (New York: Dodd, Mead, 1970), 296.
66. *FRUS, 1964–1968, Vol. III, Vietnam, June–December 1965*, Doc. 178, 475.
67. *Ibid.*, Doc. 189, 514.
68. *Ibid.*, Doc. 194, 535.
69. Sharp, 105–11.
70. Abramson, 639–41; Gibbons, 129.
71. Bird, 344; *FRUS, 1964–1968, Vol. III, Vietnam, June–December 1965*, 710n3. Johnson, apparently unwilling for some reason to disclose the full circumstances of Bundy's departure, had Bundy resigning on his last day in the White House, February 28, 1966; *The Vantage Point*, 240n. Halberstam, writing four years later, got the story wrong when he said: "In early 1966 Bundy was very uneasy with Johnson" when he had already resigned and that he was offered the Ford job in March 1966. *The Best and the Brightest*, 624–25.
72. Bird, 342.
73. See *The Pentagon Papers*, 569–72, for Bundy's May 1967 memo to Johnson on Vietnam.
74. *FRUS, 1964–1968, Vol. III, Vietnam, June–December 1965*, Doc. 212, 591.
75. *FRUS, 1964–1968, Vol. IV, Vietnam, 1966*, Doc. 70, 216.

76. Ibid., Doc.268, 726.
77. *The Pentagon Papers*, Docs. 122 and 123, 556 and 560.
78. Ibid., Doc. 129, 577–85.
79. McNamara, 270
80. Johnson, 263.
81. Halberstam, 164.
82. *The Pentagon Papers*, 493–95. McNaughton's memo was based on a January 3, 1966, draft memo by Professor Roger D. Fisher of Harvard Law School entitled "A Barrier Strategy." This memo may have given substance to an idea mentioned in McNamara's Nov. 3, 1965, draft presidential memorandum that the US might have to erect a 175-mile barrier along the 17th parallel. Gibbons, Part IV, 85.
83. *FRUS, 1964–1968, Vol. IV, Vietnam*, Doc. 235, 639n1.
84. Gibbons, 382.
85. *FRUS, 1964–1968, Vol. IV Vietnam*, Doc. 233, 635.
86. Ibid., Doc. 235, 639n4.
87. Ibid., Doc. 340, 932.
88. Ibid., Doc. 269, 738.
89. Zaffiri, 175.
90. McNamara, 246.
91. Gibbons, Part IV, 84–85.
92. McNamara, 280.
93. McNamara, 306–9.
94. In *In Retrospect*, 309, McNamara said that only Rostow and Rusk knew the identity of the author of the memo and that Rostow showed the memo to the others without revealing the author. Knowing the ways of Washington as well as he did, McNamara could hardly have believed the others did not know the identity of the author.
95. McNamara, 310.
96. McNamara remained through February 1968, succeeded on March 1 by Clark Clifford.
97. McNamara, 311.
98. Johnson, 20. On balance, it would appear McNamara was dismissed.
99. Assistant Secretary for International Security Affairs John McNaughton had been McNamara's principal resource in the Pentagon on policy matters.
100. Sharp, 94–96.
101. Ibid., 86.
102. Rusk, 458. One boggles at the thought of World War II bombing targets in Germany and Japan being selected by FDR, Cordell Hull and Henry L. Stimson sitting together at White House luncheons.
103. Zaffiri, 218–19, stated that on August 25, 1967, the members of the JCS agreed among themselves to resign en masse in protest over repeated public statements by Johnson and McNamara that the military was in full consensus with them on the conduct of the war. On further reflection, General Wheeler had a change of heart and persuaded the others to drop the idea.
104. Sharp, 68, 100, 101.
105. Sharp, 103.
106. Mark Clodfelter, *The Limits of Air Power: The American Bombing of North Vietnam* (New York: The Free Press, 1989), 85.
107. *FRUS, 1964–1968, Vol. III, Vietnam, June–December 1965*, Doc. 100, 280.
108. See Special National Intelligence Estimates (SNIEs)10-9-65, July 23, 1965, and 10–11-65, September 22, 1965, in *Ibid.*, Docs. 81, 224 and 148, 403 respectively.
109. Sharp, 102.
110. The intense debate within the administration over the bombing of POL began with the resumption of Rolling Thunder at the end of January 1966 and continued until the end of June when the first attacks were conducted, a full five months. Through leaks to the press it became public information that these discussions were going on. See Gibbons, Part IV, 360–79.
111. Sharp, 117–18; *New York Times*, June 27 and 29.
112. Clodfelter, 131. By August 1967, the DRV's air defenses included roughly 200 SAM sites, 7,000 antiaircraft guns and 80 MiG fighters.
113. John T. Smith, *The Linebacker Raids* (London: Cassell, 1998), 36.
114. *The Pentagon Papers*, Doc. 97, 440–41.
115. Johnson, 366; Sharp, 160.
116. Sharp, 202.
117. Johnson, 367–68.
118. Ibid., 266–67.
119. Clodfelter, 111. This group of scientists and academics convened by McNamara in mid–1966 concluded that Rolling Thunder had actually caused an *increase* in the gross national product of the DRV, presumably because the bombing had stimulated increased net contributions of aid from China and the USSR.
120. Sharp, 188. Testimony at the Stennis hearings.
121. McNamara and his civilian assistants held this view beginning in 1966, and this is Clodfelter's position in his well-researched *The Limits of Air Power* written in 1989.
122. Admiral Sharp's view, as expressed in *Strategy for Defeat*, is representative of that of the JCS and the air force and naval officers responsible for conducting Rolling Thunder.
123. Sharp, 251–58; Clodfelter,176, 201–202.
124. *FRUS, 1964–1968, Vol. III, Vietnam, 1965*, Doc. 100, 280.
125. Smith, 102, 110.
126. For example, during the debate over the bombing of POL, the JCS repeatedly requested authority to mine the harbors but was not supported by McNamara. Gibbons, 361–63.
127. *The Pentagon Papers*, Doc. 128, 573–77.

128. A basic difference existed as to what constituted the "funnel." The civilians tended to define it as the narrow part of North Vietnam south of the 20th parallel when, actually, the real funnel was the port of Haiphong and the two railroads to China through which almost all war materiel was funneling. In practice, it was an inverted funnel with the narrow part in the north.

129. *The Pentagon Papers*, Doc. 129, 577–85; Gibbons, Part IV, 640–69.

130. While Herring devotes several pages, 146–50, to assessing the air war, he mentions mining only twice in his book, 247–48, in describing Nixon's "drastic escalation" of the war, but nowhere assesses the results of mining. In *Why the North Won the Vietnam War*, the subject is never raised.

131. Gibbons, Part IV, 609; Johnson, 259.

132. Gibbons, Part IV, 355.

133. Pike, 76–77.

134. Duiker, *The Communist Road*, 263–65.

135. Gen. Phillip B. Davidson, who was Westmoreland's chief of intelligence during Tet, asserts in his book *Vietnam at War* (Novato, CA: Presidio, 1988), 434–41, that the Communists were most assuredly *losing* the war at this point. Duiker, in *Communist Road*, 256–65, takes a more positive view of the Communist position.

136. Duiker, *The Communist Road*, 264.

137. *Ibid.*, 266–67.

138. Detailed accounts can be found in Davidson, chapters 17 and 18; Don Oberdtorfer, *Tet!* (Garden City, NY: Doubleday, 1971); Peter Braestrup, *Big Story*. (New Haven, CO: Yale University Press, 1983); Karnow, 515–66; and Westmoreland, 310–34.

139. Davidson, 321. The Tet Offensive is usually understood to take in the period from the launch of coordinated attacks on January 30 and 31 to the final clearing of VC from Hue on February 25, but in reality, Tet was followed by a series of "mini–Tets" lasting into August.

140. *Ibid.*, 547–48.

141. *Ibid.*, 475.

142. *Ibid.*

143. *Ibid.*, 477. Also Karnow, 545. He quoted DRV Gen. Tran Do: "As for making an impact in the United States, it had not been our intention—but it turned out to be a fortunate result."

144. Westmoreland, 230–31.

145. Westmoreland, 234; *New York Times*, November 20 and November 22; Davidson, 435. In reality, while the crossover point may have been reached with respect to the Viet Cong, the deployment of regular North Vietnam forces in South Vietnam more than offset any reduction in guerrilla forces.

146. The *New York Times* November 20 article quoted Westmoreland as saying: "If U.S. bombing of North Vietnam and progress in other areas continues, the U.S. may be able to start withdrawing troops in two years," and in its November 22 article the *Times* said Westmoreland believed the war had entered a new phase when the end begins to come into view but did not forecast military victory in the classic sense.

147. Westmoreland, 315; Davidson, 435.

148. Braestrup, 85. Peter Arnett, an Associated Press correspondent, typified this attitude when he said, "Considering the record over the years, we had little faith in what General Westmoreland stated...."

149. *Ibid.*, 9

150. Oberdorfer, 183.

151. Braestrup's *Big Story* and Oberdorfer's *Tet!* are valuable sources on media coverage of Tet and are cited frequently here. Of the two, *Big Story*, published in 1978, is far more exhaustive and objective than *Tet!* published in 1971.

152. While the correspondents treated Khe Sanh as a part of Tet, it did not fit the objectives of Tet, which were aimed at population centers.

153. Braestrup, 121, quoting Gen. Bruce Clarke (USA, ret.) who visited Vietnam during the Tet offensive.

154. In his memoir *Muddy Boots and Red Socks* (New York: Times Books, 1993), 160–61 and 189, Malcolm Browne persisted in stating that the U.S. Embassy had been *captured* by the Viet Cong when it had been an accepted fact for 25 years that they never penetrated the building. Browne was an AP reporter in Saigon in the early 1960s but was not present in Vietnam during the Tet Offensive.

155. Braestrup, Chapter 4; *New York Times*, February. 3.

156. Oberdorfer, 250–51 and 272–73. NBC followed on March 10 with the one-hour *Frank McGee Sunday Report* entirely devoted to Vietnam. The report opened with flashbacks of optimistic statements by Johnson, McNamara and Westmoreland followed by film clips of the Tet fighting selected for their dramatic impact, and though it was aired at a time when the Tet offensive had unquestionably been defeated, no mention of this crept into the commentary.

157. Braestrup, 188–90, 509.

158. *Ibid.*, 505; *New York Times*, Gallup poll report, February. 14.

159. Braestrup, 500.

160. *Ibid*, 506.

161. *Ibid.*, 484–89.

162. Herbert Y. Schandler, *The Unmaking of a President: Lyndon Johnson and Vietnam* (Princeton, NJ: Princeton University Press, 1977), 81–85.

163. 313–22.

164. Westmoreland, 313.

165. Duiker, 266; Westmoreland, 328.

166. Braestrup, 179, 188–90.

167. Davidson, 551.
168. Westmoreland, 316.
169. Davidson has a detailed account of the siege, 551–71. Also, see *Semper Fidelis: The History of the United States Marine Corps* (New York: Macmillan,1980).
170. Davidson, 552, Westmoreland, 347.
171. Braestrup, 508.
172. Westmoreland, 351–52. Schandler, 94–99. As Schandler put it, the request for additional troops had to be "teased," out of Westmoreland by several messages from Wheeler.
173. Some reports give the figure as 10,500 while others give it as 11,000.
174. *New York Times*, February 13.
175. 387.
176. Schandler, Chapter Six, 105–20.
177. Westmoreland, 355–56.
178. *The Pentagon Papers*, Doc. 132, 615–21.
179. Johnson, 397.
180. *Ibid.*, 399.
181. *Ibid.*, 402.
182. *Ibid.*, 403.
183. Oberdorfer, 265–66, 286–87. The Pentagon dovecote included Deputy Secretary of Defense Paul Nitze, Assistant Secretary for International Security Affairs Paul Warnke, (McNaughton's successor), Undersecretary of the Air Force Townsend Hoopes, Assistant Secretary for Public Affairs Phillip Goulding, Assistant Secretary for Systems Analysis Alain Enthoven, and analysts Leslie Gelb and Daniel Ellsberg. Gelb was the principal editor of the Pentagon Papers, assisted by Daniel Ellsberg, who later leaked them to the *New York Times*.
184. Johnson, 407.
185. *Ibid.*, 407.
186. *Ibid.*, 415.
187. Westmoreland, 359.
188. Johnson, 415.
189. *Ibid*.
190. Clifford, 40 and 67. Clifford had obtained a direct commission as lieutenant (junior grade), USNR, in April 1944 at the age of 37. His progression to navy captain in 21 months may have established a new record for rapid advancement for one who had never served on a ship.
191. Walter Isaacson and Evan Thomas, *The Wise Men: Six Friends and the World They Made*, (New York: Simon & Schuster,1986), 644–45. In the summer of 1964 Johnson assigned McGeorge Bundy the task of assembling a group of elder Establishment statesmen, originally labeled the President's Consultants on Foreign Affairs or the Peace Panel but later called the Senior Advisory Group. Ostensibly to advise the president on Vietnam, it was actually nothing more than a campaign ploy intended to show Johnson's putative bipartisanship and desire for peace. Regarding the group as too unwieldy, Johnson seldom called them together but frequently consulted with individual members, mainly Dean Acheson and John McCloy. The Wise Men at the November 1967 meeting included Dean Acheson, George Ball, McGeorge Bundy, Douglas Dillon, Arthur Dean, Cabot Lodge, Robert Murphy, Gen. Omar Bradley, Gen. Maxwell Taylor, Abe Fortas and Clifford.
192. Taylor, 377–78. Clifford, 454–55.
193. The San Antonio Formula was enunciated by Johnson in a speech in that city on September 29, 1967, in which he stated the U.S. was willing to stop all bombing of the North when this would lead to productive discussions, assuming that while discussions proceeded, North Vietnam would not take advantage of the bombing cessation. Johnson, 267. In his confirmation testimony before the Senate Armed Services Committee, Clifford, without consulting anyone in the administration, gave his own interpretation of the phrase "not take advantage" which had the effect of softening it and making it more ambiguous. Schandler, 130–32.
194. See note 183.
195. For an inside account of how the Pentagon bureaucracy worked to influence Clifford, see Townsend Hoopes, *The Limits of Intervention*. (New York: McKay, 1969), Chapters 8, 9 and 10. See also Schandler, Chapter Seven.
196. Clifford, Chapter 28.
197. Isaacson and Thomas, 696–703.
198. Karnow, 562.
199. Schandler, 237–40.
200. Johnson, 427.
201. Goodwin, 352, 357–58, 364.
202. Johnson, 495.
203. As related earlier, while the bombing limit was announced as the 20th parallel, after April 2 no bombing was conducted north of the 19th parallel. This tacit limitation became public knowledge, again trapping the U.S. within its own self-imposed restraints.
204. Nixon, *The Memoirs of Richard Nixon*, 347. In fact, it was only after his inauguration that Nixon, with Kissinger's support, began to develop his Vietnam policy.
205. *Ibid.*, 318.
206. Clifford, 530.
207. Points 2 and 3 were pursuant to the San Antonio Formula.
208. Abramson, 667–72; Clifford, 567–69.
209. Johnson, 518. As related earlier in the chapter "The Kennedy Years," Harriman followed a similar procedure in the 1961–62 Geneva negotiations on Laos, exchanging explicit U.S. concessions for tacit Communist agreements.
210. Clifford, 525.
211. It was disingenuous of Clifford, writing in 1991, to assert that an earlier cessation of the bombing could have produced peace in six months when in fact fruitless negotiations con-

tinued throughout the period November 1968 to April 1972 when no strategic bombing of North Vietnam took place. The only way a peace could have been produced before the 1968 election would have been through acceptance of North Vietnam's terms. Clifford's public statements during the Nixon administration calling for a rapid and total unilateral withdrawal and his virulent opposition to the Thieu regime would indicate he might have been willing to meet North Vietnam's terms in 1968 if only to assure the election of a Democrat.

212. Clifford, 570; Abramson, 667–68.
213. Berman, *No Peace, No Honor.* (New York: The Free Press, 2001), 32–36; Clifford, 581–93; Abramson, 671–72; Karnow, 585–86, et al.
214. Clifford, 585–96.
215. Berman, *No Peace — No Honor*, 36, 43, 188 and 246. The underlying thesis of the book is that Nixon betrayed Thieu even though Berman repeatedly cited Nixon's unswerving loyalty to Thieu as the principal reason for the drawn-out negotiations in which, ultimately, the Communists were forced to abandon their demand for Thieu's ouster.
216. Johnson, 520–21.
217. Goodwin, 100, 269–70.
218. Goodwin, 174.
219. Johnson, 20.
220. Johnson, 68.
221. Johnson, 428–29.

Chapter 6

1. http://thewallusa.com/stats/index.html. U.S. military casualties in Southeast Asia, deaths by calendar year: Through 1963—195; 1964—206; 1965—1,863; 1966—6,144; 1967—11,153; 1968—16,589; 1969—11,614; 1970—6,083; 1971—2,357; 1972—640; 1973—168; 1974—178; 1975—160. A further 834 deaths, shown as post–1975, are those that died from wounds incurred during the war or for which a specific year could not be determined.
2. Richard M. Nixon, *The Memoirs of Richard Nixon* (London: Arrow, 1978), 340.
3. *Ibid.*; Henry Kissinger, *The White House Years* (Boston: Little, Brown, 1974), 14–16.
4. Kissinger, 263–64.
5. Nixon, 347. In speeches and interviews during the 1968 campaign, e.g., *New York Times*, March 11, Nixon pledged to end the war in Vietnam if elected but steadfastly refused to explain how this would be achieved. This led to media reports that he had a "secret plan." In *The Memoirs of Richard Nixon*, 298, Nixon stated, "A regular part of my campaign speech was the pledge: 'New leadership will end the war and win the peace in the Pacific.'" He went on to deny that he ever said during the campaign that he had a plan, much less a secret plan.
6. *Ibid.*, 348–49.
7. *Ibid.*, 392.
8. *New York Times*, January 17, 1989.
9. Kissinger, 256.
10. Johnson, 267. The full cessation of bombing of North Vietnam announced on October 31, 1968, was based on the San Antonio Formula of September 29, 1967, the objective of which was to initiate peace talks.
11. *New York Times*, May 9.
12. Nixon, 391–92. Kissinger, 270–71.
13. *New York Times*, May 15.
14. Kissinger, 271–72.
15. *Ibid.*
16. *New York Times*, September 17.
17. *Ibid.*, September 22.
18. Kissinger, 303.
19. *Ibid.*, 284.
20. *New York Times*, June 19. Clark Clifford was in the forefront of those demanding a rapid withdrawal. His June 18 statement calling on Nixon to withdraw all combat forces by the end of 1970 was thrown back at U.S. negotiators in Paris by the Communists.
21. Kissinger, 437, 520–21.
22. Gibbons, Part II, 209n5; Kissinger, 250.
23. Lewis Sorley, *A Better War* (New York: Harcourt Brace, 1999), 101–2. U.S. military intelligence soon detected the flow through Sihanoukville but until the sanctuaries were attacked by U.S. and ARVN forces in 1970, the CIA deprecated the importance of Sihanoukville, maintaining that the Ho Chi Minh Trail was sufficient to support the entire Communist war effort. Documents captured in the 1970 raids proved that military intelligence had been correct.
24. Kissinger, 250–51.
25. Sorley, 117–18; Kissinger, 247.
26. Kissinger, 250. At the chargé d'affaires level.
27. Nixon's critics continue to nurture the thesis advanced by William Shawcross in his book *Sideshow: Kissinger, Nixon and the Destruction of Cambodia* (New York: Simon & Schuster, 1979), that Nixon was directly responsible for the slaughter of an estimated 1.5 million innocent Cambodians by the Communist Khmer Rouge after they took Phnom Penh in 1975, allegedly because his bombing of Cambodia drove the otherwise peaceable Khmer Rouge "agrarian reformers" into a demonic frenzy of retribution on their fellow citizens. For a detailed rebuttal, see Peter W. Rodman, "Sideswipe: Kissinger, Shawcross and the Responsibility for Cambodia," *The American Spectator* 14, no. 3 (March 1981).
28. Westmoreland, 222.
29. Clifford, 550–51.

30. Westmoreland, 235.
31. Nixon, 392.
32. Kissinger, 276.
33. Westmoreland, 221–22. Near the end of 1967 when the first M-16s for the ARVN began to arrive, priority was given to airborne, ranger, and marine units which constituted the general reserve after which the ARVN 1st Infantry Division was equipped.
34. *Ibid.*, 222, and Sorley, 172.
35. Westmoreland, 100.
36. Braestrup, 338.
37. *Ibid.*, 379.
38. Colby, 270.
39. Braestrup, 85.
40. Davidson, Chapter 20, provides a brief biography of Abrams.
41. Zaffiri, 118.
42. *Ibid.*, 210.
43. *Ibid.*, 324–25.
44. Davidson, 571–72.
45. *Ibid.*, 614.
46. *Ibid.*, 571.
47. Zaffiri, 326. During 1969, some 11,600 U.S. service personnel died in Vietnam. In 1967, the figure was 11,153.
48. Colby was to become director of the CIA in 1973.
49. Colby, 208.
50. *Ibid.*, 269–70.
51. *Ibid.*, 190–92.
52. *Ibid.*, 256.
53. *Ibid.*, 310.
54. *Ibid.*, 244, 247–48.
55. *Ibid.*, 331.
56. Davidson, 460. General Davidson called the program ineffective because, "It never succeeded in identifying and locating the heart of the Viet Cong underground movement," but that was never the objective as the "heart of the VC underground movement" was never located in the villages of South Vietnam.
57. Karnow, 601–2; Colby, 360
58. Kissinger, 459.
59. *Ibid.*, 458.
60. *Ibid.*, 458–61.
61. *Ibid.*, 461–62; 467.
62. *Ibid.*, 467.
63. Nixon, 448.
64. Davidson, 623–35.
65. *Ibid.*
66. *New York Times*, May 1 ff.
67. *New York Times*, April 20. The Vietnam Moratorium Committee announced it was disbanding. The leaders said money sources had run dry and that the "political fad" of large demonstrations had run its course, acknowledging that Nixon's withdrawal policy had "knocked the legs" from under the nonradical movement.
68. Kissinger, 507.
69. *Ibid.*, 513.
70. *Ibid.*, 984

71. Davidson, 637–51.
72. Kissinger, 987–1010.
73. Sorley, Chapter 15.
74. Davidson, 651–59.
75. In no previous war would an American newspaper ever have presumed to speculate about an impending U.S. military operation. It is difficult to visualize this happening prior to, say, the St. Lo breakout or the Inchon landing, but during the Vietnam War, some of the antiwar press showed little compunction in publishing leaked information on U.S. military plans and operations from antiwar sources in the government.
76. Davidson, 643 and 649.
77. Kissinger, 1005.
78. Davidson, 650.
79. *New York Times*, February 3.
80. Kissinger, 278–82.
81. *Ibid.*, 438–39, 443–46. Kissinger stated that the offer made February 21 to withdraw all U.S. forces was a *new* point when he had already made this offer in the first meeting with Xuan Thuy on August 4.
82. Nixon, 348–49, 468, 583, 701; Kissinger, 282, 1180,
83. Kissinger, 976. Kissinger justified this concession on the basis that domestic pressures for withdrawal were such that leaving residual forces in Vietnam, as in Korea, was out of the question anyway, but at that point it was highly doubtful that Hanoi had arrived at the same conclusion with equal certainty.
84. The PRG was formed in June 1969 to elevate the status of the National Liberation Front in the Paris talks to that of a "government," and effectively it supplanted the NLF. It was quickly recognized by the socialist bloc nations. It was a bitter pill to the Thieu government to be forced to negotiate with what it regarded as a sham alternative government of South Vietnam.
85. Kissinger, 977–78.
86. Nixon, 468–69; Kissinger, 980–81.
87. Kissinger, 981.
88. Kissinger, 1018–19.
89. Kissinger's visit and China's invitation to Nixon to visit China in early 1972 were announced by Nixon in a TV address on July 15, 1971.
90. Kissinger, 1023.
91. *Ibid.*, 1024–25.
92. *New York Times*, July 2 and for the following two weeks carried numerous statements by administration critics, inevitably including Harriman and Clifford, and by its own columnists hailing the Binh proposal, and the paper editorialized on July 2 that the Communist offer "may open the way for a breakthrough."
93. Kissinger, 1021.
94. *Ibid.*, 1027–31.
95. *Ibid.*, 1042.

96. *Ibid.*, 1039–40. The proposal had been hand-passed to Xuan Thuy by General Walters on October 11, but Hanoi had not replied.
97. *Ibid.*, 1044.
98. Sorley, 155. This new strategy was embodied in COSVN Resolution 9, a copy of which was captured by U.S. troops. As noted earlier, this change in Communist strategy caused Abrams also to shift away from large-unit operations in 1969.
99. Nixon, 584, 593. On April 26, in the midst of the Easter Offensive, Nixon announced a withdrawal of 20,000 troops by July 1, leaving 49,000.
100. *Ibid.*, 316–17. Since no B-52s were based in Vietnam and naval forces at sea were not considered "in country," this augmentation in air support had only a small effect on the head count of forces remaining in Vietnam.
101. *Ibid.*, 306.
102. Davidson, 673–705.
103. Nixon, 586–90, 601–3; Kissinger, 1174–86. Also Davidson, 702. By the end of May, the U.S. had more than doubled its air force fighter-bomber strength in Southeast Asia from 190 to 409, B-52s had gone from 83 to 171 and navy carriers from two to six (and eventually, seven.) The sortie rate in March was 4,237 and in May, 18,444.
104. Kissinger, 1120–21 and Chapter 26.
105. *Ibid.*, 1169–74.
106. Nixon, 605–6; *New York Times*, May 13. In a May 12 Paris news conference, Le Duc Tho rejected Nixon's peace proposal.
107. Smith, 61–115; Nixon, 606–7
108. *New York Times*, May 10.
109. *Ibid.*, May 14.
110. The Moscow summit was held May 22–31 and resulted in the signing of the first SALT treaty.
111. *New York Times*, May 12.
112. Gareth A. Porter, *A Peace Denied* (Bloomington: Indiana University Press, 1975), 113.
113. Davidson, 680–706.
114. Sorley, 339.
115. Porter, 103–8.
116. Davidson, 673.
117. *Ibid.*, 733.
118. Nixon, 689.
119. *Ibid.*, 697.
120. Nixon defeated McGovern 60.7 percent to 37.5 percent, only slightly less decisive than Johnson's 1964 win over Goldwater.
121. Nixon, 701–2, 718; Kissinger, 1308–9.
122. Kissinger, 1310.
123. Nixon, 718; Alexander M. Haig, Jr., *Inner Circles: How America Changed the World: A Memoir.* (New York: Warner, 1992). 300.
124. Haig, 300.
125. Kissinger, 1310.
126. *Ibid.*

127. *Ibid.*,1315. Kissinger could not have actually believed this fiction, but he knew he could never negotiate the North Vietnamese troops out of South Vietnam.
128. Haig, 292–93.
129. Kissinger, 1304–5; *NYT*, June 29, June 30. Private talks were actually resumed July 19.
130. *Ibid.*, 1313.
131. Chapter 31, "From Stalemate to Breakthrough," 1301–59, Chapter 32, "The Troubled Road to Peace," 1360–94 and Chapter 33,"Peace Is at Hand," 1395–1470.
132. Nixon, 701.
133. Kissinger, 1337.
134. *Ibid.*, 1338–41; Haig, 294–96.
135. Kissinger, 1341–59.
136. Nixon, 697.
137. Kissinger,1362–63.
138. *Ibid.*, 1368 and 1375. On November 18, the Thieu government submitted a list of 69 modifications it wanted in the draft text of the agreement.
139. Nixon, 702–3
140. Kissinger, 1388–90.
141. *Ibid.*, 1397–98.
142. *Ibid.*, 1399.
143. Nixon, 705.
144. *Ibid.*, 718.
145. Kissinger, 1415–46.
146. *Ibid.*, 1448–49, Haig, 308–9.
147. Kissinger, 1452–54; *NYT*, Dec. 22.
148. The official North Vietnamese figure for civilian deaths was 1,318 for Hanoi and 305 for Haiphong. These were hardly numbers that would support the charge of indiscriminate carpet bombing of heavily populated areas. Western journalists who visited Hanoi after the bombing concluded that the damage had been "grossly overstated." Karnow, 653. Far greater numbers of civilians had been killed by the Communists in indiscriminate rocket attacks on South Vietnamese cities, in Hue where about 3,000 South Vietnamese civilians were executed during Tet and in the deliberate shelling of refugee columns during the Easter Offensive.
149. Kissinger, 1454.
150. *Ibid.*, 1457–59.
151. Smith, Chapter 10, 116–41. Planning for the Linebacker II B-52 raids was done at SAC headquarters in Omaha, based on World War II and Korean War strategic bombing experience prior to the existence of SAMs. The loss of 11 B-52s in the first four days was attributed to the tactics prescribed which proved to be faulty for the conditions faced in North Vietnam. Beginning with the fifth day, December 22, the raids were planned and controlled by Eighth Air Force headquarters on Guam, and through a combination of new tactics and North Vietnam's diminishing stock of SAMs, only four B-52s were lost in the remaining seven days of bombing.
152. Porter, 165.

153. Kissinger,1462.
154. *Ibid.*, 1469.
155. For the full text of the agreement, see *New York Times*, January 25, 1973.

Chapter 7

1. Duiker, *Communist Road*, 302. The Communist hierarchy clung tenaciously to the myth of the "general uprising" and talked of "a revolutionary high tide throughout the country" which would sweep away the "corrupt and oppressive Thieu regime," but at no time in the course of the 16-year Second Indochina War was the general uprising anything more than an illusion on the part of a Politburo that had come to believe its own propaganda.
2. Davidson, 738.
3. Karnow, 648–49. In the closing months of 1972 when it was apparent that an agreement was near, the U.S. conducted Operation Enhance Plus, a crash program to get as much materiel as possible into South Vietnam before the cease-fire, increasing the base for supplying replacements. About $2 billion worth was shipped in the period.
4. Nixon assured Thieu in writing three times, on October 19, November 14 and January 16 of his intention to enforce the agreement against violations by North Vietnam. Kissinger, 1369; Nixon, 718, 749–50.
5. Duiker, *Communist Road*, 304.
6. *Ibid.*, 303–4.
7. Kissinger, *Years of Upheaval* (London: Weidenfeld and Nicholson and Michael Joseph, 1982), 37–41. Later, the Byrd Amendment barred direct or indirect assistance unless specifically authorized by Congress. 326–27.
8. Nixon, 812.
9. Kissinger, *Years of Upheaval*, 315–27.
10. Duiker, *The Communist Road*, 307.
11. *Ibid.*, 308–9.
12. *Ibid.*, 309–13.
13. *Ibid.*, 313–14.
14. *Ibid.*, 314–18; See also Davidson, 752–91, for an account of the military events of the final 16 months which brought an end to the Republic of Vietnam.
15. Kissinger, *Years of Upheaval*, 304–9.
16. *Ibid.*, 356–59.
17. In almost 30 years, the constitutionality of the act has yet to be tested in the courts.
18. Robert Mann, *A Grand Delusion: America's Descent into Vietnam* (New York, Basic Books, 2000), 718, 721.
19. Frank Snepp, *Decent Interval* (New York: Random House, 1977), 563–64. Another 65,000 Vietnamese escaped on their own, bringing the total to over 130,000. Colby, 353, agrees with this figure.

20. Duiker, *The Communist Road*, 331–32; Duiker, *Vietnam Since the Fall of Saigon*. revised edition (Ohio State Center for International Studies: Monograph in International Studies, Southeast Asia Series, N. 56A, January 1990), 8, 15–20.
21. Duiker, *Vietnam Since the Fall*, 9. Most accounts agree with the "hundreds of thousands" estimate. Sheehan, in *After the War Was Over*. (New York: Random House, 1991), 79, uncritically accepted the figure as "nearly 100,000" from unspecified SRV sources.
22. Duiker, *Vietnam Since the Fall*, 11–12. In contrast, Ngo Dinh Diem successfully conducted a similar program to resettle several hundred thousand refugees from the north in 1954–55, but these were largely peasants and were provided better support from government and private sources.
23. *Ibid.*, 45–47.
24. *Ibid.*, 13. Doubts as to the loyalties of the Chinese led the Hanoi regime to apply especially stringent measures against that community. This led to a mass exodus from Vietnam of ethnic Chinese which the regime did nothing to discourage. In May 1978 China cancelled all remaining aid projects and withdrew its technicians. Duiker, 43–51.
25. *Ibid.*, 34.
26. *Ibid.*, 31–43,
27. Sheehan, 17
28. Duiker, *Vietnam Since the Fall*, 48.
29. *Ibid.*, 96–97, 112–13, 118.
30. *Ibid.*, 98–99.
31. *Ibid.*, 110–12.
32. In *After the War Was Over*, 84–85, Sheehan played back Hanoi's line that the SRV was the injured party and invaded Cambodia only "after persistent Khmer Rouge attacks on Vietnamese border areas over a two year period had killed approximately 30,000 SRV troops, an equivalent number of civilians, destroyed thousands of homes and public buildings and forced the abandonment of border farmlands." Since he provided no authority for these assertions, one can only assume he unskeptically accepted what he was told by SRV officials. He goes on to state, 85, again without citing his authority, that after the Khmer Rouge were defeated, the U.S. connived with China "to rebuild the Khmer Rouge into a potent guerrilla force." This is a far different Sheehan from the skeptical correspondent for UPI and *New York Times* in Saigon during the war who accepted almost nothing he was told by American officials.
33. Duiker, *Vietnam Since the Fall*, 127.
34. Sheehan, *After the War Was Over*, 80.
35. *Ibid.*, 17. Sheehan stated that Soviet aid to Vietnam was "worth about $2 billion annually during the 1980s" No source for this information is furnished.

36. *Ibid.*, 19.
37. Duiker, *Vietnam Since the Fall*, 32.
38. A July 2002 estimate of the population of Vietnam is given in the *CIA World Factbook — 2002* as 81.1 million. http://www.cia.gov/cia/publications/factbook/. The 1960 population was estimated at approximately 28 million.

Bibliography

Abramson, Rudy. *Spanning the Century: The Life of W. Averell Harriman: 1891–1986.* New York: William Morrow, 1992.
Acheson, Dean. *Present at the Creation.* New York: W. W. Norton, 1969.
Anderson, David L. *Trapped by Success: The Eisenhower Administration and Vietnam, 1953–61.* New York: Columbia University Press, 1991.
Arnold, James R. *The First Domino: Eisenhower, The Military, and America's Intervention in Vietnam.* New York: William Morrow, 1991.
Asprey, Robert B. *War in the Shadows: The Guerrilla in History.* Vol. 2. Garden City, NY: Doubleday, 1975.
Berman, Larry. *Lyndon Johnson's War.* New York: Norton, 1989.
_____. *No Peace, No Honor.* New York: The Free Press, 2001.
_____. *Planning a Tragedy.* New York: Norton, 1982.
Bird, Kai. *The Color of Truth: McGeorge Bundy and William Bundy, Brothers in Arms; A Biography.* New York: Simon & Schuster, 1998.
Braestrup, Peter. *Big Story.* Garden City, NY: Anchor Press, 1978.
Browne, Malcom W. *Muddy Boots and Red Socks.* New York: Times Books, Random House, 1993.
Bullock, Alan. *Hitler and Stalin: Parallel Lives.* New York: Knopf, 1992.
Buttinger, Joseph. *A Dragon Defiant: A Short History of Vietnam.* Newton Abbot, Great Britain: David & Charles, 1973.
_____. *The Smaller Dragon: A Political History of Vietnam.* New York: Praeger, 1958.
Cady, John F. *The History of Post-War Southeast Asia: Independence Problems.* Athens: Ohio University Press, 1974.
Charlton, Michael, and Anthony Moncrieff. *Many Reasons Why: The American Involvement in Vietnam.* New York: Hill and Wang, 1978.
Clifford, Clark. *Counsel to the President.* New York: Random House, 1991.
Clodfelter, Mark. *The Limits of Air Power: The American Bombing of North Vietnam.* New York The Free Press, 1989.
Colby, William. *Lost Victory.* Chicago: Contemporary Books, 1989.
Cooper, Chester L. *The Lost Crusade.* New York: Dodd Meade, 1970.
Courtois, Stephane, et al. *The Black Book of Communism: Crimes, Terror, Repression.* Cambridge: Harvard University Press, 1999.
Dallek, Robert. *An Unfinished Life: John F. Kennedy 1917–1963.* New York: Little, Brown, 2003.
Davidson, Gen. Phillip B. *Vietnam at War.* San Rafael, CA: Presidio Press, 1988.
Doyle, Edward, et al., *The Vietnam Experience: America Takes Over, 1965–67.* Boston: Boston Co., 1982.

_____. *The Vietnam Experience: A Contagion of War*. Boston: Boston Co., 1983.
Duiker, Wm. J. *The Communist Road to Power in Vietnam*. Boulder, CO: Westview Press, 1981.
_____. *Ho Chi Minh*. New York: Hyperion, 2000.
_____. *Vietnam Since the Fall of Saigon*. Ohio State Center for International Studies: Monograph in International Studies, Southeast Asia Series, No. 56A, January 1990.
Duncanson, Dennis J. *Government and Revolution in Vietnam*. London: Oxford University Press, 1968.
Eden, Anthony. *Full Circle: The Memoirs of Anthony Eden*. Boston: Houghton Mifflin, 1960.
Eisenhower, Dwight D. *Mandate for Change 1953–1956*. Garden City, NY: Doubleday, 1963.
Ellsberg, Daniel. *Papers on the War*. New York: Simon & Schuster, 1972.
Fall, Bernard B. *Hell in a Very Small Place*. Philadelphia: Lippincott, 1966.
_____. *The Two Viet-Nams*. New York: Praeger, 1963.
_____. *Viet-Nam Witness 1953–1966*. New York: Praeger, 1966.
Fifield, Russell H. *Americans in Southeast Asia: The Roots of Commitment*. New York: Thomas Y. Crowell, 1973.
Fitzgerald, Frances. *Fire in the Lake: The Vietnamese and the Americans in Vietnam*. New York: Vintage, 1972.
Gelb, Leslie H. *The Irony of Vietnam: The System Worked*. Washington, DC: Brookings, 1979.
Gibbons, William C. *U.S. Government and the Vietnam War, Part I, 1945–1961*. Washington, DC: United States Government Printing Office, 1984.
_____. _____, *Part II, 1961–1964*. Princeton, NJ: Princeton University Press, 1986.
_____. _____, *Part III, January–July 1965*. Princeton, NJ: Princeton University Press, 1990.
_____. _____, *Part IV, July 1965–January 1968*. Princeton, NJ: Princeton University Press, 1995.
Gilbert, Marc Jason, ed. *Why the North Won the Vietnam War*. New York: Palgrave, 2002.
Goodwin, Doris Kearns, *Lyndon Johnson and The American Dream*. New York: Signet, 1976.
Goodwin, Richard N. *Triumph or Tragedy: Reflections on Vietnam*. New York: Vintage, 1966.
Grant, Zalin. *Facing the Phoenix*. New York: W. W. Norton, 1991.
Haig, Alexander M., Jr., with Charles McCarry. *Inner Circles: How America Changed the World: A Memoir*. New York: Warner, 1992.
Halberstam, David. *The Best and the Brightest*. New York: Random House, 1972.
_____. *Ho*. New York: Random House, 1971.
_____. *The Making of a Quagmire*, revised ed. New York: Alfred A. Knopf, 1964, 1965, 1988.
Hammer, Ellen J. *The Struggle for Indochina: 1940–1955*. Stanford, CA: Stanford University Press, 1966.
Hendrickson, Paul. *The Living and the Dead: Robert McNamara and Five Lives of a Lost War*. New York: Vintage, 1997.
Herring, George C. *America's Longest War: 1950–1975*. New York: Wiley, 1979.
_____. _____. Second edition. New York: Knopf, 1986.
Hilsman, Roger. *To Move a Nation*. Garden City, NY: Doubleday, 1967.
Hoopes, Townsend. *The Limits of Intervention*, New York: McKay, 1970.
Iacocca, Lee, with William Novak. *Iacocca: An Autobiography*. New York: Bantam, 1984.
Isaacs, Arnold R. *Without Honor: Defeat in Vietnam and Cambodia*. Baltimore: Johns Hopkins University Press, 1983.
Isaacson, Walter. *Kissinger: A Biography*. New York: Simon & Schuster, 1992.
Isaacson, Walter, and Evan Thomas *The Wise Men: Six Friends and the World They Made*. New York: Simon and Schuster, 1986.
Joes, Anthony James. *The War for South Viet Nam*. New York: Prager, 1990.
Johnson, Lyndon B. *The Vantage Point: Perspectives of the Presidency 1963–1969*. New York: Holt, Rinehart and Winston, 1971.
Kahin, George McT. *Intervention: How America Became Involved in Vietnam*. New York: Knopf, 1986.
Kaiser, David. *American Tragedy: Kennedy, Johnson and the Origins of the Vietnam War*. Cambridge, MA: Belknap Press, 2000.
Karnow, Stanley. *Vietnam: A History*. New York: Penguin, 1983.
Kendrick, Alex. *The Wound Within*. Boston: Little, Brown, 1974.

Kissinger, Henry. *Ending the Vietnam War*. New York: Simon & Schuster, 2003.
_____. *The White House Years*. Boston: Little, Brown, 1979.
_____. *Years of Upheaval*. London: Little, Brown, 1982.
Lacouture, Jean. *Ho Chi Minh: A Political Biography*. New York: Random House, 1968.
_____. *Vietnam: Between Two Truces*. New York: Random House, 1966.
Lamb, David. *Vietnam, Now: A Reporter Returns*. New York: Public Affairs, 2002.
Lanning, Michael Lee, and Dan Cragg, *Inside the VC and the NVA*. New York: Fawcett Columbine, 1992.
Lansdale, Edward G. *In the Midst of Wars: An American's Mission to Southeast Asia*. New York: Harper & Row, 1972.
Lewy, Guenter. *America in Vietnam*. New York: Oxford University Press, 1978.
Lind, Michael. *Vietnam: The Necessary War*. New York: The Free Press, 1999.
Lodge, Henry Cabot. *The Storm Has Many Eyes: A Personal Narrative*. New York: Norton, 1973.
Mann, Robert. *A Grand Delusion: America's Descent into Vietnam*. New York: Basic Books, 2000.
McCullough, David. *Truman*. New York: Simon & Schuster, 1992.
McGlothen, Ronald. *Controlling the Waves: Dean Acheson and U.S. Foreign Policy in Asia*. New York: Norton, 1993.
McMaster, H. R. *Dereliction of Duty: Johnson, McNamara and the Joint Chiefs of Staff, and the Lies that Led to Vietnam*. New York: Harper/Collins, 1997.
McNamara, Robert S. *In Retrospect: The Tragedy and Lessons of Vietnam*. New York: Times Books, 1995.
Millett, Allan R. *Semper Fidelis: The History of the United States Marine Corps*. New York: Free Press, 1991.
Newman, John M. *JFK and Vietnam*. New York: Warner, 1992.
Nixon, Richard M. *The Memoirs of Richard Nixon*. London: Arrow Books, 1978.
Oberdorfer, Don. *Tet! : The Story of a Battle and Its Historic Aftermath*. Garden City, NY: Doubleday, 1971.
Palmer, Gen. Bruce. *The 25-Year War: America's Military Role in Vietnam*. Lexington: University of Kentucky Press, 1984.
Patti, Archimedes L. A. *Why Viet Nam?* Berkeley: University of California Press, 1980.
The Pentagon Papers, as published by *The New York Times*. New York: Bantam, 1971.
Pike, Douglas. *Viet Cong: The Organization and Techniques of the National Liberation Front of South Vietnam*. Cambridge, MA: M.I.T. Press, 1966.
Podhoretz, Norman. *Why We Were in Vietnam*. New York: Simon & Schuster, 1982.
Porter, Gareth. *A Peace Denied*. Bloomington: Indiana University Press, 1975.
Prochnau, William. *Once Upon a Distant War*. New York: Times Books, 1995.
Pyle, Richard, and Horst Faas. *Lost Over Laos*. Cambridge, MA: Da Capo, 2003.
Reeves, Richard. *President Kennedy: Profile of Power*. New York: Simon & Schuster, 1994.
Roy, Jules. *The Battle of Dien Bien Phu*. New York: Pyramid, 1966.
Rusk, Dean. *As I Saw It*. New York: Norton, 1990.
Schandler, Herbert Y. *The Unmaking of a President: Lyndon Johnson and Vietnam*. Princeton, NJ: Princeton University Press, 1977.
Schlesinger, Arthur M., Jr. *Robert Kennedy and His Times*. Volume 2. Boston: Houghton Mifflin, 1978.
_____. *A Thousand Days: John F. Kennedy in the White House*. Cambridge, MA: Riverside Press, 1965.
Schultzinger, Robert D. *A Time for War: The United States and Vietnam 1941–1975*. New York: Oxford University Press, 1997.
Scigliano, Robert. *South Vietnam: Nation Under Stress*. Boston: Houghton Mifflin, 1963.
Shaplen, Robert. *The Lost Revolution*. New York: Harper & Row, 1965.
_____. *The Road from War: Vietnam 1965–1970*. New York: Harper & Row, 1970.
Shapley, Deborah. *Promise and Power: The Life and Times of Robert McNamara*. Boston: Little, Brown, 1993.
Sharp, Adm. U.S. Grant. *Strategy for Defeat: Vietnam in Retrospect*. Novato, CA: Presidio, 1978.

Sheehan, Neil. *After The War Was Over: Hanoi and Saigon*. New York: Random House, 1991.
_____. *A Bright Shining Lie: John Paul Vann and America in Vietnam*. New York: Random House, 1988.
Smith, John T. *The Linebacker Raids*. London: Cassell, 2000.
Snepp, Frank. *Decent Interval*. New York: Random House, 1977.
Sorley, Lewis. *A Better War*. New York: Harcourt Brace, 1999.
Spector, Ronald H. *Advice and Support: The Early Years 1941–1960*. Washington, DC: Center of Military History, U.S. Army, 1983.
Stevenson, Charles A. *The End of Nowhere: American Policy Toward Laos Since 1954*. Boston: Beacon, 1972.
Summers, Col. Harry G., Jr. *On Strategy: A Critical Analysis of the Vietnam War*. Novato, CA: Presidio, 1982.
_____. *On Strategy: The Vietnam War in Context*. Carlisle Barracks, PA: Strategic Studies Institute, U.S. Army War College, 1981.
Taylor, Gen. Maxwell D. *Swords into Plowshares*. New York: Norton, 1972.
Tuchman, Barbara W. *Stilwell and the American Experience in China 1911–45*: New York: Bantam, 1972.
U.S. Department of Defense. *U.S.-Vietnam Relations, 1945–1967*. Washington, DC: United States Government Printing Office, 1971.
U.S. Department of State. *Foreign Relations of the U.S., 1961–1963, Volume XXIV, Laos Crisis*. Washington: United States Government Printing Office, 1994.
_____. _____, *1955–1957, Volume I, Vietnam*. Washington, DC: USGPO, 1985.
_____. _____, *1958–1960, Volume I, Vietnam*. Washington, DC: USGPO, 1986.
_____. _____, *1961–1963. Volume I, Vietnam-1961.* Washington, DC: USGPO, 1988.
_____. _____, *1961–1963, Volume II, Vietnam-1962*. Washington, DC: USGPO, 1990.
_____. _____, *1961–1963, Volume III, Vietnam, January-August-1963*. Washington, DC: USGPO, 1991.
_____. _____, *1961–1963, Volume IV, Vietnam, August-December-1963.* Washington, DC: USGPO, 1991.
_____. _____, *1964–1968, Volume I, Vietnam, 1964*. Washington, DC: USGPO, 1992.
_____. _____, *1964–1968, Volume II, Vietnam, January-June, 1965*. Washington, DC: USGPO, 1996.
_____. _____, *1964–1968, Volume III, Vietnam, June-December, 1965*: Washington, DC: USGPO, 1996.
_____. _____, *1964–1968, Volume IV, Vietnam, 1966*. Washington, DC: USGPO, 1998.
Westmoreland, Gen. William C. *A Soldier Reports*. Garden City, NY: Doubleday, 1976.
Zaffiri, Samuel. *Westmoreland*. New York: William Morrow, 1994.

Index

Abrams, Creighton 135; adopts new tactics 187–88; agrees to bombing halt 174; background of 186; and Cambodian incursion 191; contrasts with Westmoreland 186–87; and Hamburger Hill 187; ordered to upgrade ARVN 184; proposes to bomb Cambodian sanctuaries 183; receives new mission statement 184, 187; succeeds Westmoreland 168
Acheson, Dean 40, 64, 132, 170, 231n51
America(n) *see* United States of America
Annam 11, 14, 18, 19, 20
Antiwar movement 139–44, 177, 179, 181, 183, 187, 196, 197; and Cambodian incursion 191; on college campuses 142–43; and DRV 145, 198, 200; and 1968 Democratic National Convention 172; and Kent State 192; and military draft 142–43, 240n48; and mining of ports 200; in New Hampshire primary 164; organizations in 141, 240n49; and Phoenix program 190; reaction to Linebacker I 200; reaction to Linebacker II (Christmas bombing) 208; in Senate 140–41, 203; in State and Defense 164
Ap Bac, battle of 84
Armed Forces Council 118
ARVN (Army of the Republic of Vietnam) 31, 59, 84–85, 86, 108–9, 117, 127–28; in Buddhist crisis 89, 235n132; and Cambodian incursion 191; and coup plotting 94, 235n135; and clear-and-hold 137; in counterinsurgency plan 76–77; and Easter offensive 187, 198–99, 201; and final PAVN offensive 212–13; and Lam Son 719, 193–94; and near defeat in 1965 129, 134; reorganization and training of 54–55; strength of 126, 185; and U.S. takeover of ground war 136–37; and Tet offensive 159–63, 164–66; and Vietnamization 137, 183–85, 192, 194
Associated State of Vietnam 24, 39; and Bao Dai 47; Diem as premier of 48; and Elysée Agreement 42, 47; status of after Geneva Accords 25, 48; and U.S. recognition of 42–43

Ball, George 238n78; appointment as undersecretary of state 64; argues for compromise settlement in Viet Nam 130; and Deptel 243 90, 92
Bao Dai 25, 39, 50; abdication 47; and appointment of Diem as premier 48; and Associated State of Vietnam 47; and Geneva Accords 24; as Japanese puppet 18
Barrel Roll, Operation 74
Bay of Pigs 60, 62, 70, 76, 78
Binh, Madame Nguyen Thi: as foreign minister of PRG 195; presents eight-point peace proposal 195; presents new seven-point peace proposal 197; proposal hailed by *New York Times* 245n92
Binh Xuyen sect 49–50
Blum, Leon: and Popular Front government 16
Borodin, Michael 12
Boun Oum, Prince 68–69
Brezhnev, Leonid 30, 200; and Brezhnev Doctrine 224
Britain: attitude to colonialism 35; and Geneva Accords 24, 46; and post-WWII occupation of Vietnam 19, 39; and SEATO 47
Browne, Malcom 84, 242n154
Bruce, David K. E. 179, 182
Buddhism 85–87, 89, 103, 114, 117–18, 119, 160, 234n116, 235n121
Bundy, McGeorge 31, 62, 64, 114, 122; appointment as national security advisor 61; and bombing strategy 123–24; and communications with Lodge 97–99; and Deptel 243 92; and 44-battalion request 130–31; as

253

LBJ advisor 106, 114, 123, 175, 238n39; and memo of 1/27/65 with McNamara to LBJ 123; and NSAM 52 77; and NSAM 273 106; resignation of 146–47; and Rostow 66; and trip to Vietnam 31, 123; and Wise Men 243n191
Bundy, William 125, 237n26; appointment as assistant secretary of defense 64; as assistant secretary of state for Far Eastern affairs 110; and 44-battalion request 130; and NSC working group 122
Bunker, Ellsworth 151, 162, 163, 166, 191

C. Turner Joy, U.S.S.: and Tonkin Gulf incident 116
Cambodia 10, 18, 44, 46, 47, 56, 68, 194; Communist Party in 23; and diplomatic relations with U.S. 42, 182; as French protectorate 11; and Geneva Accords 24; incursions by U.S.-ARVN 191–92; infiltration trails, sanctuaries in 71–73, 74, 134, 148, 167, 221, 244n23; invasion by SRV 217, 247n32; and overthrow of Sihanouk 190; U.S. bombing of 182–83, 207; U.S. military operations in ended by Congress 214; *see also under* Khmer Rouge; Pol Pot; Sihanouk
Cao Dai sect 28, 49, 85
Carter, Jimmy 224; attempts to negotiate with SRV 218
Catholics 10, 28, 49, 85–86, 100, 231n66
Central Intelligence Agency *see* CIA
Central Office of South Vietnam *see* COSVN
Chennault, Anna: as Republican activist 174
Chennault, Claire 36
Chiang Kai-Shek: defeat of 22, 42; and 1927 purge of Communists 13
China: Communist victory in 22; Ho, arrest of 17; Ho sent to 12, 14, 16; and post-WWII occupation of Vietnam 19, 38; role in Vietnam history 10; and Sino-French agreement 20
China, People's Republic of (PRC) 42, 51; and Cambodia 182, 190; cultural revolution in 136; and DRV 210, 214, 217, 241n119, 247n24; embargoes trade with SRV 217; and Geneva Accords 24; and Geneva Conference on Laos 71, 74; invades SRV 217; and limited war 112; Nixon visit to 196, 245n89; and potential intervention in Indochina wars 43, 45, 70, 136, 153–54, 158, 221, 239n23; and potential intervention in Laos 75; and rail lines from DRV 130, 158, 222, 242n128; recognizes DRV 22; and tensions with Soviet Union 68, 136, 199; and U.S. 42, 183, 158, 196, 225, 230n46, 245n89
Churchill, Winston 34
CIA (Central Intelligence Agency) 55, 75, 97, 107, 109, 122, 154, 169, 235n134, 236n182; and W. Bundy 64; and Cambodia 190; and Church Committee 225; Colby as Saigon station chief 82, 232n105; Conein as agent of 89; and CORDS 188–89; and coup plotting 89, 94, 95, 100; and Hilsman 65; and Lansdale 48, 49, 50, 96; in Laos 68, 71, 74; McCone as director of 90, 235n128; McCone misgivings on Rolling Thunder 111, 124, 156; and Michigan State University 52; in post–Deptel 243 White House meetings 92; and Sihanoukville 244n23
Civil Guard 52, 54–55, 56–57, 76–77, 185
clear-and-hold: ARVN in 137; as strategy 134, 137–38, 139
Clifford, Clark 184; as advisor to LBJ 151–52, 167; appointment as secretary of defense 167, 169; attitude to Thieu 174, 198; background 168–70, 243n190; and LBJ 3/31/68 speech 170–71; and peace negotiations 173, 243n211; position on disengagement 195, 198, 244n20, 245n92; and post–Tet task force 167, 169–70; and Truman 169; and Wise Men 169, 170, 243n191
Cochin China: French conquest of 10; Japanese in 18, 228n36; status of 20
Colby, William 80, 232n105, 234n101; as CIA station chief in Saigon 57; as CORDS head 189; as Komer deputy 188; and Phoenix program 189–90; and strategic hamlets 82–83
Collins, J. Lawton 54; recommends removal of Diem 48–49
Comintern (Communist International) 12, 13, 41; and Great Terror 15; Ho as agent of 12, 14, 15, 17, 228n24; sends Ho to China 12, 16; Sixth Congress of 13–14; Seventh Congress of 15
commodity import program (CIP): suspension of 97
Communist containment policy of U.S. 43–45, 59, 106, 112, 132, 221; in Laos 68; in NSC-64 and NSC-124/2 230n46; in NSC-68 44; in NSC 5429 231n59; and Truman Doctrine 42; *see also* National Security Action Memoranda 52, 273, 288
Communist International *see* Comintern
Conein, Lucien: role of in Diem coup 89, 93, 94, 98
Congress, U.S. 43, 51, 53, 112, 181; antiwar sentiment in 178, 179, 187, 213; bars counteractions to Soviet imperialism 224; bars military action in or over Indochina 214; bars U.S. ground forces in Laos and Cambodia 193; and Byrd Amendment 347n7; cuts appropriations for Republic of Vietnam 214; and LBJ maneuvers to mislead 132, 176, 239n23; and legislation to force withdrawal 197, 203, 207–8; passes War Powers Act 214; and peace proposals 197; and reaction to RMN 5/8/72 speech 201; repudiates U.S. commitments in Indochina 223; and Tonkin Gulf resolution 115–117, 140, 238n49
CORDS *see* pacification
COSVN (Central Office for South Vietnam) 211; formed 23

Index 255

counterinsurgency 55, 65, 78; plan 57, 59, 76–77; Committee (Special Group [CI]) 65, 123
Cronkite, Walter 163
cultural revolution 136
Cuong De 45n6

Dai Viet (Dai Viet Dan Dang-Greater Vietnam Nationalist Party) 13, 38
Dang Lao Dong *see* Vietnamese Worker's Party
deGaulle, Charles 34; and neutralization of Indochina 115
Democratic National Convention (1968) 172
Democratic Republic of Vietnam (DRV, North Vietnam, Hanoi, Communists) 22, 58, 130, 131; and cease-fire violations 211, 223; decision to build socialism 25; and Easter offensive 198–99, 201–2; and final offensive 212–13; and Four Points 30, 125, 144, 145, 155, 206; and Geneva Accords 24–25; and Geneva Conference on Laos 70–73; and Ho Chi Minh 11, 27, 32; and Indochinese federation 217; Kissinger postwar visit to 211; lacks incentive to negotiate 145; and land reform 25, 229n71; negotiations to end bombing 173–74, 180–181; negotiations with France 20; and Nghe An uprisings 14, 25; and NLF 27–29; objectives in Laos 74, 220; objectives in South Vietnam 25, 26, 30, 159–60, 180, 195, 198, 210; as one-party state 21, 42, 228n50; and Pathet Lao 68, 70, 74; and peace negotiations (*see under* Kissinger; Le Duc Tho); and postwar governance of South Vietnam 215–16; and post-WWII relations with U.S. 38–42; and PRC 22, 210, 214, 217, 241n119, 247n24; proclaimed by Ho 18–19, 32; and PRP, 29; and reaction to LBJ 3/31/68 speech 171; and regroupment 49; rejects 17-nation peace proposal 125; and Resolution 15, 26, 56, 220; and Sihanouk alliance with 191; and strategic hamlets 83; and Tet Offensive 159–60; U.S. bombing of (*see* Linebacker I and II; Rolling Thunder); and USSR 30–31, 158, 199, 214–15, 218, 223, 241n119, 247n35
Deptel 243 90–93, 99, 102, 105, 235n137; controversy over 92–93; LBJ disapproval of 105; Lodge actions on 93–95; origin of 90; text of 91–2
Dewey, A. Peter 39
Diem, Ngo Dinh (Ngo Dinh Diem) 19, 25, 27, 28, 30, 57, 59, 110, 231n71; and bilateral security treaty with U.S. 78; and Buddhists 85–87; and counterinsurgency plan 76–77; in Deptel 243 91; and Durbrow 57, 58, 76; and elections 57–58; as founder of Republic of Vietnam 50–51, 102; governing philosophy of 51, 102; and land reform 52–53, 231n86; and Lansdale 48, 50, 59, 75–76; and LBJ visit 76; as liberator 51–52; and Lodge 90, 93–96, 98–100; and Mansfield report 81–82; and opposition to increased U.S. presence 94, 103; overthrow and death of 99–101, 103, 177, 182, 220–21, 236n150; and plebiscite, denial of 26, 51; as premier of Associated State of Vietnam 47–48; and press opposition to 84; and ranger units 54–55; and regrouped refugees 49; and rejection of U.S. recommendations 58–59, 80; and sects 49–50; and security, preoccupation with 55–56; and strategic hamlets 82–83, 188; and Taylor-Rostow mission 79
Dien Bien Phu 24, 46, 67, 162, 165–66, 228n63
Domino Theory 44–45, 113, 132; and NSAM 288 111
Don, Tran Van 98, 108, 235n135
Dong Minh Hoi (Vietnam Revolutionary League) 13, 19, 38; formed 17
DRV *see* Democratic Republic of Vietnam
Dulles, John Foster 46, 58, 64; and SEATO 47
Durbrow, Eldridge 55–56, 231n107; as ambassador 58; and counterinsurgency plan 57, 76; and Lansdale report 76

Easter offensive 187, 194; DRV objectives of 198, 201–2; U.S. reaction to 199–200
EDC (European Defense Community): and France 45; influence of on U.S. policy 45
Eden, Anthony 46
Eisenhower, Dwight D. 106, 132; actions on Laos 68, 237n6; and Kennedy briefing on Laos 68; LBJ seeks support of, 144; pledges support to Diem 48, 58; policy in Vietnam 106, 175
El Salvador 225
Ellsberg, Daniel 243n183
Ely, Paul 48, 54
Elysée Agreements 42, 47
enclave strategy 205; ARVN role in 138; as option 134, 138, 140; as proposed by Gavin and Taylor 138
Enthoven, Alain 243n183

Farmgate, Operation 81
Fatherland Front 228n46
final offensive (Ho Chi Minh campaign) 213
First Indochina War 22, 33; begins 21; and Dien Bien Phu 24, 67, 165; ends 24; and Navarre plan 24; U.S. role in 43–44
Fishel, Wesley 52
Flaming Dart I and II, Operations 123
flexible response 78
Fontainebleau conference 20
Ford, Gerald 214
Ford Foundation: McG. Bundy joins 146
Ford Motor Company: and McNamara 63
Forrestal, Michael 97, 106, 235n138; appointment of as Bundy assistant 65; and Deptel 243 90; and opposition to Nolting 88
Fortas, Abe: as LBJ advisor 151; as one of Wise Men 243n191
Four Points: announced by Pham Van Dong 204, 229n92; DRV commitment to 144, 145–46, 155; Hanoi flexes on 206; text of 30

France (French government, Paris) 52, 54; and Bao Dai 18, 47; conquest of Vietnam by 10–11; defeat of in WWII 16, 40; departure from Vietnam 47, 50, 54; and Diem 47–48, 50; and EDC 45, 231n51; and First Indochina War 21–24; and Geneva Accords 24, 46; Ho's negotiations with 20; Patti attitude to 230n9; Popular Front government of 16; and post–WWII goals in Vietnam 20; and SEATO 47, 69; and sects 49; and Sino-French agreement of 1946 20; and U.S. 40–41, 42–46; and Vichy government 16, 18
French Communist Party (FCP): and EDC 45; formed 12; Ho joins 12; on Indochina War 40
French Indochina 11, 50, 230n46, 231n51; British occupation of 19; Chinese occupation of 19; French sovereignty in 40, 42–44; Japanese in 16, 18; OSS role in 22, 36–39; potential intervention in by PRC 43, 70; Roosevelt and 34–35; U.S. policy toward 35, 38, 39–40, 42–45; in WWII 35
French Union 20, 24, 42, 47; troop strength in Indochina 24
Fulbright, William: as antiwar senator 138, 140–41, 237n6, 240n41

Galbraith, J. Kenneth 235n128
Gallagher, Philip E. 38
Gavin, James M. 133; and enclave strategy 138, 140
Gelb, Leslie 243n183
Geneva Accords 38, 47, 49, 59, 204; and Britain 46; DRV attitude to 24; and France 46; provisions of 24, 67; U.S. attitude to 46, 53–54
Geneva Conference on Laos 69–73; as diplomatic defeat for Kennedy 73–74, 75, 103, 220, 233n61; Harriman role in 70–73; outcome of 73–74; Soviet role in 71
Giap, Vo Nguyen 14, 16, 18; and Dien Bien Phu 24; in DRV government 22; and Easter offensive 202; in First Indochina War 21, 23; and Khe Sanh 166; and removal from Politburo 202; and revolutionary war doctrine 159
Gilpatrick, Roswell: and Deptel 243 90, 92, 236n141; and Vietnam Task Force 76
Goldwater, Barry 107, 116
Goodwin, Doris Kearns 239n17
Gracey, Douglas 39
Great Britain *see* Britain
Great Society 115, 132, 133, 139, 176, 222, 239n23

Haig, Alexander: on Christmas bombing 207; delivers Nixon letter to Thieu 209; as Kissinger aide 205; as Nixon military advisor 207
Haiphong: bombing of by U.S. 35, 153, 154–56, 200, 207–8; casualties in 246n148; importance of as port 157–58, 242n128;

mining of 158; *see also* Linebacker I and II; Rolling Thunder
Halberstam, David 60, 64, 84, 86, 92, 96, 149, 236n141
Hanoi (city): bombing of by U.S. 153, 154–56, 200, 207–8; casualties in 246n148; Chinese occupation of 38; and Patti mission to 38; U.S. consulate in 38; Vietminh seizure of power in 18, 38
Harkins, Paul: and coup plotting 94–95, 99; and Khan-led coup 108–9; as MACV chief 81, 234n92; and opposition to Diem coup 105, 107; replacement of 114, 133
Harriman, W. Averell 61, 65, 233n45; as ambassador-at-large 65, 131, 237n8; as chief Paris negotiator 173–74; and Deptel 243 90–92; and Geneva Conference on Laos 70–74, 75, 233n42, 240n41; and influence on Vietnam policy 207n7; and LBJ 106; and opposition to Diem 90, 97, 235n128; and opposition to Nixon policy 195, 198, 245n92; and opposition to Nolting 88, 95
Heath, Donald 39, 48
Helms, Richard 191; and Deptel 243 92, 236n141
High National Council 118–19
Hilsman, Roger 64, 108, 234n116; appointed director of INR 65; and Deptel 243 90, 92–93, 235n138, 236n141; ouster of 106, 237n8
Ho Chi Minh 21, 27, 41, 47; adulation of 27, 32; arrests of 15, 17; in China 12, 16–17; as Comintern agent 12, 14–15, 17; death and legacy of 31–33; decline in influence of 27, 31; and dissolution of ICP 19; as DRV president 22, 25; DRV proclaimed by 19, 38; early life 11; and Great Terror 15; and Ho-Sainteny agreement 20; ICP founded by 14; and involvement of with AGAS 36; joins FCP 12; and negotiations with France 20; as Nguyen Tat Than 11; and Patti 37–38; Resolution 15 26; and Thanh Nien 12; and U.S. support, attempts to gain 38, 41; Vietminh Front organized by16; writings of 41
Ho Chi Minh Trail 71, 233n45; as objective of Lam Son 719, 193; proposals to block 135, 139, 150, 158, 221–22, 244n23
Hoa Hao 28, 49, 85
Hoopes, Townsend: as Pentagon dove 243n183, 243n195
Hue 18, 212; and Buddhist crisis 85–86, 89; and Tet offensive 163, 165
Humphrey, Hubert: and 1968 presidential campaign 172–74
Hurley, Patrick 38

Ia Drang Valley, battle of 85
Indochinese Communist Party (ICP): becomes Dang Lao Dong 22; dissolution of 19; is founded by Ho 14; in Laos 67; recognition of by Comintern 15
Indonesia 43, 44

Institute for Defense Analyses: and Jason studies 150, 157
International Control Commission (ICC) 54; in Laos 67, 71, 73

Japan: in Indochina 16, 35, 37; and Indochinese coup d'état 18; post-WWII importance of Indochina to 46
Jason Study Group: and evaluation of Rolling Thunder 150, 157; on infiltration barrier 150
Johns Hopkins University: LBJ speech at 125
Johnson, Harold K.: report of trip to Vietnam 124, 126
Johnson, Lyndon B., and Johnson administration 31, 101; and Communism 106, 116; containment policy of predecessors, LBJ adherence to 106, 221, 237n6; as dissembler 132; and Eisenhower 106, 144; and enmity to R.F. Kennedy 114, 140; and Great Society 115, 132, 133, 139, 176, 222, 239n24; and Johns Hopkins speech 125; as Kennedy's vice president 64, 105, 177; and liking for secrecy 62, 126, 132; and Lodge 106, 114, 144; and McNamara resignation 151–52; and Nixon 178, 192, 202; opinion polls on 163; presidential campaign of 106, 116; role of summarized 174–76; and Rusk 62, 66, 152, 170; and Taylor appointment as ambassador 114; and withdrawal from presidential race 171
Johnson, Lyndon B., and Vietnam: bombing of DRV (see Rolling Thunder); bombing halt, partial 170; bombing halt, total 173, 198; bombing pauses 125, 145–46; Chinese intervention, fear of 112, 135, 153–54, 158; Diem coup, disapproval of 106; errors in conduct of war 133, 220–22; escalation, phase I 131–32; escalation, phase II 147; 44-battalion request 129–32; Komer appointment 188; limited war 5, 112, 133, 134, 176, 221–22; Marine offensive operations authorized by 138; mining, refusal to authorize 158, 200; objectives as restated by McNaughton 113; objectives in Vietnam: per NSAM 273 106, per NSAM 288 111–12, 149; peace talks, efforts to start 125, 145, 146, 243n193; reprisal air strikes 31, 116, 120, 123; reserves, refusal to call up 132, 147, 166; and San Antonio formula 171, 243n193, 243n207, 244n10; sanctuaries, refusal to authorize attacks on 135, 182, 221; speech of 3/31/68 170; Tonkin Gulf Resolution 115–17, 128; troop deployments to Vietnam 126–28; visit to Vietnam 76, 78, 105; and Wise Men 169, 243n191
Joint Chiefs of Staff (JCS) 81, 108, 111, 134, 135; recommendations ignored 120, 121, 122, 126, 127, 131, 146; Taylor as chairman 78; withdrawals, agrees to begin 181

Kahin George McT. 109
Karnow, Stanley 91

Katzenbach, Nicholas 151
Kennan, George 140
Kennedy, John F., and Kennedy administration 59; and appointment of Lodge 88, 102; and appointments to foreign policy posts 60–66; inaugural address of 60; sensitivity of to press 83–84, 100, 234n110, 234n112; and Taylor 78
Kennedy, John F., and Laos: Eisenhower briefing on 68; failure of diplomacy in 73–74, 75, 103, 220, 233n61; Geneva Conference on 69–73; goal of neutrality for 69; intervention in planning for 69, 75
Kennedy, John F., and Vietnam: additional military advisors sent to 77, 80, 139; counterinsurgency plan 57, 59, 76–78; Deptel 243 90–93; Diem coup 93–95, 97–100, 103, 177, 221; Diem death, reaction to 100; Lansdale report on 75–76; objectives in Vietnam, per NSAM 52 77–78, 80, 106, 112; Special Forces, deployment of 77; Taylor-Rostow mission to 78–81; Vietnam Task Force recommendations to JFK 77; withdrawal from Vietnam, alleged plan for 82, 97, 177, 234n97, 236n169
Kennedy, R. F. 94, 99, 114, 152, 238n40; as Johnson adversary 140, 164, 170
Kent State 192
Khan, Nguyen: decline of 117, 119; government of 110, 114, 123; and Lodge 110; ouster of 119, 144; and overthrow of Minh government 83, 108–9; and Taylor 118–19
Khe Sanh, siege of 165–66
Khmer Issarak 228n59
Khmer Rouge: formed 23, 228n59; and murder of Cambodians 244n27; and Sihanouk 183
Kim, Le Van 108, 110, 235n135
King, Martin Luther: as antiwar activist 143
Kissinger, Henry: appointed national security advisor 178; and Beijing, secret trip to 196; and Christmas bombing 207; criticizes Lam Son 719 193; plans Vietnam strategy with Nixon 179; and postwar visit to Hanoi 211; and secret trip to Moscow 200; supports Cambodian incursion 191; and troop withdrawals 181
Kissinger, Henry, and peace negotiations with DRV: invites secret negotiations 194; negotiations of 1970 195–96; proposal of 5/31/71 196; negotiations of June–July 1971 196–97; believes secret talks disadvantageous to U.S. 197; failed meeting of 5/2/72 200; negotiations of July–Oct. 1972 204–6; agrees to arbitrary negotiating schedule 205; "peace is at hand" 207; failure to persuade Thieu 206; negotiations of November–December 1972 207; final negotiations 208; and "no residual forces" concession 195; and "no withdrawal of PAVN" concession 196
Komer, Robert: 162; and CORDS 188–89; as pacification head 137, 159

Korea 42; troops of in Vietnam 126
Korean War 43, 230n46; and China 45; influence of on U.S. policy in Vietnam 46; as limited war 112
Kosygin, Alexei 31, 131
Khrushchev, Nikita 70; overthrown by Brezhnev 30; and peaceful coexistence 26
Kuomintang (Chinese Nationalist Party) 12, 13, 17, 227n23; as Vietminh source of arms 22

Lacouture, Jean 29
Ladejinsky, Wolf 231n82
Laird, Melvin: advises against Cambodian incursion 191; advises against Christmas bombing 207; announces reduction in draft 181; appointed secretary of defense 178
Lam Son 719, Operation: outcome of 193–94; planning for 193
Langdon, William 37
Lansdale, Edward G. 52, 57, 78, 79, 80, 96, 149, 231n60; and Diem 48, 50, 231n66, 231n82, 231n84; as pacification spokesman for Lodge 145, 240n26; in Philippines 48; and report on Vietnam 75–76
Lao Dong see Vietnamese Worker's Party
Lao Issara 228n59
Laos: bombing in 74, 221; coalition government of 74; Communist victory in (1975) 74, 217; Communists in 23, 67, 70, 228n59; DRV objectives in 71, 73, 115; Eisenhower on 68; as French protectorate 11, 66; and Geneva Accords, failure of 67, 204; Geneva Conference on 69–73; inclusion in DRV's Indochinese federation 217; and infiltration barrier 150; infiltration trails through 68, 71, 73, 74, 135, 220, 221; military operations in ended by Congress 214; Operation Lam Son 719 in 192–93; and Pathet Lao 67, 68, 228n59; and SEATO, renunciation by 47; strategic location of 68; and U.S. actions after Geneva Accords 68; and U.S. planning to intervene in 70, 75, 120
Le Duan: as chairman of Central Committee 26; and COSVN 23, 26; death of 216; influence of on Resolution 15, 26; and Le Duc Tho 195; as leader of DRV 27, 31, 229n76; and postwar governance of South Vietnam 216; removes Giap from Politburo 202
Le Duc Tho: as close ally of Le Duan 195
Le Duc Tho, and peace negotiations: begins secret meetings with Kissinger 195; introduces nine-point proposal, June 1971 196; failed meeting of 5/2/72 200; rejects Nixon proposal of May 1972 246n106; negotiations of July–October 1972 204–6; presses for accelerated schedule 205; negotiations of November–December 1972 207; final negotiations 208
Le Hong Phong 15, 227n21, 230n100
League for the Independence of Vietnam see Vietminh Front

Lenin, V. I. 32, 33
Lien Viet Front 20, 22, 28
limited war 5, 112, 133, 134, 176, 221–22
Linebacker I and II, Operations 157–58, 222; effect of on DRV 208; Nixon announces start of I 200; planning for 246n151; start of II 208
Lodge, Henry Cabot 40, 105; appointed ambassador to Vietnam, by JFK 88, by LBJ 144; attitude of to Diem 90, 102; attitude of to negotiations 145; background of 88; and Diem telephone call during coup 99; and end of first tour 114; heads Paris delegation 179; role in coup plotting 93–99; supports bombing of DRV 120; and Wise Men 243n191
Lon Nol: as prime minister of Cambodia 190
Lovett, Robert 61, 63
Lu Han 38

MAAG (Military Assistance and Advisory Group) 48, 59; arrival of in Saigon 39; and counterinsurgency plan 57; in Laos 69; staff levels of 53–54; training orientation of 54–55
MACV (Military Assistance Command-Vietnam): established 80, 106; foresees 1972 enemy offensive 193; and planning of Lam Son 719 194; role of in Khan-led coup 108–9; takes control of ground war 136–37, 184; and Tet offensive 161, 163; Westmoreland as commander of 133
Maddox, U.S.S.: and Tonkin Gulf incident 116
Malaya 43, 44, 45, 47; as purported origin of strategic hamlets 82, 234n101
Manila formula 180
Mansfield, Mike 115, 190; and alleged plan of JFK to withdraw from Vietnam 234n97; and Mansfield amendment 197; report on Vietnam 81
Mao Zedong 16, 25, 27, 32, 42
Marshall, George C. 62; and Marshall Plan 42
McCarthy, Eugene: as antiwar senator 141; in New Hampshire primary 164
McCloy, John J. 132; and Wise Men 243n191
McCone, John A. 96, 110, 111; and bombing of DRV 124, 127, 156; and Deptel 243 90, 92, 99, 105, 235n128
McGarr, Lionel: and counterinsurgency plan 57, 59; as MAAG chief 55
McGovern, George: as antiwar senator 141; defeated by Nixon 246n120; interviews Mme. Binh 197; as presidential candidate 202, 204
McNamara, Robert S. 64, 114, 115, 185, 186, 238n39; appointed secretary of defense 63; and bombing strategy 124, 127, 195 (see also Rolling Thunder); and departure from administration 151–52; and deployment of troops 126, 129–31, 147; and Deptel 243 90–92; and Diem coup, opposition to 105;

early hawkishness of 129, 147; and escalation, phase I 131; and escalation, phase II 147; gains ascendancy on Vietnam 63, 80; and Honolulu conferences: July 1962 81, November 1963 105, April 1965 127; and infiltration barrier 149–51; initiates Pentagon Papers 151; and joint memo with Bundy of 1/27/65 123, 134; and NSAM 288 111–12; and plans to phase out of Vietnam 81, 97; recommends reserve call-up 130; recommmends stabilizing war 148, 151; and relations with LBJ 106, 175; rephrase NSAM 288, attempt to 149; and Taylor-Rostow report 79–80; and Tonkin Gulf incident 116, 238n49; trips to Vietnam and recommendations from: September 1963 96–97, December 1963 105, March 1964 110–111, May 1964 120, July 1965 131, November 1965 147, October 1966 148, July 1967 162; and U.S. objectives in Vietnam 113, 115; and Westmoreland minimum essential-optimal troop request 148
McNamara-Taylor mission 97
McNaughton, John: as assistant secretary of defense 64, 129; and bombing strategy 124; and infiltration barrier 149, 241n82; restates U.S. objectives in Vietnam 113
Mekong River and delta 9; and pacification in 189
Michigan State University 52
Military Assistance and Advisory Group *see* MAAG
Military Assistance Command-Vietnam *see* MACV
Military Revolutionary Council (MRC) 101, 107, 117
Minh, Duong Van: and coup to oust 108–9; and Diem coup 101; and Military Revolutionary Council 101, 107; and surrender of South Vietnam 213
Minh Mang, Emperor 10
mining of ports 158; Nixon orders 200; as recommended by JCS 120, 130, 148; remining of in Linebacker II 207
Morse, Wayne 115; as antiwar senator 139–40
Moscow 40, 41, 125; Ho in 12, 13; Kissinger secret trip to 200; summit meeting in 199–201, 246n110; *see also* Soviet Union
Mountbatten, Lord Louis 38

Napoleon III (Louis Napoleon) 10
National Front for the Liberation of South Vietnam *see* NLF
National Security Action Memoranda (NSAMs): *No. 52* 77, 80, 106, 112; *No. 111* 80; *No. 273* 106, 107, 112; *No. 288* 111–12, 149; *No. 328* 126
National Security Council memos: NSC-64 of 4/24/50 230n46; NSC-68 of 4/7/1950 44, 237n6; NSC 124/2 of 6/25/52 230n46
National United Front of Vietnam *see* Lien Viet

Nationalist movements (in Indochina) 13
NATO (North Atlantic Treaty Organization) 42, 43, 47
Navarre Plan: and Dien Bien Phu 23–24
negotiations (peace): between France and DRV 20–21; during Johnson administration (*see* Johnson, Lyndon B.); during Nixon adminstration (*see* Kissinger; Le Duc Tho; Nixon)
New Frontier 60, 62, 65, 66
New York Times 92, 96, 125, 127; antiwar position of 115; and Ap Bac battle 84; backs RFK peace proposal 141; and coverage of antiwar activities 141, 143; and Diem 52, 86, 89; on first Nixon peace proposal 181; opposes Lam Son 719 193–94; opposes Linebacker I renewal of bombing 201; opposes Linebacker II 208; and Rolling Thunder 155; on secret bombing of Cambodia 183; on troop withdrawal 181; on Westmoreland post–Tet troop request 167
Nghe An: 1930 uprising 14; 1956 uprising 25
Ngo Dinh Diem *see* Diem, Ngo Dinh
Ngo Dinh Khoi 19
Ngo Dinh Nhu *see* Nhu, Ngo Dinh
Nguyen Ngoc Tho 101, 109
Nguyen Tat Than *see* Ho Chi Minh
Nguyen Van Linh 218
Nguyen Van Thieu *see* Thieu, Nguyen Van
Nhu, Ngo Dinh (Ngo Dinh Nhu): as advisor to Diem 77, 87; American opposition to 89, 90, 94; and Buddhist crisis 85, 87; death of 100, 236n186; in Deptel 243 90, 91; and strategic hamlets 82–83, 234n101; and Xa Loi raid 89, 235n132
Nixon, Richard M., and Nixon administration: appoints cabinet 178–79; and Beijing trip 159, 196, 246n98; and Moscow summit 199, 201, 246n110; and 1968 campaign 172; and 1972 campaign 204, 246n120; takes office 177; and triangular diplomacy 225; and Watergate 211, 212, 223
Nixon, Richard M., and Vietnam: and bombing of Cambodian sanctuaries 182–83; and Cambodian incursion 190–91; Congress overrides 1973 veto 214; develops disengagement strategy 179, 186; and domestic pressures to end war 179, 203; and flawed peace 210–11, 223; and intent to enforce peace 207, 208, 211, 212, 223; and mining 157–58; and 1968 negotiations to end bombing 173–74, 244n215; orders Linebacker I 200; orders Linebacker II (Christmas bombing) 207; peace proposal (8-point) of 5/69 180; peace proposal of 10/70 196; peace proposal of 5/72 200, 204; and relations with Thieu 195, 203, 207, 208–9; resigns 212; response to Easter offensive 199, 200–201; reveals secret talks 197; and "secret" plan to end war 172, 243n204, 244n5; and troop withdrawals 181, 192, 199, 204; and Vietnamization 184

260 Index

NLF (National Liberation Front, National Front for the Liberation of South Vietnam, Viet Cong, VC) 53, 109, 125; and doctrine of General Uprising 28, 159–60, 247n1; formed 27–29, 229n83; joins Paris peace talks 173; and People's Revolutionary Party 29; program of 29; and strategic hamlets 83; supplanted by PRG 245n84; and Tet Offensive 159–60

Nolting, Frederick: appointed ambassador to Republic of Vietnam 76; replacement of 88; reports Diem rejection of U.S. proposals 80; in White House meetings on overthrow of Diem 94

Norodom Sihanouk see Sihanouk, Prince Norodom

North Vietnam see Democratic Republic of Vietnam (DRV)

NSAM see National Security Action Memoranda

O'Daniel, John M.: as MAAG chief 39, 54
Office of War Information (OWI) 37
OSS (Office of Strategic Services): role of in Vietnam 22, 36–38, 230n12

Pac Bo 17
pacification: and appointment of Komer 159, 188; and CORDS 188–89; failure to recognize need for 57, 77, 80, 137, 188, 222; and Lansdale 240n26; McNamara recommends 148; as part of Nixon policy 184, 187; and strategic hamlets 82; and Tet offensive 159, 189

Pathet Lao: and aftermath of 1954 Geneva Conference 73–74; formed 28, 67, 228n59; and Geneva Conference on Laos 69–73; Souphanouvong as leader of 67; and Soviet arms airlift to 68

Patti, Archimeded L.A.: as OSS officer in Vietnam 37–38

PAVN (People's Army of Vietnam) 55, 138, 147, 150, 157, 170, 186; in Cambodia 182–83, 190, 192; and Easter offensive 198–99, 201; and failure of U.S search-and-destroy strategy 135; and final offensive (Ho Chi Minh campaign) 212–13; in First Indochina War 23–24; and Hamburger Hill 187; and Khe Sanh 162, 165–66; and Lam Son 719 192, 194; occupies portions of South Vietnam 180, 202, 203–4; post–Tet role 161; puts down Nghe An uprising 25; re-equipping of by PRC 55, 231n97; role of in Tet offensive 160, 164; and sanctuaries 112; and U.S. strategy to defeat 134–35, 139, 162; USSR as principal arms supplier to 31, 158, 200, 223, 241n119; violates 1968 understanding 174

Pentagon Papers: Gelb as editor 243n183; initiated by McNamara 151; publication of 196

People's Army of Vietnam see PAVN

People's Liberation Armed Forces (PLAF) see Viet Cong

People's Republic of China (PRC) see China, People's Republic of

People's Revolutionary Party (PRP) 109, 234n107; formation, role, relationship to DRV 29

People's Self Defense Forces 185, 188
Petain, Henri Philippe 16
Pham Van Dong 14, 16; in DRV government 23, 26; and Four Points 30, 125; and Geneva Conference 24
Phan Boi Chau 227n6
Philippines 35, 45; and Hukbalahaps 43, 44, 48
Phnom Penh 190–91
Phoenix program 189
Phoumi Nosavan: and Harriman 71, 73; joins coalition government 73; as leader of Laos rightist forces 68–69, 71
Phuc Quoc (Viet Nam Restoration League) 13
Pierce Arrow, Operations I and II 120
Pike, Douglas: on strategic hamlets 83
PLAF see Viet Cong
plebiscite see reunification plebiscite
Pol Pot 217
PRC see China, People's Republic of
press, press relations: adverse trend in 84; and Buddhist crisis 87, 89; Kennedy administration sensitivity to 84, 100, 234n110; opposition to Nhu 89, 93; role of Halberstam, Sheehan, and Browne in 84; and Tet offensive 161–62, 166
Provisional Revolutionary Government (PRG) 29, 195, 205; formed 245n84; in postwar South Vietnam 215; signs peace agreement 209

Rally of the French People (RPF) 45
Reagan, Ronald 6, 225
Red River and delta 9, 23
refugees: regroupment of 49; and Tet offensive 162, 165, 189
Reinhardt, G. Frederick: as ambassador to South Vietnam 58
Republic of Vietnam (RVN) see South Vietnam
Resolution 15: adoption of by central committee 26; effect of 27, 220
Reston, James 81
reunification plebiscite 59; Diem denial of 26, 51; and Geneva Accords 24–25
Revolutionary Path 41
Richardson, John 96
Ridgway, Matthew 133, 239n23
Rockefeller, Nelson 178
Rogers, William P.: appointed secretary of state 178; opposes Cambodian incursion 191; signs peace agreement 209
Rolling Thunder, Operation: begins 124; civilian management of 136, 152–53, 222; criticism of: by Taylor 124, by McCone 124, 127, 156; description and evaluation of

152–57; ends 173; and Jason studies 150, 157; LBJ restrictions on 127, 153–55, 156, 157, 158; McNamara recommends stabilizing 148, 151; objectives of 124, 154; and partial halt 170; pauses in 125, 145; and planning for 120–22; U.S. losses in 155
Roosevelt, Franklin D. 34–35
Rostow, Walter 76, 151; appointed Bundy deputy 66; becomes national security advisor 66, 147; and bombing 153, 156; rejects mining 158; and Taylor-Rostow mission 78
Rusk, Dean: appointed secretary of state 61–62; and JFK attitude to 62; and Lodge appointment 88; and Lodge, communications with 96, 101; and relations with LBJ 106, 170, 175; and Taylor, communications with 119, 121
Rusk, Dean, and Vietnam: and alleged plan of JFK to withdraw 234n97; bombing target selection 152; commitment of U.S. in 115; Deptel 243 90–92; loses primacy to McNamara 80; and NSC Working Group 122; opposes bombing pauses 146; and partial bombing halt 170; and Phase I escalation 130; and Taylor-Rostow mission recommendations 125

Saigon Military Mission (SMM): and Lansdale 48, 231n66
Sainteny, Jean: and Ho-Sainteny agreement 20
San Antonio formula 171, 244n10; Clifford interpretation of 169, 243n193
Schlesinger, Arthur, Jr.: on alleged plan of JFK to dismiss Rusk 62; on alleged plan of JFK to withdraw 81, 234n97; on appointment of Lodge 88, 235n126; on Geneva Conference on Laos 70, 74, 233n61
SEATO (Southeast Asia Treaty Organization) 47; and Laos 69; as legal basis for U.S. involvement 112
Second Indochina War 208; ends 213; and general uprising 28, 159–60, 247n1; and Laos 74, 233n61; and Resolution 15 26, 56, 220; U.S. begins direct intervention in 31; and U.S. defeat in 1; *see also* Vietnam War
sects 49; *see also* Binh Xuyen; Cao Dai; Hoa Hao
Shaplen, Robert: on factionalism in Vietnam 102
Sharp, Ulysses Grant, Jr. 127, 147, 239n85; as critic of slowly ascending tempo strategy 152; opposes infiltration barrier 150; and Rolling Thunder 156, 241n122; and Tonkin Gulf incident 116
Shaw, Rudolph 36
Sheehan, Neil 84, 235n132, 247n21, 247n32, 247n35
Sihanouk, Prince Norodom: allies self with PRC 191; breaks diplomatic relations with U.S. 182; does not object to U.S. bombing 183; opposes presence of PAVN 183; overthrown 190–91; permits Viet Cong bases 182; restored as king 218
Sihanoukville 244n23; is closed by Lon Nol government 191, 193; Sihanouk permits Viet Cong use of 182
slowly ascending tempo (graduated overt military pressure): civilian support of 122, 124, 133, 152, 154, 158; ineffectiveness of as strategy 124, 145, 155, 157, 222; McNamara proposes to abandon 148; McNamara recommends 111, 120, 122; planning for 111, 120, 122; *see also* Rolling Thunder
Smith, Walter Bedell 46
Socialist Republic of Vietnam (SRV): diplomatic recognition by U.S. 218; economic policies of 216; formed 215; invades Cambodia 217; and PRC, relations with 217
Souphanouvong, Prince: joins coalition government 67, 73; as Pathet Lao leader 67
South Vietnam (Republic of Vietnam, RVN, Saigon): becomes independent republic 50; Communist offensives in (*see under* Easter offensive; final offensive; Tet offensive); Diem as liberator 51; elections in 50, 57, 144; and Geneva Accords 46, 47; joins Paris peace talks 173; land reform in 52–53; Lansdale in 48; Laos as corridor to 71, 73, 74, 103; limited war strategy, effect on 134, 139; PAVN occupies portions of 180, 196, 202, 203–4; post–1975 Communist government of 215–16; and progress under Diem 59; as SEATO protocol state 47, 69; sects in 49–50; strategic hamlets in 82–83; Thieu assumes power in 144; Viet Cong activity in 36, 78, 83, 89, 127, 181, 191, 197, 201, 205, 213, 222; and Vietnamization 179, 183–84; U.S. objectives in 58, 59, 77, 134
Southeast Asia Treaty Organization *see* SEATO
Souvanna Phouma, Prince: as premier of Laos 68, 73
Soviet Union (USSR, Soviet government, Moscow) 51; and arms airlift to Pathet Lao 68; as arms supplier to DRV 31, 158, 199, 224, 241n119; breakup of 218, 225; and Brezhnev Doctrine 224; and DRV, rapprochement with 30; and economic aid to DRV 214, 218, 247n35; and Geneva Conference on Laos 69–73; and Khrushchev, overthrow of 30; and Khrushchev peaceful coexistence policy 26, 30; launches proxy war 3, 6, 30, 224; and Moscow summit 199–201, 246n110; in NSC-68 44; post–Vietnam War imperialism of 224, 225; and PRC, tensions with 136; and Tito 41
Special Forces, U.S. Army: deployment of by JFK 77
Special Group (CI) 235n128; formed by JFK 78
Spock, Benjamin 143
State Department, U.S. 73, 75, 100; and Buddhist crisis 86, 89; and civilian control of

war 131, 152, 155, 175; and criticism of Diem by 102; and Diem coup 108; efforts to open peace talks 145; Europeanist faction in 40; and Ho Chi Minh 41; and Lodge 102; and nation-building program in Indochina 46; Rogers appointed secretary of 178; Rusk appointed secretary of 61; and Vietnam 35, 38, 39, 58
Stevenson, Adlai E. 61, 64
strategic hamlets 82–83, 188, 234n101
Sukarno 43
Summers, Harry G., Jr.: on blocking Ho Chi Minh Trail 136; on limited war 112
Sûreté 15

Tan Viet (New Vietnamese Revolutionary Party) 13
Taylor, Maxwell 65, 110, 132; as ambassador to South Vietnam 114, 118–19, 121, 144; background of 78; and bombing of DRV 31, 121, 122, 124; as chairman of JCS 78, 120, 133; and deployment of combat troops 126–27, 131; and Deptel 243 90–92; and Diem coup 99, 100, 105, 235n128; and enclave strategy 126, 138; JFK attitude to 78; as LBJ advisor 248; opposes peace talks 145; as Westmoreland sponsor 133
Taylor-Rostow mission 78–79, 110; McNamara-Rusk recommendations on 79–80; and NSAM 111 80
Tchepone: as target of Lam Son 719 193
Tet Offensive 135, 138, 242n139; ARVN in 160–166; brings U.S. policy of disengagement 169–72; and civilian executions of, in Hue 246n148; consequences of, in South Vietnam 185, 187, 189; consequences of on U.S. troop deployments 166–68; description and evaluation of 159–66; press coverage of 162–66
Thailand (Siam) 45; Ho in 14; as SEATO member 47
Thanh Nien (Vietnamese Revolutionary Youth League): dissolution of 14; formed by Ho 12; as future Communist Party 13
Thich Quang Duc: immolation of 87
Thich Tri Quang 114; and Buddhist unrest 85–86, 235n131
Thieu, Nguyen Van (Nguyen Van Thieu) 108; assumes power 144; balks at negotiations 203, 205, 206; Cambodian incursion supported by 191; Communist insistence on removal of 195, 197, 201, 204; Communists drop demand for removal of 206; creates People's Self Defense Forces 185, 188; demands changes to peace agreement 206, 246n138; and distrust of Kissinger 205; Kissinger resentment of 206; Nixon affirms support of 195, 207, 208, 247n4; Nixon's alleged betrayal of 244n215; as obstacle to peace 198; opposes total bombing halt 174; and Phoenix program 189; and program of

four no's 211; receives Nixon ultimatum 209; resigns 213
Thompson, Sir Robert: and strategic hamlets 234n101
Tito, Josip Broz 61
Tonkin: as French protectorate 10, 20
Tonkin Gulf Resolution 115, 116–17; LBJ interpretation of 123; and McNamara 116, 238n49
Trotskyites 13
Truman, Harry S. 35, 115; containment policy of 42, 44, 106, 132; and decision to aid France 43–44, 106; and OSS 38; and Truman Doctrine 62, 111; *see also under* Communist containment policy of U.S.
Truong Chinh 14; in DRV government 22; and land reform program 25, 26

United States of America (U.S. Government, America, Washington): air war strategy of (*see* Rolling Thunder); antiwar movement in 139–44; attitude to Khan government 118–19; attitude to Minh government 108; attitude to plebiscite 51; Communist containment policy of 42, 44, 62, 106, 111, 230n46, 237n6; consequences of defeat in Vietnam 224–25; and Diem, support of 48, 77–78, 102, 105; and Domino Theory 44, 111, 113, 132, 230n46; and errors in conduct of war 221–22; and European Defense Community 45; factors in final defeat of 223; final role of, 1975 213–14; and France, decision to support 43; ground war strategy of 134–37, 138–39; intervention in Vietnam begins 31; and Laos crisis 68–74; and limited war 4, 112, 133, 134, 176, 221–22; maneuvered out of Laos 71–74, 220; objectives as restated by McNaughton 113; objectives in Vietnam (*see* National Security Action Memoranda); and Operation Enhance Plus 247n3; and peace negotiations (*see under* Kissinger; Nixon); and peace talks, efforts to start 125, 145, 243n193; position at Geneva (1954) 46; position on neutralization of Indochina 115; and post-WWII policy in Vietnam, arguments in support of 39–42; post-WWII role in Vietnam 22, 23; shifts in policy of 42–43, 92; and troop withdrawals 181, 192, 199, 204, 246n99; and withdrawal of support from 90–100, 103, 220; and WWII air attacks on Vietnam 35
U.S. Defense Department (Pentagon) 58, 79, 92; antiwar officials in 164, 167, 243n183; Clifford as secretary 117, 169; gains ascendancy on Vietnam 108, 114; Laird as secretary 178, 181, 191, 207; McNamara as secretary 97–99, 100
U.S. State Department 73, 75, 100; and Buddhist crisis 86, 89; and civilian control of war 131, 152 155, 175; and criticism of Diem by 102; and Diem coup 108; efforts to

open peace talks 145; Europeanist faction in 40; and Ho Chi Minh 41; and Lodge 102; and nation-building program in Indochina 46; Rogers appointed secretary of 178; Rusk appointed secretary of 61; and Vietnam 35, 38, 39, 58
USSR *see* Soviet Union

Van Tien Dung: commands final PAVN offensive 213
Vichy government 16, 18, 34
Viet Cong (VC, NLF, PLAF) 53, 55, 77, 82, 84, 111, 112, 117, 123, 126, 127, 128, 140; and ARVN 59, 129; and Bien Hoa raid 121; and Cambodian sanctuaries, U.S. bombing of 182–83; CORDS effect on 189; counterinsurgency plan to defeat 57; and crossover point 135, 148, 242n45; and failure of search-and-destroy 135; minimal role of in Easter offensive 201; and pacification 137, 148, 161; and Phoenix effect on 189; and Tet offensive 159–63, 164–65, 242n139, 242n154; *see also* NLF
Vietminh Front (League for the Independence of Vietnam) 17, 230n11, 230n12, 231n67; and Dien Bien Phu 23; and First Indochina War 23; formed by Ho 16; and Japanese 18, 19, 20; and negotiations with France 20; numerical strength of 21, 24; program of 17, 21; seizes power (1945) 18; and suppression of opposition 19, 32
Vietnam: August revolution in 18; Chinese role in history of 10; French conquest of 10; partition of 24, 46, 47; physical description of 9–10; reunification of 24–25, 26, 30, 32, 51, 56, 74, 228n57; *see also* French Indochina
Vietnam War: consequences of U.S. defeat in 224–25; errors in conduct of 221–22; factors in U.S. defeat 223
Vietnamese Nationalist Party *see* VNQDD
Vietnamese Revolutionary League *see* Dong Minh Hoi
Vietnamese Revolutionary Youth League *see* Thanh Nien
Vietnamese Worker's Party (VWP, Dang Lao Dong): founded 22; and NLF 27, 29; and PRP 29; renaming of 215; and Resolution 15 of Fifteenth Plenum 26; reunification strategy of 27

Vietnamization 137, 151, 192, 194; Easter offensive aims at defeat of 198; goals of 184; neglect of in 1965–67 184; Nixon policy of 179, 181, 184, 187; strengthens ARVN 199, 201
VNQDD (Viet Nam Quoc Dan Dang, Vietnamese Nationalist Party) 13, 14, 17, 19, 21, 38
Vo Nguyen Giap *see* Giap, Vo Nguyen
Voice of America 93
Vung Tau Charter 117
VWP *see* Vietnamese Worker's Party

Wallace, George 172
Warnke, Paul: as Pentagon dove 152, 243n183
Washington Post 127
Watergate 6, 211, 212, 223
Westmoreland, William C. 114, 128; background of 133; becomes Army chief of staff 185; chooses search-and-destroy strategy 134; and escalation, phase I 129; escalation, phase II 147; and failure of search-and-destroy 135–36; and infiltration barrier 246–47; and pacification 137, 159, 188; and post–Tet troop request 166–68; and press relations 162, 186, 242n148; requests for troops by 126–27, 129, 148, 239n17; and takeover of ground war 136, 184; and Tet offensive 162, 163, 164
Wheeler, Earle (Bus) 127, 131, 133, 153; and post–Tet troop request 166–68
Williams, Samuel T.: as MAAG chief 54–55
Wilson, Jasper: and Khan-led coup 108
Wilson, Woodrow 34
Wise Men 169, 170, 243n191
World Bank: McNamara named president of 152
World War II: and defeat of France 16; and Indochina 35

Xa Loi temple: raid on 89
Xuan Thuy 194, 195, 196, 245n81, 246n96

Yen Bay insurrection 14

Zhang Fa Kui (Chang Fa-kwei) 17
Zhou Enlai 24

www.ingramcontent.com/pod-product-compliance
Lightning Source LLC
Chambersburg PA
CBHW020859020526
44116CB00029B/576